Climate Justice

Climate
Justice

Ethics, Energy, and Public Policy

James B. Martin-Schramm

Fortress Press   Minneapolis

CLIMATE JUSTICE
Ethics, Energy, and Public Policy

Cover image: Martin Ruegner / The Image Bank / Getty Images
Cover design: Paul Boehnke
Book design: Zan Ceeley, Trio Bookworks

Library of Congress Cataloging-in-Publication Data

Martin-Schramm, James B.
  Climate justice : ethics, energy, and public policy / James B. Martin-Schramm.
    p. cm.
  Includes bibliographical references and index.
  ISBN 978-0-8006-6362-9 (alk. paper)
  1. Human ecology—Religious aspects—Christianity. 2. Environmental justice—Religious aspects—Christianity. 3. Climatic changes. 4. Global warming. I. Title.
  BT695.5.M374 2010
  241'.691—dc22
                              2009034471

14   13   12   11   10   1   2   3   4   5   6   7   8   9   10

For my teachers in Christian Ethics,
with respect and deep appreciation

Robert Stivers

James Burtness

Beverly Harrison

Larry Rasmussen

Contents

Preface

Just over a year ago, my family was required to evacuate our home because the Upper Iowa River was threatening to breach the dikes that protect our community in northeastern Iowa. The eight inches of rain that had fallen the day before were racing through our steep watershed. As a result, the river rose rapidly and ultimately crested at a point five *feet* above the previous record flood stage and just below the top of the dikes. The earlier record had been set in 1993, the year our family moved to Decorah from New York City. Thus, within the span of fifteen years, our community experienced two "500-year" flood events.

Our Changing Global Climate

A recent report issued by the U.S. Global Change Research Program provides evidence that the deluges our community has experienced have become more frequent over the past forty years and will become more severe over the course of the twenty-first century.[1] The intensity of heavy downpours is related to an increase of water vapor in the atmosphere, which is just one example of the impact of global warming on the United States. Other examples include fewer frost days, reduced snow cover, retreating glaciers, and less sea ice.

This governmental report, which was produced by a team of expert scientists and reviewed by a blue-ribbon panel, notes that some of the changes that have taken place in the United States have occurred sooner than previous assessments had predicted. The scientists project these changes will soon be joined by more intense hurricanes, reduced precipitation in the Southwest, and rising sea levels along the Atlantic and Gulf coasts.[2] These changes will pose serious challenges for agriculture and ecosystems due to rapidly changing growing seasons and the impact of heat stress on plants and animals. Reduced snowpack and rising sea levels will also threaten freshwater supplies. Other threats to human health will be posed by an increase in disease, reduced air quality, and the increased likelihood of severe weather events.[3]

Over the past three decades, the average winter temperature in the Midwest and northern Great Plains has increased more than 7°F.[4] Nationally, the average temperature has increased more than 2°F. The U.S. Global Change Research Program projects an additional increase during this century of approximately 7°F to 11°F under a scenario of higher greenhouse gas emissions or approximately 4°F to 6.5°F under a lower-emissions scenario.[5] The authors of the report depict the implications of these temperature increases in many ways. It was sobering for me to view their projections for the climate of Illinois, the state of my birth, which borders Iowa, where my family now lives. By the middle of the century, Illinois will likely experience a climate similar to what the residents of northern Louisiana experience today; by the end of the century, Illinois could experience a climate more like present-day southeastern Texas.

As the twentieth century marked a period of rapid technological change, it is becoming all too clear that the twenty-first century will mark a period of rapid ecological change. This change will pose unprecedented challenges for human communities and the ecological systems that sustain them.

I recently had the privilege to attend a consultation on climate change convened by the Lutheran World Federation. All of the participants spoke to some extent about the impact of climate change on the places where they live. Rev. Tore Johnsen, chair of the Sámi

Church Council in Norway, spoke eloquently about the challenges facing indigenous communities living in the Arctic regions. The polar areas of the planet have experienced the most rapid rate of warming and are already reeling from the consequences. Johnsen described the impact climate change is having on the Sámi people in the Arctic Circle and lamented that global warming might destroy cultures that have lived sustainably in this region for millennia.[6] These cultures are dependent on key species in these Arctic ecosystems. The report of the U.S. Global Change Research Program projects that two-thirds of the world's polar bears will have disappeared by the middle of this century and that there will be no wild polar bears in Alaska in seventy-five years.[7]

Other colleagues at the consultation focused on the impact of climate change on various nations in Asia, Africa, Latin America, and Europe. A biblical scholar from Zimbabwe emphasized that extended periods of drought were amplifying the suffering of people in her much-beleaguered nation. A colleague from Brazil spoke about the changing climate of the Amazon and its impact on human and other natural communities in this vital region of the world. An ethicist from India emphasized that global warming will produce a huge wave of climate refugees displaced by rising sea levels.

An important theme emerged from these conversations: All over the world, those who are the most affected and least able to adapt to global climate change are also those who have least contributed to the problem. To date, the vast majority of global greenhouse gas emissions have been produced by the few who are rich, rather than by the many who are poor. Thus, the costs associated with mitigating greenhouse gas emissions and adapting to global climate change raise important ethical questions about *climate justice*. There are *inter*generational dimensions that involve our ethical obligations to future generations. There are also *intra*generational dimensions that demand an equitable distribution of the burdens associated with mitigation of greenhouse gas emissions and adaptation to global climate change.

Book Outline and Audience

This book grapples with various issues related to climate justice. It begins in the introduction by confronting the challenges posed by the industrialized world's addiction to fossil fuels. The combustion of coal, oil, and natural gas is the main cause of global warming. In addition, the exploitation, protection, and distribution of fossil fuel energy supplies pose a host of other social, political, economic, and environmental problems.

The first chapter identifies various resources that can empower an ethical response to climate justice issues. I commend and utilize the ethic of ecological justice that emerged from discussions in the World Council of Churches during the 1970s and was developed further in various social policy statements of the Presbyterian Church, (U.S.A.) and the Evangelical Lutheran Church in America from the 1980s through today. I trace the biblical and theological foundations for this ethic and its related moral norms of sustainability, sufficiency, participation, and solidarity. I also identify guidelines that can be used to amplify the ethic of ecological justice as it is applied to evaluate energy options and climate policy proposals.

The next two chapters utilize these ethical resources to ethically assess conventional energy options (coal, oil, natural gas, and nuclear power) in the United States as well as alternative energy options (energy efficiency and a variety of renewables). I give attention to the public policies that have encouraged a dependence on fossil fuels and nuclear power and identify policies that will be vital to a sustainable energy future. There is no question that this will be a long and daunting process, but there is also no question that global climate change cannot be held to an ecologically sustainable level unless new energy options emerge to power economies around the world.

I then use the ethic of ecological justice and a list of guidelines I have developed to ethically assess current climate policy proposals in the international community and the United States. This has been a challenging task, since both are moving targets. When this book went to press, the U.S. House of Representatives had just narrowly passed the landmark American Clean Energy and Security Act of 2009, which utilizes a cap-and-trade system to reduce U.S. greenhouse gas emissions 83 percent from 2005 levels by 2050. By the time this book is published the fate of a similar bill in the Senate will presumably be known, and thus whether Congress will have been able to pass landmark climate legislation. On the international front, nations were still establishing their negotiating positions in advance of the United Nations Climate Change Conference in Copenhagen in December 2009. While the details in these complicated national debates and international negotiations are constantly changing, I have tried to focus on the major ethical questions related to these proposals that will likely endure for years to come.

The book closes on a more personal and practical note as I discuss the work my college is doing to reduce its greenhouse gas emissions. As a charter signatory of the American College and University Presidents' Climate Commitment, Luther College has pledged to make sustainability a part of every student's learning experience and also to achieve "climate neutrality" as soon as possible. I discuss the barriers and opportunities associated with achieving our interim goal of cutting our carbon footprint in half, ideally by the time the college celebrates its sesquicentennial in 2011.

This book is written primarily for a U.S. audience, but I hope it will prove useful to readers in other settings. I focus on the United States because historically it is the largest emitter of greenhouse gases and also because I am a U.S. citizen. The rest of the world is waiting for the United States to assume responsibility and take leadership with regard to climate justice. This work is a contribution toward that end.

My aim is to be helpful to a wide circle of readers. I hope the book will be useful to scholars within the fields of Christian ethics and public policy, but I also have written the book in a way that I hope makes it accessible to students in classrooms, other adult learners in a variety of settings, and also to activists. The ethic of ecological justice that I utilize throughout this project provides a common moral vocabulary for discussions about the ethical aspects of climate change in various venues of civil discourse. One does not have to be a Christian to embrace the moral norms of sustainability, sufficiency, participation, and solidarity. While any discussion of energy or climate policy raises a host of social, political, economic, and environmental concerns, the reality is that these discussions always involve ethical questions about how to balance competing goods and minimize related harms. I believe the ethic of ecological justice and its associated moral norms are valuable ethical resources that can be employed productively with integrity by many.

Companion Website

Finally, I am very pleased that Fortress Press has created a website for this book (www.fortresspress.com/martinschramm). Students and instructors will find additional resources to help in their study of the ethical and environmental issues raised in this book. A study guide will help students in their review of the material in the text. A research guide will assist students in their further study, providing them with guidelines on how to write a research paper and how to find more information on energy options and climate policy proposals, including links to key sources on the web. Instructors will also find additional resources to help with their teaching of this text in their courses, including teaching notes, exam questions, and links for additional web resources.

Ethical Foundations

In my view, ethics is inherently an interdisciplinary enterprise. As a result, most of my dialogue partners in this project have been energy experts, policy analysts, and representatives of various nongovernmental organizations. As a white, male, middle-class citizen of the United States, however, I have tried to locate and integrate analyses of energy and climate issues that are written by or focus on the welfare of the poor and disadvantaged. Like Jesus, Christians must stand with "the least of these" (Matthew 25:40) and advocate for the poor and oppressed in present and future generations, who are often the victims of environmental injustice and who are least able to adapt to the global warming that is disproportionately affecting them.

My Lutheran heritage undoubtedly shapes my analysis and recommendations in this volume. Like any religious tradition, Lutheranism is a broad movement that has been expressed in many different ways in various parts of the world for centuries. Some expressions have contributed to social and political disaster, especially in Germany during the Nazi era and in South Africa under apartheid. Perhaps it is because I spent most of my youth growing up in both of these nations that I have tried to recover Lutheran traditions that contribute to the common good. I want to comment briefly here on two aspects that I think shape my views.

The first is Martin Luther's claim that God is very much at work in the world outside of the church. While there is much that is problematic about Luther's doctrine of the two kingdoms and what Lutherans later termed the "orders of creation," I think Luther's insight about God's work in the world is critical. As one surveys the advance of freedom, equality, and justice over the span of the past five hundred years, there is no question that many of these efforts were advanced and achieved by leaders who often had no association with Christian traditions, and often were opposed by representatives of them. Though Dietrich Bonhoeffer's radical christocentrism is decidedly unfashionable in our postmodern era, I resonate with his view that this cosmic Christ is the source of all that is good, true, and beautiful. It is precisely this conviction that led Bonhoeffer to work with a wide variety of people in the conspiracy who sought only one goal: the restoration of democracy and the rule of law in Germany. I see God at work in all of those people around the world who are working tirelessly to address the dangers posed by global climate change while also addressing the needs of so many who remain poor.

The second aspect of the Lutheran tradition that shapes my thinking in this volume is Luther's theological anthropology, which is most often summed up in the Latin phrase *simul iustus et peccator* (simultaneously saint and sinner). Luther believed human beings are, on the one hand, saints justified by faith before God and, on the other hand, sinners who remain in bondage to the devil. This view leads to the rejection of overly optimistic and pessimistic views of human nature. Human beings are capable of much good, but also much evil. This view produces a more realistic assessment of human potential. A realistic perspective is vital when it comes to grappling with energy options and climate policy proposals. Massive investments in fossil fuel and nuclear power infrastructure will not be abandoned overnight. Nations will not accept obligations to reduce greenhouse gas emissions if they do not perceive those reductions to be in their interests. We must not let the perfect become the enemy of the good. There is only so much that can be done at any one time. I realize that this incremental and gradualist approach can be abused, and that it has been used to suppress the revolutionary and egalitarian aspirations of the abolition, suffrage, and gay rights movements. Nevertheless, I think a realistic perspective is vital to reflection about energy and climate policy. It is not possible to turn things around on a dime. It took centuries for industrialized nations to put the world into this climate predicament, and it will take at least decades to hold the rate of global warming to a point that might prevent ecological collapse.

For us to do this, however, bold and dramatic action is needed today. I believe realistic reflection on the current state of climate science leads to this radical conclusion. Realism and bold, decisive action are not mutually exclusive.

Notes and Acknowledgments

The impetus for this book came from courses I have been teaching at Luther College. I have been team-teaching an interdisciplinary course titled "Stewardship and Sustainable Development" for more than a decade. For the past seven years, the course has focused on U.S. energy policy. Over these years, I have had the good fortune of working with excellent students and colleagues who have taught me much and have pushed me to expand my understanding. I can't imagine a better setting for an ethicist than a liberal-arts college. I have taught with sociologists, economic historians, chemists, physicists, biologists, and experts in international business during my time at Luther. It is precisely because ethics is an interdisciplinary exercise that it is so helpful to have students majoring in diverse fields in the classroom. I only hope they have learned as much from me as I have learned from them.

The modicum of expertise I developed in this course led to a wonderful opportunity in the fall of 2007. The Advisory Committee on Social Witness Policy (ACSWP) of the Presbyterian Church (U.S.A.) invited me to serve as the lead writer on a revision of an existing energy policy statement that had been developed in the early 1980s. Prompted by two recent wars in the Middle East and the new findings of climate scientists, leaders of the denomination decided they needed to update their energy policy statement within the context of global warming. I worked closely with the committee that fall and developed a study document and various recommendations, which were ultimately adopted by the 218th General Assembly of the Presbyterian Church (U.S.A.) in June 2008 under the title *The Power to Change: U.S. Energy Policy and Global Warming*.[8] Much of this work served as the foundation for the following introduction and the chapters on energy options. I am grateful to ACSWP for its permission to use this work in this volume.

I have presented portions of the research for this book in various venues over the past two years. These include presentations about energy options for the Theological Educators for Presbyterian Social Witness at a meeting in Richmond, Virginia, and also for participants in a workshop that I taught with Larry Rasmussen and Melanie Harris at Ghost Ranch in New Mexico. I have given formal papers on this topic at the annual meetings of the American Academy of Religion and the Society of Christian Ethics, as well as the Paideia Texts and Issues Lecture Series at Luther College. I have had the opportunity to give presentations about climate policy issues at consultations sponsored by the Evangelical Lutheran Church in America and the Lutheran World Federation. On all of these occasions, I have benefited enormously from the feedback I received. Ethics is most productive when it is conducted by a community of moral deliberation.

Earlier drafts and portions of the chapters in this book have been published in print or online in various journals and publications. I am grateful to Fred Gaiser, Kaari Reierson, Karen Bloomquist, and Susan Perry for their permission to use these materials in this volume.[9] Like all writers, I am indebted to these editors for their keen insights and editorial suggestions. This is especially true with regard to my editors at Fortress Press, Michael West, Ross Miller, and Marissa Wold Bauck.

I also want to thank several people who have shaped and encouraged my work on this project. It would be hard to find a more enthusiastic and tireless advocate for justice issues than Chris Iosso, Coordinator of the Advisory Committee on Social Witness Policy of the Presbyterian Church (U.S.A.). I thoroughly enjoyed working with Chris and his colleague, Belinda Curry, as well as Gloria Albrecht and other members of ACSWP. To my knowledge, the PCUSA is the only denomination in the United States that has produced a social statement on energy policy. I also thank Ron Duty and Karen Bloomquist for including me in consultations related to climate change convened by the Evangelical Lutheran Church in America and the Lutheran World Federation. I learned so much from my colleagues at these gatherings. One of these dialogue partners was Barbara Rossing, a good friend who provided very helpful responses to drafts of each chapter.

I want to thank several members of Luther College's faculty who gave me feedback or sent me information on various aspects of this project Eric Baack, Jon Jensen, Kirk Larsen, Craig Mosher, Todd Pedlar, Uwe Rudolf, Peter Scholl, Tim Schweitzer, Tex Sordahl, and John Tjostem. I have also been fortunate to work with many excellent students, staff, regents, consultants, and other friends of the college on Luther's energy and greenhouse gas reduction efforts. Thanks to Luther's President, Rick Torgerson, and also to Peg Armstrong-Gustafson, Bill Craft, Larry Grimstad, Rob Larson, Caleb Mattison, Paul Roeder, Megan Selvig, Arne Sorenson, Diane Tacke, Rich Tenneson, Jay Uthoff, Todd Velnosky, and Tom Wind. It is a privilege to work with so many talented and supportive colleagues.

I have received substantial institutional support from Luther College to work on this project. I was granted a yearlong sabbatical during the 2007–2008 academic year and was recently appointed the first research chair in Luther's new Center for Ethics and Public Life. This three-year position permits me to devote half of my professional time to teaching and the other half to research. The center has enabled me to work closely with a student research assistant this past year. I express my sincere thanks to Brandon Reed for his excellent work researching various aspects of climate policy proposals, and also for his work on the index for this volume. Smart, dedicated, and mature students like Brandon are a sure source of hope for the future.

When immersing oneself in the sobering realities of climate change, it is important to have people who keep you grounded and help keep things in perspective. My wife, Karen, has been an endless source of support and encouragement. Our sons, Joel and Joshua, have also been very supportive and provide one of my primary motivations for addressing the topic of climate justice. Their generation and those that follow face a rate of warming that will be unprecedented in human history. My brothers-in-law, Mark and Mike Schramm, have a sense of humor that keeps me from getting too morose about the future as they make this world a better place as conscientious contractors. The same goes for my friends Tim Peter and Brad Miller. Tim needles me playfully about my preoccupations with global warming and campus sustainability, and Brad has patiently endured too many bike rides where I have bent his ear talking endlessly about the prospect of Luther College acquiring a wind turbine.

This book is dedicated to my teachers in Christian ethics over the years. Bob Stivers first introduced me to the field when I was an undergraduate at Pacific Lutheran University in Tacoma. I thought I was going to study business as my brothers did, but Bob got his mitts on me, and I got hooked on the humanities in general, and ethics in particular. Over the years, it has been a joy to shift from being a student of Bob's to being a colleague. James Burtness was one of my professors at Luther Northwestern Theological Seminary. I was immediately attracted to the precision of his thinking and the passion behind his ethical reflection. I was honored to be one of his research assistants and expanded my knowledge of Dietrich Bonhoeffer through this work and in his courses. Finally, I was truly blessed to work with Beverly Harrison and Larry Rasmussen at Union Theological Seminary. Both of them helped me navigate my doctoral studies in the most expeditious and productive ways. My work with Bev led to opportunities I could never have imagined in the field of ethics and population policy. My work with Larry has led to lots of work in the field of environmental ethics and a much deeper interest in the work of Dietrich Bonhoeffer. I doubt anyone else had a better doctoral advisor. These four teachers have profoundly shaped my life both inside and outside of the classroom over the course of my academic career. I dedicate this work to them in gratitude and out of a sense of responsibility to them.

James B. Martin-Schramm
Decorah, Iowa
September 14, 2009

Abbreviations

ACESA	American Clean Energy and Security Act of 2009
ACSWP	Advisory Committee on Social Witness Policy (PCUSA)
ACUPCC	American College and University Presidents' Climate Commitment
Btu	British thermal unit
CAFE	Corporate Average Fuel Economy
CCS	Carbon capture and sequestration
CDC	Centers for Disease Control and Prevention
CDM	Clean Development Mechanism
CentCom	U.S. Central Command
CFTC	Commodity Futures Trading Commission
CH_4	Methane
CO_2	Carbon dioxide
CO_2eq	Carbon dioxide equivalent
CSIRO	Commonwealth Scientific and Industrial Research Organization
CST	Concentrated solar thermal
DOE	U.S. Department of Energy
EERS	Energy efficiency resource standard
EIA	U.S. Energy Information Administration
EISA	Energy Independence and Security Act

ELCA	Evangelical Lutheran Church in America
EPA	U.S. Environmental Protection Agency
EPRI	Electric Power Research Institute
EU	European Union
EU ETS	European Union Emission Trading System
FERC	Federal Energy Regulatory Commission
FY	Fiscal year
GAO	Government Accountability Office
GDP	Gross domestic product
GDR	Greenhouse Development Rights
GHG	Greenhouse gas
GNP	Gross national product
Gt CO_2eq	Gigatonnes of carbon dioxide equivalents
GW	Gigawatt
GWP	Global warming potential
HFC	Hydrofluorocarbon
IPCC	Intergovernmental Panel on Climate Change
ITC	Federal Business Energy Investment Tax Credit
KJV	King James Version
kW	Kilowatt
kWh	Kilowatt-hour
LCWEP	Luther College Wind Energy Project, LLC
LDC	Less-developed country
LIHEAP	Low-Income Home Energy Assistance Program
MMBtu	One Million British Thermal Units
MOX	Mixed-oxide fuel
mpg	Miles per gallon
MT	Metric ton
MW	Megawatt
N_2O	Nitrous oxide
NCCC	National Council of Churches of Christ
NF_3	Nitrogen trifluoride
NRC	Nuclear Regulatory Commission
ODA	Official development assistance
PCUSA	Presbyterian Church (U.S.A.)
PFC	Perfluorocarbon
PPA	Power purchase agreement
ppb	Parts per billion
ppm	Parts per million
PTC	Federal Renewable Electricity Production Tax Credit
PV	Photovoltaic
RCI	Responsibility–Capacity Index
REC	Renewable Energy Certificate
REDD	Reducing emissions by preventing deforestation and forest degradation
REPI	Renewable Energy Production Incentive

RES	Renewable electricity standard
RFS	Renewable Fuels Standard
RMI	Rocky Mountain Institute
RPS	Renewables portfolio standard
SF_6	Sulfur hexafluoride
t CO_2	Ton of carbon dioxide
TAR	Third Assessment Report (IPCC)
TW	Terrawatt
TWh	Terrawatt hour
UNFCCC	United Nations Framework Convention on Climate Change
USDA	U.S. Department of Agriculture
USGS	U.S. Geological Survey
WCC	World Council of Churches
WW	*Word and World*

Introduction

> *In the beginning when God created the heavens and the earth,*
> *the earth was a formless void and darkness covered the face*
> *of the deep, while a wind from God swept over the face of the*
> *waters. Then God said, "Let there be light"; and there was light.*
>
> GENESIS 1:1-3

Wind. Light. Creation. To imagine the fullness of God is to talk about energy. From beginning to end, the Bible is replete with images of energy and divine activity. In the first verses of Genesis, "a wind from God swept over the face of the waters," inaugurating God's creation of the world (Genesis 1:2).[1] In the last chapter of Revelation, "the river of the water of life" flows from the throne of God to water the trees of life that grow along its banks, and whose twelve kinds of fruit are for the healing of the nations (Revelation 22).

Religious Understandings of Energy

Energy is central to God's work as Creator, Redeemer, and Sanctifier. In the first creation account, God works for six days to create the world, which God proclaims "very good" (Genesis 1:31). The second creation account emphasizes that the first human being *(Adam)* is created from energy-intensive and life-sustaining humus *(adamah)* (Genesis 2). God's redeeming and liberating work is also described in dramatic and energetic ways. After parting the Red Sea, God leads the freed Hebrew slaves in a pillar of cloud by day and a pillar of fire by night (Exodus 13:21). The prophet Amos compares God's quest for justice to the powerful force of a waterfall and the might of a raging river that clears everything from its path (Amos 5:24). Finally, God's gift of the Holy Spirit on the day of Pentecost is preceded by "a sound like the rush of a violent wind," after which "tongues, as of fire" rested on each of the disciples (Acts 2:1-3).

The authors of the Synoptic Gospels all discuss Jesus' ministry in terms of power. They utilize the Greek noun δύναμισ *(dunamis)* to describe the power with which Jesus performs miracles (Mark 6:2; 9:39), they associate this power with God (Mark 12:24; 14:62), and they emphasize that Jesus transfers this power to his disciples (Luke 9:1; Matt. 25:15). When a woman plagued by hemorrhages touches Jesus' cloak, it becomes clear that Jesus is filled with a redemptive and healing power because she is immediately healed of her disease. Sensing that "power had gone forth from him," Jesus praises the woman for her faith and blesses her (Mark 5:25-34). Divine power is redemptive energy.

God also provides energy in abundance for all whom God has made (Psalms 145:15). The birds of the air and the fish of the sea first receive the same blessing God bestows on human beings—to be fruitful and multiply (Genesis 1:22). As the people of God wander in the wilderness after the Exodus, God sends "enough" manna each day to sustain the community (Exodus 16). The jubilee legislation in Exodus and Leviticus stressed the needs of the poor and wild animals to eat from fields left fallow every seven years because all creatures are entitled to the energy they need to live. In the Gospel of John, Jesus proclaims that he has come so that all "may have life, and have it abundantly" (John 10:10). Jesus demonstrates this in the feeding of the five thousand, where all are fed and twelve baskets of food are left over (Mark 6:39-44). Paul summarizes, "God is able to provide you with every blessing in abundance, so that by always having enough of everything, you may share abundantly in every good work" (2 Corinthians 9:8). Abundance and sufficiency are linked.

There can be no greater measure of God's abundant provision than the energy provided by Earth's sun. Each hour of every day, the sun delivers more energy to Earth than human beings consume in an entire year.[2] Renewable energy sources can provide almost six times more power than human communities currently consume from all energy sources.[3] Unlike virtually all other species, however, human beings in the modern era have not learned how to live in harmony with current solar energy that we receive each day from the sun. Instead, human communities have grown and some have prospered over the past three centuries by tapping into banked solar energy that has been buried for millions of years as fossil fuels beneath Earth's surface.

Moral Challenges in Energy Use

Today, heavy reliance on these fossil fuels (coal, oil, and natural gas) has produced grave threats to justice, peace, and the integrity of creation. The related challenges posed by global climate change are unprecedented in human history. If the world takes a business-as-usual approach and continues a fossil-fuel-intensive energy path during the twenty-first century, the Intergovernmental Panel on Climate Change (IPCC) projects current concentrations of greenhouse gases could more than quadruple by the year 2100. The last time Earth had such a level of greenhouse gases in the atmosphere was fifty million years ago, when no permanent ice existed anywhere on the planet, even in Antarctica.[4] If present trends continue, the IPCC's best estimate is that the global average surface temperature will increase 4.0°C (7.2°F) by the end of the twenty-first century (Fig. 0.1), but the upper range of this estimate projects warming could reach 6.4°C (11.5°F).[5] Putting these changes into perspective, the global average surface temperature has increased only 0.74°C (1.37°F) since 1850.[6]

This rapid rate of global warming will raise sea levels, endangering millions of people living in low-lying areas, despoil freshwater resources, widen the range of infectious diseases like malaria, reduce agricultural production, and increase the risk of extinction for 25 percent to 30 percent of all surveyed species.[7] The U.S. Climate Change Science Program claims, "We are very likely to experience a faster rate of climate change in the next 100 years than has been seen over the past 10,000 years."[8]

FIG. 0.1   Multimodel Averages and Assessed Ranges for Surface Warming

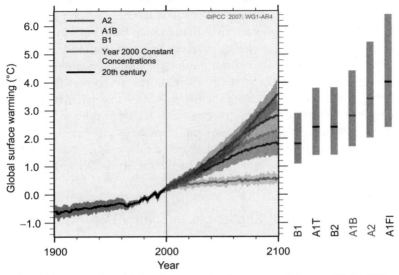

The solid lines are multimodel global averages of surface warming (relative to 1980–1999) for IPCC emission scenarios A2, A1B, and B1, shown as continuations of the twentieth-century simulations. Shading denotes the ±1 standard deviation range of individual model annual averages. The orange line is for the experiment where concentrations were held constant at year 2000 values. The gray bars at right indicate the best estimate (solid line within each bar) and the likely range assessed for the IPCC's six emission scenarios. Scenario A1F1 (far-right bar) reflects the consequence of "business as usual" emissions.

Source: Intergovernmental Panel on Climate Change, "Summary for Policymakers," in Climate Change 2007: The Physical Science Basis; Contribution of Working Group I to the Fourth Assessment Report of the Intergovernmental Panel on Climate Change, ed. S. Solomon et al. (New York: Cambridge University Press, 2007), fig. SPM.5, p. 14, accessed at http://www.ipcc.ch/pdf/assessment-report/ar4/wg1/ar4-wg1-spm.pdf. Unfortunately, it was not possible to reprint this graph in its original color version.

These findings have prompted scientists all over the world to plead for reductions in greenhouse gas (GHG) emissions. James Hansen, the leading climate scientist in the United States, argues that following a business-as-usual approach for ten more years "guarantees that we will have dramatic climate changes that produce what I would call a different planet."[9] Hansen warns, "Recent greenhouse gas emissions place the Earth perilously close to dramatic climate change that could run out of our control, with great dangers for humans and other creatures."[10] To avoid ecological catastrophe, many scientists and policy makers are urging that global warming be held to less than 2°C (3.6°F) above preindustrial levels.[11]

Together with people all around the world, Christians at the outset of the twenty-first century must respond to this climate crisis by developing a new way of living in harmony with Earth's energy resources and in solidarity with all of God's creatures. This moral obligation involves our commitment to the poor and marginalized among the present generation, but it especially includes our responsibilities to future generations. Actions taken or not taken today will affect the welfare of the planet for centuries to come.

Those of us living in the United States have a unique moral responsibility to change our energy consumption practices in the face of global climate change. According to the World Resources Institute, the United States is responsible for nearly 30 percent of the carbon dioxide (CO_2) emissions produced by the combustion of fossil fuels from 1850 to 2002.[12] Even though China now leads the world in annual CO_2 emissions—with 24 percent of the total, compared with the United States at 21 percent—the United States still leads the world in CO_2 emissions on a per capita basis, according to a 2008 report issued by the Netherlands Environmental Assessment Agency. Each person in the United States produces 19.4 metric tons of carbon dioxide (t CO_2) per year, compared with 11.8 t CO_2 per person in Russia, 8.6 t CO_2 in the European Union, 5.1 t CO_2 in China, and only 1.8 t CO_2 per person in India.[13] Given statistics like these, there is no question that as a nation and as individuals, citizens of the United States must accept moral responsibility to deal with the negative consequences associated with fossil fuel consumption and global warming.

The challenges are daunting, and to many, they appear insurmountable. Certainly, several Christian traditions support a hard-eyed realism with regard to the nexus of issues related to energy policy and global climate change. Empowered, however, by a just, good, and gracious God, we must resist the temptation of despair. Among the wealthy and powerful, such despondency can be self-serving, because it leads to moral paralysis. This "cheap despair" changes nothing and preserves the status quo from which the wealthy and powerful currently benefit. Empowered by God's costly grace, Christians must work tirelessly with others as individuals, within church denominations, and as global citizens to live in harmony with the energy resources God has so abundantly provided.

The rest of this introductory chapter explores more fully various problems associated with reliance on fossil fuels and also examines in greater detail the recent findings of climate scientists.

Problems Related to Fossil Fuel Energy Sources

Energy is a key factor in advancing well-being and realizing human potential. Advances in the creative and efficient use of modern, fossil fuel energy sources have been at the heart of progress in affluent industrial nations, enabling advances in living standards to levels never experienced before in history. Energy is vital for growing and providing food for the world, for facilitating advances in health technologies, for powering transportation and industry, and for enabling the growth of the information and communications revolution. As technologies have advanced, energy costs as a share of economic output have tended to decline. This has created the foundation for sizable growth in living standards, reducing the burden of human toil and turning what were once conveniences into virtual necessities for those in the industrial and industrializing worlds.

Nevertheless, roughly one-third of the world's population (over two billion people) still lacks access to adequate supplies of energy, particularly electricity. This lack of access impairs human health and welfare, wastes environmental resources, and limits development in countless ways. For cooking, reliance on inefficient wood stoves leads to emission of large amounts of carbon monoxide and particulate matter, creating high levels of indoor air pollution that induce respiratory illness and shorten lives. Deforestation brings its own tragedies. Without electricity, there is no refrigeration to cool vaccines, no power for lights and computers needed to expand education, and limited connection to the wider world. This lack of access impairs human health and welfare, wastes environmental resources, and limits development in countless ways. Thomas Friedman argues persuasively, in his recent book *Hot, Flat, and Crowded,* that addressing "energy poverty" is one of the keys to reducing all forms of poverty around the world.[14]

While one-third of the world's population experiences serious problems associated with *too little access* to modern supplies of energy, all nations are grappling with various problems associated with *too much use* of fossil fuel energy sources by the rest of the world.

Social Problems

Even in the United States, where environmental regulations have slowed the rate of emissions related to the increasing use of fossil fuels, the American Lung Association estimates over 150 million people live in areas where the air quality puts their health at risk.[15] Vehicle emissions are the leading cause of this air pollution.[16] The 240 million cars, trucks, and buses on U.S. roads today emit a noxious cloud of pollutants consisting of large and fine particulate matter, volatile organic compounds, ozone, nitrogen oxide, and carbon monoxide.[17] These pollutants are a leading cause of asthma, lung cancer, and other respiratory diseases, cardiopulmonary disease, low-birth-weight babies, and increased infant mortality.[18] Each year, diesel exhaust alone is responsible for over 125,000 cancer cases in the United States, and nearly 100,000 Americans die annually from causes attributable to smog.[19] These health impacts are concentrated in cities all over the country, but they have a particularly harsh and unjust effect on vulnerable populations such as asthmatics, the elderly, the very young, and those who live near busy highways, refineries, and polluting industries. People who are poor and racial minorities bear a disproportionate and unjust share of this burden.[20] Around the world, the global toll from air pollution is much worse, likely exceeding a million deaths annually. This is particularly the case if we include indoor air pollution, which has a significant impact on women and children, who spend more time indoors.

Health issues associated with coal mining and the burning of coal to generate electricity are especially sobering. Next to petroleum, coal is the second largest source of energy in the world.[21] Each year, more than 6,000 coal miners are killed in China's coal mines.[22] Since 1900, more than 100,000 people have been killed in coal mine accidents in the United States, and black lung disease is estimated to have killed twice as many miners over the same period of time.[23] Accounting for nearly half of all electricity generation, coal-fired power plants in the United States produce two-thirds of all sulfur dioxide (the leading cause of acid rain), 22 percent of all nitrogen oxides (a major contributor to smog), approximately 40 percent of carbon dioxide (the principal greenhouse gas), and 40 percent of all emissions of mercury (a potent neurotoxin that accumulates in body tissues).[24] The Centers for Disease Control and Prevention (CDC) reports that one in twelve women in the United States have an unsafe level of mercury in their blood, and that as many as 630,000 babies per year could be at risk for health problems. The Environmental Protection Agency has issued advisories in forty-four of the fifty states regarding high mercury levels in various kinds of fish.[25]

Economic Problems

For various reasons, energy prices have risen sharply in the United States over the past two decades (Fig. 0.2). Persons in low-income households (especially elderly residents, the disabled, and children) are most vulnerable to rising costs and often must choose between paying their energy bills or buying food and medicine. Congress created the Low Income Home Energy Assistance Program (LIHEAP) in 1981 precisely to address this need. Families receiving LIHEAP assistance must have income below 150 percent of the federal poverty level. Two-thirds of LIHEAP families earn less than $8,000 per year. Sadly, funding levels for the program have not kept pace with the growing number of households eligible for assistance. In recent years, Congress has authorized sufficient funding to provide LIHEAP assistance for only 15 percent of the eligible population.[26] The American Recovery and Reinvestment Act of 2009 that President Obama signed into law as a major economic stimulus bill provided only a 20 percent increase to LIHEAP's budget.[27]

The rising cost of petroleum fuels has affected all Americans. The average price of gasoline more than doubled from less than $2 a gallon in 2002 to over $4 a gallon in 2008.[28] This has had a disproportionate impact on people who are poor. Poor households with incomes below $15,000 a year typically spend more than 10 percent of their income on gasoline.[29] While prices dropped back to lower levels in 2009, many analysts believe this price reduction will be short-lived. U.S. oil production peaked in the 1970s, and ever since, imports have been rising steadily to meet demand. Today, the United States imports approximately two-thirds of the oil it consumes. Net imports of crude oil in 2008 cost $354 billion and represented over 52 percent of the nation's $677 billion international trade deficit in goods and services (Fig. 0.3).[30] These are dollars the United States could spend to reduce serious and unjust deficits in health care coverage or to invest in inner-city education and poverty alleviation. Instead, the rapidly increasing demand for oil in China and India is pushing the U.S. cost of imported oil even higher. As a result, the needs of the poor get shortchanged because the United States spends more and more money each year to purchase oil.

There are other significant costs related to U.S. oil supplies. Various studies estimate the United States spends between $55 billion and nearly $100 billion each year on the military to secure its oil supplies

FIG. 0.2. U.S. Consumer Energy Expenditures

Total Energy, 1970-2006

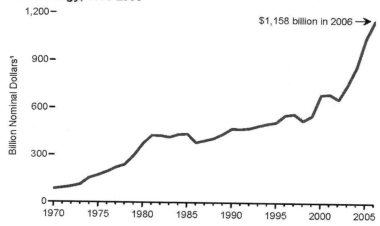

$1,158 billion in 2006 →

Expenditures[3] by Energy Type, Indexed, 1970-2006

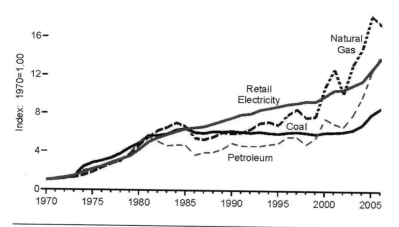

[1] See "Nominal Dollars" in Glossary.
[2] Wood and waste; excludes ethanol and biodiesel.
[3] Based on nominal dollars.
[4] Liquefied petroleum gases.

Source: Energy Information Administration, Annual Energy Review 2008, DOE/EIA-0384(2008) (Washington, D.C.: EIA, June 2009), fig. 3.5, p. 76, accessed online at http://www.eia.doe.gov/aer/pdf/aer.pdf.

around the world.[31] These estimates do not include more than $100 billion spent each year since 2003 for the war in Iraq, which has the world's third largest proven reserves of oil.[32] With the number of civilian and military deaths in Iraq at or above 100,000 people, those who mourn the loss of their loved ones are a reminder that the human toll far exceeds the economic costs of this war.[33] Nevertheless, when these costs are added to the cost of federal and state subsidies to the oil industry, and combined with estimates of health care costs related to fossil fuel pollution, some analysts argue that the true cost of a gallon of gasoline at the pump ranges from $8 to $11 per gallon.[34]

Political Problems

Recently, the National Petroleum Council warned that international energy development and trade are more likely to be influenced by geopolitical considerations and less by market factors.[35] President Bush acknowledged this reality in his 2006 State of the Union address when he remarked, "America is addicted to oil, which is often imported from unstable parts of the world."[36] More recently, President

Fig. 0.3. Value of U.S. Fossil Fuel Imports

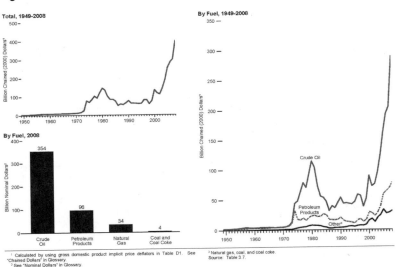

1 Calculated by using gross domestic product implicit price deflators in Table D1. See "Chained Dollars" in Glossary.
2 See "Nominal Dollars" in Glossary.
3 Natural gas, coal, and coal coke.
Source: Table 3.7.

Source: Energy Information Administration, Annual Energy Review 2008, DOE/EIA-0384(2008) (Washington, D.C.: EIA, June 2009), fig. 3.7, p. 80, accessed online at http://www.eia.doe.gov/aer/pdf/aer.pdf. For definitions of "chained" and "nominal" dollars, see the glossary at the end of Annual Energy Review 2008.

Obama lamented in his 2009 Address to the Joint Session of Congress that "we import more oil today than ever before."[37] In recent years, over half of U.S. oil imports have come from four leading suppliers: Canada (19 percent), Saudi Arabia (12 percent), Mexico (11 percent), and Venezuela (10 percent). Nigeria, Algeria, Angola, Iraq, Brazil, and Kuwait round out the other top ten suppliers.[38] While the United States enjoys primarily positive foreign relations with its neighbors, Canada and Mexico, it has strained relationships with Saudi Arabia and Venezuela. In addition, the relationship between blood and oil is all too clear in Iraq's civil strife, and it is becoming more apparent as the level of violence and civil unrest grows in nations like Nigeria and Angola, where oil wealth is not being spread broadly to all residents of these oil-exporting nations. A recent report by Amnesty International claims the exploitation of oil reserves in the Niger Delta has produced a "resource curse" for the 31 million people in the region who suffer from pollution related to the production and from human rights abuses related to its control.[39]

Once oil has been extracted from beneath the ground, transporting the oil can lead to another set of political problems. More than half the world's oil passes through a few potential "choke points," including the Suez Canal, the Bosporus, and the Straits of Hormuz and Malacca.[40] A significant disruption of oil shipments through any of these points could wreak havoc on the world's economy. Nine out of the last ten recessions in the United States were preceded by oil price shocks related to supply disruptions.[41] Many analysts fear that Iran may lay siege to tankers in the Strait of Hormuz if the United States or Israel attacks the facilities Iran has built to enrich uranium.

With demand for natural gas rising around the world, Russia's control of natural gas supplies raises concerns for many nations in Europe and Central Asia. Recently Russia signed a deal to build a pipeline from Turkmenistan through Kazakhstan, which will feed Russia's network of pipelines to Europe. The deal seeks to thwart efforts by the United States and other European nations to build oil and gas pipelines that would avoid Russia by connecting to Europe through Azerbaijan and Turkey. Recently, Russia reduced the flow of natural gas to Georgia, which reduced supplies for countries in Eastern Europe that are fed by the same pipeline. Many European nations fear Russia will use its virtual monopoly over natural gas resources for political purposes.[42]

This brief overview reveals a host of social, economic, and political problems associated with heavy reliance by the United States on fossil fuels. There are also serious environmental problems. Oil spills around the world despoil waters and harm wildlife. Mountaintop coal mining in Appalachia erodes hillsides, ruins scenic lands, and degrades surface streams and groundwater supplies. Emissions of nitrogen oxides and particulate matter from fossil fuel combustion play havoc with respiratory systems. Volatile organic compounds in petroleum fuels produce cancers and other diseases. Sulfur dioxide emissions from the burning of coal produce acid rain that destroys forests and significantly reduces agricultural production around the world.

Global Warming and Climate Change

While these are all serious problems, they pale in comparison to the unprecedented perils posed by global warming and climate change. After nearly two decades of intensive study, scientists around the world have reached a much greater consensus about these phenomena, their causes, and likely impacts. The United Nations established the Intergovernmental Panel on Climate Change (IPCC) in 1988 to review and assess the most recent scientific, technical, and socioeconomic information relevant to climate change. The IPCC has issued periodic reports and issued its Fourth Assessment Report in four installments during 2007. Over 1,200 authors contributed to the report, and their work was reviewed by more than 2,500 scientific experts.[43] Since each report for policy makers is approved line by line in plenary sessions, the IPCC's findings are arguably the least controversial and most accepted assessments of climate change in the scientific community. As a result, their findings are also relatively conservative.

The IPCC Fourth Assessment Report in 2007 finally persuaded many that global warming is real, that it is caused by human activity, and that it will very likely produce climate change in the twenty-first century that will be unprecedented in human history. The following are some of the key findings reprinted directly from the IPCC reports.

Human and Natural Drivers of Climate Change[44]

- Global atmospheric concentrations of carbon dioxide, methane, and nitrous oxide have increased markedly as a result of human activities since 1750 and now far exceed preindustrial values determined from ice cores spanning many thousands of years (see fig. 0.4).
- Carbon dioxide is the most important anthropogenic greenhouse gas. The global atmospheric concentration of CO_2 has increased from a preindustrial value of about 280 ppm to 379 ppm in 2005. The atmospheric concentration of CO_2 in 2005 exceeded by far the natural range over the past 650,000 years (180 to 300 ppm) as determined from ice cores.
- The primary source of the increased atmospheric concentration of CO_2 since the preindustrial period results from fossil fuel use, with land use change providing another significant but smaller contribution.
- The understanding of anthropogenic warming and cooling influences on climate has improved since the Third Assessment Report, leading to *very high confidence* (greater than 90 percent probability) that the globally averaged net effect of human activities since 1750 has been one of warming.

Direct Observations of Recent Climate Change[45]

- Warming of the climate system is unequivocal, as is now evident from observations of increases in global average air and ocean temperatures, widespread melting of snow and ice, and rising global mean sea level (see fig. 0.5).
- Eleven of the past twelve years (1995 to 2006) rank among the twelve warmest years in the instrumental record of global surface temperature.
- At continental, regional, and ocean basin scales, numerous long-term changes in climate have been observed. These include changes in Arctic temperatures and ice, widespread changes in precipitation amounts, ocean salinity, wind patterns and aspects of extreme weather, including droughts,

FIG 0.4 Changes in Greenhouse Gases from Ice Core and Modern Data

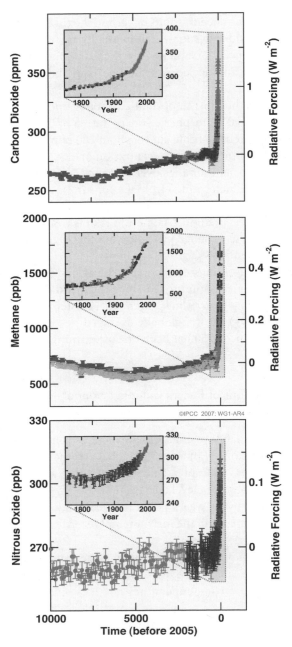

Atmospheric concentrations of carbon dioxide, methane, and nitrous oxide over the past 10,000 years (large panels) and since 1750 (inset panels). Measurements are shown from ice cores (symbols with different colors for different studies and atmospheric samples (red lines). The corresponding radiative forcings are shown on the right axes of the large panels.

Source: Intergovernmental Panel on Climate Change, "Summary for Policymakers," in Climate Change 2007: The Physical Science Basis; Contribution of Working Group I to the Fourth Assessment Report of the Intergovernmental Panel on Climate Change, ed. S. Solomon et al. (New York: Cambridge University Press, 2007), fig. SPM.1, p. 3, accessed at http://www.ipcc.ch/pdf/assessment-report/ar4/wg1/ar4-wg1-spm.pdf. Unfortunately, it was not possible to reprint this graph in its original color version.

Fig. 0.5. Changes in Temperature, Sea Level, and Northern Hemisphere Snow Cover.

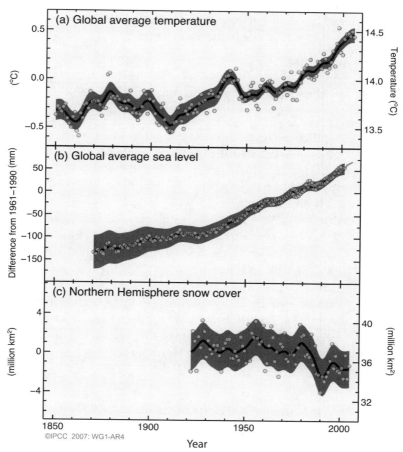

©IPCC 2007: WG1-AR4

Observed changes in (a) global average surface temperature, (b) global average sea level from tide gauge (blue) and satellite (red) data, and (c) Northern Hemisphere snow cover for March through April. All changes are relative to corresponding averages for the period 1961–1990. Smoothed curves represent decadal average values, while circles show yearly values. The shaded areas are the uncertainty intervals estimated from a comprehensive analysis of known uncertainties (a and b) and from the time series (c).

Source: Intergovernmental Panel on Climate Change, "Summary for Policymakers," in *Climate Change 2007: The Physical Science Basis; Contribution of Working Group I to the Fourth Assessment Report of the Intergovernmental Panel on Climate Change*, ed. S. Solomon et al. (New York: Cambridge University Press, 2007), fig. SPM.3, p. 6, accessed at http://www.ipcc.ch/pdf/assessment-report/ar4/wg1/ar4-wg1-spm.pdf. Unfortunately it was not possible to reprint this graph in its original color version.

heavy precipitation, heat waves, and the intensity of tropical cyclones.

- Average Arctic temperatures increased at almost twice the global average rate in the past 100 years.

Projections of Future Changes in Climate [46]

- Continued greenhouse gas emissions at or above current rates would cause further warming and induce many changes in the global climate system during the twenty-first century that would *very likely* be larger than those observed during the twentieth century.
- This assessment gives best estimates and likely ranges for globally average surface air warming in six emissions scenarios. For example, the best estimate for the low scenario is 1.8°C (3.2°F), and the best estimate for the high scenario is 4.0°C (7.2°F).
- Past as well as future anthropogenic CO_2 emissions will continue to contribute to warming and sea level rise for more than a millennium, due to the timescales required for removal of this gas from the atmosphere.

Current Knowledge of Future Impacts [47]

- Drought-affected areas will likely increase in extent. Heavy-precipitation events, which are very likely to increase in frequency, will augment flood risk.
- In the course of the century, water supplies stored in glaciers and snow cover are projected to decline, reducing water availability in regions supplied by meltwater from major mountain ranges, where more than one-sixth of the world population currently lives.
- The resilience of many ecosystems is likely to be exceeded this century by an unprecedented combination of climate change, associated disturbances (for example, flooding,

Impact of Climate Change on the United States

The U.S. Global Change Research Program published a major report in 2009 on the impact of global climate change on the United States. What follows are some of the key findings excerpted directly from the study:

- The U.S. average temperature has risen more than 2°F over the past 50 years and is projected to rise more in the future; how much more depends primarily on the amount of heat-trapping gases emitted globally and how sensitive the climate is to those emissions.
- Precipitation has increased an average of about 5 percent over the past 50 years. Projections of future precipitation generally indicate that northern areas will become wetter, and southern areas, particularly in the West, will become drier.
- The amount of rain falling in the heaviest downpours has increased approximately 20 percent on average in the past century, and this trend is very likely to continue, with the largest increases in the wettest places.
- Many types of extreme weather events, such as heat waves and regional droughts, have become more frequent and intense during the past forty to fifty years.
- The destructive energy of Atlantic hurricanes has increased in recent decades. The intensity of these storms is likely to increase in this century.
- In the eastern Pacific, the strongest hurricanes have become stronger since the 1980s, even while the total number of storms has decreased.
- Sea level has risen along most of the U.S. coast over the past fifty years and will rise more in the future.
- Cold-season storm tracks are shifting northward, and the strongest storms are likely to become stronger and more frequent.
- Arctic sea ice is declining rapidly, and this is very likely to continue.

Source: Thomas R. Karl, Jerry M. Melillo, and Thomas C. Peterson, eds., *Global Climate Change Impacts in the United States* (New York: Cambridge University Press, 2009), 27, accessed at http://downloads.globalchange. gov/usimpacts/pdfs/climate-impacts-report.pdf.

drought, wildfire, insects, ocean acidification), and other global change drivers (for example, land use change, pollution, over-exploitation of resources).

- Approximately 20 to 30 percent of plant and animal species assessed so far are likely to be at increased risk of extinction if increases in global average temperature exceed 1.5°C to 2.5°C (see Fig. 0.6).
- Globally, the potential for food production is projected to increase with increases in local average temperature over a range of 1°C to 3°C, but above this it is projected to decrease.
- Many millions more people are projected to be flooded every year due to a rise in sea level by the 2080s. The numbers affected will be largest in the mega-deltas of Asia and Africa, while small islands are especially vulnerable.
- Poor communities can be especially vulnerable, particularly those concentrated in high-risk areas. They tend to have more limited adaptive capacities and are more dependent on climate-sensitive resources such as local water and food supplies.[48]

In summary, the IPCC's Fourth Assessment Report concluded that the scientific evidence of global warming is "unequivocal" and that that panel has "very high confidence" that human activities have contributed to this warming since 1750.[49] The Earth's global average surface temperature has increased 0.74°C (1.37°F) since 1850, and the rate of temperature increase has been accelerating since 1970.[50] The IPCC reported that the concentration of the principal greenhouse gas, CO_2, increased from preindustrial levels of 280 parts per million by volume (ppm) to 379 ppm in 2005. At the end of 2008, atmospheric concentrations of CO_2 stood at 386 ppm, and the concentration of all six greenhouse gases stood at over 460 ppm of carbon dioxide equivalent (CO_2eq).[51]

Climate Sensitivity Thresholds

After the IPCC issued its Third Assessment Report in 2001, many scientists believed that limiting CO_2 concentrations to 450 ppm and all greenhouse gases to 550 ppm CO_2eq would be sufficient to forestall the worst consequences of climate change. In fact, the U.S. Global Change Research Program published a major report in 2009 on the impact of

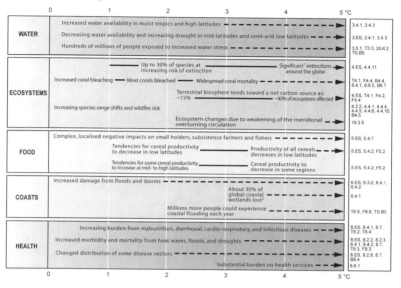

	0	1	2	3	4	5 °C	
WATER	Increased water availability in moist tropics and high latitudes						3.4.1, 3.4.3
	Decreasing water availability and increasing drought in mid-latitudes and semi-arid low latitudes						3.ES, 3.4.1, 3.4.3
	Hundreds of millions of people exposed to increased water stress						3.5.1, T3.3, 20.6.2, TS.B5
ECOSYSTEMS			Up to 30% of species at increasing risk of extinction		Significant[†] extinctions around the globe		4.ES, 4.4.11
	Increased coral bleaching — Most corals bleached — Widespread coral mortality						T4.1, F4.4, B4.4, 6.4.1, 6.6.5, B6.1
				Terrestrial biosphere tends toward a net carbon source as: ~15% ──── ~40% of ecosystems affected			4.ES, T4.1, F4.2, F4.4
	Increasing species range shifts and wildfire risk						4.2.2, 4.4.1, 4.4.4, 4.4.5, 4.4.6, 4.4.10, B4.5
				Ecosystem changes due to weakening of the meridional overturning circulation			19.3.5
FOOD	Complex, localised negative impacts on small holders, subsistence farmers and fishers						5.ES, 5.4.7
		Tendencies for cereal productivity to decrease in low latitudes		Productivity of all cereals decreases in low latitudes			5.ES, 5.4.2, F5.2
		Tendencies for some cereal productivity to increase at mid- to high latitudes		Cereal productivity to decrease in some regions			5.ES, 5.4.2, F5.2
COASTS	Increased damage from floods and storms						6.ES, 6.3.2, 6.4.1, 6.4.2
				About 30% of global coastal wetlands lost[‡]			6.4.1
				Millions more people could experience coastal flooding each year			T6.6, F6.8, TS.B5
HEALTH	Increasing burden from malnutrition, diarrhoeal, cardio-respiratory, and infectious diseases						8.ES, 8.4.1, 8.7, T8.2, T8.4
	Increased morbidity and mortality from heat waves, floods, and droughts						8.ES, 8.2.2, 8.2.3, 8.4.1, 8.4.2, 8.7, T8.3, F8.3
	Changed distribution of some disease vectors						8.ES, 8.2.8, 8.7, B8.4
					Substantial burden on health services		8.6.1
	0	1	2	3	4	5 °C	

Source: Intergovernmental Panel on Climate Change, "Summary for Policymakers," in Climate Change 2007: Impacts, Adaptation and Vulnerability: Contribution of Working Group II to the Fourth Assessment Report of the Intergovernmental Panel on Climate Change, ed. M. L. Parry et al. (Cambridge: Cambridge University Press, 2007), fig. SPM.2, p. 16, accessed at http://www.ipcc.ch/pdf/assessment-report/ar4/wg2/ar4-wg2-spm.pdf.
†"Significant" is defined here as more than 40 percent.
‡Based on average rate of sea level rise of 4.2 mm/yr from 2000 to 2080.

global climate change that focused on this 450 ppm CO_2 threshold, though it noted that scenarios that stabilize emissions below that level "offer an increased chance of avoiding dangerous climate change."[52] Today, an increasing number of scientists and policy makers are urging that global concentrations of CO_2 be reduced from their current level and stabilized at 350 ppm or lower, in order to limit the total increase in global surface temperature from preindustrial levels to no more than 2°C.[53]

Converting greenhouse gas (GHG) concentrations to future temperature changes is currently limited by scientific uncertainty about the sensitivity of the planet's climate system. Climate sensitivity is defined as the global mean temperature increase that would result in the long run if CO_2 concentrations were to double from their preindustrial level of approximately 278 ppm. If climate sensitivity is low, then a doubling of carbon dioxide levels to 550 ppm might produce only 1°C of warming. If climate sensitivity is high, then 4.5°C of warming might result from the doubling of CO_2 concentrations. The IPCC Fourth Assessment Report estimates climate sensitivity "*likely* to be in the range 2°C to 4.5°C with a best estimate of about 3°C, and is *very unlikely* to be less than 1.5°C."[54] According to the Worldwatch Institute, there is about a 75 percent risk that stabilizing greenhouse gas concentrations at 550 ppm CO_2eq would lead to warming exceeding 2°C. If concentrations are stabilized at 475 CO_2eq, the risk of exceeding 2°C is reduced to 50 percent.[55] That amounts to flipping a coin.

The IPCC Fourth Assessment Report reviews a variety of GHG emission scenarios and related temperature stabilization levels. For the best chance of limiting the temperature increase to 2.0°C to 2.4°C, the IPCC emphasizes that global GHG emissions must peak before 2015 and then fall 85 percent by 2050 to within a range of 350 to 400 ppm for CO_2 and 445 to 490 ppm CO_2eq for all greenhouse gases.[56]

Research published after the IPCC's Fourth Assessment Report has raised concerns that these recommended temperature and GHG concentration thresholds may be too high to forestall dangerous climate change. In 2008, the most famous climate scientist in the United States, James Hansen, made the following recommendation in a coauthored article published in the *Open Atmospheric Science Journal*: "If humanity wishes to preserve a planet similar to that on which civilization developed and to which life on Earth is adapted, paleoclimate evidence and ongoing climate change suggest that CO_2 will need to be reduced from its current 385 ppm to at most 350 ppm, but likely less than that."[57]

Across the Atlantic, in England, the former cochair of the IPCC, Sir John Houghton, expressed his concern that "the 2°C target as currently pursued will almost certainly turn out to be inadequate."[58] Houghton arrived at this conclusion after observing record-low summer sea ice volume during 2008 in the Arctic Ocean. Some climate scientists now predict the Arctic Ocean could be completely ice free by 2015, eighty years ahead of the IPCC's most recent projections.[59] In 2009, a group of scientists at the International Scientific Congress on Climate Change presented findings that sea levels may rise twice as much by the end of the century as was projected in the IPCC's Fourth Assessment Report. One of the scientists remarked, "We are at the very least in the worst-case scenario of the IPCC. There's no good news here."[60]

In July 2009, the Commonwealth Scientific and Industrial Research Organization (CSIRO), an Australia-based research group, published a report that shows the amount of carbon stored in frozen soils at high latitudes is double previous estimates and could, if emitted as carbon dioxide and methane, lead to a significant increase in the global average surface temperature by the end of this century. The scientists warn that if only 10 percent of the permafrost melts, an additional 80 ppm CO_2eq would be released into the atmosphere, resulting in an additional 0.7°C of global warming. The scientists warn that rapid thawing of the permafrost will create a negative feedback loop, which will only spur even greater warming.[61]

Virtually all climate scientists agree that global warming is real and that the concentration of greenhouse gases in the atmosphere poses unprecedented challenges from climate change for human communities.[62] A recent study in the United States published in the prestigious *Proceedings of the National Academy of Sciences* notes warming will take place for a thousand years even after GHG emissions stop. The report concludes, "Irreversible climate changes due to carbon dioxide emissions have already taken place, and future carbon dioxide emissions would imply further irreversible effects on the planet, with attendant long legacies for choices made by contemporary society."[63]

Conclusion

Clearly, global warming and related climate change brought on by the combustion of fossil fuels and some land use practices pose grave threats to justice, peace, and the integrity of creation. The information provided by the IPCC raises at least two fundamental ethical issues. The first is an *inter*generational question: What are our obligations to future generations with regard to reducing or mitigating the challenges posed by climate change? The second is an *intra*generational question: How do we equitably distribute the burdens associated with mitigating greenhouse gas emissions and adaptation to global climate change among present generations? A recent report of the United Nations Development Programme reframes these questions in a more provocative way:

Climate change demands urgent action now to address a threat to two constituencies with little or no political voice: the world's poor and future generations. It raises profoundly important questions about social justice, equity and human rights across countries and generations . . . . Dangerous climate change is the avoidable catastrophe of the 21st Century and beyond. Future generations will pass a harsh judgment on a generation that looked at the evidence on climate change, understood the consequences, and then continued on a path that consigned millions of the world's most vulnerable people to poverty and exposed future generations to the risk of ecological disaster.[64]

This book grapples with these issues of climate justice and focuses primarily on the ethical responsibilities of industrialized nations, especially the United States. The first chapter offers biblical and ethical resources for grappling with these ethical questions. The subsequent chapters use these resources to assess the ethics of diverse energy options as well as international and U.S. climate policy proposals.

1. Ethical Resources

But let justice roll down like waters,
and righteousness like an ever-flowing stream.

AMOS 5:24

In the end, without environmental stewardship, there can be no
sustainable prosperity and no sustainable social justice.

GORDON BROWN
PRIME MINISTER OF THE UNITED KINGDOM[1]

As we have seen, global warming and related climate change pose grave dangers to human communities and the planet as a whole. Christians in the World Council of Churches (WCC) have been wrestling with the nexus between social justice and environmental issues for decades. In fact, it was the WCC that elevated the concept of sustainability to a social norm when it challenged its members and the international community in 1974 to create a "just, participatory, and sustainable society."[2] In ethics, norms like "do no harm" and "love your neighbor" are general ethical guidelines for moral behavior. While most Christian moral norms are drawn from the Bible, they have also been developed from Christian theology, the moral wisdom acquired through experience, and important scientific findings discovered through God's gift of reason.

Justice and Environmental Issues

Faced with the prospects for nuclear war, rapid population growth, deepening poverty, and growing environmental degradation, members of the WCC began in the 1970s to consult the sources of scripture, tradition, reason, and experience to develop various ethical resources to grapple with complicated and interconnected problems related to social justice and environmental well-being. In 1979, a WCC conference on "Faith, Science and the Future" identified and gave explicit attention to four moral norms: sustainability, sufficiency, participation, and solidarity.[3] In 1983, the sixth assembly of the WCC encouraged all of its member communions to use these norms in their pursuit of "justice, peace, and the integrity of creation."

In 1984, with its publication of *Accelerated Climate Change: Sign of Peril, Test of Faith*, the WCC became one of the first organizations in the world to call attention to the dangers of global warming.[4] This study demanded an integrated and twofold response. First, it distinguished between "the luxury emissions of the rich" and the "survival emissions of the poor." It emphasized that social justice is key to any strategy to combat climate change. Second, it noted that related environmental problems reveal that nature has become a "co-victim with the poor." The statement declared, "Earth and people will be liberated to thrive together, or not at all." Quite presciently, the WCC also emphasized, "*We must not allow either the immensity or the uncertainty pertaining to climate change and other problems to erode further the solidarity binding humans to one another and to other life.*"[5]

Some of the participants in these WCC conversations were also engaged in ethical reflection about various policy issues in their own countries. Presbyterians in the United States addressed issues related to energy policy in a comprehensive policy statement adopted in 1981, *The Power to Speak Truth to Power*.[6] This important social policy statement promoted an "ethic of ecological justice" that attempted to unite in one broad scope of moral concern the ethical obligations Christians have to present and future generations, as well as to all human and natural communities. Four norms rooted in Scripture and Christian theology were identified as central to this ethic: justice, sustainability, sufficiency, and participation.

The ethic of ecological justice and its related norms were developed further a decade later in 1990, when the Presbyterian Church (U.S.A.) (PCUSA) approved a major study on environmental policy entitled *Restoring Creation for Ecology and Justice*.[7] This study recast the norm of justice in terms of solidarity and honed the application of the other norms to environmental issues. As new scientific studies further confirmed the phenomenon of global warming, and as the prospects grew for a second war in oil-rich Iraq, delegates at the PCUSA's 214th General Assembly in 2002 approved a proposal to revise the 1981 statement on U.S. energy policy.[8] In 2008, the PCUSA's 218th General Assembly approved *The Power to Change: U.S. Energy Policy and Global Warming*.[9] The document utilized the ethic of ecological justice and the related moral norms of sustainability, sufficiency, participation, and solidarity to assess U.S. energy options and to formulate related policy recommendations.

The Evangelical Lutheran Church in America (ELCA) drew, in part, on the work of the WCC and the PCUSA as it developed a series of social statements on various issues beginning in the early 1990s. The ELCA's statement on environmental issues in 1993 emphasized that justice "means honoring the integrity of creation, and striving for fairness within the human family." It also called on members of the ELCA to "answer the call to justice and commit ourselves to its principles—participation, solidarity, sufficiency, and sustainability."[10] All four of these principles are referred to in the ELCA's 1995 statement on peace issues and also in the ELCA's 1999 statement on economic justice issues.[11] These four principles are also referred to explicitly in a draft social statement on genetics that is scheduled for action by the ELCA's Churchwide Assembly in 2011.[12] This study claims, "These four principles could be said to articulate a core ethics of 'faith active in love through justice' for ELCA social policy."[13]

While the ELCA has utilized the four dimensions of justice that emerged from WCC discussions in the 1970s, the National Council of Churches of Christ has developed the notion of an ethic of ecological justice that emerged from reflection on U.S. energy policy among Presbyterians in the 1980s. Today the council's "Eco-Justice Program" enables "national bodies of member Protestant and Orthodox denominations to work together to protect and restore God's Creation." The program defines ecojustice as "all ministries designed to heal and defend creation, working to assure justice for all of creation and the human beings who live in it."[14]

This book uses the ethic of ecological justice and its related moral norms to conduct an ethical assessment of energy options and climate policy proposals. These resources offer a sophisticated ethic to grapple with social and environmental issues that are intertwined. They also offer a common moral vocabulary with which to engage in ethical reflection and public discourse about various energy and climate policy proposals. The remainder of this chapter explores the concept of ecojustice in greater detail and traces the biblical and theological foundations for sustainability, sufficiency, participation, and solidarity in Jewish and Christian traditions. The chapter concludes by identifying additional guidelines that will further enable ethical assessments of energy options and climate policy proposals.

The Ethic of Ecological Justice

The ethic of ecological justice is a biblical, theological, and tradition-based ethic that emphasizes four moral norms: sustainability, sufficiency, participation, and solidarity.[15] This ethic addresses human-caused problems that threaten both human and natural communities and considers both human and natural communities to be ethically important. The word *ecological* lifts up moral concern about other species and their habitats; the word *justice* points to the distinctly human realm and human relationships to the natural order.

Justice
The norm of justice used in the title of this ethical perspective is an inclusive concept. Its full meaning is given greater specificity by the four norms of sustainability, sufficiency, participation, and solidarity. Justice is, however, a norm in its own right with a distinct history in Christian ethics and Western philosophy. In Christian traditions, justice is rooted in the very being of God. It is an essential part of God's community of love and calls human beings to make fairness the touchstone of social relations and relations to other species and ecosystems. Justice is not the love of Christ (*agape*). Justice involves

a calculation of interests. Justice has a more impersonal quality than love, because social groups are more its subject than individuals. Nevertheless, justice divorced from love easily deteriorates into a mere calculation of interests and finally into a cynical balancing of interest against interest. Without love inspiring justice, societies lack the push and pull of care and compassion to move them to higher levels of fairness. Love forces recognition of the needs of others. Love judges abuses of justice. Love lends passion to justice. Justice, in short, is love worked out in arenas where the needs of each individual are impossible to know.

The biblical basis for justice with its special sensitivity for the poor starts with God's liberation of the poor and oppressed slaves in Egypt and the establishment of a covenant, one of whose cardinal features is righteousness (Exodus 22:21-24). The biblical basis continues in the prophetic reinterpretation of the covenant. Micah summarized the law: "to do justice, and to love kindness, and to walk humbly with your God" (Micah 6:8). Amos was adamant that God's wrath befell Israel for its unrighteousness. Important for Amos among the transgressions of Israel were injustice and the failure to care for the poor (Amos 2:6; 8:4-8; 5:11). Isaiah and Jeremiah were no different (Isaiah 10:1-2; Jeremiah 22:13-17).

In the Christian scriptures, the emphasis on justice is muted in comparison to that of the prophets, but the concern for the poor may be even stronger. Jesus himself was a poor man from a poor part of Israel. His mission was among the poor and directed to them (Luke 4:16-20). He blessed the poor and spoke God's judgment on the rich (Luke 6:20-26; Matthew 5:1-14).

The early church carried this tradition beyond the time of Jesus. Paul's concern is frequently for the weak members of the community. This is his concern as he addresses a question that now seems quaint: eating meat sacrificed to idols (1 Corinthians 8). He affirms the new freedom in faith that is one important foundation for political freedom. Freedom is not, however, a license to ignore or prosecute the weak in the pursuit of one's own consumption.

Paul is even more emphatic on equality, which with freedom is the backbone of the modern concept of justice. His statement on the ideals of freedom and equality are among the strongest in the entire biblical witness (Galatians 3:28). His commitment to freedom and equality is in no way diminished by his more conservative interpretations in actual situations where he may have felt the need to moderate his ideals for the sake of community harmony. Thus, while Paul seems to advise an inferior role for women (1 Corinthians 14:34-36) and urges the slave to return to his master (Philemon), his ringing affirmation of equality in Galatians has through the ages sustained Christians concerned about justice.

In the Christian community in Jerusalem (Acts 1–5), equality was apparently put into practice and also involved sharing. In this practice, these early Christians set themselves apart from the prevailing Roman culture.

For Aristotle, justice meant "treating equals equally and unequals unequally."[16] This simple statement of the norm of justice hides the complexities of determining exactly who is equal and who is not and the grounds for justifying inequality. In modern interpretations of justice, however, it leads to freedom and equality as measures of justice. It also leads to the concept of equity, which is justice in actual situations where a degree of departure from freedom and equality are permitted in the name of achieving other social goods. So, for example, most societies give mentally and physically impaired individuals extra resources and justify it in the name of greater fairness. This is a departure from equal treatment, but not from equitable treatment. The problem, of course, is that self-interested individuals and groups will always ask for departures from freedom and equality and use spurious justifications. This is one reason justice needs love as its foundation and careful scrutiny of claims for justice.

In summary, justice in Christian thought is the social and ecological expression of love and means a special concern for the poor, a rough calculation of freedom and equality, and a passion for establishing equitable relationships. The ethical aims of justice in the absence of other considerations should be to relieve the worst conditions of poverty, powerlessness, exploitation, and environmental degradation and provide for an equitable distribution of burdens and costs. The moral norms of sustainability, sufficiency, participation, and solidarity help to flesh out more fully what an ethic of ecological justice might entail.

Sustainability

Sustainability may be defined as the long-range supply of sufficient resources to meet basic human needs and the preservation of intact natural communities. It expresses a concern for future generations and the planet as a whole, and emphasizes that an acceptable quality of life for present generations must not jeopardize the prospects for future generations.

Sustainability is basically good stewardship and is a pressing concern today because of the human degradation of nature. It embodies an ongoing view of nature and society, a view in which ancestors and posterity are seen as sharing in present decisions. The present generation takes in trust a legacy from the past with the responsibility of passing it on in better or at least no worse condition. A concern for future generations is one aspect of love and justice. Sustainability precludes a shortsighted stress on economic growth that fundamentally harms ecological systems and any form of environmentalism that ignores human needs and costs.

There are several significant biblical and theological foundations for the norm of sustainability. The doctrine of creation affirms that God as Creator sustains God's creation. The creation is also good independently of human beings (Genesis 1). It is not simply there for human use, but possesses an autonomous status in the eyes of God. The goodness of matter is later picked up in Christian understandings of the incarnation and the sacraments.[17]

Psalm 104 is a splendid hymn of praise that celebrates God's efforts at sustainability: "When you send forth your spirit . . . you renew the face of the ground" (Psalms 104:30). Similarly, Psalm 145 rejoices in the knowledge that God gives "them their food in due season" and "satisfies the desire of every living thing" (Psalms 145:15-16). The doctrine of creation also emphasizes the special vocation of humanity to assist God in the task of sustainability. In Genesis, the first creation account describes the responsibility of stewardship in terms of "dominion" (Genesis 1:28), and the second creation account refers to this task as "to till [the garden] and keep it" (Genesis 2:15). In both cases, the stress is on humanity's stewardship of *God's* creation. The parable of the Good Steward in Luke also exemplifies this perspective. The steward is not the owner of the house but manages or sustains the household so that all may be fed and have enough (Luke 12:42). The Gospels offer several other vivid metaphors of stewardship. The shepherd cares for the lost sheep. The earth is a vineyard, and humanity serves as its tenant.

The covenant theme is another important biblical and theological foundation for the norm of sustainability. The Noahic covenant (Genesis 9) celebrates God's "everlasting covenant between God and every living creation of all flesh that is on the earth" (Genesis 9:16) The biblical writer repeats this formula several times in subsequent verses, as if to drive the point home. The text demonstrates God's concern for biodiversity and the preservation of all species.

It is the Sinai covenant, however, that may best reveal the links between the concepts of covenant and sustainability. Whereas the prior covenants with Noah and Abraham were unilateral and unconditional declarations by God, the Sinai covenant featured the reciprocal and conditional participation of humanity in the covenant: "If you obey the commandments of the Lord your God . . . then you shall live" (Deuteronomy 30:16). Each of the Ten Commandments and all of the interpretations of these commandments in the subsequent Book of the Covenant were intended to sustain the life of the people of God in harmony with the well-being of the earth (Exodus 20–24).

At the heart of the Sinai covenant rested the twin concerns for righteousness (justice) and stewardship of the earth. Likewise, the new covenant in Christ is very much linked to these twin concerns as well as to the reciprocal relation of human beings.

In Romans 8:18, the whole creation suffers and in 8:22 "groans in travail." But suffering, according to Paul, does not lead to despair: "The creation waits with eager longing for the revealing of the children of God" (Romans 8:19), and "in this hope we are saved" (Romans 8:24). Suffering, as in the suffering of Jesus Christ on the cross, points beyond to the hope that is already partially present. Part of this hope is a return to the good stewardship of Genesis 1 and 2 before the fall in Genesis 3.

Sufficiency

The norm of sufficiency emphasizes that all forms of life are entitled to share in the goods of creation. To share in the goods of creation in a Christian sense, however, does not mean unlimited consumption, hoarding, or an inequitable distribution of the earth's goods. Rather, it is defined in terms of basic needs, sharing, and equity. It repudiates wasteful and harmful consumption and encourages humility, frugality, and generosity.[18]

This norm appears in the Bible in several places. As the people of God wander in the wilderness after the exodus, God sends "enough" manna each day to sustain the community (Exodus 16:4). Moses instructs the people to "gather as much of it as each of you need" (Exodus 16:16). The norm of sufficiency is also integral to the set of laws known as the jubilee legislation. These laws fostered stewardship of the land, care for animals and the poor, and a regular redistribution of wealth. In particular, the jubilee laws stressed the needs of the poor and wild animals to eat from fields left fallow every seven years (Exodus 23:11). All creatures were entitled to a sufficient amount of food to live.

In Christian scriptures, sufficiency is linked to abundance. Jesus says, "I came that you may have life, and have it abundantly" (John 10:10). Jesus rejects the notion, however, that the "good life" is to be found in the abundance of possessions (Luke 12:15). Instead, the good life is to be found in following Christ. Such a life results not in the hoarding of material wealth but rather in sharing it so that others may have enough. Acts 1–5 reveals that this became the model for what amounted to the first Christian community in Jerusalem. The believers distributed their possessions "as they had need" (Acts 2:45). Paul also emphasizes the relation of abundance to sufficiency: "God is able to provide you with every blessing in abundance, so that you may always have enough" (2 Corinthians 9:8).

The norm of sufficiency is also supported by biblical and theological understandings of wealth, consumption, and sharing. Two general and not altogether compatible attitudes dominate biblical writings on wealth and consumption. On the one hand, there is a qualified appreciation of wealth, and on the other, a call to freedom from possessions that sometimes borders on deep suspicion.[19] The Hebrew scriptures generally take the side of appreciating wealth, praising the rich who are just and placing a high estimate on riches gained through honest work.

Both sides are found in the teachings of Jesus. The announcement of the coming community of God carries with it a call for unparalleled righteousness, freedom from possessions, and complete trust in God. The service of God and the service of riches are incompatible (Matthew 6:24; Mark 8:36; 9:43-48; 10:17-25; Luke 12:15; 8:14; 11:18-23; 19:1-10). Jesus himself had no possessions and prodded his disciples into the renunciation of possessions and what later has been called "holy poverty," that is, poverty that is freely chosen as a way of life (Matthew 8:20; Mark 1:16; 6:8-9; Luke 9:3; 10:4).On the other side, Jesus took for granted the owning of property and was apparently supported by women of means (Luke 8:2). He urged that possessions be used to help those in need (Luke

6:30; 8:2-3; 10:38-39). He was fond of celebrations, talking often about feasts in the community of God.

The biblical witness on consumption follows much the same pattern. The basic issue has been between self-denial and contentment with a moderate level of consumption.[20] The side of self-denial evolved into the monastic movement of later ages. The way of moderation is expressed well in 1 Timothy 6:6-8: "There is great gain in godliness with contentment; for we brought nothing into the world, and cannot take anything out of the world; but if you have food and clothing, with these we shall be content."

Sharing is an implication of neighbor love, hoarding a sign of selfishness and sin. Jesus repeatedly calls his disciples to give of themselves, even to the point of giving all they have to the poor. He shares bread and wine with them at the Last Supper. Paul in several letters urges Christians elsewhere to share with those in the Jerusalem community.

Sufficiency and sustainability are linked, for what the ethic of ecological justice seeks to sustain is the material and spiritual wherewithal to satisfy the basic needs of all forms of life. They are also linked through the increasing realization that present levels of human consumption, especially in affluent countries, are more than sufficient and in many respects are unsustainable. Only an ethic and practice that stress sufficiency, frugality, and generosity will ensure a sustainable future.

Finally, the norm of sufficiency offers an excellent example of how human ethics is being extended to nature. The post–World War II stress on economic growth has been anthropocentric. Economists and politicians have been preoccupied by human sufficiency. The anthropocentric focus of most Christian traditions has reinforced this preoccupation.

With increasing environmental awareness, however, this preoccupation no longer seems appropriate. And while other species are not equipped to practice frugality or simplicity—indeed, to be ethical at all in a human sense—the norm of sufficiency does apply to humans in how they relate to other species. To care is to practice restraint. Humans should be frugal and share resources with plants and animals because they count in the eyes of God. All of creation is good and deserves ethical consideration. The focus on sufficiency is part of what it means to practice justice.

Participation

The norm of participation likewise stems from the affirmation of all forms of life and the call to justice. This affirmation and this call lead to the respect and inclusion of all forms of life in human decisions that affect their well-being. Voices should be heard, and, if creatures are not able to speak, which is the case for other species, then humans will have to represent their interests when those interests are at stake.[21] Participation is concerned with empowerment and seeks to remove the obstacles to participating in decisions that affect lives.

The norm of participation is also grounded in the two creation accounts in Genesis. These accounts emphasize the value of everything in God's creation and the duty of humans to recognize the interest of all by acting as good stewards. Through their emphasis on humanity's creation in the image of God, the writers of Genesis underline the value of human life and the equality of women and men.

The prophets brought sharp condemnation upon kings and people of Israel for violating the covenant by neglecting the interests of the poor and vulnerable. They repudiated actions that disempowered people through the loss of land, corruption, theft, slavery, and militarism. The prophets spoke for those who had no voice and could no longer participate in the decisions that affected their lives (Amos 2:6-7; Isaiah 3:2-15; Hosea 10:12-14).

With Jesus comes a new emphasis: the kingdom or community of God (Mark 1:14-15). While the community of God is not to be equated to any community of human beings, it nevertheless is related. It serves as a general model for human communities and is to some degree realizable, although never totally.

The community of God has its source in a different kind of power, God's power of love and justice. This power alone is capable of producing genuine and satisfying human communities and right relations to nature's communities. The community of God cannot be engineered. Technology, material consumption, and economic growth may enhance human power but offer little help in developing participatory communities. Reliance on these powers alone can in fact make matters worse by creating divisions.

Jesus also stressed the beginning of the community of God in small things, such as seeds that grow. He gathered a community largely of the poor and needy. He gave and found support in a small inner group of disciples. In this day of complex technologies, large corporations that dominate globalization, and mammoth bureaucracies, Jesus' stress seems out of place to many. In their pell-mell rush to increase the size and complexity of social organizations and technological processes, humans are missing something, however. For effective community and participation, size counts and must be limited in order for individuals to have significant and satisfying contacts.

The concern for the poor evident in the Gospels is another support for the norm of participation. Without some semblance of justice, there can be little participation in community. Extremes of wealth and poverty and disproportions of power create an envious and angry underclass without a stake in the community. Equality of worth, rough equality of power, and political freedom are prerequisites for genuine communities.

In the early church, small communities flourished. The Jerusalem church, while poor, had a remarkable sense of sharing. Paul's letter to the Romans contains perhaps the most ideal statement of community ever written (Romans 12). He also talked about the church as the body of Christ. It has many members, all of whom are united in Christ. Differences between Jew and Greek, male and female, slave and free are unimportant (Galatians 3:28). He repeatedly used the Greek word *koinonia*, rich in communal connotations, to describe the house churches he established.

All this is not to romanticize the early church. There was enough conflict for us to avoid sentimentalizing the notion of participation. It is difficult—more so in industrialized societies, even with their full range of communications—to achieve participatory communities. A multitude of decisions, each requiring expert technical judgments and having wide-ranging consequences, must be made in a timely way. Popular participation in decisions, especially when there is conflict, as there is in environmental disputes, can paralyze essential processes. Expedience often results in the exclusion of certain voices and interests. Impersonal, functional ways of relating become easy and further reduce participation.

The norm of participation calls for a reversal of this trend. At minimum, it means having a voice in critical decisions that affect one's life. For environmental problems, it means having a say—for example, in the selection of energy and resource systems, the technologies these systems incorporate, and the distribution of benefits and burdens these systems create. All this implies free and open elections, democratic forms of government, responsible economic institutions, and a substantial dose of good will.

Finally there is the difficult problem of how to bring other species and ecosystems into human decision making. In one sense, they are already included, since there is no way to exclude them. Humans are inextricably part of nature, and many human decisions have environmental consequences that automatically include other species and ecosystems. The problem is the large number of negative consequences that threaten entire species and systems and ultimately the human species, for humans are dependent on other species and functioning ecosystems. The task is to reduce and eliminate where possible these negative consequences. One reason is obviously pragmatic. Humans are fouling their own nests. Beyond this anthropocentric reason, however, it helps to see plants, animals, and their communities as having interests that humans should respect. They have a dignity of their own kind. They experience pleasure and pain. The norm of participation should be extended to include these interests and to relieve pain—in effect, to give other species a voice. Humans have an obligation to speak out for other forms of life that cannot defend themselves.

Solidarity

The norm of solidarity reinforces this inclusion as well as adding an important element to the inclusion of marginalized human beings. The norm highlights the communal nature of life in contrast to individualism and encourages individuals and groups to join in common cause with those who are victims of discrimination, abuse, and oppression. Underscoring the reciprocal relationship of individual welfare and the common good, solidarity calls for the powerful to share the plight of the powerless, for the rich to listen to the poor, and for humanity to recognize its fundamental interdependence with the rest of nature. The virtues of humility, compassion, courage, and generosity are all marks of the norm of solidarity.

Both creation accounts in Genesis emphasize the profound relationality of all of God's creation. These two accounts point to the fundamental social and ecological context of existence. Humanity was created for community. This is the foundation of solidarity. While all forms of creation are unique, they are all related to each other as part of God's creation.

Understood in this context and in relation to the concept of stewardship in the Gospels, the *imago Dei* tradition that has its origins in Genesis also serves as a foundation for solidarity. Creation in the image of God (*imago Dei*) places humans not in a position over or apart from creation but rather in the same loving relationship of God with creation. Just as God breathes life into the world (Genesis 7), humanity is given the special responsibility as God's stewards to nurture and sustain life.

In their descriptions of Jesus' life and ministry, the Gospels provide the clearest examples of compassionate solidarity. Jesus shows solidarity with the poor and oppressed; he eats with sinners, drinks from the cup of a Gentile woman, meets with outcasts, heals lepers, and consistently speaks truth to power. Recognizing that Jesus was the model of solidarity, Paul used the metaphor of the body of Christ to emphasize the continuation of this solidarity within the Christian community. Writing to the Christians in Corinth, Paul stresses that by virtue of their baptisms, they are all one "in Christ." Thus if one member suffers, all suffer together; if one member is honored, all rejoice together (1 Corinthians 12:26). It would be hard to find a better metaphor to describe the character of compassionate solidarity.

The norm of solidarity also finds its home in a theology of the cross. The cross is the central symbol in Christianity. It points to a God who works in the world not in terms of power *over* but power *in, with, and under*. This is revolutionary. It upsets normal ways of conceiving power. God suffers with all living things that groan in travail (Romans 8). In the words of Jesus, "The last shall be first, and the first shall be last" (Matthew 19:30; Mark 10:31; Luke 13:30). The one who "was in the form of God . . . emptied himself, taking the form of a servant" (Philemon 2:6-7). The implication is clear. Christians are called to suffer with each other and the rest of the creation, to change their ways, and to enter a new life of solidarity and action to preserve and protect the entire creation.

These four moral norms sketch the broad outline of an ethic of ecojustice. These norms are complemented by the following guidelines, which will be utilized in conjunction with the norms in the following chapters to engage in an ethical assessment of energy options and climate policy proposals.

Energy Policy Guidelines

Ethics involves careful, systematic reflection on moral questions. These moral questions arise in a variety of contexts from the intimacy of the home to public debates about policy questions. As I noted at the outset, Christian ethics is guided by several general moral norms, but the two that are most important are love and justice. We have explored in this chapter how various social and environmental problems have led Christian communities to develop an expanded ethic of ecological justice. It is not hard to see how the related moral norms of sustainability, sufficiency, participation, and solidarity might inform discussions about energy options and energy policy. For example, there is nothing sustainable about the world's dependency on fossil fuels, which poses grave threats to justice, peace, and the integrity of creation. The norm of sustainability urges us to find ways to live more sustainably by relying on current solar energy and the geothermal heat of the planet. The moral norm of sufficiency, however, reminds us that access to energy supplies is one of the things people need to escape a life of poverty and deprivation. Where sustainability emphasizes the welfare of future generations, sufficiency reminds us that we must also be concerned about the welfare of present generations, especially the poor.

The norms of participation and solidarity address how we meet and distribute our dual responsibilities for present and future generations. Given the absolute centrality of energy to modern ways of life, there are enormous economic interests at stake in any debates about energy options and energy policy. Those who benefit from the status quo will use their power to maintain their privilege and control. The norm of participation, however, values the participation of all and seeks to overcome obstacles to their empowerment. It is not easy to implement this norm, but it is vital given the power of special interests and lobbyists in the energy field. The norm of solidarity also insists that any efforts to meet our dual obligations to present and future generations be made in a way that is just. It is not fair for present generations to burden future generations with rapidly rising levels of greenhouse gases and the ecological and social devastation that scientists warn will be the consequence of global warming and climate change. Solidarity demands that present generations make sacrifices for the welfare of future generations, but solidarity also demands that this burden be shared equitably among those in the present generation. One of the solutions to the climate crisis is to capture the social and ecological costs of greenhouse gas (GHG) emissions in the prices of coal, oil, and natural gas. This will drive up the cost of energy for all people, but it will have a regressive impact on people who are poor. Solidarity insists that the rich bear a disproportionate share of this burden so that the poor do not.

In these and other ways, the four ecojustice norms provide a general means to assess energy options and sketch out new directions in energy policy. Ethicists often develop additional guidelines or criteria that are consistent with general norms in order to apply these norms to specific issues and policy questions. The task force that developed the 1981 Presbyterian statement on U.S. energy policy developed a list of guidelines to assess energy options. These guidelines fleshed out various dimensions of sustainability, sufficiency, participation, and solidarity. Robert Stivers was the chair of this task force. He and I recently revised these guidelines in our book, *Christian Environmental Ethics: A Case Method Approach*.[22] What follows is a brief description of these twelve guidelines:

- **Equity** concerns the impact of policy decisions on various sectors of society with special concern for the poor and vulnerable. Burdens and benefits should be assessed and distributed so that no group gains or loses disproportionately.
- **Efficiency** is the capability of an energy policy or alternative to provide power with the input of fewer resources. It also means frugality in consumption and a decrease in pollution. New technologies are essential to satisfying this guideline.
- **Adequacy** addresses the complex problem of supply. Policies and energy alternatives should be sufficient to meet basic energy needs. The meeting of basic needs takes priority until they are satisfied, then gives way to other guidelines, especially frugality and conservation.
- **Renewability** refers to the capacity of an energy option to replenish its source. Reliance on renewable sources should take priority.
- **Appropriateness** refers to the tailoring of energy systems to a) the satisfaction of basic needs, b) human capacities, c) end uses, d) local demand, and e) employment levels. Energy decisions should lead to a variety of scales and level of technical complexity.

- **Risk** concerns the measurable potential of an energy policy or alternative to harm human health, social institutions, and ecological systems. Low risk options are preferable.
- **Peace** points to the potential of an energy policy to decrease the prospects of armed conflict. While international cooperation is essential to a sustainable energy future, energy dependence should be avoided to prevent disruption of supplies.
- **Cost** refers to monetary costs as well as other social and environmental costs. All costs should be included in the prices consumers pay for energy.
- **Employment** concerns the impact of a policy or alternative on employment levels, skills, and the meaningfulness of work. Policies and systems should stimulate the creation of jobs and new skills.
- **Flexibility** points to the capacity of policies and options to be changed or reversed. High flexibility is preferable, and systems subject to sudden disruption should be avoided.
- **Timely decision-making** refers to the processes used to set energy policies and choose alternatives. Processes should allow for those affected to have a voice without leading to endless procrastination.
- **Aesthetics** points to beauty as one aspect of a flourishing life. Policies and alternatives that scar the landscape should be avoided.

Many of these guidelines are related to several ecojustice norms, but it is also possible to see how they flesh out particular norms. For example, the guidelines regarding renewability, risk, peace, flexibility, and aesthetics are all aspects of the norm of sustainability. The adequacy, efficiency, and cost guidelines all probe dimensions of the norm of sufficiency. The guidelines that address timely decision making, employment, and the appropriateness of various energy technologies are all expressions of the norm of participation. Finally, the emphasis on equity in the very first guideline reflects the central emphasis of the norm of solidarity. I use the four ecojustice norms and these twelve energy policy guidelines in the following two chapters to engage in a comprehensive ethical assessment of U.S. energy options and related public policies.

Guidelines for Ethical Assessment
of Climate Policies

After assessing U.S. energy options, the next two chapters in this book focus on climate policy. As I emphasized in the introduction, the current pace and projected increase in global warming are unprecedented in human history. Scientific studies released after the Intergovernmental Panel on Climate Change's Fourth Assessment Report have often been accompanied by increasingly loud and alarming warnings from scientists. All of this information is motivating policy makers and people around the world to step up efforts to develop effective climate policies. These policy proposals differ in many ways, but in general they all grapple with the following questions:

- What level of GHG concentrations would offer the greatest likelihood of avoiding ecological catastrophe, and how rapidly should nations reduce their emissions to achieve such a target?
- Who should bear responsibility for reducing emissions in the future, and to what extent does this depend on emissions in the past as well as the capacity to bear the costs associated with reducing emissions in the present?
- What are the best means to reduce GHG emissions, and how can they be employed in the most comprehensive, cost-effective, and just manner?
- When does it make more sense to invest resources to mitigate emissions in the present versus investing resources to help communities and nations adapt to climate change in the future?
- How can financial and technological resources be transferred to industries and nations that lack the means to invest in GHG mitigation and climate change adaptation strategies?
- How will reductions in GHG emissions be verified within a nation and between nations?
- How can climate policies be applied fairly so that they do not hinder economic competitiveness within or between nations?

This list of questions is illustrative, not definitive, and the best way to answer any of the questions is not self-evident. In some questions, the ethically normative dimensions are articulated, but in others, they are implicit. How should Christian communities answer these questions? What ethical resources could Christians utilize to assess competing climate policy proposals?

The ethic of ecojustice and its related moral norms can be utilized in general ways to conduct an ethical assessment of international and national climate policy proposals. For example, the ecojustice norm of sustainability precludes shortsighted emphases on economic growth that fundamentally harm Earth's climate in the future, but it also excludes any approaches to climate policy that don't address the suffering of over two billion people who are trapped in poverty today. Sustainability emphasizes the importance of healthy, interdependent communities for the welfare of present and future generations.

The ecojustice norm of sufficiency emphasizes that all of creation is entitled to share in the goods of creation. This means, most fundamentally, that all forms of life are entitled to those things that satisfy their basic needs and contribute to their fulfillment. Insofar as the norm of sufficiency repudiates wasteful and harmful consumption and emphasizes fairness, it represents one dimension of distributive justice. Many nations in the developing world are implicitly appealing to the norm of sufficiency as they demand the "right to development" and insist they not be required to make the same rate or level of reductions in GHG emissions as citizens of wealthy, developed nations.

The ecojustice norm of participation stresses that the interests of all forms of life are important and must be heard and respected in decisions that affect their lives. Those who champion the norm of participation should be worried about the growing number of lobbyists who are representing special interests with regard to climate policy. Today there are four global-warming lobbyists for every member of Congress in the United States. According to the Center for Public Integrity, more than 770 companies and organizations spent at least $90 million and hired more than 2,300 representatives to address U.S. climate policy in 2008. The largest player was the American Coalition for Clean Coal Electricity, which spent $9,945,276, dwarfing the next largest funder, Air Products and Chemicals, Inc., which spent $1,365,000.[23]

The ecojustice norm of solidarity highlights the kinship and interdependence of all forms of life and encourages support and assistance for those who suffer. Solidarity calls the powerful to share the plight of the powerless, the rich to listen to the poor, and humanity to recognize its fundamental interdependence with the rest of nature. The norm of solidarity supports intragenerational transfers of resources from the rich to the poor so that they can adapt to climate change both now and in the future, but it also calls present generations to make sacrifices for future generations as a matter of intergenerational ethical responsibility.

These four moral norms sketch the broad outline of an ethic of ecojustice and can be applied generally to debates about climate policy. As is the case with energy policy, however, additional ethical criteria are needed to assess particular climate policy proposals. I have developed the following guidelines to help expand and apply the ethic of ecojustice and its related moral norms to various climate policy proposals that are discussed later in this volume.[24] Different ethical guidelines address the temporal, structural, and procedural dimensions of these policy proposals.

Temporal Dimensions

- **Current urgency.** Given the fact of global warming and the dire consequences associated with rapid climate change, climate policy proposals should be evaluated on the extent to which they address what Martin Luther King Jr. famously termed "the fierce urgency of Now."[25]
- **Future adequacy.** The proposed level and timetable of reductions in GHG emissions must be sufficient to avoid catastrophic consequences associated with climate change.
- **Historical responsibility.** A greater share of the burden associated with reducing GHG emissions must fall on those who have been major emitters in the past.
- **Existing capacity.** Those with more financial and technological resources should bear a greater share of the cost associated with reducing emissions than those who have much less.
- **Political viability.** A morally praiseworthy climate proposal must have sufficient political support to make it realistic and viable.

Structural Dimensions

- **Scientific integrity.** Climate policies must be based on the best current science and have the capacity to be revised in light of future scientific findings.
- **Sectoral comprehensiveness.** An ethically adequate climate policy should spread GHG reduction requirements over all sectors of an economy (agriculture, heavy industry, transportation, and so on), rather than lay the burden or blame on one or more particular industries.
- **International integration.** Since the planet's atmosphere does not recognize political boundaries, national climate policies must be consistent with international agreements and be integrated with them.
- **Resource sharing.** Morally praiseworthy climate proposals should contain mechanisms to transfer resources from the rich to the poor, so the poor can bear the cost and acquire the technologies necessary to mitigate emissions in the present and adapt to climate change in the future.
- **Economic efficiency.** Climate policies that achieve the greatest measures of ecological and social well-being at the least economic cost are morally preferred.

Procedural Dimensions

- **Policy transparency.** It is vital that all parties be able to comprehend the impact of a climate policy upon them and to discern how and by whom the policy will be implemented.
- **Emissions verifiability.** With several principal greenhouse gases and emission sources spread around the world, climate policies must identify ways to verify emission reductions with a high degree of confidence and accuracy.
- **Political incorruptibility.** The auctioning of emission allowances and/or the collection of taxes on GHG emissions will generate major fiscal obligations that the rich and powerful will seek to avoid, as well as enormous revenue streams that some will try to misappropriate. Climate policies must be

designed so that they cannot easily be corrupted by the rich and abused by the powerful.

- **Implementational subsidiarity.** While the focus must be on global reductions of greenhouse gas concentrations, better climate policies will utilize the principle of subsidiarity to empower those closest to the source of the emissions to decide how best to achieve the reductions.

As was the case with the energy policy guidelines, many of these climate policy guidelines reflect aspects of different ecojustice norms, but they also can be associated with particular norms. For example, the guidelines of current urgency and future adequacy clearly address the norm of sustainability. So too do the guidelines that emphasize the scientific integrity of climate policy proposals and the verification of emission reductions. The norm of sufficiency is addressed in part by the guidelines that emphasize economic efficiency and sectoral comprehensiveness. Sufficiency is also addressed when the guidelines of historical responsibility and existing capacity are employed to place more of the burden for reducing GHG emissions on those who have the most financial capacity to bear it. The participation norm is fleshed out in the guidelines that emphasize policy transparency, political incorruptibility, international integration, implementational subsidiarity, and political viability. Finally, the guidelines of resource sharing, historical responsibility, and existing capacity all address the norm of solidarity and the equitable distribution of the financial burdens and moral responsibilities associated with reducing GHG emissions and adapting to climate change.

Conclusion

The following chapters utilize the ecojustice norms and these two sets of guidelines to ethically assess conventional and alternative U.S. energy options as well as climate policy proposals that have been and continue to be debated at the international level and within the U.S. Congress.

2. Conventional Energy Options

Energy is the world's biggest industry, by far . . . . All told, the global energy game is nearly a $2 trillion-a-year business.

VIJAY V. VAITHEESWARAN

ENERGY AND ENVIRONMENT CORRESPONDENT, *THE ECONOMIST*[1]

Our excessive reliance on a fossil-fuel based economy is destroying our planet's resources, impoverishing the poor, weakening the security of nations, and choking global economic potential.

BAN KI-MOON

SECRETARY-GENERAL OF THE UNITED NATIONS[2]

The world clearly needs new energy options, because current patterns of production and consumption are creating conditions that pose grave threats to justice, peace, and the integrity of creation. This is especially true with regard to global warming and the challenges posed by climate change. The Intergovernmental Panel on Climate Change (IPCC) emphasized in its Fourth Assessment Report published in 2007 that carbon dioxide emissions from fossil fuel combustion represented 56.6 percent of all global annual anthropogenic (human-caused) greenhouse gas (GHG) emissions from 1970 to 2004.[3] The impact of energy-related GHG emissions is even greater in the United States. The U.S. Environmental Protection Agency reports energy-related activities were the primary source of 86.3 percent of all U.S. anthropogenic GHG emissions in 2007, the last year for which full data are available.[4]

This chapter focuses on conventional U.S. energy options: coal, oil, natural gas, and nuclear power. It utilizes the four ecojustice norms and twelve energy guidelines described in the previous chapter to conduct an ethical assessment of these energy sources. The impact of existing energy policies and the potential for policy reform are discussed within this chapter and the next one, which focuses on alternative energy options.

Ecojustice Norms and Energy Policy Guidelines

Ecojustice Norms

- Sustainability
- Sufficiency
- Participation
- Solidarity

Energy Policy Guidelines

- Equity
- Efficiency
- Adequacy
- Renewability
- Appropriateness
- Risk
- Peace
- Cost
- Employment
- Flexibility
- Timely decision making
- Aesthetics

Conventional, Nonrenewable Energy Sources
in the United States

The U.S. Energy Information Administration (EIA) reports that 92.6 percent of the nation's primary energy consumption in 2008 was provided by coal, oil, natural gas, and nuclear power (fig. 2.1).[5] Primary energy is energy embodied in sources that human beings must capture or extract before the energy can be traded, used, or transformed. U.S. primary energy sources are utilized in different sectors of the economy and have been steadily growing over the last sixty years (fig. 2.2). In 2008, electricity generation (40.1 percent) was the largest consumer of primary energy supplies, followed by transportation (27.8 percent), the industrial sector (20.6 percent), and finally the residential and commercial sectors (10.8 percent).[6]

Fig. 2.1. U.S. Primary Energy Consumption by Source and Sector, 2008 (Quadrillion Btu)

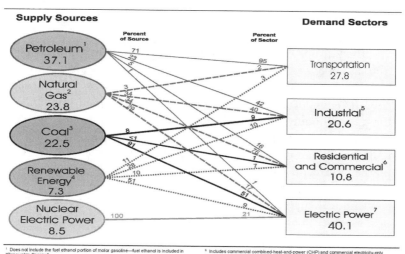

Source: Energy Information Administration, *Annual Energy Review 2008*, DOE/EIA-0384(2008) (Washington, D.C.: EIA, June 26, 2009), fig. 2.0, p. 37 accessed at http://www.eia.doe.gov/aer/pdf/aer.pdf.

Fig. 2.2. U.S. Energy Consumption by Sector

Total Consumption by End-Use Sector, 1949-2008

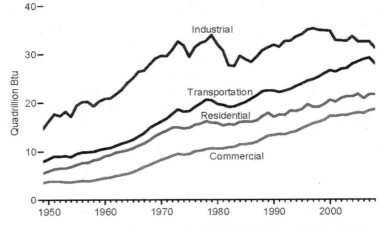

Source: Energy Information Administration, *Annual Energy Review 2008*, DOE/EIA-0384(2008) (Washington, D.C.: EIA, June 26, 2009), fig. 2.1a, p. 38, accessed at http://www.eia.doe.gov/aer/pdf/aer.pdf.

The EIA updated the reference case scenario it uses to make projections about energy supply and demand in the future after Congress passed the American Recovery and Reinvestment Act in February 2009. This important piece of legislation was designed to stimulate the U.S. economy, in part through several provisions to increase renewable energy production. Despite large anticipated investments in renewable energy, the EIA expects coal, oil, natural gas, and nuclear power to grow in volume and continue to supply 84 energy of U.S. energy in 2030.[7] Clearly, it will not be easy to shift away from these conventional energy options to a more sustainable energy path. We next assess each of these options in some detail.

Coal

The United States almost doubled its consumption of coal between 1970 and 2008. The vast majority of this coal during this time period has been consumed by the electric power sector (fig. 2.3).[8] The EIA reports that coal was used to generate 49 percent of U.S. electricity in 2008.[9] Coal is the most abundant fossil fuel in the world, and the United States has more reserves than any other nation. At current rates of consumption, the nation's coal supply has been projected to last over 250 years, though a recent study by the U.S. Geological Survey (USGS) indicates that considering only economically recoverable coal reserves may cut this length of time in half.[10] Nevertheless, given this large domestic resource, utilities in recent years have proposed building 151 new coal-fired power plants to meet rising demand. Early in 2007, the EIA estimated the nation would need 290 new plants to meet projected demand by 2030. Since then, at least 95 out of nearly 200 coal-fired power plants proposed by electric utilities have been canceled or postponed due to an April 2007 Supreme Court ruling that gave the Environmental Protection Agency authority to regulate carbon dioxide (CO_2) emissions.[11] These legal issues, combined with community opposition and financial uncertainty over possible carbon regulations in the future, are forcing electric utilities to reconsider major investments in coal-fired power plants.

Fig. 2.3. U.S. Coal Production and Use by Sector, 1949–2008

U.S. Coal Overview

U.S. Coal Consumption by Sector

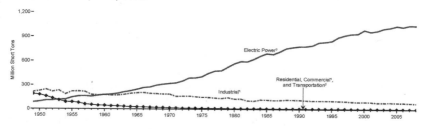

Source: Energy Information Administration, *Annual Energy Review 2008*, DOE/EIA-0384 (2008) (Washington, D.C.: EIA, June 26, 2009), fig. 7.1, p. 206, and fig. 7.3, p. 210, accessed at http://www.eia.doe.gov/aer/pdf/aer.pdf.

Viewed through the lens of the ecojustice norms and energy guidelines, coal provides the United States with a large domestic energy resource that reduces dependency on foreign supplies and thus reduces the chance for armed conflict. Coal also provides considerable employment in the mining, rail, and utility industries, and generates electricity at low economic costs. As the nation's dependency on foreign oil grows, many are also eager to tap the flexibility of this resource by converting coal into a liquid transportation fuel or into synthetic natural gas. These advantages are overwhelmed, however, by the fact that coal is a nonrenewable and carbon-intensive fossil fuel whose combustion is producing enormous GHG emissions. Coal-fired power plants alone produce approximately 40 percent of U.S. CO_2 emissions.[12] While these emissions will have a significant and inequitable impact on future generations through global climate change, they also have a deleterious impact on present generations through mercury pollution, acid rain, fly ash disposal, and the aesthetic destruction of mountaintops and valleys. Even though it may be cost-effective to provide 7 percent of the U.S. coal supply via mountaintop removal mining, the social, ecological, and aesthetic destruction it wages on communities is incalculable.[13] Continued dependence on coal-fired electricity generation violates the norms of sustainability and solidarity.

Cognizant of these flaws, the coal and utility industries are promoting a new generation of "clean coal" technologies. In fact, all of the remaining eighty-seven proposed new power plants intend to utilize one of four different technologies that either improve combustion or gasify coal, thus modestly increasing the efficiency of coal-fired power plants from approximately 38 percent to over 50 percent.[14]

The most important technology on the horizon, however, is carbon capture and sequestration (CCS). At some locations around the world, CO_2 is already being captured and pumped underground to force more oil out of the ground. The gas is not being permanently sequestered, however. Eventually, the gas is free to find its way back to the surface and up into the atmosphere. Given its contribution to global warming and climate change, the only way to responsibly expand coal-based generation in the future will be if the related carbon emissions can be permanently sequestered.

Research is under way to accomplish that goal, but even proponents of this technology acknowledge that it is at best fifteen years away from widespread commercial application.[15] Close scrutiny must be brought to bear on this research, because concentrations of CO_2 pose real risk to human and ecological health, for both present and future generations. Deep ocean storage risks acidifying water and damaging aquatic ecosystems. Storage underground as a gas poses risks to human populations, because CO_2 is heavier than air and can cause suffocation at concentrations of 7 percent to 8 percent by volume.

The scale of any significant amount of carbon capture and sequestration is daunting. A recent report by the Massachusetts Institute of Technology concludes, "If 60 percent of the CO_2 produced from U.S. coal-based power generation were to be captured and compressed to a liquid for geologic sequestration, its volume would about equal the total U.S. oil consumption of 20 million barrels per day."[16] A single 1,000-megawatt (MW) power plant can emit as much as 6 million tons of CO_2 per year. Over the course of a sixty-year operating life, such a plant would emit the equivalent of 3 billion gallons of oil. Compressed to a liquid, this amount of CO_2 would require an area of underground geological storage that is six times larger than what the oil industry calls a "giant" oil field.[17] The Pew Center on Global Climate Change claims the United States can store the current emissions from coal-fired power plants in depleted oil and gas reservoirs for several decades, and that other potential geological reservoirs have the potential to store current levels of emissions for over three hundred years.[18]

Theoretically, it may be possible to store this much CO_2 underground, but currently none of the 617 coal-fired power plants in the United States either capture or sequester carbon dioxide.[19] This has led the Pew Center to urge the federal government and electricity generators to develop ten to thirty CCS demonstration projects around the country over the next ten to fifteen years.[20] In June 2009, one of the most prominent attempts to demonstrate this technology received conditional support from the Obama administration. The FutureGen project in Mattoon, Illinois, would be the first commercial-scale CCS project in the country. The 275 MW power plant would originally capture 60 percent of its emissions but could be upgraded later to capture 90 percent. The Department of Energy has pledged just over $1 billion for the project, which is currently estimated to cost $2.4 billion if it is completed by 2013 or 2014.[21] While it is not known whether it will be possible to permanently sequester CO_2 from U.S. coal-fired power plants, different studies estimate CCS will increase the cost of coal-fired electricity by 40 percent to 100 percent.[22]

It is possible that China will complete two large CCS pilot projects before the United States brings the FutureGen project on line. China is the world's largest coal producer, and it uses about half of its coal to generate electricity. China now leads the world in GHG emissions. Even if all the other nations in the world cut their emissions 80 percent by 2050, scientists predict the global average temperature will still increase 2.7°C if China continues to produce emissions at the same rate as it does today.[23] The Obama administration has made CCS cooperation a major part of bilateral climate change negotiations between the two nations. Without agreement between the world's two largest polluters, any attempt to develop a climate agreement to replace the Kyoto Protocol, (the limited but currently binding international agreement to reduce GHG emissions), is doomed to fail.

As we have seen, the energy guidelines and ecojustice norms reveal a host of issues associated with the combustion of coal. While coal adequately supplies a large share of U.S. primary energy consumption at currently low economic costs, the social and ecological costs of this nonrenewable and inefficient resource are significant. The benefits coal provides to current generations in terms of low energy costs and related employment are offset by the huge risk future CO_2 emissions pose with regard to global warming and climate change. Given the fact that CO_2 is the principal greenhouse gas, and that the combustion of coal produces enormous emissions, the ecojustice norms of sustainability and solidarity justify a moratorium on all new coal-fired power plants until it can be demonstrated that carbon capture and sequestration can be done in a verifiable and permanent way. In the meantime, the nation should use the next two decades to reduce demand for electricity by practicing energy conservation and investing in energy efficiency and renewable energy.

Oil

Petroleum products including gasoline and diesel power the nation's transportation sector and also serve as a primary feedstock in the plastics and chemical industries. While the United States now produces far more coal and natural gas than oil, imported oil makes petroleum the largest primary source of energy in the United States, providing 39 percent of the nation's energy.[24] Over 96 percent of the vehicles in the United States run on petroleum products.[25] The United States consumes 25 percent of the world's petroleum supply and imports 66 percent of the oil it consumes.[26] In 2008, the United States imported 12.9 million barrels of oil per day and consumed 19.4 million barrels per day (fig. 2.4).

Fig. 2.4. U.S. Petroleum Production and Consumption

Overview, 1949–2004

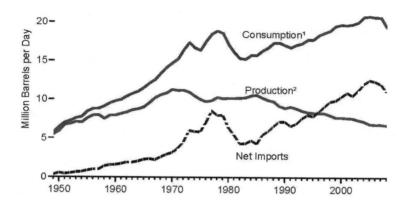

Crude Oil and Natural Gas Plant Liquids Production, 1949–2004

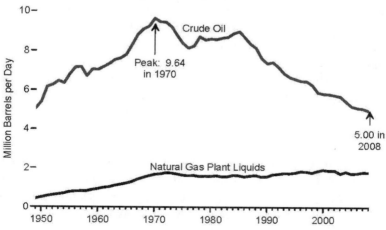

Source: Energy Information Administration, *Annual Energy Review 2008*, DOE/EIA-0384(2008) (Washington, D.C.: EIA, June 26, 2009), fig. 5.1, p. 128, accessed at http://www.eia.doe.gov/aer/pdf/aer.pdf.

Energy expert Daniel Yergin says, "We are so dependent on oil, and oil is so embedded in our daily doings, that we hardly stop to comprehend its pervasive significance."[27] Yet we must. If present trends continue, recent studies indicate that the 800 million vehicles on the world's roads today will grow to 2 billion vehicles by 2030.[28] This growth in vehicle ownership will produce a rapid increase in petroleum demand.

The drilling, refining, distribution, and combustion of petroleum products (along with other fossil fuels) pose several grave threats to peace and planetary welfare. Before I present evidence to support this stark thesis, I confess that I am certainly part of the problem. Together, my wife and I have owned ten cars over the past twenty-five years and driven over 300,000 miles. We are part of the 92 percent of U.S. households that own a car that travels an average of 12,000 miles a year.[29] In fact, we have owned two cars for much of our married life and do so now. Like most Americans, we use these vehicles primarily to get to work and to shop for household goods, but we have also driven many miles over the years to attend our sons' sports events. In fact, we have added two more drivers to the road by teaching both of our sons to drive.

Cars help us be the relational creatures we are. They help us maintain social relationships with family and friends who are both far and near. They also help us appreciate (to some extent) God's beautiful world, which often whizzes by at high speeds. I relish the solitude and scenic beauty that accompanies me on many of my trips in Iowa, Minnesota, and Wisconsin. I also cherish the great experiences our family has enjoyed as we traveled across the country on various vacations. In a recent national poll, 39 percent of Americans said they "love" their car.[30] While my wife and I may not be willing to go that far, the reality is we can't easily imagine our lives without a car.

While many of us may not be able to conceive of how we could live our lives without a car, it appears the world may soon have to find some alternative way to fuel the vehicles we drive. Unlike coal, the world's proven reserves of oil may soon be inadequate to fuel growing consumption demands much longer. U.S. oil production peaked in the 1970s, and many predict that global oil production will peak within the next two or three decades, if it has not done so already. In fact, oil giant BP reported in its annual *Statistical Review of World Energy* that the world's proven oil reserves fell in 2008 for the first time in ten years. The company noted that this level of reserves would supply the world market for forty-two years at current production levels.[31] Once conventional oil production peaks, the U.S. Energy Information Administration (EIA) expects global production to decline precipitously.[32] If global oil production peaks in 2026 at approximately 42 billion barrels per year, the EIA projects global production in 2050 to be approximately 6 billion barrels per year, which is a decline of approximately 85 percent. This rapid change in the availability of oil has the potential to spur inflation, plunge economies into recession, and ignite conflict around the world. While it is possible to extract oil from oil shale and tar sands, and even to convert coal to synthetic petroleum, all of these options have high costs both economically and environmentally. Clearly, the world needs to find alternative fuels to power the transportation sector.

Fig. 2.5. Global Oil Production Scenarios

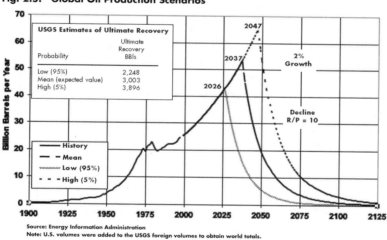

Source: Energy Information Administration
Note: U.S. volumes were added to the USGS foreign volumes to obtain world totals.

Source: John H. Wood, Gary R. Long, and David F. Morehouse, "Long-Term World Oil Supply Scenarios," Energy Information Administration Web site, August 18, 2004, fig. 2, accessed at http://www.eia.doe.gov/pub/oil_gas/petroleum/feature_articles/2004/worldoilsupply/oilsupply04.html. R/P refers to the Reserves-to-Production ratio, which is the remaining amount of a non-renewable resource, expressed in years.

As we have seen, there is a significant link between oil and geopolitics that poses a direct threat to peace, democracy, and justice. The link between oil, war, and geopolitics is not new. At the turn of the twentieth century, Great Britain decided to convert its Royal Navy from a coal-burning fleet to an oil-burning fleet. This led Winston Churchill to help form the Anglo-Persian Oil Company, which invested heavily in what today is Iran.[33] In 1940, Japan occupied

French Indochina (Vietnam) and joined the Axis powers of Germany and Italy. These actions led the United States and Britain to launch an oil boycott against Japan. Cut off from oil, Japan invaded and captured the Dutch East Indies (Indonesia), which ignited the war in the Pacific.[34] During World War II, the United States was the world's leading oil producer, supplying over 85 percent of the oil the Allied forces consumed during the war.[35] By 1943, however, it became clear that the United States was rapidly depleting its domestic supplies. In 1944, the State Department issued the *Foreign Petroleum Policy of the United States,* which sought "a broad policy of conservation of Western Hemisphere petroleum reserves" and "substantial and orderly expansion of production in Eastern Hemisphere sources of supply, principally the Middle East."[36]

From that point on every U.S. president has emphasized the strategic importance of Middle Eastern oil. A State Department report issued during the Truman administration described Saudi Arabia's oil resources as a "stupendous source of strategic power, and one of the greatest material prizes in human history."[37] During the Cold War, the Eisenhower administration promised to use U.S. combat forces to defend countries in the Middle East from Soviet aggression and provided military assistance to friendly regimes. The Nixon administration supplied advanced weaponry worth billions of dollars to Saudi Arabia and Iran in the early 1970s,[38] but when the Shah of Iran fell, President Jimmy Carter decided to abandon the use of surrogates to protect America's access to oil from the Persian Gulf. President Carter told Congress that the United States would use "any means necessary, including military force," to secure oil from this area.[39] In 1983, the Reagan administration established the U.S. Central Command (CentCom) to project military power into this region.[40] In 1990, President George H. W. Bush deployed CentCom troops in Saudi Arabia and utilized CentCom and other military forces to repel Iraqi troops from the oil fields of Kuwait. What is clear from this brief history is that Operation Iraqi Freedom, which was launched in March 2003, is only the latest in a series of U.S. military engagements in the Persian Gulf.[41] Given the fact that the United States continues to import about 25 percent of its oil from the Middle East, it will likely not be the last.

U.S. dependence on oil from the Middle East in particular is ironic, self-defeating, and counterproductive. It is ironic because the U.S. military is the nation's largest consumer of oil. In 2006, the defense establishment spent $13.6 billion to consume 340,000 barrels of oil per day, representing 1.5 percent of total U.S. energy consumption.[42] In 2006, the average U.S. soldier in Iraq and Afghanistan consumed on a daily basis 16 gallons of oil either directly or indirectly through the use of Humvees, tanks, trucks, helicopters, and air strikes.[43] It is a bitter irony that some wars in the future may be fought in part to secure the oil to fight them.

U.S. dependence on Persian Gulf oil is self-defeating because some of the money the United States expends to import oil from this region has wound up in the pockets of those committed to sponsoring terrorism around the world. Fifteen of the nineteen terrorists who hijacked planes and crashed them into the World Trade Center and the Pentagon were citizens of Saudi Arabia. Osama bin Laden is a Saudi, and oil money has helped finance al Qaeda. In 2005, the United States spent nearly $40 billion to import oil from the Persian Gulf while at the same time it financed a war on terror.[44] To some extent, every gallon of gas purchased in the United States helps fund terrorists.[45]

U.S. dependence on foreign oil is counterproductive because it often requires that the United States do business with nations that do not support democracy. Tom Friedman refers to this as the First Law of Petropolitics: "In oil-rich petrolist states, the price of oil and the pace of freedom tend to move in opposite directions."[46] As we have seen, Nigeria and Angola are experiencing civil unrest because their oil wealth has not been spread very broadly. In addition, Vladimir Putin in Russia and Hugo Chavez in Venezuela are taking steps to shore up their personal power in ways many believe will undermine democracy in these nations. All of these realities pose dangers to democracy and thus violate the norm of participation.

In addition to social, economic, and political problems associated with heavy reliance on oil in the United States, there are also serious environmental problems. The impact on air pollution has already been noted. Oil-related water pollution also is important. Every year, tankers shipping oil to foreign markets spill large amounts of oil in the oceans, which fouls beaches, threatens freshwater supplies, and causes significant harm to wildlife. Globally, there have been at least eight spills of over a million gallons in the past fifteen years. The largest spill in U.S. waters occurred in 1989, when the *Exxon Valdez* ran aground in Alaska's Prince William Sound. This spill of almost 11 million gallons caused extensive environmental damage and cost the company over $2 billion to clean up.[47] Sadly, the U.S. Minerals Management Service projects a 94 percent likelihood that a spill of similar proportions will occur along the West Coast of the United States by 2020.[48]

The storage of gasoline and diesel fuel on land also poses dangers to water quality. In 1992, the U.S. Environmental Protection Agency reported that approximately 25 percent of underground storage tanks at gas stations around the nation were leaking. This precipitated a vigorous cleanup campaign, but numerous communities around the nation have had their groundwater supplies polluted. More recently, the American Petroleum Institute has reported that at least 35 percent of their member distribution centers have leaks in above- and below-ground tanks that threaten water supplies.[49]

The most significant environmental dangers posed by U.S. (and global) oil consumption, however, are related to global warming and climate change. The combustion of petroleum products produces 43 percent of U.S. CO_2 emissions.[50] Approximately 67 percent of these emissions are attributable to the vehicle transportation sector of the U.S. economy.[51] While we enjoy the convenience of our cars and drive ever more miles every year, we pass the ecological consequences of our driving on to future generations who have no control over our actions. This clearly violates the norms of sustainability and solidarity.

To recap, the energy guidelines offer a largely negative assessment of oil. While energy-intensive and inexpensive petroleum products have powered the U.S. and global economies for decades, thus increasing the number of jobs and raising standards of living for many, it appears the days of cheap oil may be coming to a rapid end. The cost of this flexible resource has started to climb in recent years and appears likely to increase rapidly as the world approaches and surpasses peak global oil production. This will increase the risk of global conflict, threaten world peace, and imperil the poor—who will inequitably bear the rising cost of petroleum products. Finally, as was noted in the introduction, the combustion of nonrenewable petroleum fuels produces a host of air pollutants that adversely affect human health and also cloak many urban areas in a veil of harmful smog that also mars the aesthetic quality of the landscape.

The ecojustice norms also lead to a serious critique of oil. Dwindling supplies indicate that this is not a sustainable energy source that will be adequate in the future to meet global demand. In addition, the GHG emissions associated with the combustion of petroleum products not only violate the norm of sustainability, they also violate the norm of solidarity. It is not fair to burden future generations with the consequences of our oil consumption today. While inexpensive oil supplies have helped many human communities better meet their basic needs, there is little question that this resource is not being used efficiently, and for many, its use serves far more than basic needs. In addition, the global warming associated with petroleum combustion is imperiling the ecological welfare of many species, which increasingly struggle to satisfy their basic needs. Both of these realities violate the norm of sufficiency. Finally, there is no question historically that there is an inverse relationship between oil wealth and democratic power. Insofar as petroleum products have helped to concentrate power in the hands of the few and have thus thwarted the democratic will of the many, these developments also violate the norm of participation. Viewed through the lens of the ecojustice norms and the energy policy guidelines, there is little question that reducing U.S. dependence on oil and developing alternative transportation fuels both need to become national priorities.

Natural Gas

Natural gas is the most desirable fossil fuel, because it is about half as carbon intensive per unit of energy as coal or oil, and it is a highly flexible resource that can be utilized in a variety of end uses and sized to scale. After petroleum, natural gas is the second largest source of primary energy in the United States. While natural gas is normally 70 percent to 90 percent methane, it can also include ethane, propane, butane, and pentane.[52]

Prices for natural gas have oscillated wildly in recent years, in part due to market manipulation by companies like Enron, but mostly because of the increase in natural-gas-fired electricity generation (fig. 2.6). Utilities have invested in gas-fired power plants for various reasons. They are ideal for responding to peak electricity demands throughout the year because they can be brought on line quickly. In addition, they are more economical to build than coal-fired or nuclear power plants, and it is easier for utilities to secure the necessary environmental permits. This increased demand for natural gas due to electricity generation in recent years has driven up the cost of heating homes and businesses as well as the cost of production in agriculture and other industries where natural gas serves as an important energy source or chemical feedstock.

Fig. 2.6.   U.S. Natural Gas Consumption and Real Prices by Sector

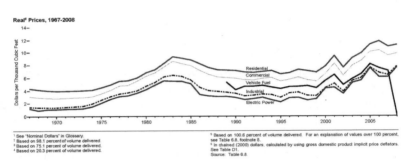

¹ See "Nominal Dollars" in Glossary.
² Based on 98.1 percent of volume delivered.
³ Based on 75.1 percent of volume delivered.
⁴ Based on 20.3 percent of volume delivered.

⁵ Based on 100.6 percent of volume delivered. For an explanation of values over 100 percent,
see Table 6.8, footnote 8.
⁶ In chained (2000) dollars, calculated by using gross domestic product implicit price deflators.
See Table D1.
Source: Table 6.8.

Source: Energy Information Administration, *Annual Energy Review 2008*, DOE/EIA-0384(2008) (Washington, D.C.: EIA, June 26, 2009), fig. 6.5, p. 194, and fig. 6.8, p. 200, accessed at http://www.eia.doe.gov/aer/pdf/aer.pdf.

Recently, however, natural gas prices have fallen to almost record lows because of reduced economic activity during the global recession as well as increased discoveries of natural gas in the United States. These new supplies are due to advanced horizontal drilling technology, chemicals, and large amounts of pumped water that are used to fracture rock in huge coal shale beds found throughout North America.[53] The Natural Gas Supply Association reports that these unconventional sources now supply 10 percent to 12 percent of U.S. demand but have the potential to supply one-quarter of U.S. demand in the future.[54] The Potential Gas Committee, the official governmental authority on gas supplies in the United States, reported in June 2009 that new shale gas discoveries have increased the nation's estimated gas reserves by 35 percent.[55] The Natural Resources Defense Council, however, reports there are cases around the United States where water contamination has been linked to hydraulic fracturing activities. The Energy Policy Act of 2005 exempted hydraulic fracturing from requirements under the Safe Drinking Water Act, but recently Democratic lawmakers have introduced legislation to overturn this previous decision.[56] The American Petroleum Institute claims a ban on hydraulic fracturing would result in a 45 percent reduction in natural gas production by 2014, force the United States to import more liquefied natural gas, and harm the economy.[57]

Application of the energy guidelines produces a mixed assessment of natural gas. On the one hand, it is far less polluting than the other fossil fuels, and it is playing an increasingly important role, especially in electric power generation. Natural gas is also used in many other ways by a wide variety of people in the U.S. economy. It serves as the primary heating fuel for most of the U.S. population, it provides a source of heat and a chemical feedstock for various industries, and it fuels many backyard barbecue grills. There is no question that this is a very flexible, efficient, and appropriate fuel source that supplies a major percentage of U.S. primary energy. Since most natural gas is still produced domestically, and the transport of natural gas supplies takes place through buried pipelines, this fuel source poses far less risk to peace and human health. It also does not mar the aesthetic quality of landscapes, for example, in the way mountaintop coal removal does.

On the other hand, even though natural gas is less carbon intensive than coal and oil, it is still a fossil fuel and the source of a significant amount of GHG emissions. Natural gas also is not a renewable resource. Even though U.S. natural gas reserves have been increasing recently, experts predict global production will peak in the first half of this century and be followed by even higher prices. The majority of global supplies are unevenly concentrated in the Middle East and Russia, so the potential for conflict will increase over access to this valuable energy resource in the future. The United States now imports a growing percentage of natural gas from Canada, Mexico, and the Caribbean—increasingly in the form of liquefied natural gas, which is dangerous to transport and vulnerable to terrorists.

The ecojustice norms of sustainability, sufficiency, and solidarity require us to use this valuable resource wisely as a bridge to a future in which fossil fuels play a diminishing role. Key to this effort will be to replace the role natural gas plays in electrical power generation with investments in electricity generated by renewable energy systems. This would free up natural gas for a variety of purposes, including its use as a lower-carbon transportation fuel. Many taxi fleets and mass-transit vehicles around the world are already powered by natural gas. Others have proposed using natural gas to fuel small delivery trucks and even personal automobiles. Some have also proposed increasing natural gas supplies by gasifying coal and mining methane hydrates sequestered on the ocean floor into natural gas, but this would be expensive economically and environmentally. It would be more prudent to capture and utilize methane that is already being emitted into the atmosphere via livestock waste lagoons and municipal landfills, because methane is twenty-one times more potent a greenhouse gas than carbon dioxide.[58] Nevertheless, there is little question that the U.S. economy will need to utilize increasing amounts of natural gas if it is going to replace coal and oil consumption, and thereby reduce GHG emissions. The ecojustice norms all support increasing supplies and consumption of natural gas if these supplies can be garnered in a socially and ecologically responsible way. The efficient use of this valuable resource is the least expensive and most immediate way to increase natural gas supplies.

Nuclear Power

The most controversial conventional energy source in the United States is probably nuclear power. I give extended attention to it because many believe increased investments in nuclear power are essential to reduce GHG emissions in the United States, while others believe the drawbacks far outweigh any potential gains that would be achieved through additional investments in this energy source.

Currently 104 commercial reactors produce 20 percent of the nation's electricity and serve approximately 50 million people (fig. 2.7).[59] About 50 of these reactors have recently received twenty-year license renewals, and approximately 40 more are expected to submit relicensing applications by 2013. The Nuclear Regulatory Commission (NRC) has approved all relicensing requests to date.[60] While no new reactors have come on line in the United States since 1996, 30 are now on the drawing boards, due to a variety of tax, insurance, and production subsidies made available to the industry via the federal Energy Policy Act of 2005.[61] Globally, 439 nuclear power reactors are in operation, generating approximately 15 percent of the world's electricity. Around the world, 35 new reactors are under construction, and almost all of these are in Asia.[62]

Fig. 2.7. U.S. Nuclear Generating Units

Operable Units,[1] 1957–2008

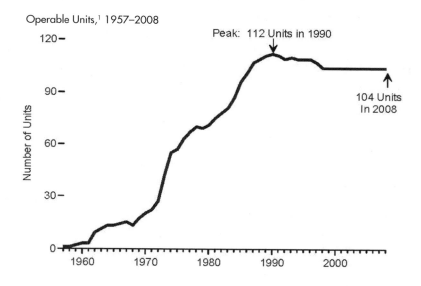

Full-Power Operating Licenses Issued,[2] 1957–2008

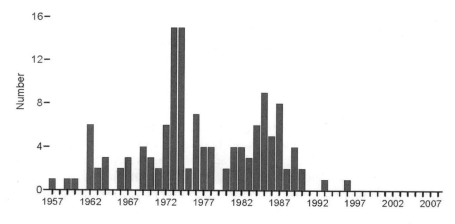

Source: Energy Information Administration, *Annual Energy Review 2008*, DOE/EIA-0384(2008) (Washington, D.C.: EIA, June 26, 2009), fig. 9.1, p. 274, accessed at http://www.eia.doe.gov/aer/pdf/aer.pdf.

Together with coal-fired power plants, nuclear power reactors are the backbone of the nation's base load electricity supply. In other words, they produce electricity twenty-four hours a day throughout the year and seldom have to be taken off line for maintenance. On the one hand, nuclear power plants extract an enormous amount of energy from the nuclear fuel they utilize. On the other hand, nuclear power plants, like coal-fired power plants, are relatively inefficient because a great deal of the energy they utilize from nuclear fission is lost as heat. Thus, while nuclear power plants largely satisfy the adequacy guideline, they fall short when viewed in terms of the efficiency guideline. Like coal-fired power plants, nuclear power plants are also huge facilities that cost billions of dollars to construct. As such, they are not very flexible facilities, in contrast to natural gas power plants that can be easily powered up and down.

Given that we face the prospect of rapid climate change, the primary strength of nuclear power is that it produces virtually no GHG emissions once reactors are operational and construction is completed. This is very attractive from the perspective of the sustainability norm. While construction costs are very high, operational costs have been relatively low. In addition, while the region around Chernobyl in Russia had to be abandoned and cordoned off due to high radiation levels after a reactor melt-down and explosion, the nuclear power industry in the United States has never suffered such a major catastrophe. The Nuclear Regulatory Commission proudly emphasizes that there has been no loss of life associated with the operation of the nation's commercial nuclear reactors in the history of the industry. These facts lead to a favorable conclusion when nuclear power is assessed in relation to energy guidelines pertaining to the adequacy of sufficient energy production, operational risk, and operational costs.

The primary weakness of nuclear power is that the United States has not figured out how to dispose of the highly radioactive waste that is produced by the reactors. Spent nuclear fuel contains many highly radioactive elements such as cesium, strontium, technetium, neptunium, and various forms of plutonium. Some of these elements will remain radioactive for a few years, but many will be radioactive for millions of years.[63] U.S. law requires that any permanent disposal of high-level nuclear waste must protect human health and safety for up to a million years.[64] Human civilizations based on agriculture are approximately ten thousand years old. It is not hard to see how this failure to deal with nuclear waste is a violation of the solidarity norm and the risk guideline when viewed in a long-term perspective.

Currently, there are about 55,000 metric tons (MT) of high-level nuclear waste from nuclear power reactors stored in over 120 locations in thirty-nine states that require permanent disposal.[65] This waste is primarily in the form of spent fuel rod assemblies, which are piling up in cooling ponds and in aboveground concrete storage casks because the federal government has failed to open an underground geological repository to receive this waste. Congress mandated in 1987 that Yucca Mountain in Nevada become the site for this facility. Its original opening in 1998 has been postponed several times for both scientific and political reasons, and it is now slated to open no sooner than 2020. This delay violates the guideline of timely decision making. The Department of Energy (DOE) has also spent $13.5 billion researching Yucca Mountain since 1983 and estimates that developing and operating the facility will cost at least $96.2 billion over its lifetime, assuming it opens in 2020 and closes in 2133. The agency also projects that transporting the waste to the site over the life of the facility will cost an additional $195 billion.[66] That's a lot of money simply to deal with waste disposal. Nuclear power is not a low-cost energy source.

If and when the facility does open, it will be too small to accommodate the amount of spent nuclear fuel produced to date. As a result, the Department of Energy recently notified the President and Congress that the United States needs a second underground geological repository to store the increasing amount of commercially produced spent nuclear fuel and other high-level radioactive waste. The agency proposes that Congress increase the amount that can be stored at Yucca Mountain from the current limit of 70,000 MT to at least 130,000 MT in order to meet this need.[67] If Congress decides not to open or expand the storage capacity of Yucca Mountain, the DOE estimates it will take twenty-eight to thirty-seven years to locate, design, and build an alternative underground repository.[68]

Utilities that own and operate nuclear reactors have filed over seventy lawsuits against the DOE for failing to take possession of their spent nuclear fuel under the terms of the Nuclear Waste Policy Act. Since 1982, ratepayers served by these utilities have been paying one-tenth of a cent per kilowatt-hour into a federal fund that is to be used to build a permanent geological storage facility. The proceeds in the fund now exceed $30 billion, and utilities are suing to be reimbursed for the costs associated with storing their wastes on-site. The DOE is currently liable for $11 billion even if the Yucca Mountain facility opens in 2020.[69] The federal government has settled twenty-nine of the cases that have been filed against the DOE, which has resulted in payments of approximately $1 billion thus far to the utilities.[70] Several state legislatures are now considering bills that would stop, reduce, or place in escrow the ratepayer contributions to the federal waste disposal fund until Yucca Mountain or another facility opens.[71]

As a solution to the liability issue, the DOE recently proposed to Congress that DOE take possession of the waste on an interim basis until a final waste disposal solution is determined.[72] The agency estimates it would cost $743 million to operate such an interim storage facility from 2015 to 2025.[73] This short approval and operations time frame is highly optimistic, given the recent experience of a similar private venture. In 2006, the NRC granted a license to Private Fuel Storage, LLC, to construct an interim storage facility large enough to accommodate 40,000 MT of spent nuclear fuel on a portion of the 18,000-acre Skull Valley Goshute Indian Reservation near Salt Lake City, Utah. This highly controversial project had been reviewed by the NRC and debated by the citizens of Utah for ten years after Private Fuel Storage filed its license application with the NRC in 1997. Ultimately, the project was scuttled when the Bureau of Indian Affairs and the Bureau of Land Management both issued decisions against different aspects of the project.[74]

President Obama's proposed budget for the 2010 fiscal year reduced federal funding for Yucca Mountain by $90 million to a total of $197 million. This reduction of funds ensures that no further study will take place at the site. The requested funds will be utilized by the DOE to respond to queries from the NRC as it processes the DOE's licensing request for the Yucca Mountain facility.[75] U.S. Secretary of Energy Steven Chu has reassured members of the Senate Budget Committee that he supports expansion of nuclear power in the United States and intends to establish a "blue-ribbon" commission of experts to evaluate storage options for nuclear waste and make recommendations to the administration. He believes dry-cask storage of spent nuclear fuel at reactors provides a safe solution for decades until a new long-term storage strategy can be formulated.[76] The vast majority of these casks are stored near lakes and major waterways in the United States. The only nuclear plant in Iowa was nearly marooned during the record floods in 2008. While employees could ultimately have been ferried to the facility by helicopter, the facility was fortunate that the floodwaters stopped rising before they breached the facility's interim storage facility for spent nuclear fuel.

It is clear from this brief history of Yucca Mountain that the United States has not yet determined how to safely dispose of its high-level nuclear waste. This clearly violates the norms of sustainability and solidarity. It is not fair to burden future generations with this highly toxic waste. In addition, the endless delays in finding a permanent disposal solution also violate the guideline of timely decision making. The energy guidelines pertaining to cost, risk, and appropriateness illuminate additional concerns related to nuclear power.

For example, with regard to cost, the Associated Press reported in 2009 that utilities are not setting aside enough money to decommission and dismantle nuclear reactors when they become too radioactive to operate. Large reductions in stock market valuations and other investments have left about half of the reactors in the United States without sufficient funds for this ultimate task. According to the study, the average cost to dismantle a reactor is currently estimated at $450 million, but the typical plant owner has only $300 million available to do the job. This information has sparked fears that some utilities may walk away from their responsibilities or may no longer be in business when decommissioning is necessary, thus burdening taxpayers with these expenses.[77]

Cost, in fact, is the main obstacle facing the nuclear power industry. The editors of *The Economist* summarized the situation famously in a cover story on the industry in 2001 when they quipped, "Nuclear power, once claimed to be too cheap to meter, is now too costly to matter."[78] In 2008, the average cost to build a 1,500 MW nuclear power plant was over $7 billion, which is a huge sum for utilities and their financiers.[79] A recent study estimates the cost of electricity from a new nuclear power plant at 14¢ per kilowatt-hour (kWh), compared with 7¢ per kWh from a wind farm, and this does not include additional costs related to waste disposal, accident insurance, and plant decommissioning.[80] While safety concerns receive the bulk of the attention, the simple fact is that high costs are the main reason nuclear power will have difficulty expanding in the future. The DOE attempted to overcome this barrier in 2009 by offering $18.5 billion in loan guarantees to four power companies proposing to build seven new nuclear reactors in the United States by 2016.[81] Lacking such federal guarantees, the Canadian province of Ontario recently suspended a $22 billion plan to build what would have been the first two new nuclear reactors in North America in over thirty years.[82]

Another source of concern revolves around rising levels of operating costs. While it is true that nuclear power plants do not emit greenhouse gases during operation, they are not a renewable form of energy, because they rely on enriched uranium for fuel, and conventional uranium supplies are limited. The International Atomic Energy Agency estimates that eighty years' worth of uranium is left at current rates of consumption, and prices recently have been climbing.[83]

While cost factors are a major limitation, risk and safety issues do remain important as well. Recent discoveries of steel embrittlement and leaks of radioactive tritium into groundwater supplies from aging reactor facilities raise concerns about the safety risks associated with operating these facilities beyond the length of their original operating licenses.[84] While reactor facilities are heavily guarded, many fear what would happen if terrorists managed to damage a reactor or casks entombing spent fuel rods outside the reactor building. Others ask whether nuclear power is an appropriate way to produce the steam used to propel the generators that produce electricity. The complexity and danger of this energy source are so great that it is regulated by an independent body within the federal government, the Nuclear Regulatory Commission.

Advocates within the industry point to new reactor designs, which they believe will make nuclear reactors much safer to operate in the future.[85] Some also encourage the United States to reprocess its spent nuclear fuel in order to reduce the waste burden and to recycle the energy that remains in spent fuel rod assemblies. President Jimmy Carter abandoned reprocessing in the 1970s over concerns about nuclear proliferation and because he believed it was too expensive. The federal Energy Policy Act of 2005 reversed this policy by authorizing $580 million for research and development of nuclear reprocessing and transmutation processes.[86] Recently, the Department of Energy announced it will remove 9 MT of plutonium from hundreds of the nation's nuclear warheads and refabricate the plutonium into a mixed uranium and plutonium oxide (MOX) fuel that can be utilized in commercial nuclear reactors.[87]

France reprocesses over 1,000 MT of spent nuclear fuel every year from its fifty-nine reactors, but it never built breeder reactors that were supposed to burn up the plutonium and other high-level nuclear waste left over after reprocessing. With breeder reactors out of the picture, France is utilizing a MOX fuel that consists of 8 percent plutonium and 92 percent depleted uranium in about 20 percent of the nation's reactors. This MOX fuel contains almost five times as much plutonium as conventional, enriched uranium fuel, which increases the risk of unexpected chain reactions during operation and reprocessing. In addition, spent MOX fuel is three times as hot as spent uranium fuel and thus needs to be placed in cooling ponds for 150 years before it can be chopped up and vitrified in glass logs before it is placed in an underground waste repository like Yucca Mountain. These used fuel assemblies are starting to pile up at France's reprocessing facility in La Hague and have as yet no permanent home in an underground geological repository, though France hopes to open a proposed facility in 2025.[88]

Given the extremely toxic nature of high-level nuclear waste, the ecojustice norm of solidarity and the energy guideline of equity require that the issue of long-term waste be resolved. It is not fair to burden future generations with highly toxic waste. At the same time, the norm of sustainability and the adequacy guideline remind us that nuclear power provides a significant amount of the U.S. electricity supply and does not produce GHG emissions that imperil generations in the future. Like natural gas, nuclear power may be best viewed as a resource that can bridge the gap to a more sustainable energy future. Unless and until the waste issue can be resolved, however, it would be best to bring intense scrutiny to bear on proposals to relicense existing reactors and to put a moratorium on the construction of new reactors. If the waste and related safety issues cannot be resolved with a very high degree of confidence and integrity, nuclear power should be phased out.

Conclusion

This assessment of conventional energy options in the United States is sobering. It is easy to understand why some refer to coal, oil, natural gas, and nuclear power as "fuels from hell."[89] I am reluctant to label them this way, because they have fueled so much growth and prosperity over the past two centuries. The reality, however, is that this economic wealth has not been distributed very well, and it has only been garnered by undermining the ecological health of the planet. The long-term projections for global warming during the twenty-first century certainly do conjure up hellish images. We desperately need alternative energy options. I am reluctant to call these "fuels from heaven," but it is easy to understand why many view them this way. We turn now to assess the huge potential of alternative and renewable energy options.

3. Alternative and Renewable Energy Options

The difference between what we do and what we are capable of doing would solve most of the world's problems.

MAHATMA GANDHI

The U.S. Energy Information Administration (EIA) reports that only 7 percent of the nation's primary energy supply in 2008 was provided by renewable energy sources (fig. 3.1). Of this total, hydroelectric power (34 percent) led the way, followed by wood (28 percent), liquid biofuels (19 percent), wind (7 percent), municipal and agricultural wastes (6 percent), geothermal (5 percent), and solar (1 percent).[1] Under the EIA's long-term reference case scenario, which accounts for changes to U.S. energy policy associated with adoption of the American Recovery and Reinvestment Act of 2009, renewable sources will grow in volume but represent only 16 percent of U.S. energy in 2030.[2]

As we have seen, electricity generation consumes over 40 percent of all U.S. primary energy supplies. Currently, renewable energy sources generate only 8 percent of U.S. electricity (fig. 3.2). Hydroelectric dams generate 6 percent, and all other sources—including

Fig. 3.1. Renewable Energy as a Share of Total U.S. Primary Energy Consumption, 2008

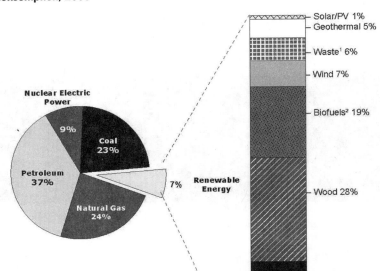

Source: Energy Information Administration, *Annual Energy Review 2008*, DOE/EIA-0384(2008) (Washington, D.C.: EIA, June 26, 2009), fig. 10.1, p. 282, accessed at http://www.eia.doe.gov/aer/pdf/aer.pdf.

wind and solar—provide the other 2 percent. Based on current U.S. policies, the Pew Center on Global Climate Change claims renewables will be able to supply 14 percent of U.S. electricity in 2030, but hydropower will still produce 6 percent, and all other sources will generate only 8 percent (fig. 3.3).

If policies are changed, however, both in terms of incentives and mandates, the same study claims wind and solar energy could grow from generating less than 2 percent of the U.S. electricity supply in 2008 to supply almost 20 percent in 2030 (fig. 3.4). To achieve this goal, wind turbines and solar electric systems would have to be installed over the next two decades at two to three times the rate they

Fig. 3.2. U.S. Electricity Production (TWh/yr.) by Energy Source, 2007

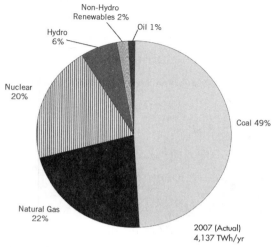

Note: TWh/yr + terawatt hours per year.

Source: Paul Komor, *Wind and Solar Opportunities: Challenges and Opportunities,* Solutions White Paper Series (Arlington, Va.: Pew Center on Global Climate Change, June 2009), fig. 1, p. 3, accessed at http://www.pewclimate.org/docUploads/wind-solar-electricity-report.pdf. Data for chart from Energy Information Administration, *Annual Energy Outlook 2009,* DOE/EIA-0383(2009), March 2009, p. 2.

Fig. 3.3. U.S. Electricity Production Projection, 2030: Business as Usual

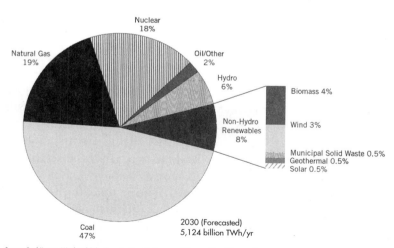

Source: Paul Komor, *Wind and Solar Opportunities: Challenges and Opportunities,* Solutions White Paper Series (Arlington, Va.: Pew Center on Global Climate Change, June 2009), fig. 3, p. 27, accessed at http://www.pewclimate.org/docUploads/wind-solar-electricity-report.pdf. Data for chart from Energy Information Administration, *Annual Energy Outlook 2009,* DOE/EIA-0383(2009), March 2009, p. 56.

were installed in 2008, which was a record year.[3] Other studies are even more optimistic. A report by the American Solar Energy Society claims renewable energy, combined with investments in energy efficiency, can provide 50 percent of U.S. electricity by 2030.[4]

Fig. 3.4.   U.S. Electricity Production Projection, 2030: High Wind and Solar

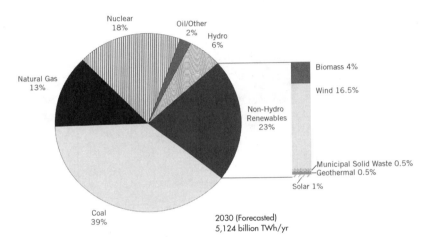

Source: Paul Komor, *Wind and Solar Opportunities: Challenges and Opportunities*, Solutions White Paper Series (Arlington, Va.: Pew Center on Global Climate Change, June 2009), fig. 6, p. 32, accessed at http://www.pewclimate.org/docUploads/wind-solar-electricity-report.pdf.

Two things will become clear in this chapter. On the one hand, renewable energy sources have enormous potential. On the other hand, eliminating dependence on conventional energy sources will not be easy nor take place overnight. U.S. energy supplies will invariably involve a mix of energy sources during the twenty-first century, but there is no question that the transition to cleaner and renewable energy sources must be achieved as soon as possible. The prospects of global climate change in particular require this. The European Renewable Energy Council and Greenpeace International claim, "The U.S. can cut carbon dioxide emissions from domestic fossil fuel use 83 percent by 2050, while still greater additional net emissions cuts can be achieved through changes in land use and agricultural practices."[5] That is a lofty claim but a worthy goal.

An Initial Ethical Assessment

Before assessing various alternative and renewable energy options in detail, I want to begin with a general, overall ethical assessment. It should not be surprising that energy efficiency and renewable energy sources fare better than fossil fuels and nuclear energy when they are assessed in light of the ecojustice norms and energy policy guidelines.

Ecojustice Norms and Energy Policy Guidelines

Ecojustice Norms

- Sustainability
- Sufficiency
- Participation
- Solidarity

Energy Policy Guidelines

- Equity
- Efficiency
- Adequacy
- Renewability
- Appropriateness
- Risk
- Peace
- Cost
- Employment
- Flexibility
- Timely decision making
- Aesthetics

For example, the norm of sustainability and the renewability guideline are satisfied when we take advantage of the various energy resources offered by the sun, the kinetic energy in waves and tides, and the heat and constant temperature of geothermal energy from the earth. The norm of sufficiency is well addressed through efforts to promote energy conservation, and the efficiency guideline is obviously satisfied when investments in energy technologies make human activities more productive. The solidarity norm and equity guideline are fulfilled insofar as these investments also reduce the burden of greenhouse gas (GHG) emissions for future generations. Moreover, investments in renewable energy and energy efficiency should also improve the prospects for peace by increasing domestic energy supplies and by diminishing reliance on nuclear energy and the risks it poses. In addition, most renewable energy technologies are portable and thus relatively flexible. Finally, the norm of participation and the appropriateness guideline are expressed through individual acts of energy conservation and the prospect that renewable energy technologies offer for decentralized power generation. Proponents claim millions will benefit from the boom of new jobs in the renewable energy sector.

There are certainly significant areas of concern, however. Since renewable energy sources currently provide so little supply both nationally and globally, will they have the capacity to meet demand and satisfy the adequacy guideline in the future? This is no small matter. Access to affordable energy sources is vital to human well-being. Given the high prices and relatively meager production of some renewable energy technologies, many currently fail to satisfy the cost and efficiency guidelines. There are also legitimate concerns about the environmental consequences of some approaches to renewable energy production. As we shall see, corn-based ethanol currently requires large amounts of fossil fuel inputs, is water intensive, and increases the risk of soil erosion. Debates also whirl around whether the cost of new renewable energy technologies will drive up energy prices, which will have a regressive impact on the poor and possibly provoke a recession. Finally, aesthetic concerns are rising as more and larger wind turbines occupy greater swaths of land and are also being constructed offshore.

With this general ethical assessment in mind, we turn now to assess the potential of specific alternative and renewable energy sources in greater detail. We begin by looking at energy conservation and energy efficiency. After that, we assess the prospects of solar, wind, biomass, hydroelectric, geothermal, marine, and hydrogen as renewable and sustainable energy options.

Energy Conservation and Efficiency

The two alternative energy "sources" of conservation and efficiency offer the United States the most substantial and immediate way to maximize supplies and decrease annual GHG emissions. Energy conservation taps the moral virtue of frugality and seeks to make wise use of precious energy resources through behavioral changes in lifestyle practices. Energy efficiency utilizes available technology to use less energy to produce goods and services. Taken together, energy conservation and energy efficiency are vital hallmarks of good stewardship and a sustainable energy future.

The disruptions in oil supply and resulting price shocks during the 1970s triggered a national commitment to energy conservation and efficiency in the United States. During this period, some of the nation's smokestack industries also moved offshore. As a result, per capita energy use has stayed about the same over the past thirty years while energy consumption per dollar of gross domestic product in 2008 was 53 percent below what it was in 1970 (fig. 3.5). In other

Figure 3.5. U.S. Energy Consumption, 1948–2008

Energy Consumption per Person

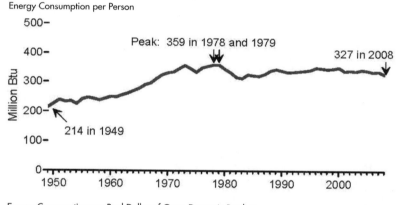

Energy Consumption per Real Dollar of Gross Domestic Product

words, we have doubled the value of the goods and services produced in the U.S. economy without increasing the average amount of energy each person in the U.S. consumes. Compared with 1973, the United States saves more energy today than it produces from any single energy source, including oil.[6]

The potential to save even more energy in the future is significant. U.S. energy use per dollar of gross domestic product is almost double that of other industrialized countries. For example, energy use per capita in the United States is twice that of citizens of countries in the European Union.[7] As a result, the United States leads the world in carbon dioxide (CO_2) emissions per household.[8] The U.S. Department of Energy conservatively estimates that increased efforts at energy efficiency could cut national energy use by 10 percent in 2010 and by approximately 20 percent in 2020. The American Council for an Energy-Efficient Economy more optimistically estimates that adoption of new policies and laws could lower national energy demand by 18 percent in 2010 and by 33 percent in 2020.[9] When these investments in energy efficiency are coupled with increased renewable energy production, other studies indicate the United States could halve the CO_2 emissions related to electricity generation by 2020.[10]

Cost-effective technologies exist today to substantially reduce energy consumption in all of the nation's energy sectors (industrial, commercial, residential, and transportation) and thus boost U.S. energy supplies. For example, the Rocky Mountain Institute (RMI) recently released a report that identified a large "electric productivity gap" in the United States. Measured in terms of dollars of gross domestic product per kilowatt-hour consumed, some states, including California and New York, are three and a half times more productive in their use of electricity than other states like Mississippi and South Carolina.[11] RMI defined the electric productivity gap as the difference in electric productivity between the top ten states and the national average. This gap totaled 1.2 million gigawatt-hours, which is equivalent to 31 percent of 2005 electricity sales and more than 75 percent of coal-fired generation in 2007. The report concludes, "If states begin to implement energy efficiency measures to close the electric productivity gap now, the nation can reduce electricity consumption by 34 percent from business as usual in 2020, while maintaining 2.5 percent annual GDP growth."[12] Reducing U.S. electricity consumption and related GHG emissions by more than one-third within a matter of just a few years via investments in energy efficiency would be an enormous accomplishment.

A recent advertisement by IBM about the efficiency of electrical transmission grids confirms RMI's findings at both the national and international levels:

> As a result of inefficiencies in this [electrical transmission] system, the world's grids are now incredibly wasteful. With little or no intelligence to balance loads or monitor power flows, they lose enough electricity annually to power India, Germany, and Canada combined for an entire year. If the U.S. grid alone were just 5 percent more efficient, it would be like permanently eliminating the fuel and greenhouse gas emissions from 53 million cars.[13]

Experience reveals, however, that regulatory and legislative action is necessary to achieve significant gains in energy efficiency. A series of state and federal efficiency standards beginning in the late 1970s dramatically improved the efficiency of U.S. refrigerators, central air conditioners, and gas furnaces (fig. 3.6). The disruptions in oil supply and resulting price shocks during the 1970s triggered a national commitment to energy conservation and efficiency in the United States. In 1975, Congress drafted and President Richard Nixon signed into law the nation's first Corporate Average Fuel Economy (CAFE) standards. These standards required automakers to double the average fuel economy of cars from 13.6 miles per gallon (mpg) in model year 1974 to 27.5 mpg in model year 1985. Similar fuel economy standards were adopted for light trucks. As a result, U.S. oil imports dropped from 46.5 percent in 1977 to 27 percent in 1985.[14]

Unfortunately, this trend did not continue. The 27.5 mpg standard for cars remained the same after 1985, and the standard for light trucks increased only from 20 mpg in 1989 to 21.6 mpg in 2006.[15] As a result, U.S. fuel economy standards have lagged well behind standards in virtually all other industrial countries for two decades. For example, back in 2002 new vehicles in Japan had to achieve approximately 46 mpg; in the European Union, the level was 37 mpg; and in China the standard was 29 mpg. All of these countries have increased their requirements today but the average fuel economy of U.S. vehicles still

Fig. 3.6.   U.S. Appliance Efficiency Driven by State and Federal Standards, 1972–2006

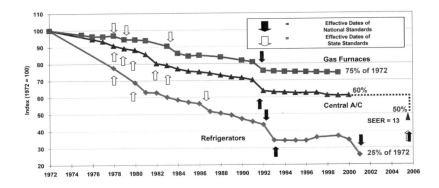

The Energy Efficiency Ratio (EER) is the ratio of *output* cooling in Btu/hr and the input power in watts at a given operating point. The dotted line reflects a period when a more stringent standard was debated between federal agencies and in the courts after it was proposed in 2001. In 2004 the Second Circuit Court of Appeals ruled the proposed standard should be placed in force in 2006, as proposed.

Source: John Randolph and Gilbert M. Masters, *Energy for Sustainability, Technology, Planning, Policy* (Washington, D.C.: Island, 2008), fig. 17.8, p. 686.

Fig. 3.7.   Auto Efficiency Standards in Various Countries

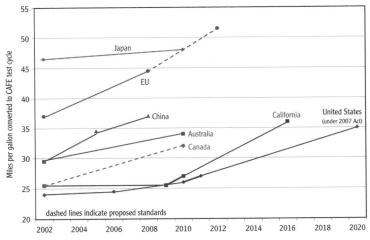

Source: John Randolph and Gilbert M. Masters, *Energy for Sustainability, Technology, Planning, Policy* (Washington, D.C.: Island, 2008), fig. 13.13, p. 510.

fails to achieve the level China mandated in 2002, let alone the higher standards achieved in Japan and the European Union (fig. 3.7).[16]

One of the reasons automobile manufacturers and autoworker unions have vigorously opposed increases in the CAFE standards is that light trucks (which include most minivans and SUVs) now make up about 50 percent of the new vehicle fleet, compared with only 10 percent in 1975. It is much harder to achieve significant fuel economy increases in these large, heavy vehicles, which U.S. drivers have come to favor. Federal tax policy has played a role in this shift to large, heavy vehicles. In 2003, President George W. Bush signed into law a tax bill that included a tax credit of up to $100,000 for those who purchased vehicles weighing more than 6,000 lbs. Depending on a person's tax bracket, this loophole could reduce the purchase of a General Motors Hummer by tens of thousands of dollars. The meager tax credits offered to purchasers of gasoline–electric hybrid vehicles or cars powered by alternative fuels paled in comparison.[17]

President Bush charted a different course in 2007, when he signed into law the Energy Independence and Security Act (EISA), which included the first major increase in the nation's CAFE standards in over twenty years.[18] Yet in contrast to the initial CAFE legislation, which resulted in a 100 percent increase in fuel economy in a decade, the new legislation mandated only a 40 percent increase over thirteen years. Automakers were required to increase the national fleetwide average fuel economy of cars and light trucks from 24.5 mpg in 2007 to 35 mpg in 2020. Experts projected the law would reduce U.S. oil imports by 1.2 million barrels per day and level off at approximately 10 million barrels per day in 2030, instead of continuing to grow beyond 12 million barrels per day.[19]

In 2009, President Barack Obama unveiled new fuel economy standards that surpassed the EISA standards mandated in 2007. These increases were prompted by California's petition to implement more stringent fuel economy standards and also by an April 2007 Supreme Court ruling that gave the Environmental Protection Agency (EPA) the authority to regulate CO_2 emissions. After weeks of negotiations between regulators and automakers, the Obama administration announced new national fuel economy standards that meet California's higher expectations. The standards require automakers to achieve a 5 percent annual increase in fuel economy for model years 2012 through 2016 and a national fleetwide average fuel economy for cars and light trucks of 35.5 mpg by 2016, which is four years ahead of what would have been achieved under the CAFE increase mandated in 2007. The change is expected to save 1.8 billion barrels of oil over five years but cost consumers an additional $600 per vehicle.[20]

While regulatory and legislative action can increase the number and variety of energy-efficient products in the marketplace, consumers do not have to wait to invest in energy efficiency or to practice energy conservation. Trading in a sedan that gets 24 mpg in combined city and highway driving for a hybrid sedan that gets 36 mpg improves energy efficiency by 50 percent and cuts related GHG emissions in half. Counterintuitively, the Union of Concerned Scientists points out that trading in a SUV that gets 14 mpg for a model that gets only 16 mpg saves almost as much fuel over the course of 15,000 miles as trading in a 35 mpg car for the most efficient hybrid that consumes 51 mpg.[21] These gains can be further increased if citizens conserve fuel by choosing to drive fewer miles every year.

Similar gains can be made by reducing energy consumption in the buildings where people live and work. The American Institute of Architects reports that the energy consumed to heat and power buildings across the United States produces 48 percent of the nation's GHG emissions.[22] Adjusting thermostats, sealing leaks, installing insulation, and investing in more efficient lights, appliances, furnaces, and air conditioners could substantially reduce energy consumption in our homes and business settings.

Viewed through the lens of the ecojustice norms and energy guidelines, there is no question that energy conservation and efficiency should become national priorities. Personal acts of energy conservation reflect the norms of sufficiency and participation, but they also enhance the norm of solidarity and the equity guideline through sacrifices made on behalf of others. Energy conservation is an area where one can exercise greater personal responsibility without waiting for government to act.

That said, there is no substitute for government standards mandating increases in the energy efficiency of various products, including major appliances and vehicles. And, as we've seen, it has not always been easy to increase these standards. All of the ecojustice norms encourage participation in politics to consistently ratchet up energy efficiency standards. Investments in energy conservation and energy efficiency not only keep energy costs down for the poor, they also offer the fastest way to reduce the nation's carbon footprint and GHG emissions. This is clearly consistent with the sustainability norm and the cost guideline. While reduced consumption of energy resources due to energy conservation could reduce the gross domestic product and add to unemployment, these consequences should be offset by the acquisition of new appliances and vehicles that are more energy efficient. Finally, the practice of energy conservation and investments in energy efficiency advance the prospects for peace by helping make the United States less energy dependent, and they also offer ways to increase adequate energy supplies at very low levels of risk, and often at very low costs.

It will not be possible to rely on energy conservation and energy efficiency alone to reduce GHG emissions, but these efforts are a critical first step. Every home owner, business, agricultural producer, industrial manufacturer, and transporter of goods and services should first become more conservative in their use of energy and invest in energy efficiency before even beginning to consider substantial investments in renewable energy technologies. The next step is to consider several forms of renewable energy.

Solar Energy

According to the European Renewable Energy Council, every day, the sunlight that reaches Earth provides 2,850 times more energy than human communities currently consume.[23] Clearly, the potential of solar energy is enormous. The sun's energy can be utilized in a variety of ways with different technologies. Residential solar thermal collectors capture and store the sun's energy in water. According to a study by the Department of Energy, these systems could provide half of the space heating and 65 percent to 75 percent of the domestic hot water needed for U.S. homes.[24] Solar chillers use thermal energy to cool and dehumidify air, much as conventional air conditioners do. While the name of the technology may sound like an oxymoron, solar chillers have been successfully demonstrated and will make major inroads in the near future.[25]

Concentrated solar thermal (CST) collectors are often located in desert regions and use mirrors to focus the sun in order to produce high-temperature heat for industrial processes or steam that can be used to generate electricity. The U.S. Southwest is ideally suited for this technology. Over the course of a year, the amount of solar energy that falls on an area the size of a basketball court in the Southwest is equivalent, in thermal energy terms, to 650 barrels of oil. [26] A recent report indicates that seven states in this region of the United States could together theoretically use concentrated solar power to produce ten times more electricity than is produced from all electricity generators in the nation today.[27] Of course, this would require enormous investments in transmission capacity, and sadly, an estimated 45 percent of the electricity would be lost in transmission if it were sent all the way to the East Coast.[28]

While it currently costs 11¢ to 15¢ per kilowatt-hour to produce electricity via CST systems, costs are expected to decline over the next decade as new projects come on line, driving down the costs of production.[29] Projects totaling 6,000 megawatts (MW) of capacity are now in the pipeline for California, Arizona, and Florida.[30] Recently, the U.S. Department of the Interior announced it was fast-tracking the development of solar energy on public lands and establishing solar-energy study areas in six states in the Southwest. Federal officials expected these actions to spur the construction of thirteen commercial-scale solar plants by the end of 2009.[31] At the same time, federal studies are under way regarding the environmental impact of CST systems in arid regions. Like all power plants, CST systems use significant amounts of water for cooling, and their construction on fragile desert soils could imperil the habitat of threatened and endangered species.

Photovoltaic (PV) cells are the most visible solar-energy technology. Their installation is growing rapidly around the world while their costs are declining dramatically (fig. 3.8). These cells convert sunlight into electricity and can be utilized in a variety of scalable applications. They are often the least expensive way to bring electricity to remote locations, but most PV installations today are connected to the electricity grid. Global production of PV cells has grown sixfold since 2000, rising largely in response to public policies that encourage their use. In 2008, Europe led the world with 65 percent of installed capacity; Japan was second with 15 percent, and the U.S. was a distant third at 8 percent. The significant growth of the PV markets in Spain and Germany are due to feed-in tariff policies in both countries, which require utilities to purchase the electricity produced by solar-power projects at guaranteed, long-term prices that are currently above the market average.[32]

Fig. 3.8. Solar Photovoltaic Overview

World Annual Photovoltaic Production, 1975–2007

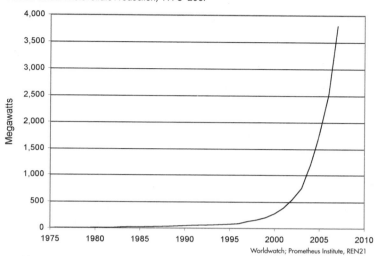

Worldwatch; Prometheus Institute, REN21

World Average Photovoltaic Module Cost per Watt, 1975–2006

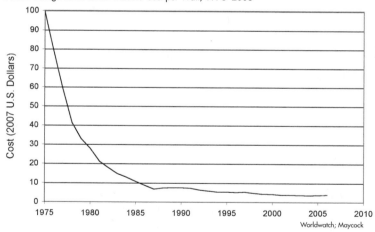

Worldwatch; Maycock

Source: Jonathan G. Dorn, "Solar Cell Production Jumps 50 Percent in 2007," Eco-Economy Indicators (Earth Policy Institute), December 27, 2007, accessed at http://www.earth-policy.org/Indicators/Solar/2007.htm.

According to a study by the International Energy Agency, PV could meet 55 percent of future U.S. electricity demand.[33] U.S. investors in all solar technologies can benefit from the federal Business Energy Investment Tax Credit (ITC), which provides a federal tax credit equivalent to 30 percent of eligible equipment costs. This tax credit can then be utilized to lessen the federal tax obligation of the business. Investors in some states can also benefit from renewable energy system cash rebates available through sponsoring utilities or government agencies, which often cover an additional 20 percent to 30 percent of the system's cost.[34] Lawmakers in several states have proposed feed-in tariffs patterned after the successful policies in Spain and Germany.[35] Wisconsin and Washington have limited programs, and Vermont is the most recent state to adopt a feed-in tariff.[36]

One of the obvious drawbacks of PV is that it is limited by the amount of sunlight that strikes a particular point on Earth over the course of a day. As a result, PV has the lowest capacity factor of all renewables, at 14 percent.[37] Manufacturing and installation costs still remain relatively high, despite more than a decade of rapid growth in the industry: The installed cost of PV systems ranges from 25¢ to 40¢ per kilowatt-hour. The cost per watt continues to drop rapidly, however, especially with the development of new thin-film technologies. Researchers are also actively exploring energy storage solutions via molten salt for CST power plants and in the batteries of all-electric and gasoline–electric hybrid cars.[38] Another potential drawback is that PV cells are currently constructed with rare elements as well as toxic chemicals and heavy metals. These materials are used widely in the semiconductor industry, however, where new techniques are emerging to maximize material efficiency and reduce environmental and safety risks.

When viewed through the lens of the ecojustice norms and energy guidelines, solar energy has much obvious strength but several significant weaknesses. Obviously, the sustainability norm and renewability guidelines are satisfied via investments in various forms of solar energy. The sufficiency and solidarity norms and the equity guideline are also addressed when energy consumers install solar systems to meet their own needs and thus reduce GHG emissions that imperil future generations. The participation norm and the appropriateness and flexibility guidelines are met when individuals are empowered to make investments in residential or small commercial solar systems. These systems can normally be installed by a workers in aesthetically pleasing ways, and often create new jobs in the process. Moreover, the social and ecological risks associated with solar power pale in comparison to the dangers we have noted regarding conventional energy options. Finally, solar systems have an enormous potential to increase U.S. energy supplies, which increases the prospects for peace.

The reality, however, is that most solar systems are still very expensive in comparison with other forms of renewable and nonrenewable electricity generation, and are viable only with various types of subsidies. While such subsidies are not new and have supported the fossil fuel and nuclear industries for years, these subsidies are always vulnerable to changes in political leadership. The participation norm and the guideline of timely decision making require sustained political support for these subsidies, and that is no small matter. Financial incentives are necessary because the cost of most solar systems is still quite high and thus not affordable to many. This violates the sufficiency norm and the cost and equity guidelines. One of the keys to unlocking the potential of solar energy will be continued progress in lowering the cost of these systems. Another key impediment is the fact that solar energy, like wind energy, is not dispatchable. That is, these types of energy create electricity only when the sun shines. Until some cost-effective methods are developed to store solar energy and then release it when the sun has set, solar energy will fail to satisfy the adequacy guideline.

Despite the huge potential offered by solar energy, we must still face the fact that solar energy currently supplies only 1 percent of U.S. electricity and an even smaller fraction of domestic hot-water and space-heating needs. The ecojustice norms and energy guidelines, however, justify significant investments in this vital source of renewable energy.

Wind Energy

Every day, the energy from the sun heats the planet, which then cools as the sun sets over different regions. This heating and cooling of the earth produces wind. The wind that blows across the planet is being converted into electrical energy by turbines at a record pace in the United States (fig. 3.9) and around the world (fig. 3.10). For example, the U.S. wind energy industry installed 4,000 MW of new generation capability in the first half of 2009, which outpaced the previous record of 2,900 MW that was installed in 2008.[39] In recent years, only natural gas-fired power plants have added more capacity to the U.S. power grid than have wind farms.[40] The United States has led the world in wind energy installations since 2005.[41] Even with turbine and component prices rising with global demand, installations with an excellent wind resource can often generate electricity at a lower cost (3¢ to 5¢ per kilowatt-hour) than natural-gas-fired power plants.[42]

The U.S. wind resource is distributed around the nation, but the most abundant winds are in the Great Plains region. Theoretically, North Dakota, Kansas, and Texas together could furnish the nation with all the electricity it currently consumes.[43] The Department of

Fig. 3.9. U.S. Nonhydroelectric Power Sources, 1989–2008

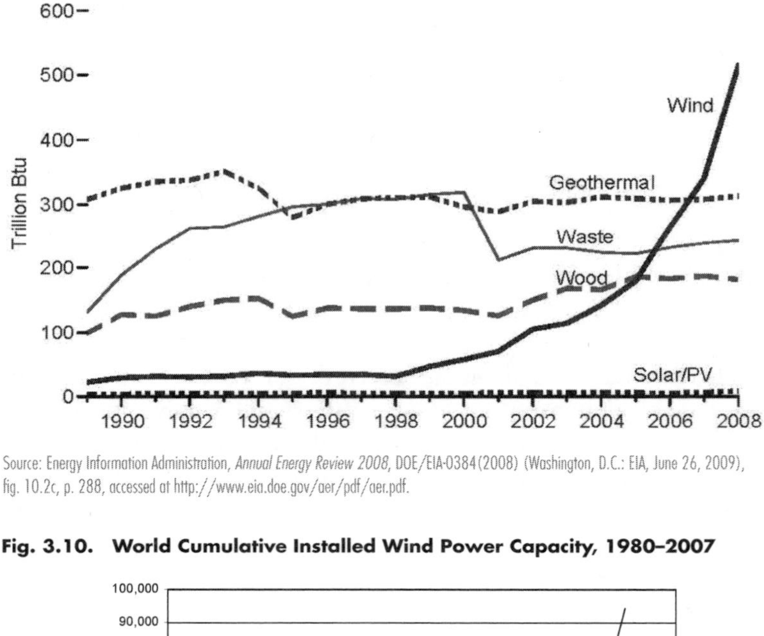

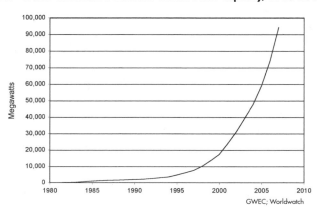

Source: Energy Information Administration, *Annual Energy Review 2008*, DOE/EIA-0384(2008) (Washington, D.C.: EIA, June 26, 2009), fig. 10.2c, p. 288, accessed at http://www.eia.doe.gov/aer/pdf/aer.pdf.

Fig. 3.10. World Cumulative Installed Wind Power Capacity, 1980–2007

Source: Jonathan G. Dorn, "Global Wind Power Capacity Reaches 100,000 Megawatts," *Eco-Economy Indicators* (Earth Policy Institute), March 4, 2008, accessed at http://www.earth-policy.org/Indicators/Wind/2008.htm.

Energy estimates that the U.S. offshore wind resource could support as much generating capacity as currently exists in all of the nation's coal-fired, natural gas, and nuclear power plants.[44] The United States has a huge wind resource.

The U.S. wind industry has been driven both by carrots and sticks. One of the key incentives is the federal Renewable Energy Production Tax Credit (PTC), which is indexed for inflation and currently provides eligible investors with a tax credit of approximately 2¢ per kilowatt-hour each year for ten years. The importance of this public policy to the wind industry has been proven repeatedly, because new installed capacity has dropped precipitously when Congress has failed to reauthorize the program.[45] Investments in the wind industry set record levels in 2008 after Congress reauthorized the PTC but began to slow down in the second quarter of 2009 as the global recession forced corporations to tighten belts and as credit markets froze up. In response, the Obama administration expanded federal incentives for investors in wind energy and other renewables through provisions in the American Recovery and Reinvestment Act of 2009. One of the key changes is that project investors now can receive either a 30 percent Business Energy Investment Tax Credit (ITC) in the first year on eligible energy equipment or a grant from the Treasury Department for the same amount in lieu of the PTC. Analysts expect these changes to breathe new life into the U.S. wind industry in 2010 and beyond.[46]

Federal subsidies have played a key role in the U.S. energy industry for decades. According to a recent report by the federal Government Accountability Office (GAO), U.S. subsidies for oil, coal, natural gas, nuclear power, and large hydro projects totaled approximately $500 billion from 1950 to 1977. The GAO estimates the federal government spent $18.2 billion in tax expenditures to subsidize electricity production between fiscal year (FY) 2002 and FY 2007. Of this total, approximately $13.7 billion was provided to the fossil fuel sector (75 percent), and only $2.8 billion (14.8 percent) was provided to the renewable-energy sector. Renewables received an even smaller percentage of research and development funds. The GAO estimates the federal government doled out $11.5 billion for research and development between FY 2002 and FY 2007. The nuclear power sector received $6.2 billion (54 percent), the fossil fuel sector received $3.1 billion (27 percent), and the renewables sector received only $1.4 billion (12 percent).[47] This pattern has to be changed radically in order for the United States to embark on a sustainable energy future. A recent study indicates the tide has begun to change, but a greater shift toward and increase of subsidies for renewable energy is needed.[48] I offer more remarks about this subject in some policy recommendations at the end of this chapter.

Investments in renewable energy in general, and wind energy in particular, have also been driven by government mandates. These have come in the form of various renewables portfolio standards (RPS) that have been established by legislatures in more than half the states in the nation (fig. 3.11). These laws mandate in various ways that an increasing percentage of electricity be produced renewably over a period of years and decades. It is no coincidence that Texas leads the nation in terms of installed wind capacity, because it also has one of the most aggressive RPS laws in the nation. The state of Colorado was the first state to establish an RPS via a voter referendum in 2004. It requires investor-owned utilities to purchase or produce 20 percent of their electricity from renewable generators by 2020.[49] The success of these diverse RPS mandates in various states has prompted calls for a national renewable electricity standard (RES). For example, in 2009, the American Wind Energy Association urged Congress to adopt an

Fig. 3.11. U.S. State Renewables Portfolio Standards, September 2009

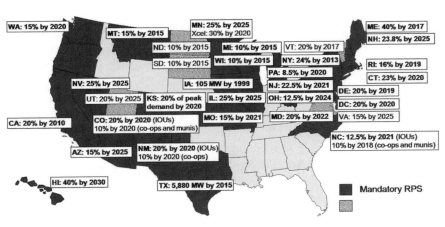

Source: Ryan Wiser and Galen Barbose, Lawrence Berkeley National Laboratory, Berkeley, Calif., September, 2009, most recent and previously unpublished map revision received via personal communication with author. For an earlier version of this map, see *Renewable Portfolio Standards in the United States: A Status Report with Data through 2007* (Berkeley, Calif.: Lawrence Berkeley National Laboratory, April 2008), fig. 1, p. 3, accessed at http://eetd.lbl.gov/ea/ems/reports/lbnl-154e.pdf.

RES of 25 percent by 2025.[50] Debates were taking place in Congress over less aggressive RES proposals when this book went to press.

One of the main drawbacks to wind power, as with solar, is its intermittent nature. The wind industry is vigorously exploring storage options so that wind energy can be dispatched on an hourly basis, rather than just when the wind blows. Another important drawback concerns the lack of transmission capacity. While there is plenty of wind resource in the nation, too often the wind farms that harvest this energy are long distances from major metropolitan centers and thus require the construction of new transmission lines. Recent studies estimate that 15,000 miles of new lines need to be built at a cost of $80 billion to transmit electricity to the Northeast from wind farms in the Midwest.[51] Public resistance to the construction of new transmission lines is hampering the construction of a smarter grid that can handle the flows of energy from new wind farms.

Some opponents of transmission lines fear that the electromagnetic fields in these lines may harm human health, but there is no dispute that the combustion of fossil fuels is definitely having an adverse effect on human health today and will only get worse in the future.[52] Others oppose the construction of large wind farms for aesthetic reasons, but the impact of wind turbines on the landscape pales in comparison to the ravages of mountaintop coal mining or the dangers posed by global warming. Finally, while there has been increased avian mortality associated with early turbine designs and the unwise siting of some wind farms in migratory bird flyways, studies indicate that the vast majority of avian mortality is caused by housecats, vehicles, cell phone towers, and birds flying into windows.[53]

Viewed through the lens of the ecojustice norms and the energy guidelines, wind energy shares many of the strengths of solar energy and fewer weaknesses. There is no question that increasing amounts of wind-generated electricity are helping to reduce U.S. GHG emissions and thus satisfy the sustainability norm and renewability guideline. In addition, the increasing size and productivity of commercial-scale wind turbines have made it possible for wind energy, in some U.S. locations, to actually become the lowest-cost energy source when fossil fuel costs have been high. The rapid growth of the wind industry in the United States has also increased employment in many areas, producing thousands of new jobs in the construction and maintenance industries, and an increasing number of domestic manufacturing jobs. These will only grow if the United States adopts an aggressive RES in the range of 20 percent by 2020 or 25 percent by 2025. Land lease payments to American farmers have also had a beneficial effect, boosting farm incomes while not significantly impeding agricultural production. Finally, wind farms fairly easily meet the risk and flexibility guidelines. Turbines can be installed or removed in a matter of days, and there is little risk associated with their operation. I often tell my students about an opportunity I had to visit Iowa's only nuclear power plant a couple after the terrorist attacks in September 2001. Our vehicle was searched upon entry, and once we were inside the facility, I counted at least nine men with machine guns providing security for the facility. A colleague of mine who produces emergency evacuation plans for nuclear power plants visited the same facility a year earlier. The presence of an unidentified plane in nearby airspace resulted in an alert that placed two men with anti-aircraft guided missile launchers on top of the reactor facility. To my knowledge, there are no guards with machine guns or shoulder-fired guided missile launchers providing security at any of the nation's wind farms.

As with solar, one of the wind industry's primary weaknesses is that it relies heavily on federal subsidies and available credit to overcome the fact that it is a very capital-intensive industry. Sustained political support for policies that support the renewable energy sector in general, and the wind industry in particular, will be vital to success. The participation norm and the guideline for timely decision making require this. The intermittent nature of wind reduces the capacity factor of wind farms relative to coal-fired or nuclear power plants, so it is hard for wind to satisfy the efficiency and adequacy guidelines. Key to the latter guideline will be the development of storage systems that enable the industry to supply power in a cost-effective manner at all times of the day, not only when the wind is blowing. These storage systems are emerging but can't arrive fast enough.

Another important issue the industry faces is growing opposition to the installation of wind farms near highly populated areas or in favorite viewsheds along the horizon. A large amount of land is needed for installation of enough wind turbines to displace even one-fourth of the production from a large coal-fired or nuclear power plant. In addition, transmission losses are reduced if these wind farms are installed closer to electricity load centers. These realities are prompting an increasing number of complaints from those who oppose the aesthetic impact of turbines. While it is true that many people are mesmerized by the rotation of turbines in the wind, many others dislike them and are increasingly mustering organized opposition to them. Somehow, the wind industry must counter this growing force, perhaps by visually reminding Americans of the aesthetic impact of coal mining and the impact on air quality caused by the combustion of fossil fuels.

On balance, the ecojustice norms and energy guidelines clearly support continued and substantial investments in wind energy.

Biomass Energy

The oldest source of energy for human activities accounts for over half of the renewable energy currently produced in the United States. Biomass energy takes two primary forms. *Biopower* is produced when agricultural and forestry residues are used to generate heat and power. *Biofuels* are produced when crops and other plants are fermented into transportation fuels. When the feedstocks for biopower and biofuels are grown and harvested sustainably, biomass energy is truly renewable and carbon neutral. This is because the CO_2 that is released had previously been absorbed from the atmosphere by the plants. If carbon capture and sequestration (CCS) technology is developed and perfected, biomass energy could actually become carbon *negative,* since plants scrub CO_2 out of the air, and CCS would permanently remove it from the planetary carbon cycle.

The forest products industry is the largest producer of biopower, because it burns forest residues to produce heat and electricity. This is why wood is currently the second largest source of renewable energy in the United States. At other sites around the nation, crop residues and switchgrass are burned with coal to produce electricity, thus reducing the net emission of CO_2. Studies indicate that up to 15 percent of all coal could be replaced with biomass if upgrades are made to coal-fired power plants. Still another use of biomass is to capture methane from the decomposition of organic matter found in landfills, sewage treatment plants, and livestock facilities. Using this methane to produce heat or power is much wiser and more lucrative than letting this potent greenhouse gas enter the atmosphere.

Corn-based ethanol is currently the largest source of biofuel in the United States (fig. 3.12). The industry benefits from a tax credit of 51¢ per gallon available to blenders of ethanol and a tariff of 54¢

per gallon on imported fuel ethanol. In 2007, the industry received $3 billion in federal subsidies, which represented two-thirds of all subsidies for renewable energy.[54] As a result, the industry has grown rapidly in recent years. It has been a boon to many farmers when corn prices have risen, but also a bust when corn prices have fallen.[55] The industry has certainly benefited rural communities when corn prices

Figure 3.12. Biofuels Overview

Fuel Ethanol and Biodiesel Production, 2008

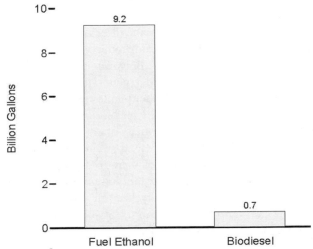

Fuel Ethanol Consumption, 1981–2008

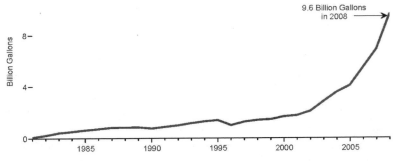

Source: Energy Information Administration, *Annual Energy Review 2008*, DOE/EIA-0384(2008) (Washington, D.C.: EIA, June 26, 2009), fig. 10.3, p. 290, accessed at http://www.eia.doe.gov/aer/pdf/aer.pdf.

have been high, because just one ethanol facility that produces 40 million gal. per year can inject as much as $140 million into the local economy.[56] Today, approximately one-third of the U.S. corn harvest is utilized for ethanol production, and that percentage has been rising.[57] This ethanol is blended with gasoline. Most gasoline in the United States contains 10 percent ethanol, and the industry would like to increase this to 15 percent.

Yet there are many problems with corn-based ethanol production. Almost all corn in the nation is planted, fertilized, cultivated, and harvested with machinery powered by fossil fuels. The fermentation and transportation of corn-based ethanol is also fossil fuel intensive. As a result, burning corn-based ethanol in gasoline tanks lowers GHG emissions by only 13 percent.[58] There are also other environmental problems. The production of ethanol is water intensive and thus puts significant stress on local groundwater resources. Nitrogen fertilizer applications pollute surface water supplies, especially in the Mississippi River, and thus further contribute to a toxic algae bloom in the Gulf of Mexico. Finally, there is good reason to fear that soil erosion will increase as rising corn prices encourage farmers to plant on some of the 35 million acres currently set aside for soil and wildlife conservation.[59]

Economically, the increased use of corn for transportation fuel is driving up the cost of grain for livestock producers, as well as the cost of food in grocery stores. Recently, global grain prices reached their highest levels in a decade. During this period, the United States was able to purchase only about half the grain it bought to distribute as food aid in 2000.[60] The United Nations Food and Agriculture Organization has warned that rising food prices and reduced food supplies are increasing the likelihood of social unrest in developing countries.[61] In 2006, the rapidly increasing price of corn tortilla flour led to riots in some parts of Mexico.[62] Recently, the United Nations Special Rapporteur on the Right to Food called for a five-year moratorium on the production of first-generation liquid biofuels made from food crops such as corn, wheat, palm oil, and rapeseed (the source of canola oil).[63]

Obviously there are serious problems associated with the way biofuels are currently being produced in the United States and in some other parts of the world. Even if the entire corn crop were devoted to production of corn-based ethanol, it would replace only 12 percent of U.S. gasoline consumption. Allocating the entire soybean crop to biodiesel production would replace only 6 percent of the nation's diesel consumption.[64] Key to biofuel production in the future will be new feedstocks and conversion technologies. While important technological challenges still need to be overcome, the potential of cellulosic ethanol is considerable, because it produces ethanol from portions of plants not used for food and also from fast-growing trees and perennials like switchgrass. Studies indicate that one-third of the nation's current petroleum demand could be satisfied if cellulosic ethanol were to become commercially viable.[65]

The U.S. Energy Policy Act of 2005 established the nation's first Renewable Fuels Standard (RFS) when it mandated that 7.5 billion gal. of renewable fuels be produced by 2012. When Congress passed the Energy Independence and Security Act (EISA) in 2007, it increased the RFS to at least 36 billion gal. of renewable fuels by 2022. EISA stipulated that 21 billion gal. of the total must be advanced biofuels, defined as renewable fuel other than corn-based ethanol that is derived from renewable biomass and achieves a 50 percent reduction in GHG emissions relative to the fuels replaced. Congress further stipulated that 16 billion gal. of these 21 billion gal. of advanced biofuels must be cellulosic biofuel, and at least 1 billion gal. must be biodiesel.[66] This left 15 billion gal. of the 36 billion gal. total available for conventional corn-based ethanol, but Congress stipulated that production at new facilities must achieve at least a 20 percent reduction in GHG emissions relative to the fuels replaced.[67]

EISA is a landmark piece of legislation for many reasons, but one of the most important aspects is that it requires the federal government to determine which fuels qualify as advanced biofuels on the basis of the *life cycle* GHG emissions associated with each fuel. According to the Environmental Protection Agency (EPA), "lifecycle GHG emissions are the aggregate quantity of GHGs related to the full fuel cycle, including all stages of fuel and feedstock production and distribution, from feedstock generation and extraction through distribution and delivery and use of the finished fuel."[68]

A major study on this topic, published in the prestigious journal *Science,* arrived at the following conclusion concerning indirect life cycle emissions associated with land use changes around the world: "Converting rainforests, peatlands, savannas, or grasslands to produce food crop–based biofuels in Brazil, Southeast Asia, and the United States creates a 'biofuel carbon debt' by releasing 17 to 420 times more CO_2 than the annual greenhouse gas (GHG) reductions that these biofuels would provide by displacing fossil fuels."[69] This finding produced howls of protest from the renewable-fuels industry in the United States, especially from producers of corn-based ethanol and soy-based biodiesel. These outcries reached a fevered pitch when the EPA published draft rules to implement the revised national biofuels mandate in May 2009. Per the terms of EISA, these rules proposed measuring not only the direct GHG emission impacts of advanced biofuels, but also the international impact of indirect, life cycle GHG emissions.

In June 2009, in a demonstration of the power of the U.S. farm lobby, several members of the U.S. House of Representatives that represent large agricultural states refused to support pending landmark energy and climate policy legislation in the House unless the EPA was prohibited from considering the indirect GHG emissions of advanced biofuels. To secure much-needed votes of support for the American Clean Energy and Security Act of 2009 (which will be discussed in detail later in chapter five), the chairman of the House Energy and Commerce Committee agreed to include a provision that would require at least five years of further study by the National Academy of Sciences about how to measure indirect emissions. At the end of the study period, the EPA, Department of Energy, and Department of Agriculture can each veto the findings, in which case the EPA would be barred for at least fifty years from considering indirect emissions with regard to advanced biofuels.[70]

If and when agreement is reached on whether and how to count indirect emissions, the new RFS will displace only about 15 billion gal. of petroleum-based fuels in 2022, which represents about 11 percent of the projected national gasoline and diesel consumption in that year.[71] A recent study published in *Science* argues it is better to use biomass to generate biopower in the form of electricity than to convert it to biofuels in the form of ethanol. This is primarily due to the inefficiency of the internal combustion engine relative to electric-battery-powered vehicles. The authors of the study found that bio-electricity used for battery-powered vehicles would deliver 80 percent more miles of transportation per acre of crops, while also providing double the GHG offsets to mitigate climate change.[72] Studies like this one indicate that humanity's oldest energy source, biomass, still has considerable utility, but perhaps not in the ways many assume.

One of the most intriguing areas of biomass research is the potential of algae for biofuel production. Given that algae are one of the primordial forms of life on Earth and one of the fastest-growing forms of plant life, it makes eminent sense to explore ways algae might be a key to renewable energy production. There are over eight thousand species of algae, and many of them produce more than 50 percent of their weight in oil. Carbon dioxide, sunlight, and nutrient-rich water are the main feedstocks for algae production.[73] Recently, Exxon Mobil Corporation announced it was investing $600 million in a research partnership with Synthetic Genomics to explore the feasibility of producing liquid transportation fuels from algae. According to Exxon, algae could produce 2,000 gal. of biofuel per acre, compared with only 650 gal. per acre from palm oil plants, 450 gal. from sugarcane, and just 250 gal. of corn-based ethanol per acre.[74] Many research efforts are focused on using captured CO_2 emissions from coal-fired power plants to grow algae to produce ethanol, biodiesel, and jet fuel. A Chinese firm has recently embarked on such a project, and the Chinese government has suggested this might be a fruitful avenue for collaborative research with the United States.[75]

Other intriguing research projects are focused on tapping the potential of human sewage for biofuel production. For example, a researcher at the University of Minnesota is working in conjunction with a regional planning agency to design and construct a demonstration algae-to-fuel plant at the Metropolitan Council Wastewater Treatment Plant near St. Paul, Minnesota.[76]

An assessment of biomass energy from the perspective of the ecojustice norms and energy guidelines yields conclusions similar to those discussed with regard to solar and wind energy. Sunlight, nutrients, and water are necessary to sustain virtually all forms of life on Earth. Biomass is humanity's oldest primary energy source and offers enormous potential for the future. Utilized appropriately and grown renewably, biomass energy can substantially reduce GHG emissions from fossil fuels and thus satisfy the sustainability and solidarity norms. Insofar as biomass can be produced by farmers in virtually every region of the world, it can also meet the sufficiency and participation norms, as well as the employment and appropriateness guidelines. Given the demonstrated linkage between war and oil, the sustainable development of liquid transportation biofuels surely helps to satisfy the peace guideline, but an enormous increase will be necessary to meet the adequacy guideline.

The norms and guidelines do identify important concerns, however. Not the least of these are questions about whether current approaches to U.S. biofuel production are sustainable and renewable. For example, there is little question that changes need to be made in U.S. ethanol production in order to satisfy the sustainability norm and renewability guideline. Huge investments in corn-based ethanol plants that are currently mothballed due to the economy do not reflect well in terms of the cost and flexibility guidelines. In addition, the use of food crops to produce biofuels is raising food prices for the poor and thus violates the sufficiency and solidarity norms, as well as the equity and cost guidelines. Finally, like solar and wind, the biofuels industry has been shaped and significantly affected by federal legislative mandates and financial incentives. The boom and bust of the U.S. corn ethanol industry reveals, and the participation norm requires, that considerable care be taken in formulating wise policies to promote sustainable production of liquid biofuels.

Hydropower

Several dams in the Pacific Northwest and the northeastern region of the United States are responsible for the largest source of renewable energy in the United States, producing 6 percent of the nation's electricity supply (fig. 3.13). As the graphs below indicate, however, increased use of wood, biofuels, and wind power are increasing the amount of renewable energy that is being consumed in the United States. The vast majority of hydro power comes from several large dams along major rivers, especially in the western region of the country. These dams were almost entirely subsidized by various federal and state subsidies, and in many cases were very expensive to build. One advantage these facilities have over other power plants is that the amount of electricity can be increased or decreased relatively easily by adjusting the amount of water released to the turbines. This flexibility is important when accommodating the intermittent production of other renewable energy sources like solar and wind.[77] A major disadvantage of large hydropower projects has been their toll on fish habitats, especially in the Pacific Northwest. Several species of fish in the region are either threatened or on the verge of extinction.

Remarkably, only 3 percent of the eighty thousand dams in the United States are used to generate electricity. The Department of Energy reports that hydropower capacity could be doubled in the

Fig. 3.13. Hydroelectric Power Overview, 1949–2008

Renewable Energy Total Production and Major Sources

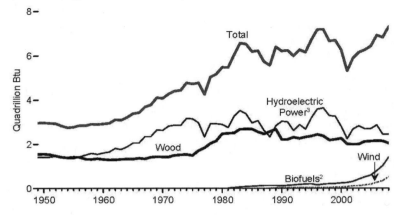

Electric Power Sector Total and Hydoelectric Power, 1949–2008

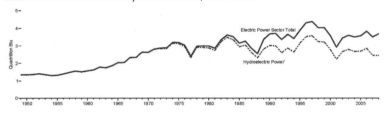

Source: Energy Information Administration, *Annual Energy Review 2008*, DOE/EIA-0384(2008) (Washington, D.C.: EIA, June 26, 2009), fig. 10.1, p. 282, and fig. 10.2c, p. 288, accessed at http://www.eia.doe.gov/aer/pdf/aer.pdf.

United States by installing generators at some of the dams that do not have them and by installing more generators at dams already producing electricity. A significant share of this electricity could be generated at smaller hydroelectric dams that were taken out of production decades ago when their productive capacity was eclipsed by large coal-fired and nuclear power plants.[78]

Viewed through the lens of the ecojustice norms and energy guidelines, there is no question that hydropower is a vital source of renewable energy. The potential to double U.S. hydropower production is very significant, since hydro power currently supplies more renewable energy than any other single source in the United States (fig. 3.13). Doubling hydro power capacity would clearly satisfy the sustainability and solidarity norms and the adequacy guideline, so long as it can be done in a way that does not further endanger the extinction of many aquatic species. The low operational cost of hydroelectric power is key to the economic vitality of those parts of the country that benefit from this inexpensive source of energy, so it satisfies the equity, cost, and employment guidelines. It may be necessary, however, to remove some smaller dams in order to bolster the prospects for the recovery of endangered and threatened species. The sufficiency norm requires that such steps be given serious consideration despite the loss in renewable electricity generation. In sum, hydropower is a key to a sustainable energy future in the United States, but its potential is limited, and there are legitimate ethical concerns associated with expanding production.

Geothermal Energy

The temperature at Earth's core is nearly as hot as the surface of the sun. Geothermal power plants tap some of this heat to create steam, which powers turbines. Rock transfers heat slowly, however, so these power plants have to be located in select "hot spots" where it is easier to tap and harness this heat for electricity generation. The United States has abundant geothermal resources and leads the world in geothermal electric power capacity installed at plants in four western states (fig. 3.14). The Geothermal Energy Association estimates that

Fig. 3.14. U.S. Geothermal Resource Map

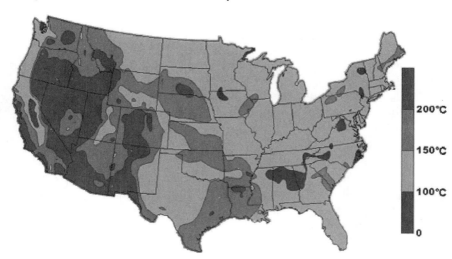

200°C

150°C

100°C

0

Source: U.S. Department of Energy, Energy Efficiency and Renewable Energy Program, "U.S. Geothermal Resource Map," accessed at http://www1.eere.energy.gov/geothermal/geomap.html (July 2, 2009).

this current capacity could grow tenfold by 2025.[79] Other reports estimate that up to 20 percent of the nation's electricity could be produced by geothermal power plants by 2030.[80] According to a recent report by the Massachusetts Institute of Technology, advanced geothermal power could produce 100 gigawatts (GW) of electricity over the next fifty years. That is enough electricity to replace all of the U.S. nuclear power plants that will need to be retired over this period of time; it is also enough to replace a large share of the nation's coal-fired power plants that will need to be phased out due to their carbon emissions.[81] Clearly, geothermal energy offers enormous potential as an alternative source of base load power.

Some of the drawbacks of geothermal power have been high costs associated with drilling, but new techniques are beginning to reduce these factors. Like most power plants, geothermal plants use water for cooling, and this can be in short supply in the arid regions of the Southwest where most of the potential for U.S. geothermal power exists. Another concern is that small amounts of CO_2, mercury, and hydrogen sulfide are often released during drilling. While these emissions pale in comparison to those emitted by coal-fired power plants, they can have a significant impact nevertheless. The emissions of hydrogen sulfide from a new geothermal power plant near Reykjavik, Iceland, have been blamed for an increase of black soot and the rapid degradation of rubber in tires, suspensions, and steering systems of vehicles driving on roads near the plant. Related mercury emissions have also resulted in severe damage to vegetation in areas near and downwind from the plant.[82]

Another serious concern revolves around the risk of earthquakes triggered by drilling. Since the best geothermal resources are normally found near active seismic areas, there are legitimate concerns that drilling will cause both small and large earthquakes. In 2006, the drilling of a well 3 mi. below the surface of Basel, Switzerland, triggered an earthquake that measured 3.4 on the Richter scale. The quake was felt throughout Basel and resulted in immediate cessation of the exploration project. After citizens of California reported a higher incidence of earthquakes in areas where exploratory drilling had been taking place, state officials halted the drilling out of a concern that it could trigger a major quake in the state.[83]

While the best geothermal power sources are located in the West, all areas of the United States are suitable for geothermal heat pumps.

These pumps utilize the constant temperature of earth or groundwater near the surface of the ground as a heat source in winter and a heat sink in summer to regulate indoor temperatures. The EPA claims geothermal heat pumps are "the most energy efficient, cost-effective, and environmentally clean space conditioning technology available."[84] According to the Department of Energy, geothermal heat pumps have the potential to supply 15 percent of the nation's energy needs by 2050.[85] Heat pump sales are growing at about 15 percent a year and could expand further if this technology were routinely incorporated into the construction of new homes and buildings.[86]

There is no doubt that geothermal energy could significantly increase U.S. energy supplies and thus satisfy the sustainability norm and adequacy guideline. Inexpensive geothermal heat pump technologies that can be utilized by the owners of homes and businesses clearly satisfy the cost and efficiency guidelines as well as the sufficiency and participation norms. Key to tapping the full potential of geothermal power production, however, will be whether new drilling technologies will permit the safe and dependable generation of electricity from geothermal power plants. The participation norm and risk guideline demand that residents in the drilling area be heard and assured that their safety will not be placed in jeopardy. The sustainability norm also requires that geothermal power plants not despoil or reduce the water resources in the area.

Marine Energy

Like the geothermal energy beneath the ground, an enormous amount of marine energy exists in the waves, tides, and currents of the oceans that cover 70 percent of the planet. Since seawater is eight hundred times as dense as air, even small movements of seawater contain significant amounts of energy. Globally, wave energy is estimated to be equivalent to present world energy demand. Nationally, the Electric Power Research Institute (EPRI) estimates that near-shore wave resources in the United States could theoretically generate eight times more electricity than all the nation's hydroelectric dams.[87] More recently, an EPRI researcher conservatively estimated that ocean energy near U.S. shores could meet as much as 10 percent of U.S. electricity demand, which is about half the electricity produced by nuclear power plants.[88]

Historically, the most common form of marine energy has been tidal power, which involves using dams to trap water in a bay or estuary and then releasing it through turbines at low tide. Tide mills were common in Western Europe during the Middle Ages but fell out of favor during the coal-fired Industrial Revolution. Today, efforts are under way to recapture the energy contained in tides. Tidal projects in New York City's East River and in the Puget Sound near Tacoma have the potential to power thousands of homes in these cities, but they are still at the experimental stage.[89]

Several companies are currently developing different wave energy conversion technologies, but these are all definitely in the testing phase. One of the key factors slowing the growth of the industry is the delay many companies experience in securing required permits due to environmental concerns. There are at least twelve state and federal agencies in the United States that have some level of jurisdiction over ocean energy projects. One of the environmental concerns these agencies consider pertains to the impact high-voltage transmission lines on the ocean floor could have on ocean ecosystems. Another concern is that wave energy conversion devices might interfere with the migration of fish and whales.[90] Delays in permitting have led at least one company to cancel its ocean energy research initiatives.[91]

A 2006 report by the British Carbon Trust estimates the costs of tidal power at 20¢ to 40¢ per kilowatt-hour and the cost of wave systems at closer to 90¢ per kilowatt-hour.[92] While the cost of tidal power is similar to the cost of photovoltaic electric power, the solar-power industry is much better developed than the marine-energy industry. At its current stage of development, marine energy is clearly in its infancy and thus is not cost-competitive with most of the nation's renewable and nonrenewable energy sources. While marine energy is attractive from the perspective of the ecojustice norms and energy guidelines, much work still needs to be done to realize its potential.

Hydrogen

Finally, the ultimate alternative energy source may be hydrogen, because it is the most abundant chemical element in nature. One of the challenges, however, is that hydrogen does not exist in large quantities in its pure form; it has to be separated from water, ammonia, or even fossil fuels before it can be used as a fuel source. This is an energy-intensive process. The use of fossil energy to do this work results in GHG emissions. The only way to make hydrogen a truly clean energy source is to use renewable energy to reform the hydrogen, and this is expensive. Nevertheless, once reformed, the hydrogen can be used in a fuel cell to produce electricity with water as the only emission, or it can be burned in an internal combustion engine.

Other challenges remain, however. The platinum used in current fuel cell designs is in limited supply and expensive. Another challenge revolves around the safety of hydrogen storage. As the smallest chemical element, hydrogen easily escapes from most containers and is highly flammable.

These production, storage, safety, and cost issues will all have to be resolved before hydrogen can become a significant fuel source in the future. As with marine energy, the ecojustice norms and energy guidelines indicate hydrogen is a promising future energy source, but it also is not ready for prime time.

Policy Recommendations

This ethical assessment of the major energy options facing U.S. policy makers reveals three important truths. First, the potential supply of alternative and renewable energy sources far exceeds current and projected demand. God has truly furnished creation with energy in abundance. The second truth, however, is that the United States still relies heavily on conventional fossil fuels and nuclear power to provide approximately 93 percent of the energy we currently consume. We are not living sustainably in relationship with God's creation. This leads to the third, sad truth: Our reliance on these conventional energy sources poses grave dangers to justice, peace, and the integrity of creation. As noted, we find ourselves at a pivotal moment in history with regard to global climate change.

Public policies play a major role in either encouraging or discouraging various energy options. I close this chapter with some brief policy recommendations I believe will hasten the development of alternative and renewable energy options and thus secure a more sustainable energy future.

1. **Enact a modest carbon tax on all fossil fuels.** We need to internalize the social and environmental costs related to GHG emissions in the prices of fossil fuels. A preferred way to capture these costs is through an initial auction and continued

trade of a fixed and ultimately declining number of emissions allowances in a cap-and-trade approach applied to all sectors of the economy. I support and discuss this idea to a much greater extent later in chapter 5. A separate tax based on the carbon content of fossil fuels should complement a cap-and-trade approach, but it should not replace it, because a carbon tax lacks a guaranteed cap on total emissions.[93] Gilbert Metcalf at Tufts University has proposed a carbon tax of $15 per ton of carbon dioxide (t CO_2), which would raise the 2007 price of gasoline by approximately 25¢ per gallon and increase the 2007 prices of electricity and natural gas by 14 percent. He estimates that a tax of $15/t CO_2 would generate approximately $82 billion per year in revenue.[94] I propose a much less aggressive initial carbon tax of $5/t CO_2 that would generate approximately $27 billion per year in revenue and increase at a rate of 5 percent per year. The economic impact of the tax could be offset by a refundable environmental tax credit, which would help relieve the regressive impact of the tax on the working poor who have federal income tax obligations. The revenues raised by the tax could provide additional cash subsidies to the poor, but primarily they offer a means to substantially increase the amount of federal funds available for public transportation, increased research and development and investment in renewable energy, and incentives to purchase energy-efficient appliances and vehicles.[95] A carbon tax of $5/t CO_2 would provide almost as much tax revenue in one year as has been spent to subsidize electricity production among all industries over five years from 2002 to 2007. There is no question that passing such a tax would be politically difficult, but several other countries and even cities have managed to muster the political will to do so.[96] In fact, French President Nicolas Sarkozy recently announced plans to impose a carbon tax in 2010 on carbon emissions not currently covered by the European cap-and-trade system. The tax, set at an initial rate of €17 ($24.7) per ton of carbon dioxide emitted, will apply largely to gasoline and natural gas sales.[97]

2. **Shift subsidies and financial incentives toward the renewable energy and energy-efficiency sectors and away from the fossil fuel and nuclear-power sectors.** One vital step

in this regard would be to extend for ten years the federal production tax credit for the generation of electricity from wind, solar, geothermal, closed-loop and open-loop biomass, landfill gas, and small irrigation power facilities. A long-term congressional reauthorization would send an important signal to companies faced with making very large investments in manufacturing facilities. Certainly, Denmark and Japan have benefited from long-term policies that have stimulated the wind and solar industries in their countries. Subsidies can also influence personal consumption decisions. For example, "feebates" require purchasers of fuel-inefficient vehicles to pay a fee; these funds are then utilized to offer purchasers of fuel-efficient vehicles a rebate on the purchase price. Federal research and development grants are another important type of subsidy. These funds need to be increased, and a much larger percentage must be dedicated to renewable energy, alternative fuels, and energy efficiency. To make funding for these measures revenue neutral, the government could reduce subsidies to the oil, gas, and nuclear power industries.

3. **Adopt significantly increased efficiency standards for all energy-consuming appliances, buildings, and vehicles.** The Obama administration has recently ushered in important improvements to federal laws and rules regarding the energy efficiency of lighting products, household appliances, and building codes, as well as the nation's CAFE standards for vehicles. These increases are long overdue and much needed, and they offer the United States the least expensive way of increasing energy supplies and reducing GHG emissions. Increased efficiency and fuel economy standards should be based on the best science available and be in dialogue with the relevant industries, but ultimately legislated standards are more productive than voluntary goals negotiated with industries. In addition, public scrutiny must be brought to bear on regulatory agencies to ensure they are insulated from undue industry influence when new standards are developed.

4. **Mandate that an increasing percentage of the U.S. energy supply be produced renewably and sustainably.** As noted, over half the nation's states have adopted renewable portfolio standards that impose differing mandates on electricity

generators. Not surprisingly, most of the investment in renewable electricity generation is taking place in these states. Adoption of an aggressive national renewable electricity standard (RES) would build on this success. This idea is discussed in greater detail in chapter 5. It is important to remember, however, that unanticipated environmental problems associated with the federal Renewable Fuels Standard (RFS) indicate there can be dangers associated with ratcheting up standards too quickly. Any mandate must ensure that the energy is produced renewably and sustainably.

5. **Remove market barriers for producers of renewable energy, and encourage decentralized and distributed power generation.** These barriers include expensive and overly complicated requirements for connecting to the electricity grid, insufficient transmission line capacity, and extremely low power purchase rates based on costs from fossil fuel power plants that are not yet accountable for their impact on global warming. Germany and Spain have stimulated the renewable-electricity industry in their nations by requiring net billing and mandating "feed-in" tariffs. Such measures would stimulate investment in residential solar and wind power in the United States and help restore the nation as a leader in technological innovation. Decentralized, residential renewable energy systems and distributed generation from community wind and solar farms can relieve pressure on the power grid, create new jobs, and empower local communities. State and federal tax credits are one way to encourage investment in decentralized and distributed renewable energy production.

6. **Place a moratorium on all new coal-fired and nuclear power plants until related environmental concerns are addressed.** Given the predominant role CO_2 plays in global warming and climate change, and given that coal-fired power plants are responsible for 40 percent of U.S. CO_2 emissions, it would be irresponsible to build new coal-fired power plants until it can be demonstrated that the carbon can be captured economically and sequestered permanently. Similarly, given the extremely toxic danger that spent nuclear fuel poses to future generations for millions of years, it is irresponsible to

build new nuclear power plants until a permanent and safe means of disposing of this waste is placed into service.

7. **Limit exploration and exploitation of new fossil fuel supplies to parts of the United States where this can be done without damage to people and the environment.** As the climate in the Arctic warms and permafrost melts, it is doubtful that the economic benefits of drilling in the Arctic National Wildlife Refuge can outweigh the environmental damage this will do to one of the nation's most beautiful and wild places. Likewise, we are seeing the impact on communities of ecological devastation caused by mountaintop mining in Appalachia.

8. **Support a systemic shift to rail-based public transportation and urban planning that emphasizes mass transit.** These measures would discourage urban sprawl and the depletion of energy resources. These measures would also preserve water resources that are used to cool power plants, which is especially important in the arid Southwest. Support for public transportation will also require substantial funding to repair the nation's highways, and bridges. Efforts should be focused on increasing the quality and not the size of the nation's transportation and energy infrastructure.

9. **Revise U.S. national-security policies.** The United States needs to abandon attempts to use military interventions to control global oil resources owned by other nations. Further, the United States needs to base domestic and international climate policy on science-based international standards. Finally, the United States should strive to decouple nuclear power from nuclear weapons production so as not to encourage a new round of nuclear proliferation.

Conclusion

It will not be easy to move away from our dependence on conventional fossil fuels and nuclear power. In fact, it will be very hard. The challenge we face is daunting, and the temptation to despair is real. Only God can provide the power to change. Christian traditions remind us that it is God who created the earth and saw that it was good, and it is this same God who sustains the earth and seeks to hold its processes together. Though it is true that God judges sin and greed, Jesus reveals that love and justice are the essence of God's power. God is the inexhaustible source of energy for personal, social, and ecological transformation. Although we are complicit in the evils we face, we can repent of our own sinful misuse and abuse of the earth as we confess our sins. As recipients of God's endless mercy, this redemptive energy frees and empowers us to be good stewards of God's creation.

Clearly, energy choices, now more than ever, are moral choices. We turn our attention in the next chapters to consider the ethical issues associated with global warming that has resulted from the combustion of fossil fuel and some land use practices. While it is clear that changes in energy policy are necessary to achieve a sustainable future, no less important will be development of new climate policies at the international and national levels.

4. International Climate Policy

We have a very short window of opportunity. If we want to limit temperature increase to about 2 degrees Celsius, then emissions globally must peak by 2015.

RAJENDRA PACHAURI,
CHAIRMAN OF THE UNITED NATIONS INTERGOVERNMENTAL PANEL
ON CLIMATE CHANGE (IPCC) AND NOBEL PEACE PRIZE LAUREATE[1]

The time for delays and half-measures is over. The personal leadership of every head of State or government is needed to seize this moment to protect people and the planet from one of the most serious challenges ever to confront humanity.

BAN KI-MOON,
SECRETARY-GENERAL OF THE UNITED NATIONS[2]

If it were not for naturally occurring greenhouse gases (GHGs), Earth's average surface temperature would be approximately 60°F colder.[3] Water vapor, carbon dioxide, ozone, methane, and nitrous oxide all trap some of the sun's energy in the atmosphere and radiate it back to Earth. This greenhouse effect creates conditions for life to flourish. Without it, most of the planet would be cloaked in ice. The problem is that human activities have been increasing the amount of these GHGs in the atmosphere, and this is raising Earth's average surface temperature and causing global climate change.

Many different types of gases contribute to global warming; some occur naturally, and others have been created by human beings through industrial processes. Per the terms of the 1992 United Nations Framework Convention on Climate Change, the IPCC measures the concentrations and impact of carbon dioxide (CO_2), methane (CH_4), nitrous oxide (N_2O), hydrofluorocarbons (HFCs), perfluorocarbons (PFCs) and sulfur hexafluoride (SF_6). These GHGs vary in their capacity to produce warming, because they have different radiative properties and some stay in the atmosphere longer over time. Thus, each gas has a different global warming potential (GWP).[4] Carbon dioxide is by far the most important GHG, because anthropogenic (human-caused) emissions have significantly increased the concentration of CO_2 in the atmosphere. As a result, the other gases are measured in terms of carbon dioxide equivalents (CO_2eq) in the atmosphere.[5]

According to the IPCC's Fourth Assessment Report, published in 2007, global GHG emissions increased 70 percent between 1970 and 2004.[6] Annual GHG emissions have increased from 28.7 gigatonnes of carbon dioxide equivalents (Gt CO_2eq) in 1970 to 49.0 Gt CO_2eq in 2004 (fig. 4.1).[7] The rate of growth of these gases in the atmosphere is increasing rapidly. From 1970 to 1994, emissions increased at a rate of 0.43 Gt CO_2eq per year. From 1995 to 2004, global emissions increased more than twice as fast, at a rate of 0.92 Gt CO_2eq per year.[8] The energy supply sector is responsible for the largest growth in global GHG emissions, which grew 145 percent between 1970 and 2004.[9]

Carbon dioxide is the primary GHG emitted by fossil fuels. According to the U.S. Global Change Research Program, approximately 80 percent of anthropogenic CO_2 emissions since 1970 have come from burning fossil fuels, and the remaining 20 percent have resulted from deforestation and associated agricultural practices.[10] The present concentration of CO_2 in the atmosphere (about 385 ppm in 2008) is approximately 30 percent above its highest level over at least the past 800,000 years (about 300 ppm). If present trends continue, the U.S. Global Change Research Program projects global CO_2 levels will reach 900 ppm by the end of the twenty-first century (fig. 4.2).[11]

Fig. 4.1. Global Anthropogenic GHG Emissions, 1970–2004

a)

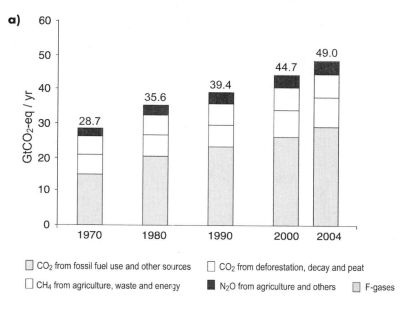

- ☐ CO_2 from fossil fuel use and other sources
- ☐ CO_2 from deforestation, decay and peat
- ☐ CH_4 from agriculture, waste and energy
- ■ N_2O from agriculture and others
- ☐ F-gases

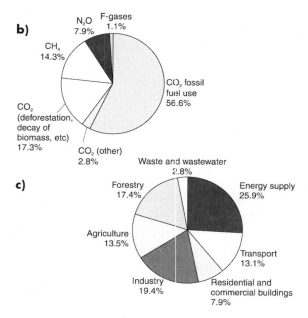

(a) Global annual emissions of anthropogenic GHGs from 1970 to 2004. (b) Share of different anthropogenic GHGs in total emissions in 2004 in terms of CO_2eq. (c) Share of different economic sectors in total anthropogenic GHG emissions in 2004 in terms of CO_2eq. (Forestry includes deforestation.)

Source: Intergovernmental Panel on Climate Change, *Climate Change 2007: Synthesis Report; Summary for Policymakers* (Geneva: IPCC, November 2007), fig. 2.1, p. 36, accessed at http://www.ipcc.ch/pdf/assessment-report/ar4/syr/ar4_syr_spm.pdf. Unfortunately, it was not possible to reprint this graph in its original color version.

Fig. 4.2. Global Carbon Dioxide Concentrations over 800,000 Years (Ice Core Data)

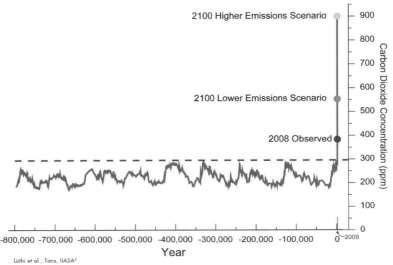

Lüthi et al., Tans, IIASA²

Analysis of air bubbles trapped in an Antarctic ice core extending back 800,000 years documents Earth's changing CO_2 concentration. Over this long period, natural factors have caused the atmospheric CO_2 concentration to vary within a range of about 170 to 300 ppm. Temperature-related data make clear that these variations have played a central role in determining the global climate. As a result of human activities, the present CO_2 concentration of about 385 ppm is about 30 percent above its highest level over at least the last 800,000 years. In the absence of strong control measures, emissions projected for this century would result in the CO_2 concentration increasing to a level that is roughly 2 to 3 times the highest level occurring over the glacial-interglacial era that spans the last 800,000 or more years.

Source: Thomas R. Karl, Jerry M. Melillo, and Thomas C. Peterson, eds., *Global Climate Change Impacts in the United States* (New York: Cambridge University Press, 2009), 13, accessed at http://downloads.globalchange.gov/usimpacts/pdfs/climate-impacts-report.pdf. Image credit: U.S. Global Change Research Program (www.globalchange.gov).

History of International Climate Policy

The international community began to address serious environmental issues during the 1970s. The first Earth Summit was held in Stockholm in 1972, and in 1979, the first World Climate Conference was held in Geneva. In 1988, the United Nations established the Intergovernmental Panel on Climate Change (IPCC), which issued its first assessment report on global warming in 1990. Based on the findings of the IPCC, the international community gathered in Buenos Aires in 1992 to draft the United Nations Framework Convention of Climate Change (UNFCCC). Most nations, including the United States, signed and ratified this general and flexible agreement.

The UNFCCC is important for several reasons. First, it publicly states that global warming and related climate change are significant problems, and it sets an ultimate objective of stabilizing GHG concentrations "at a level that would prevent dangerous anthropogenic (human induced) interference with the climate system."[12] Second, the signatories agreed to "common but differentiated responsibilities" for addressing climate change, with industrialized nations assuming responsibility for inventorying and reducing their GHG emissions.[13] Finally, all nations that ratified the convention agreed to develop national programs to slow climate change, and industrialized countries agreed to provide financial support to developing countries for these initiatives above and beyond what they already provide in foreign aid.

Kyoto Protocol

Five years later, the international community met again in Kyoto, Japan, to adopt the Kyoto Protocol. Whereas the UNFCCC encouraged industrialized countries to live up to their responsibility to reduce GHG emissions, the Kyoto Protocol committed them legally to binding reduction targets. While emission reduction targets varied among the thirty-nine industrialized countries and the European Union, the Kyoto Protocol sought to reduce overall GHG emissions to 5.2 percent below 1990 levels over a five-year period ranging from 2008 to 2012.[14] The Kyoto Protocol was adopted in Kyoto, Japan, in December 1997 and entered into force after ratification by Russia in February 2005. To date, 184 nations that are parties to the UNFCCC have signed and ratified the Kyoto Protocol.[15] In July 1997, the U.S. Senate by a 95–0 vote passed a resolution opposing any protocol that does not include binding targets and timetables for developing nations or that could "result in serious harm to the economy of the United States."[16] Vice President Al Gore signed the Kyoto Protocol on November 12, 1998, but the Clinton and subsequent Bush administrations never submitted it to the Senate for ratification.

One of the key features of the Kyoto Protocol is that it is a "cap-and-trade" system that imposes national caps on the GHG emissions of the industrialized nations identified in Annex I of the UNFCCC. These nations can trade unneeded annual emission allowances among themselves. The European Union Emission Trading System (EU ETS) was established recently for this purpose. In addition, Annex I nations can purchase "emission reduction units," which are GHG offsets that they can apply to their national emission reduction targets in one of three ways: Annex I nations can receive offsets for investing in GHG reduction projects in another industrialized nation under the Joint Implementation Mechanism of the protocol; they can receive offsets by investing in projects that reduce emissions in developing countries though the protocol's Clean Development Mechanism (CDM); and they can receive offsets for investments in various reforestation initiatives.[17]

What Is "Cap and Trade"?

A cap-and-trade system harnesses the power of markets to achieve a policy goal in a cost-effective manner. Any cap-and-trade system has several common features designed to reduce greenhouse gas (GHG) emissions. First, an emissions inventory must be established for each GHG in relationship to a baseline year. The next step is to decide the level at which emission of these gases will be capped over time. Once a cap is determined, then annual emission allowances are distributed to emitters in an amount that is equal to the cap. Emitters must surrender these allowances to the issuer in exchange for the emissions they release during an annual compliance period. If an emitter produces more emissions than it has allowances for, then the emitter has to make a decision. The emitter either has to make investments that result in fewer emissions, or it has to purchase additional allowances from companies that have already made these investments and thus have allowances to sell. By creating a market, and a price, for emission reductions, a cap-and-trade system offers an environmentally effective and economically efficient response to climate change.

Today, several industrialized nations, including France, the United Kingdom, Hungary, and Greece, are on target to meet their Kyoto obligations. Many other countries, however, are not likely to meet their targets; these include Germany, Canada, Japan, New Zealand, and Spain.[18] Thus, at best, the Kyoto Protocol has met with mixed success. On the one hand, it has demonstrated that the international community can develop a legally binding approach to reducing GHG emissions among developed nations, which also transfers some valuable financial and technological resources to developing countries. It has also demonstrated that baseline emissions can be calculated and emission allowances and GHG offsets can be tracked in a verifiable way. On the other hand, the protocol's effectiveness was fatally undermined when the United States, the world's largest historic emitter of GHGs and the largest potential market for GHG offsets, refused to ratify the protocol. In addition, a surplus of emission allowances after the fall of the Soviet Union drove down the allowance prices, and projects related to the Clean Development Mechanism have been associated with corruption and greenwashing.

Given the fact that the world's two largest emitters, China and the United States, do not have binding emission reduction obligations under the Kyoto Protocol, it is not surprising that global CO_2 emissions today are significantly higher than they were when the protocol was adopted. The lack of U.S. leadership over this last decade is extremely regrettable. Rajendra Pachauri's 2015 deadline for peak emissions is looming in the near future.

Bali Action Plan

The Kyoto Protocol was never conceived as a long-term solution to global warming. UNFCCC signatories met in Bali, Indonesia, in December 2007 to begin drafting the outline and timetable for a new international agreement that will replace the Kyoto Protocol when it expires at the end of 2012. Several ideas and proposals gained traction at the Bali conference. For example, reiteration of a Kyoto Protocol commitment to finance climate change adaptation projects through a 2 percent levy on CDM projects led to increased support among some developing nations for carbon trading related to CDM projects. Also, China for the first time expressed interest in reducing emissions via specific negotiated cuts in key industrial sectors such as electricity generation, steelmaking, aluminum production, and shipping. Under this approach, companies would work across borders to achieve the target emission reductions in these sectors, which would likely funnel significant amounts of private capital into the infrastructure of rapidly developing nations, including China. Developing nations also indicated they had become willing to discuss not only reducing emissions via afforestation (establishing forests in areas not forested for over fifty years) and reforestation initiatives (establishing forests in areas deforested before 1990), but also reducing emissions by preventing deforestation and forest degradation (REDD).[19]

The Bali Action Plan that emerged from the conference clarified that the new agreement would not depart significantly from the cap-and-trade approach of the Kyoto Protocol, but for the first time, developing nations agreed to join developed nations in reducing their emissions in a "measurable, reportable, and verifiable manner."[20] It is not clear yet what this means exactly, but it is unlikely that China, India, and other developing nations will reduce their emissions at the same rate as developed nations, nor are they likely to subject themselves to the same degree of binding commitments that they expect of developed nations. The Bali Action Plan emphasized that any new agreement that replaces the Kyoto Protocol must include stringent national GHG mitigation targets that span nearly four decades to 2050; it called for the expansion of trading in the international carbon market; and it called for review and strengthening of the Clean Development Mechanism.

Ethical Assessment of Current International Climate Policy Negotiations

Since the United Nations operates on the principle of consensus and not majority rule, it takes a very long time to develop and reach an agreement on any topic, let alone one as important and complex as global climate change. Members of the international community held ten separate meetings between the conference in Bali in December 2007 and the conference in Copenhagen in December 2009. In general, these meetings grappled with three key areas that will be central to any post-Kyoto agreement: (1) emission mitigation targets and related national obligations; (2) financing for mitigation, adaptation, and technology transfer; and (3) expanded emission allowance trading and the integrity of GHG offsets. In this section, I discuss each briefly and utilize the climate policy guidelines introduced in chapter 1 to conduct an ethical assessment of discussions thus far.

Emission Targets and National Obligations

Two key issues are related to the mitigation of GHG emissions. The first involves long-term pathway goals for emission reductions, and the second involves related national mitigation obligations. In May 2009, the United Nations released a first draft of the text that served as

Ecojustice Norms and Climate Policy Guidelines

Ecojustice Norms
- Sustainability
- Sufficiency
- Participation
- Solidarity

Climate Policy Guidelines

Temporal dimensions:
- Current urgency
- Future adequacy
- Historical responsibility
- Existing capacity
- Political viability

Structural dimensions:
- Scientific integrity
- Sectoral comprehensiveness
- International integration
- Resource sharing
- Economic efficiency

Procedural dimensions:
- Policy transparency
- Emissions verifiability
- Political incorruptibility
- Implementational subsidiarity

the basis for negotiations that began a month later in Bonn and culminated in Copenhagen in December 2009. This document offered delegates five options for achieving "a long-term aspirational global goal for emission reductions that is based on science."[21] The first alternative included various options but focused on stabilizing GHG concentrations in the atmosphere at no more than 450 ppm CO_2eq and limiting temperature increase to 2°C above the preindustrial level. To reach this goal, the text required that the parties to the agreement reduce global emissions collectively by at least 50 percent from 1990 levels by

2050. The second alternative also included various options but in general sought to stabilize GHG concentrations at "well below 350 ppm CO_2eq" and "to limit temperature increase to below 1.5° Celsius above the pre-industrial level."[22] To reach this more stringent goal, the text gave the parties the option of reducing emissions either 71 percent to 81 percent or more than 85 percent below 1990 levels by 2050. The third alternative did not state GHG concentration targets and instead focused on limiting the global temperature increase to no more than 2°C above the preindustrial level. The fourth and fifth alternatives determined a long-term goal on the basis of various factors including per capita emissions, historical responsibility for emissions, and "an equitable allocation of the global atmospheric resources."[23]

As was noted in the introduction, climate experts including Sir John Houghton and James Hansen are urging the international community to reduce GHG concentrations below 450 ppm CO_2eq and to limit total warming to less than 2°C. Thus, the guidelines for current urgency and future adequacy provide greater ethical support for the second alternative, since it seeks to stabilize emissions well below 350 ppm CO_2eq and to limit the increase in global average surface temperature to below 1.5°C. The reality, however, is that developing nations have thus far, at best, indicated a willingness to embrace the third alternative, which seeks to limit warming to no more than 2°C above the preindustrial level. Ideally, the post-Kyoto agreement will adopt a long-range goal that falls between the first two options and includes some form of binding commitment for both developed and developing nations. Even if the initial goal is less stringent than it could be, these targets can be revised in the future. The Montreal Protocol on Substances that Deplete the Ozone Layer has been amended four times over the past twenty years by the international community, and on each occasion, it imposed stricter limits on emissions that harm the ozone layer.[24]

With regard to national mitigation obligations, the draft negotiating text proposed that developed nations "shall" or "should" reduce their emissions by at least 25 percent to 45 percent below 1990 levels by 2020, and by 75 percent to 95 percent percent below 1990 levels by 2050. Similarly, the text urged developing countries as a group, "supported and enabled by technology, financing and capacity-building from developed countries," to significantly reduce their baseline emissions by as much as 15 percent to 30 percent by

2020, and 25 percent by 2050.[25] The text did not specify a baseline year for developing nations.

Todd Stern, the U.S. negotiator appointed by the Obama administration to the climate talks, was cheered with loud applause when he announced at an April 2009 meeting in Bonn, Germany, that the United States would "make up for lost time."[26] The mood changed quickly, however, when he announced the United States would only return to 1990 emission levels by 2020, though it would strive to be 80 percent below 1990 levels by 2050. Reaching 1990 levels by 2020 would require significant reductions, since U.S. GHG emissions increased 17 percent from 1990 to 2007 (fig. 4.3).[27] Nevertheless, Stern's announcement of the U.S goal to reduce emissions to 1990 levels by 2020 fell far short of the European Union's pledge to cut emissions 20 percent to 30 percent *below* 1990 levels by 2020. The U.S. position was even further short of the target that some developing nations (including China, South Africa, and the Philippines) have called for from developed nations: 40 percent to 50 percent reductions below 1990 levels by 2020.[28] I address this matter later in this chapter in a discussion of the Greenhouse Development Rights framework. Suffice it to say that the policy guidelines of historical responsibility and existing capacity demand that the United States (and other developed nations) shoulder a greater share of the burden of global GHG mitigation.

Financing for Mitigation, Adaptation, and Technology Transfer

One of the key findings of the IPCC's Fourth Assessment Report is that the impacts of global climate change will fall disproportionately on those who bear the least historical responsibility for causing the problem and have the least financial capacity to respond. Representatives of many developing nations have stated that no agreement will be reached in Copenhagen or elsewhere until this fundamental inequity is redressed. Recent studies by the World Bank and other institutions estimate that $5 billion to $10 billion is currently needed each year to help nations adapt to changing climate conditions, and this figure could grow to $100 billion per year by 2020.[29] Recently, the European Union pledged €15 billion ($21.8 billion) a year in aid to finance mitigation, adaptation, and technology transfer efforts in developing countries.[30]

Fig. 4.3. U.S. Greenhouse Gas Emissions, 1990–2007

U.S. Greenhouse Gas Emissions by Gas

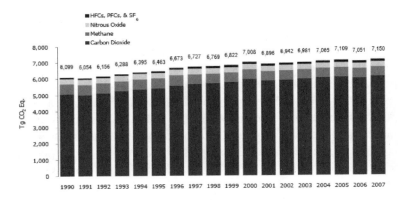

Annual Percent Change in U.S. Greenhouse Gas Emissions

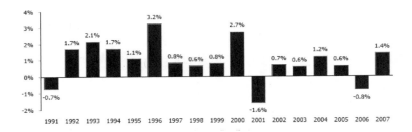

Cumulative Change in U.S. Greenhouse Gas Emissions relative to 1990

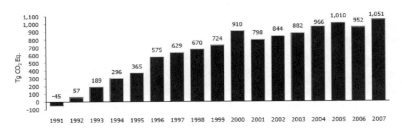

Source: Environmental Protection Agency, *Inventory of U.S. Greenhouse Gas Emissions and Sinks: 1990–2007*, EPA 430-R-09-004 (Washington, D.C.: EPA, April 2009), fig. 2-3, p. 2-27, accessed at http://epa.gov/climatechange/emissions/downloads09/InventoryUS-GhG1990-2007.pdf.

Several ideas and proposals have emerged for how these funds could be raised and what entity should distribute them. China and a large coalition of developing nations have proposed that the international community create a new organization that would be funded by industrial nations at an annual rate of 0.5 percent to 1.0 percent of their gross domestic product (GDP). These funds would be in addition to approximately $130 billion in official development assistance (ODA) that industrial nations currently make available to less-developed nations. Developed nations have publicly pledged that they will each provide ODA equivalent to 0.7 percent of their GDP, but actual rates of ODA have been running closer to 0.3 percent of GDP.[31] Advocates for poor nations are urging industrialized nations to live up to their ODA commitments and to make additional financial resources available to cope with the challenges posed by global climate change. Under China's proposal, a governing board with equal representation from developing and developed nations would determine how much funding would be provided each year in the form of grants to eligible nations for adaptation, mitigation, and technology transfer. Todd Stern, the lead U.S. climate negotiator, described China's proposal as "wildly unrealistic" and "untethered to reality" in testimony before Congress in September 2009.[32] Other ideas have been proposed. Mexico has proposed a comprehensive World Climate Change Fund, which would be open to all nations and provide assistance to any donor nation based on the size of the nation's population, its current GHG emissions, and gross domestic product. Switzerland has proposed a Multilateral Adaptation Fund that would fund climate adaptation initiatives. Brazil, South Africa, and India have made similar proposals.[33]

Raising the necessary funds for an institution that can dole out climate assistance is clearly going to be a challenge. One approach that already exists involves a 2 percent levy on all CDM projects, but developed countries have blocked a proposal by developing countries to increase this to 3 percent and also to apply the levy to projects in the former Communist countries and to the trading of emission allowances via the European Union's Emission Trading System.[34] Mexico has proposed tapping a portion of the proceeds from the auctioning of emission allowances within national cap-and-trade programs, and Norway has made a similar proposal regarding the auctioning of emission allowances under the Joint Implementation Mechanism of the Kyoto Protocol. Switzerland has advocated a global tax of $2 per metric ton (MT) on CO_2 emissions with an exemption for countries whose per capita emissions are less than 1.5 MT of CO_2 per year. Swiss estimates indicate this tax would raise $48.5 billion per year.[35] Finally, Maldives, Bangladesh, and other low-lying countries have proposed an international air travel tax that might raise $8 billion to $10 billion per year.[36]

The climate policy guidelines provide a means by which to assess proposals to help developing nations acquire resources to fund adaptation, mitigation, and technology transfer. The guidelines of historical responsibility, existing capacity, and resource sharing clearly justify placing the onus of responsibility on the backs of wealthier nations that have been the largest emitters in the past. The guidelines of international integration and economic efficiency, however, require that all nations have a seat at the table where decisions are made and that the funds be used in the most productive way possible. The guidelines of policy transparency and political incorruptibility demand that the leadership and decision-making process be above reproach and open to public scrutiny in all respects. The guidelines of industrial comprehensiveness, implementational subsidiary, and emissions verifiability require nations to develop their own mitigation and adaptation plans that will stand up to the scrutiny of other nations and whose results can be verified independently. Finally, the guideline of political viability helps to vet proposals through a lens of realism. Even if it is possible to reach an agreement, it is one thing to affirm a financial obligation and another thing to live up to it. Even a cursory review of other international agreements over the past few decades reveals that both developed and developing nations routinely fail to live up to the commitments they have made. That said, it is clear that developing nations will not entertain any binding emission reduction obligations for their own countries until developed nations make a substantial financial commitment to help them cope with the effects of climate change.

Expansion of Emission Trading and the Integrity of GHG Offsets

The expansion of GHG emission allowances and related offsets may be the most controversial aspect of any post-Kyoto agreement. For some, carbon trading raises practical concerns about verifying progress toward national mitigation obligations in developing countries and the environmental integrity of GHG offsets. For others, it just seems wrong to allow polluters to purchase the right to continue polluting. Finally, some are ideologically opposed to the trading of emission allowances because they view such trading as a dimension of neoliberal capitalism, which they believe is primarily to blame for the climate crisis. One of my colleagues in India, George Zachariah, sums up this perspective very well:

> Our prevailing policies and strategies to address the crisis posed by climate change seem to stem from faith in neoliberal capitalism. . . . Substituting fossil fuel with bio-fuel and other energy sources, carbon trading, carbon taxation, [the] Clean Development Mechanism (CDM) and the like are [all] embedded in the logic of the prevailing trajectory of economic growth as development. Climate change discourses appear to be geared towards finding solutions within capitalism. We need to have the discernment of Audre Lorde to boldly proclaim that the "Master's tools will never destroy the Master's house."[37]

This is a trenchant critique. There is no doubt that unfettered free markets have had disastrous consequences for people and the planet. There is also legitimate reason to fear that global GHG emission trading could enrich a few and bring disaster to many, just as the trading of credit default swaps played an important role recently in plunging the global economy into a recession. The question, however, is whether better regulation of markets can prevent these abuses and negative consequences. It is only because of political regulation that slavery and child labor have been banned and eliminated from most corners of the world. Similarly, environmental regulations have secured much cleaner air and water in the nations where they have been imposed and enforced. It is possible for communities to regulate their markets. For example, the Obama administration is unrolling a series of regulations on the financial sector in order to correct the laissez-faire approach of the Bush administration.

The success of any cap-and-trade system, at either the national or international level, depends in large part on the quality of regulation that is brought to bear on that system, as well as the fundamental design of the system. It is clear that a cap-and-trade approach has worked in the United States to cap and reduce the amount of sulfur dioxide emissions that cause acid rain. The Environmental Protection Agency has successfully managed this program, which has reduced emissions much faster and less expensively than had been expected.[38] The trading of emission allowances under the Kyoto Protocol's Joint Implementation mechanism has not led to significant GHG reductions, but this has had more to do with an excess availability of emission allowances after the fall of the Soviet Union than with management of the trading system. There is no question, however, that powerful economic actors will try to use the system to their advantage or at least to minimize the impact of a cap-and-trade system upon them. This is clear in the case of the European Union Emission Trading System (EU ETS), where only 5 percent of the emission allowances were auctioned initially and 95 percent were doled out for free to various companies, which often were able to parlay the allowances into windfall profits.[39] The policy guidelines of transparency and political incorruptibility must play a major role in ethical assessments of proposals for emission trading in a post-Kyoto climate agreement.

The integrity of GHG offsets will also be essential. GHG offsets can be produced in a variety of ways, including investments in renewable energy, energy efficiency, and forestry initiatives. Five key criteria have emerged for establishing the integrity of these offsets: the emission reductions achieved by these offsets must be real, additional, permanent, verifiable, and enforceable. There is significant debate among environmentalists about offsets because there is doubt about their efficacy in reducing emissions, and also suspicion that the entities that purchase them will forgo more expensive investments in energy efficiency and renewable energy. Many developing nations favor offset projects, since they offer a significant opportunity for private capital investment and infrastructure development. Currently, all CDM projects must demonstrate they will result in additional emission reductions. That is, CDM projects must be able to demonstrate that the emission reductions would not have occurred anyway due to pending economic development plans. Given this requirement, there has been significant criticism of hydroelectric projects in China that have applied for CDM certification, because China has a variety of policies and incentives in place to promote investment in hydroelectricity. Recently, the Institute for Global Environmental Studies even proposed that CDM projects in the poorest nations of the world be exempted from having to satisfy the criterion of additionality.[40] While such an exception might be justifiable for very poor nations with minimal per capita GHG emissions, the emissions verifiability guideline will be important in any assessment of the offset provisions in a post-Kyoto agreement. Offsets that lack environmental integrity will ultimately undermine political support for the system and will not help reduce global GHG emissions.

Climate Justice and the Greenhouse Development Rights Framework

To summarize thus far: It is good that the United States is now willing to discuss binding emission reduction targets, and it is good that detailed discussions have taken place about how to finance mitigation, adaptation, and technology transfer initiatives in developing countries, but the differences between developed and developing countries are still significant and may still scuttle a post-Kyoto agreement. On the one hand, poor, developing nations want rich, developed nations to make deep emission reductions while also providing billions of dollars in aid for climate assistance. On the other hand, rich, developed nations are reluctant to make binding commitments unless major developing nations such as China, India, and Brazil pledge they are willing to make significant reductions of their own. It does not help matters that all nations have been reeling from the global economic recession and tight credit markets, though global GHG emissions have been lower during this period than they otherwise would have been.

Differing Conceptions of Justice

One of the reasons it has been hard to reach agreement on a post-Kyoto climate treaty is that it is not only a political and economic issue, it is also an ethical issue about what climate justice requires. Gary Gardner, a senior researcher at the Worldwatch Institute, summarizes this well:

> Two nagging questions in particular have equity [justice] at their core: How should rights to emit greenhouse gases be allocated? And who should bear the costs of emissions reductions and adaptation to climate change?

A broad range of answers is given to these questions—each grounded in one or more climate equity principles. On emissions rights, for example, two very different principles are often cited by proponents of allocation schemes:

- The Egalitarian Principle states that every person worldwide should have the same emission allowance. . . .
- The Sovereignty Principle argues that all nations should reduce their emissions by the same percentage amount. . . .

Two other principles are often invoked to determine the economic burden of curbing climate change for different nations:

- The Polluter Pays Principle asserts that climate-related economic burdens should be borne by nations according to their contribution greenhouse gases over the years. . . .
- The Ability to Pay Principle argues that the burden should be borne by nations according to their level of wealth. . . .

The result is a thicket of principles, often conflicting, that will compete for policymakers' attention as climate negotiations unfold in the years ahead.[41]

This debate about what is just occurs because well-intentioned people don't always agree about what justice requires. In the philosophical and religious traditions of the West, justice has typically been associated with *equality*. More specifically, justice has required that similar cases be treated similarly without prejudice or discrimination. The problem is that not all cases are similar. This has led some to argue that sometimes justice must be viewed in terms of *equity*, which requires that costs be distributed on the basis of one's ability to bear the burden, and benefits distributed on the basis of need for assistance. Yet another view conceives of justice in terms of *merit* or *just deserts*. From this perspective, justice requires that people should enjoy the benefits of their labors and bear the consequences of their actions.

Thus, the ethical confusion Gardner identifies arises not only because policy makers are faced with a "thicket of principles," but also because they are operating with differing conceptions of justice. The egalitarian and sovereignty principles both tap into a conception of justice as equality. The principle of ability to pay appeals to the conception of justice as equity, and the polluter-pays principle conceives of justice in terms of merit or just deserts. Finally, differing approaches to moral theory also complicate matters. Those who primarily operate out of a deontological mind-set, which appeals to timeless principles and moral consistency, often find it hard to compromise, so the perfect can become the enemy of the good. Alternatively, those who primarily operate out of teleological mind-set can be so determined to maximize the good as they conceive it that they are willing to run roughshod over individual rights.

Key Aspects of the Greenhouse Development Rights Framework

Two organizations have recently proposed a rights-based approach to international climate policy which appeals to some of the principles Gardner identifies. In September 2007, representatives of the Stockholm Environmental Institute and EcoEquity, a think tank devoted to developing "a just and adequate solution to the climate crisis,"[42] published online *The Greenhouse Development Rights Framework: The Right to Development in a Climate Constrained World.* A second edition was published in November 2008.[43] Financial support for this project was provided by the large British relief and development organization Christian Aid,[44] as well as the Heinrich Böll Foundation in Germany, which strives "to promote democracy, civil society, human rights, international understanding and a healthy environment internationally."[45] In an official statement issued on the tenth anniversary of the Kyoto Protocol, the Executive Committee of the World Council of Churches encouraged "further deliberations and negotiations" about Greenhouse Development Rights as the international community develops an agreement to replace the Kyoto Protocol when it expires in 2012.[46]

I want to give special attention to the Greenhouse Development Rights (GDR) framework because its authors address the impasse that exists between wealthy developed countries and poor developing countries about how to develop an emergency climate stabilization program that will keep global warming less than 2°C above preindustrial levels. While developed nations that ratified the Kyoto Protocol have begun to take some responsibility for reducing GHG emissions, developing nations including China, India, and Brazil have thus far refused to accept similar binding GHG emission reductions that might constrain their ability to develop and improve the standard of living of their citizens. The GDR framework seeks to overcome this impasse by holding global warming below 2°C "while also safeguarding the right of all people around the world to reach a dignified level of sustainable human development."[47] By simultaneously addressing social justice issues and environmental issues, the GDR framework reflects an ecojustice approach.

The authors emphasize that the right to development belongs to *people* within nations and not to *nations* as a whole. Accordingly, the GDR framework utilizes the ability-to-pay principle and a development threshold based on annual personal income to allocate burden sharing associated with reducing GHG emissions and increasing sustainable human development. Individuals who fall below this threshold "are not expected to share the burden of mitigating the climate problem," but those above the development threshold "must bear the costs of not only curbing the emissions associated with their own consumption, but also of ensuring that, as those below the threshold rise toward and then above it, they are able to do so along sustainable, low-emission paths."[48] The authors of the GDR framework stress, however, that "it should be poor individuals, not poor nations, who are excused from bearing climate-related obligations."[49]

Since international efforts to grapple with climate change have focused on the obligations of nations, the GDR framework utilizes a responsibility–capacity index to translate individual responsibility into national responsibility. The GDR framework defines national *capacity* as the amount by which a country's per capita income exceeds the development threshold. Thus, "the portion of a country's GDP that [falls] below the development threshold would be exempt from being 'taxed' to pay for the global emergency program."[50] The GDR framework utilizes the polluter-pays principle to define national *responsibility* on the basis of cumulative per capita CO_2 emissions from fossil fuel consumption since 1990.[51] The authors settle on this year because this is when a general scientific consensus began to emerge about global warming and the impacts of climate change.

In the second edition of *The Greenhouse Development Rights Framework,* published in November 2008, the development threshold is lowered from $9,000 per person (calculated on the basis of purchasing power parity) to $7,500 per person, which is equivalent to $20 per day.[52] On the basis of this development threshold, figure 4.4 indicates

Fig. 4.4. National Capacity for Climate Mitigation: India, China, and the U.S.

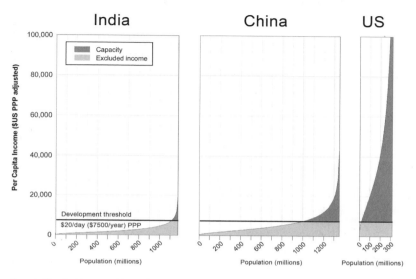

Source: Paul Baer, Tom Athanasiou, and Sivan Kartha, "Executive Summary," in *The Greenhouse Development Rights Framework: The Right to Development in a Climate Constrained World*, 2nd ed. (Berlin: Heinrich Böll Foundation, November 2008), fig. 4, p. 50, accessed at http://www.ecoequity.org/docs/TheGDRsFramework.pdf.

how national capacity for responding to the climate and development crises should be fairly allocated among India, China, and the United States. With approximately 95 percent of India's population living below the development threshold, the national capacity of India is very small compared with the huge capacity of citizens of the United States, where less than 5 percent percent of citizens live below the development threshold.

Table 4.1 calculates national responsibility on the basis of cumulative per capita CO_2 emissions since 1990 and combines this with national capacity to arrive at a responsibility–capacity index (RCI) for individual nations and groups of nations in 2010, 2020, and 2030.[53]

The authors of the Greenhouse Development Rights framework argue that the RCI offers a way for nations to fairly determine their "common but differentiated responsibilities and respective capabilities" under the UN Framework Convention on Climate Change.[54] Viewed through the lens of the RCI, the United States shoulders 33.1 percent of total global responsibility in 2010, and the nations that constitute the European Union bear 25.7 percent of responsibility, but the

Table 4.1. Percentage Shares of Total Global Population, GDP, Capacity, Responsibility, and RCI for Selected Countries and Groups of Countries.

	GDRs results for representative countries and groups						
	2010					2020	2030
	Popu-lation (percent)	GDP per Capita ($US 2005 PPP)	Capacity (percent)	Respon-sibility (percent)	RCI (percent)	RCI (percent)	RCI (percent)
EU 27	7.3	30,472	28.8	22.6	25.7	22.9	19.6
EU 15	5.8	33,754	26.1	19.8	22.9	19.9	16.7
EU +12	1.49	17,708	2.7	2.8	2.7	3.0	3.0
United States	4.5	45,640	29.7	36.4	33.1	29.1	25.5
Japan	1.9	33,422	8.3	7.3	7.8	6.6	5.5
Russia	2.0	15,031	2.7	4.9	3.8	4.3	4.6
China	19.7	5,899	5.8	5.2	5.5	10.4	15.2
India	17.2	2,818	0.7	0.3	0.5	1.2	2.3
Brazil	2.9	9,442	2.3	1.1	1.7	1.7	1.7
South Africa	0.7	10,117	0.6	1.3	1.0	1.1	1.2
Mexico	1.6	12,408	1.8	1.4	1.6	1.5	1.5
LDCs	11.7	1,274	0.1	0.0	0.1	0.1	0.1
Annex I	18.7	30,924	76	78	77	69	61
Non-Annex I	81.3	5,096	24	22	23	31	39
High Income	15.5	36,488	77	78	77	69	61
Middle Income	63.3	6,226	23	22	22	30	38
Low Income	21.2	1,599	0.2	0.2	0.2	0.3	0.5
World	100	9,929	100 %	100 %	100 %	100 %	100 %

Based on projected emissions and income for 2010, 2020, and 2030. (High, Middle and Low Income Country categories are based on World Bank definitions as of 2006. Projections based on International *Energy Agency World Energy Outlook* 2007.)

wealthy and consuming classes in the developing nations of China, India, and South Africa together bear 7 percent of the responsibility as well. Note that the GDR framework assumes China's standard of living will continue to improve, so China's RCI rating increases substantially from 5.5 percent in 2010 to 15.2 percent in 2030. Note also that the responsibilities of the United States and European Union decrease correspondingly during these two decades.

Implementation of the Greenhouse Development Rights Framework
How do these percentages of global responsibility translate into national financial obligations? The authors of the GDR framework explore two scenarios. The first involves the establishment of a World Climate Change Fund, like the one proposed recently by Mexico.

Assuming the annual requirement for climate transition funding is $1 trillion, the United States, with 33.1 percent of global responsibility, would have to provide $331 billion per year, the European Union would have to pay $257 billion, and China would have to provide $55 billion.[55] To put these numbers into perspective, $331 billion exceeds the $241 billion the United States spent in 2008 on interest to service the national debt, and it is more than half the amount the United States spent that year on national defense or social security.[56] According to the Department of State, the United States provided only $26 billion in official development assistance during 2008, and this represented a 19 percent increase from the previous year.[57] Under the GDR framework, the United States would be expected to provide almost thirteen times this amount of money in climate assistance. Politically, this level of commitment appears completely unviable.

The second scenario focuses on "national obligation wedges" to reduce global emissions to a level that is consistent with restraining maximum warming to 2°C. To meet this goal, the United States would have to reduce national emissions by over 6 percent per year to 90 percent below 1990 levels by 2050. This target level of reductions is approximately twice as aggressive as any legislation that has thus far been proposed in Congress. In addition, this scenario would require that the United States by 2025 make significant investments in emission reduction efforts in other countries to meet its national mitigation obligation under the RCI (fig. 4.5).[58] China would also need to begin making reductions, but not to the same extent as the United States, because its RCI is much lower than that of the United States (fig. 4.6). It is quite possible, if not likely, that much of the additional mitigation funded by the United States would take place in China.

The authors of the GDR framework anticipate and confront the opinion that what they propose is politically unrealistic. They argue instead that it is politically unrealistic to expect adoption of any post-Kyoto agreement until rich and poor nations can agree on a way that permits them to address and resolve both the poverty and climate crises. The authors also argue that "the demands of political realism are themselves rather labile" because "history shows, and continues to show, that they can change with remarkable rapidity."[59] They close by emphasizing that climate change is a threat that demands cooperation across the rich–poor divide and that only the moral norm of solidarity can help bridge this divide. The authors of the GDR framework make

Fig. 4.5. National RCI Greenhouse Gas Mitigation Obligation: United States

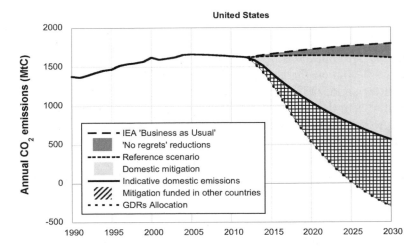

Source: Paul Baer, Tom Athanasiou, and Sivan Kartha, *The Greenhouse Development Rights Framework: The Right to Development in a Climate Constrained World*, 2nd ed. (Berlin: Heinrich Böll Foundation, September 2008), fig. 10, p. 76, accessed at http://www.ecoequity.org/docs/ TheGDRsFramework.pdf.

Fig. 4.6. National RCI Greenhouse Gas Mitigation Obligation: China

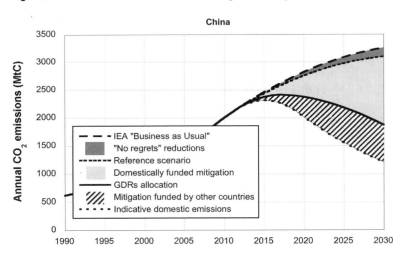

Source: Paul Baer, Tom Athanasiou, and Sivan Kartha, *The Greenhouse Development Rights Framework: The Right to Development in a Climate Constrained World*, 2nd ed. (Berlin: Heinrich Böll Foundation, September 2008), fig. 12, p. 78, accessed at http://www.ecoequity.org/docs/ TheGDRsFramework.pdf.

one thing very clear: The only thing more expensive than justice is injustice.

Conclusion

Viewed through the lens of the ecojustice norms, the Greenhouse Development Rights framework is an ethically praiseworthy contribution to the international climate policy debate. It seriously attempts to secure greater measures of sustainability by only considering mitigation strategies that will hold global warming to 2°C. It similarly satisfies the norm of sufficiency in its attempt to secure the right to development for billions of people who are still mired in poverty. It makes appropriate use of the norm of participation by emphasizing that the right to development belongs to people and not nations, and also by allocating moral responsibility for dealing with the dual climate and poverty crises to those who enjoy an income above the poverty threshold. Finally, as previously noted, the authors of the GDR framework appeal to the norm of solidarity by urging that the rich relieve the burdens of climate change and poverty from the backs of the poor.

The climate policy guidelines also yield a positive assessment of the GDR framework, though the framework pertains only to some of the guidelines, since it is not a comprehensive climate policy but rather a strategy for how to overcome one of the principal obstacles to adopting a new climate agreement. The GDR framework addresses four of the five temporal dimensions in an exemplary way. There is no question that it takes seriously the guidelines of current urgency, future adequacy, historical responsibility, and existing capacity. Despite the authors' compelling arguments about the political viability of their proposal, however, this does remain a legitimate concern. At a time when the United States is running record budget deficits, it is not realistic to expect the federal government to take on an additional climate assistance obligation that dwarfs its current level of official development assistance. Structurally, the GDR framework certainly emphasizes scientific integrity with regard to climate science, and it emphasizes that resource sharing and international integration are both key to resolving the climate and poverty crises. It says little, however, about industrial comprehensiveness and economic efficiency. In fact, critics will argue that the great economic cost associated with the measures they advocate will undermine the greater measures of social and ecological well-being they seek. Finally, the procedural dimensions of the climate policy guidelines are not addressed to a great extent in the GDR framework, because it is more of a concept than a fine-tuned policy proposal.

It is not clear yet whether the international community will embrace an approach to a post-Kyoto climate policy that reflects the GDR framework's attempt to address both the climate and development crises. There is little question, however, that such an approach would be wise and ethically justifiable when viewed through the lens of the ecojustice norms and the climate policy guidelines. I realize that many will view the GDR framework as unrealistic, but I view it as a moral corrective to policy discussions that too quickly and easily discount the interests and voices of people who are poor and disenfranchised. As a Christian ethicist, I think moral appeals to human rights concerns are essential as the international community comes to grips with the unprecedented perils posed by global warming and climate change. The GDR framework is a helpful approach to climate justice.

5. U.S. Climate Policy

We have the much larger carbon footprint per capita, and I know that in the past, the United States has sometimes fallen short of meeting our responsibilities. So, let me be clear: those days are over.

BARACK OBAMA
PRESIDENT OF THE UNITED STATES[1]

We have everything we need except political will, but political will is a renewable resource.

AL GORE
FORMER U.S. VICE PRESIDENT AND NOBEL PEACE PRIZE LAUREATE[2]

Shortly after the revised *Greenhouse Development Rights Framework* was published, the Environmental Justice and Climate Change Initiative released *A Climate of Change: African Americans, Global Warming, and a Just Climate Policy for the U.S.*[3] This study was a collaborative project between leaders of the environmental justice movement in the United States and Redefining Progress, a think tank dedicated to developing "solutions that ensure a sustainable and equitable world for future generations."[4] This study provides a valuable introduction to the focus of this chapter on U.S. climate policy, because it examines a range of options the United States could pursue and raises several important matters that deserve ethical reflection.

Envisioning a Just Climate Policy for the United States

The authors of *A Climate of Change*, J. Andrew Hoerner and Nia Robinson, emphasize at the outset that global climate change exacerbates nearly all existing inequalities and must be viewed within the context of human rights: "Climate change is not only an issue of the environment; it is also an issue of justice and human rights, one that dangerously intersects race and class. All over the world people of color, Indigenous Peoples and low-income communities bear disproportionate burdens from climate change itself, from ill-designed policies to prevent it, and from side effects of the energy systems that cause it."[5] Reflecting concerns similar to those of the GDR framework, which focuses on how the burden of reducing greenhouse gas (GHG) emissions should be distributed fairly while preserving the right to sustainable development, the Environmental Justice and Climate Change Initiative focuses on how different climate policies can affect the rights and welfare of people who are poor and the victims of racism.

Hoerner and Robinson begin by dismissing what they call "phony reductions" achieved through the European Union Emission Trading System (EU ETS) and the Kyoto Protocol's Clean Development Mechanism (CDM). They argue that both have sanctioned continued investments in fossil fuel infrastructure, ecologically damaging hydroelectric projects, and large tree plantations that jeopardize the livelihoods of local communities. They repudiate GHG offset purchases by rich nations from CDM projects in poor nations because they believe these purchases allow rich nations to avoid reducing their own consumption of fossil fuels. While the authors acknowledge that carbon trading offers a means to transfer resources to developing nations and protect the habitat of endangered species, they argue these offset projects are currently too flawed and thus result in "phony reductions."[6]

Hoerner and Robinson also repudiate "corporate windfalls" associated with cap-and-trade systems in which GHG emission allowances are distributed free to corporate polluters. This is how the vast majority of emission allowances were initially distributed when the EU ETS was established. Instead of requiring polluters to pay for the pollution they emit, Hoerner and Robinson argue that the free distribution of allowances rewards the polluters and enables only them to benefit financially from the trading of emission allowances. In this approach to climate policy, "big polluters are treated as though they have a right to pollute and taxpayers and consumers are obligated to bribe them to quit."[7] As we shall see, this is precisely how recent legislation passed and the U.S. House of Representatives proposes to distribute the vast majority of initial emission allowances.

The approach to climate policy most favored by the Environmental Justice and Climate Change Initiative is driven by the polluter-pays principle. Here the authors explore four different options and emphasize that revenue raised from polluters via any of these options needs to be returned directly to consumers, especially to people who are poor.

The first two options focus on governments imposing a fee or a tax on GHG emissions.[8] Here the goal is to capture environmental costs associated with GHG emissions in the prices of goods whose consumption results in emissions. Since a fee or a tax sets a fixed price for emissions, this predictability would help consumers and businesses make better long-range decisions about the costs and benefits of less-polluting technologies. In addition, all consumers and businesses are used to the assessment of separate fees or taxes on various kinds of economic activity, so a new emissions fee or tax would not be hard to understand.

The authors acknowledge, however, that these two strengths are matched by two significant weaknesses. The first is that few politicians are willing to propose new taxes, and many members of the public perceive new fees simply to be taxes under a different name. The second major weakness is that a fee or tax on GHG emissions does not guarantee that GHG emissions will be capped at a certain level, and a fee or tax will likely have to be significant in order for emissions to be reduced. For example, it was not until gasoline prices nearly tripled between 2001 and 2008 that drivers in the United States began to reduce their vehicle miles traveled. Sadly the revenue from this "tax" was sent to oil-exporting nations; it was not captured by the U.S. government to encourage research and development of alternative fuels or to address the regressive impact of these higher energy costs on people who are poor.

The other two options considered by the Environmental Justice and Climate Change Initiative revolve around governments establishing a firm cap on GHG emissions and then selling related emission allowances. In one case, emission allowances are auctioned to polluters by the government; in the other scenario, emission allowances are distributed for free by government to citizens, who then sell them directly to polluters. The study refers to the former as a cap-and-auction approach, and to the latter as a cap-and-dividend approach. In both cases, "collective ownership of the atmospheric commons" is viewed as "a shared birthright" for all people on the planet, in contrast to the cap-and-trade approach, "where polluting is a right that belongs to the polluter."[9] In both cases, the more a company pollutes, the more it will have to pay for the necessary emission allowances. A key weakness associated with the cap-and-auction approach is that auction prices could vary significantly in relationship to demand. While the study indicates how this problem could be addressed, corporations would still pass these costs on to consumers, and these costs would hit the poor the hardest. A key weakness associated with the cap-and-dividend approach is that it would be difficult to empower all citizens equally to sell the emission allowances allocated to them, and it would likely result in high administrative expenses.

Regardless of which route to climate policy is taken, the Environmental Justice and Climate Change Initiative advocates a Climate Asset Plan, which is designed to provide not only "climate justice" but also "common justice, justice for all."[10] One way the initiative proposes to approach these goals would be to distribute government revenues raised by fee, tax, or auction on an equal per capita basis. The authors of the study note that this approach would yield a disproportionate benefit to the poor, because the payment would represent a larger percentage of income for low-income households. Nevertheless, the authors argue that "a more nuanced approach may allow us to reap even larger benefits for justice, the economy, and African Americans."[11] They endorse distributing 62 percent of the emissions revenue on a per capita basis to all citizens, allocating an additional 18 percent for energy assistance programs such as the Low-Income Home Energy Assistance Program (LIHEAP), and applying the remaining 20 percent to promote energy efficiency.

The assessments and suspicions of the Environmental Justice and Climate Change Initiative have proven quite prescient, given recent debates about climate policy in the United States.

History of U.S. Climate Policy

It has taken at least twenty years for the United States to come to terms with the dangers posed by climate change. The nation's leading climatologist, James Hansen, began to ring the alarm bell when he testified before Congress in the summer of 1988, saying, "It's time to stop waffling so much and say that the evidence is pretty strong that the greenhouse effect is here."[12] Four years later, the United States did sign and ratify the United Nations Framework Convention on Climate Change (UNFCCC) and also participated in negotiations to draft the Kyoto Protocol during the Clinton Administration, but chose not to ratify it for reasons discussed in the previous chapter. In 2000, when Governor George W. Bush was campaigning against Vice President Al Gore for the presidency, Bush opposed the Kyoto Protocol but promised that his administration would begin regulating carbon dioxide (CO_2) emissions as a pollutant under the auspices of the Clean Air Act. Shortly after he was elected, however, Bush announced in March 2001 that he had changed his mind and no longer wanted the Environmental Protection Agency (EPA) to pursue regulation of CO_2.[13] Over the next eight years, the Bush administration muzzled climate scientists within the administration, delayed publication of important scientific studies mandated by the UNFCCC, developed a comprehensive U.S. energy policy that proposed an expansion of fossil fuels, and played an obstructionist role in international discussions about climate policy.

A host of players at the local, state, and national levels stepped into the leadership void left by the White House. For example, Greg Nickels, the mayor of Seattle, Washington, drafted the U.S. Mayors Climate Protection Agreement in 2005. Mayors who sign the agreement commit to reduce GHG emissions in their cities to 7 percent below 1990 levels by 2012. Over five hundred mayors from cities whose populations total over 44 million people are now committed to this goal, and the number continues to rise.[14] Elsewhere around the country, elected leaders in over half the states in the nation passed legislation establishing renewable portfolio standards, which mandate that an increasing percentage of electricity be produced with renewable energy.[15] At the national level, Senators Joseph I. Lieberman (Ind-Conn.) and John Warner (R-Va.) introduced America's Climate Security Act of 2007. This landmark bill in the Senate sought to establish an economy-wide, mandatory cap-and-trade law to reduce U.S. GHG emissions to 15 percent below 2005 levels by 2020 and to 70 percent below 2005 levels by 2050. The bill eventually made it through committees and to the Senate floor in June 2008. After three days of vigorous debate, the bill's proponents were able to muster only forty-eight of the sixty votes they needed to invoke cloture and bring the bill to a final vote. Even though the Lieberman–Warner bill failed in the Senate, it indicated that members of Congress were ready to address climate policy in a serious way.

The election of President Barack Obama in November 2008 was a watershed moment for the nation and a pivotal point in U.S. discussions about climate policy at both the national and international levels. Throughout his campaign, Obama expressed support for a market-based cap-and-trade system to reduce U.S. carbon emissions 80 percent below 1990 levels by 2050.[16] In February 2009, Obama released budget plans that assumed over $645.7 billion in new federal revenue would be raised by 2019 through a 100 percent auction of GHG emission allowances, assuming an initial allowance price of $20 per metric ton of CO_2. Obama's budget indicated he intended to return $525.7 billion of this revenue to taxpayers in the form of tax credits in order to address the rising cost of energy, with the rest used to fund clean-energy technologies.[17] Obama's intentions matched quite closely the Climate Asset Plan advocated by the Environmental Justice and Climate Change Initiative.

Shortly after his election, Obama ordered the EPA to review whether CO_2 emissions are pollutants subject to regulation under the Clean Air Act. While President Bush had floated this idea in 2000 in order to get elected, a 2007 Supreme Court decision had ordered the Bush administration to make a definitive determination about this matter in the last year or so of its second term. The EPA spent more than a year studying the question, but the Bush administration apparently had no desire to change the status quo, so the EPA did not make its determination public. In April 2009, the new head of the EPA in the Obama administration reviewed the EPA studies and announced that CO_2 and five other GHGs pose grave threats to public health and welfare. This finding empowers the EPA to develop and impose regulations that will reduce the emission of these GHGs throughout the U.S. economy.[18] It thus puts enormous pressure on Congress to find legislative means to reduce GHG emissions, because if Congress fails, the EPA can utilize the blunt and brute force of regulations to achieve these reductions.

American Clean Energy and Security Act of 2009

The EPA announcement in April 2009 took place shortly after Henry Waxman (D-Calif.) and Edward Markey (D-Mass.) introduced a discussion draft of the American Clean Energy and Security Act of 2009 (ACESA) in the U.S. House of Representatives.[19] Like the Lieberman–Warner legislation that had failed in the Senate, this comprehensive national climate and energy legislation called for an economy-wide cap-and-trade system along with other measures to reduce GHG emissions and help the United States build a clean-energy economy. Unlike the Senate bill, ACESA narrowly passed the House on June 26, 2009, by a vote of 219–212.[20]

This landmark bill totaled 1,428 pages and was divided into five major sections.[21] The first two sections focused on developing clean energy and increasing energy efficiency in the United States. The other three sections focused on aspects of the cap-and-trade system proposed by the bill and its effects on U.S. consumers, workers, and industries. I first summarize the content and some of the debate about the first two sections of the bill, and then go into greater detail to discuss and assess the cap-and-trade aspects of the bill.

In the initial discussion draft version of ACESA , the first section focused on various measures to develop increased supplies of clean energy in the United States. The bill provided various incentives for carbon capture and sequestration, low-carbon fuels, and electric vehicles, the development of smart electricity grids, and increased transmission capacity. The most important new policy proposal, however, was to establish a national renewable electricity standard (RES), which would require that 25 percent of all electricity in the United States be produced renewably by 2025. The second section of the bill contained provisions related to building, lighting, appliance, and vehicle energy efficiency programs. The most important new policy proposal, however, was to establish a national energy efficiency resource standard (EERS), which would require electricity and natural gas distribution companies to achieve cumulative savings of 15 percent and 10 percent, respectively, by 2020.

In the final version of ACESA that passed the House, the separate renewable electricity and energy efficiency standards were consolidated into one combined energy efficiency and renewable electricity standard. The standard requires utilities to supply 15 percent of their power sales from qualified renewable sources of electricity by 2020, and it requires an additional 5 percent to be supplied via investments in energy efficiency. State governors may reduce the renewables requirement to 12 percent, but then the efficiency requirement increases to 8 percent.[22]

As we have seen, renewable energy sources generated 8 percent of the U.S. electricity supply in 2007, with hydro projects supplying 6 percent, and wind and solar supplying only 2 percent.[23] Some environmentalists have lamented the reduced expectations of ACESA's combined standard because they believe existing state renewable portfolio standards will require the installation of sufficient renewable energy capacity to generate at least 15 percent of the U.S. electricity supply by 2020. At the same time, some members of the business community and some politicians—especially from the Southeast—believe the combined standard goes too far and will pose harm to the economy. Neither group will likely be mollified by the fact that the ACESA combined renewable electricity and energy efficiency standard that passed the U.S. House of Representatives is more rigorous than a similar standard that passed the U.S. Senate Energy and Natural Resources Committee in June 2009. The Senate version requires that 15 percent of all electricity in the United States be produced renewably by 2021. States would be allowed to fulfill up to 4 percent of the requirement through energy efficiency measures.

Given the impact that state-mandated renewable portfolio standards have had on renewable electricity production in the United States, it seems clear that a strong national RES will help the nation make a more rapid transition to a clean-energy economy. The combined renewable electricity and energy efficiency standards that have been proposed in the House and Senate are too low to prompt this transition. Ideally, advocates in the Senate will propose strengthening the Senate proposal, perhaps along the lines of mandating a combined standard of 25 percent by 2025, with 20 percent coming from renewably produced electricity and 5 percent from energy efficiency.

The cap-and-trade aspects of the bill also changed between the time the bill was first introduced and when it finally passed. Important changes were made with regard to emission targets, allowance

Ecojustice Norms and Climate Policy Guidelines

Ecojustice Norms

- Sustainability
- Sufficiency
- Participation
- Solidarity

Climate Policy Guidelines

Temporal dimensions:
- Current urgency
- Future adequacy
- Historical responsibility
- Existing capacity
- Political viability

Structural dimensions:
- Scientific integrity
- Sectoral comprehensiveness
- International integration
- Resource sharing
- Economic efficiency

Procedural dimensions:
- Policy transparency
- Emissions verifiability
- Political incorruptibility
- Implementational subsidiarity

distributions, and offset provisions. I address each of these in some detail and offer a summary assessment in light of the climate policy guidelines.

Emission Targets

ACESA limits the emissions of seven greenhouse gases. In addition to the six GHGs listed by the United Nations Framework Convention on Climate Change, the bill also covers emissions of nitrogen trifluoride (NF_3). Entities that annually emit more than 25,000 metric tons (MT) of these gases measured in terms of carbon dioxide equivalent (CO_2eq) are included in the cap-and-trade plan. The plan is estimated to cover 72 percent of U.S. emissions in 2012 and 86 percent by 2020.[24] Emission caps are imposed on electricity producers, oil refiners and importers, natural gas suppliers, and energy-intensive industries including iron, steel, cement, and paper manufacturing.[25]

The bill establishes a set of increasingly aggressive targets for reducing GHG emissions, using a baseline of 2005 emissions:

- 3 percent reduction by 2012
- 17 percent reduction by 2020
- 42 percent reduction by 2030
- 83 percent reduction by 2050

Viewed in light of U.S. recalcitrance to embrace binding emission reductions under the Kyoto Protocol, this range of increasingly aggressive targets from 2012 to 2050 is very significant. If all targets are achieved, the result would be enormous and unprecedented reductions in GHG emissions in the United States (fig. 5.1). There was only one change in these targets between the discussion draft that was introduced in April 2009 and the final version that was passed by the House during the 111th Congress in June 2009. Henry Waxman, chair of the House Energy and Commerce Committee, lowered the 2020 target from 20 percent to 17 percent in order to reduce the impact of the bill on the U.S. economy and, by doing so, increased political support for the bill in the House.

Environmentalists criticized this lowering of the near-term reduction goal and also the decision in ACESA to set 2005 as the baseline year rather than 1990, which is the baseline year under the Kyoto Protocol. As we have seen, U.S. GHG emissions increased 17 percent

Figure 5.1. Emission Reductions under the Cap-and-Trade Proposals in the 111th Congress

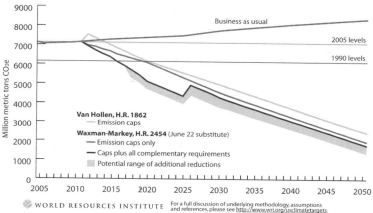

Emission Reductions Under Cap-and-Trade Proposals in the 111th Congress, 2005-2050
June 25, 2009

Source: John Larsen and Robert Heilmayr, "Emission Reductions under Cap-and-Trade Proposals in the 111th Congress" (Washington, D.C.: World Resources Institute, June 25, 2009), accessed at http://pdf.wri.org/usclimatetargets_2009-06-25.pdf.

between 1990 and 2007.[26] If the ACESA targets are adjusted for this change in the baseline year, then a 17 percent reduction from 2005 levels by 2020 would equate to only a 3.3 percent reduction below the level of U.S. emissions in 1990.[27] The Kyoto Protocol mandated that the United States reduce its emissions to 7 percent below 1990 levels by 2012. The fact that U.S. emissions under ACESA will be only 3.3 percent below 1990 levels by 2020, rather than 2012, has brought criticism from many. The following statement is an excerpt from an article published by Xinhua, China's official news agency, after the House passed ACESA: "The new move marks a major step for the U.S. government to cap and reduce greenhouse gas emissions, yet the United States still fell short of taking on its due responsibility as a developed country, much less its self-claimed 'leading role' in tackling climate change."[28] Members of the European Union (EU) also have been very disappointed with ACESA's near-term 2020 emission target. The EU has pledged to cut its GHG emissions to 20 percent below 1990 levels by 2020 and is willing to cut its emissions 30 percent below 1990 levels by 2020 if the United States accepts the same emission reduction target.

Viewed through the lens of the climate policy guidelines, the ACESA emission reduction targets fare better in terms of the future-adequacy guideline than the current-urgency guideline. One day before the House gathered for its vote on ACESA, Yvo de Boer, the executive secretary of the United Nations Framework Convention on Climate Change, gave a speech to the Spanish Parliament Commission for Climate Change. He reminded the international community (and the U.S. House of Representatives): "Science tells us that industrialized countries need to reduce emissions in the order of 25 to 40 percent below 1990 levels by 2020 if we are to avoid the worst climate impacts."[29] Clearly, the U.S. 2020 target under ACESA falls well short of this near-term goal. Also, while it is true that the binding ACESA targets become increasingly aggressive and culminate with an 83 percent reduction in 2050, the authors of the Greenhouse Development Rights framework remind us that nations like the United States should be making and financing even further reductions in order to live up to their historical responsibility and current capacity.

The political-viability guideline, however, reminds us that half a loaf is better than none. After a decade of delay and obfuscation, the United States finally appears ready to embrace binding emission reductions that become more stringent over time. The passage of ACESA is something to be celebrated, as imperfect as it is. Like most initial attempts at environmental legislation, it will have to be defended, revised, and improved over time. Nevertheless, major developing nations including China clearly think the U.S. response is insufficient. This places in jeopardy the fate of a post-Kyoto agreement. Thus, the political-viability guideline cuts both ways. Though highly unlikely, it would be best if the U.S. Senate would increase the 2020 reduction to at least 20 percent below 2005 levels, enabling the United States to nearly meet its obligations under the Kyoto Protocol. Odds are, however, that China and other nations will find the U.S. commitment to be insufficient.

Distribution of Emission Allowances

One of the key issues left unresolved in the discussion draft of ACESA was how emission allowances would be distributed. Waxman and Markey quickly discovered their bill lacked sufficient political support if allowances were to be distributed only via auction. Representatives of fossil-fuel-intensive industries and their lobbyists argued the auction cost to purchase federal GHG emission allowances would significantly drive up the prices of their goods and services, which they would have to pass on to U.S. consumers, and which would also make these industries less cost-competitive internationally. After a series of closed-door negotiations, primarily with moderate and conservative Democrats in the House, Waxman and Markey decided to auction only approximately 15 percent of the emission allowances at the outset of the program. The percentage of auctioned allowances grows steadily over time, however, to about 70 percent by 2030.[30]

Under ACESA, the electric utility industry, the nation's largest source of CO_2 emissions, would receive 35 percent of the initial GHG emission allowances for free. State-regulated local electric-distribution companies would receive 30 percent of the allowances; another 5 percent of allowances would be doled out to merchant power plants that produce electricity for the wholesale market. The allowances would be distributed according to a formula suggested by the electric utility industry that involves an even split between historic emission levels and retail sales. Another 9 percent of the allowances would be doled out to natural gas distributors. The free allowances to the electric utilities and natural gas distributors would be phased out between 2026 and 2030. Energy-intensive companies in the pulp, paper, cement, and steel industries also would receive 15 percent of the allowances for free, though these would be phased out after 2014. Oil refiners would get 2 percent of the allowances starting in 2014, but their allocation would end two years later, in 2016. The U.S. auto industry would get 3 percent of the allowances through 2017, and 1 percent from 2018 to 2025, with the stipulation that the allowances be used for increased production of electric and higher-fuel-economy vehicles. In addition, carbon capture and sequestration efforts would get 2 percent of the allowances from 2014 to 2017, and 5 percent in 2018 and beyond.[31] Other free allowances are doled out to state governments and other entities for purposes discussed later in this chapter.

News of these free distributions produced howls of protests from environmentalists, corporate watchdogs, and advocates for the poor. These groups feared the free allowances would result in corporate windfall profits, increased energy costs for the poor, and reduced effectiveness of the cap-and-trade system—exactly the concerns raised by the Environmental Justice and Climate Change Initiative.

The ACESA bill attempts to address the first two concerns by stipulating that the free emission allowances distributed to electric and natural gas utilities "shall be used exclusively for the benefit of retail ratepayers."[32] Since both industries are highly regulated in most states, this provision helps to ensure that ratepayers benefit and that electric and natural gas utilities are not able to make a windfall profit from receipt of the free allowances. Another provision of the bill devotes proceeds from the auctioning of 15 percent of the initial emission allowances toward low- and moderate-income families. These revenues would be distributed in the form of tax credits, direct payments, and electronic benefit payments to help these families cope with rising energy prices. In addition, 1.5 percent of the emission allowances are to be distributed for free to programs that provide assistance to families that need help paying their heating fuel bills, and up to 1 percent of the allowances will fund worker assistance and job-training initiatives.[33] All these provisions are appropriate ways to satisfy the resource-sharing guideline and are consistent with the Climate Action Plan proposed by the Environmental Justice and Climate Change Initiative, but only time will tell whether they will be sufficient to protect the poor. It is less clear how ACESA prevents electric utilities in deregulated states and the other industries that receive free allowances from enjoying windfall profits. What is clear is that the ACESA bill would have failed even to make it to the floor of the House if these free allowances had not been offered.

Will these free allowances undermine the environmental effectiveness of the cap-and-trade system? The Pew Center on Global Climate Change claims this is a myth because, from an environmental perspective, it does not matter how the emission allowances are distributed. The key to a cap-and-trade system is that there is a firm and declining cap that puts a price on GHG emissions.[34] Furthermore, ACESA promotes the environmental effectiveness of the cap-and-trade system by giving additional free allowances to the public and private sector to support research and development in clean energy and energy efficiency, to prevent tropical deforestation, and to fund both domestic and international adaptation to climate change.[35] The recipients of these free allowances would sell them to emitters and use the funds for these environmental initiatives. Thus, it appears the free allowances used in these ways will likely better achieve the environmental goals of the cap-and-trade system than undermine them.

Offset Provisions

Perhaps the most controversial aspect of ACESA is the provision it makes for the use of offsets in meeting annual GHG emission reductions. Offsets give covered entities a third way to comply with their annual emission limits. If their emissions exceed their limit, they can: (1) make investments in energy efficiency or renewable energy to reduce their emissions; (2) purchase emission allowances from other covered entities that have a surplus; or (3) purchase offset credits from qualifying projects.

Greenhouse Gas Offsets

Greenhouse gas (GHG) offsets are created by projects that reduce, avoid, or permanently sequester GHG emissions. Most of these projects involve one of the following measures:

- Capturing methane before it escapes from coal mines, landfills, and manure lagoons
- Biological sequestration of carbon in forestry initiatives, agricultural soils, and rangelands
- Geological sequestration of carbon dioxide beneath the earth
- Investments in renewable energy that displace investments in fossil-fuel-powered energy systems
- Reduction or avoidance of fossil fuel emissions via investments in end-use energy efficiency

---

ACESA defines qualifying offset projects as those that "result in reductions or avoidance of greenhouse gas emissions, or sequestration of greenhouse gases."[36] The bill establishes an Offsets Integrity Advisory Board and charges it with making recommendations to the EPA, which ultimately determines what domestic and international offset projects are eligible. The EPA must "ensure that such offset credits represent verifiable and additional greenhouse gas emission reductions or avoidance, or increases in sequestration."[37] In addition, the EPA must "ensure that offset credits issued for sequestration offset projects are only issued for greenhouse gas reductions that are permanent."[38] In a last-minute compromise, the bill gives the U.S. Department of Agriculture (USDA) instead of the EPA control over offsets produced through domestic agriculture and forestry practices.[39]

The bill allows all covered entities collectively to purchase up to 2 billion tons of offsets each year to meet the nation's GHG emission reduction targets. According to the EPA, U.S. emissions totaled 7.15 billion (MT) in 2007.[40] Under ACESA, domestic and international offset projects can each provide 1 billion MT of offsets per year. If there is insufficient domestic supply, EPA can raise the international limit to 1.5 billion MT, but the limit of 2 billion MT per year remains. Presumably in an attempt to stimulate and privilege the U.S. offset market, ACESA stipulates that each international offset credit beginning in 2018 will be worth only 80 percent of a domestic offset credit. Thus, a covered entity would have to submit 5 MT of international offset credits for every 4 MT of emissions they want to reduce.[41] A covered entity can use offsets to satisfy only a percentage of its annual emission reduction obligation, but this percentage changes over time.[42] At the outset of the cap-and-trade program, covered entities would be able to satisfy 30 percent of their emission reduction obligation with offsets. This percentage declines briefly from 2015 to 2021, but then it rises steadily to 63 percent in 2050.

This very large reliance on offsets to achieve U.S. goals for GHG reduction has divided the environmental community. Some groups view offsets as an essential tool to change land use practices, protect forests, and channel badly needed financial and technological resources to developing countries. Other groups view offsets as fake reductions and call them "rip-offsets" because they doubt the efficacy of offset projects to reduce global emissions and they believe offsets simply enable polluters to continue polluting.[43] As we have seen, a host of concerns have been raised about the integrity of CDM offsets. It is not easy to ensure that offset projects result in GHG emission reductions that are real, additional, permanent, verifiable, and enforceable. ACESA enjoins EPA and USDA to utilize all of these criteria along with other factors to determine the legitimacy of offset projects, but this has done little to quell the distrust and disgust of some members of the environmental community.[44]

Even if EPA and USDA are able to assure that all offset projects have high levels of environmental integrity, there is good reason to believe there will not be enough offsets available, at least in the initial years of the U.S. cap-and-trade program. A recent report produced in the United States by the National Commission on Energy Policy made the following observation: "Assuming that an average overseas project would generate 100,000 offset tons per year, this would require the approval of 10,000 projects within three years of the start of the program. To put the administrative burden in perspective, this is more than seven times the total number of projects registered under the Clean Development Mechanism (CDM) established by the United Nations as part of the Kyoto Protocol."[45] The international offset market is more developed than the U.S. offset market because the United States never ratified the Kyoto Protocol. Thus, it will take time to develop projects in the United States that could come anywhere close to meeting the potential demand of a billion metric tons per year.

While the lack of access to sufficient offsets may not trouble some environmentalists who would prefer they be abolished, the lack of offset supply has important implications for the cost of implementing ACESA. The EPA released a major study in June 2009 that calculated ACESA would cost U.S. households an additional $80 to $111 a year, or 22¢ to 30¢ per day. Offsets, however, play an important role in keeping these costs relatively low. EPA projects that the one billion ton annual limit on domestic offsets will never be reached, but it does assume that over a billion metric tons of international offsets will be used each year from 2012 to 2050. If the international offsets are not used, EPA estimates that the price of emission allowances in 2015 would increase by 89 percent from $13 per metric ton of carbon dioxide equivalent (t CO_2eq) to over $24 per t CO_2eq.[46]

This cost increase presumably would nearly double the economic impact of ACESA on U.S. households. Still, an increase of $160 to $210 per year is not insurmountable for most U.S. families, and the rising value of the emission allowance would increase the value of the various cost mitigation measures for low- and moderate-income families, discussed earlier. At the end of the day, if sufficient offsets are unavailable due to strict environmental standards or high global demand, covered entities will simply have to satisfy the cap and reduce their emissions by making investments in energy efficiency and renewable energy or purchase emission allowances from those who do. Just as the high cost of nuclear power will lead decision makers to invest in less expensive, clean-energy options, so, too, will a lack of offsets under a firm cap-and-trade system force emitters to become more efficient and greener.

Summary Assessment

Overall, the climate policy guidelines yield a fairly positive assessment of the American Clean Energy and Security Act of 2009. We look first at the temporal dimensions. While the near-term reduction target of 17 percent below 2005 levels by 2020 is inadequate viewed through the lens of the current-urgency guideline, the long-term reduction target of 83 percent below 2005 levels by 2050 is much more consistent with the future-adequacy guideline. The historical-responsibility and existing-capacity guidelines, however, justify expectations among developing nations and within the European Union that the United States accept much greater responsibility for reducing global GHG emissions. Developing nations, including China, India, Brazil, and South Africa, will never commit to binding emission reductions until the world's largest historical emitter imposes large and binding reductions upon itself. Climate justice demands more from the United States. That said, the narrow margin by which the bill passed the U.S. House of Representatives indicates ACESA may achieve the most reductions that are currently possible politically.

The structural dimensions of the climate policy guidelines appear to be well addressed in ACESA. Various aspects of the bill require revision of the cap-and-trade program if new scientific findings justify them. The bill will cover 86 percent of the U.S. economy by 2020 and thus is comprehensive in nature. Despite the protestations of some industries such as oil refiners, the bill does not lay a significantly disproportionate burden on any one industry. The expectation that a large share of U.S. emission reductions will be achieved through the purchase of international offsets is one important way that this domestic climate policy can be integrated with other global efforts. The provisions in the bill that secure financial assistance for international efforts to stop deforestation and provide adaptation assistance are one example of international integration, though critics rightly argue that the amount of this resource sharing should be much higher. As has been noted, various provisions in ACESA are designed to mitigate the financial impact of the bill on U.S. households. While a 100 percent auction of emission allowances would generate an enormous amount of revenue that could be distributed each year on a per capita basis to U.S. citizens, the income tax credits, direct payments, electronic benefits payments, and ratepayer protection provisions in the bill should still provide a significant and, hopefully, sufficient amount of resource sharing. Finally, the fact that the EPA expects ACESA to cost U.S. households only 22¢ to 30¢ per day indicates that economic efficiency was paramount for the bill's designers and supporters. In the near term, however, it appears that social well-being is weighted more heavily than ecological well-being, and this will be counterproductive in the long run. The current urgency of the planet's climate crisis must lead to a reassessment of economic efficiency. The economic and social costs of failure to adequately address the ecological consequences of the climate change that loom before us are enormous. Again, the only thing more expensive than climate justice is climate injustice.

It is hard to assess how well ACESA will meet the procedural dimensions of the climate policy guidelines, because the bill has not yet become law and thus has not been implemented. It would be hard to claim that a policy of 1,428 pages is overly transparent and easily comprehensible to the general public. Still, the bill does make it possible for industries to calculate their emission reduction obligations over time, and it includes various cost containment provisions that should help industries manage the related expenses. Insofar as these decisions must be made by emitters themselves, the guideline of implementational subsidiarity is satisfied. Given the importance offsets play as one of these cost containment provisions, the verifiability of offset emission reductions will be extremely important. The bill saddles EPA and USDA with determining which offset projects have environmental integrity, so public scrutiny of these decisions will be vital. Finally, as with any piece of legislation, lobbyists representing special interests will try to shape it to serve and protect their interests. The only way to secure greater measures of political incorruptibility in a democracy is for ordinary citizens and not-for-profit organizations to participate in policy debates in order to make their voices heard. Certainly, a wide variety of Christian denominations participated in the debate about ACESA in the House, and most advocated aggressively for its passage.

Prospects in the Senate
and the Need for U.S. Leadership

With ACESA's narrow margin of victory in the U.S. House of Representatives, attention now turns to climate policy discussions in the U.S. Senate. This book went to press in mid-September 2009, before the Senate began deliberations on a cap-and-trade bill. Given the failure of the less aggressive Lieberman–Warner bill in 2007, reaching the sixty votes necessary to pass a bill in the Senate will be an uphill battle. To pass such a bill, many are calling for changes to ACESA. For example, Senator Tom Harkin (D-Iowa) has called for a change in the way emission allowances are distributed to electric utilities under ACESA. He believes the formula, which distributes allowances half on the basis of historical emissions and half on the basis of current retail sales, will force states like Iowa to shoulder more of the nation's cost to reduce emissions, since the state gets a high percentage of its power from coal-fired power plants. He thinks it is unfair that ratepayers in the Northwest and Northeast would bear less of the national burden, since they benefit from the clean hydroelectric dams that were built in these states with federal taxpayer dollars.[47]

A host of other concerns about ACESA have been raised by legislators and lobbyists. Senator Bernie Sanders (Ind-Vt.) and Frank Lautenberg (D-N.J.) want to replace ACESA's weakened 2020 emissions target of 17 percent below 2005 levels with a more stringent target of 20 percent below 2005 levels. Consumer and environmental groups want the Senate to spell out more clearly how residential electric and natural gas ratepayers would receive benefits from any free allowances distributed to local distribution companies. Forestry advocates want to ensure the Senate bill has specific offset provisions for forestry, which are lacking in the House cap-and-trade bill. To quell concerns about the trading of emission allowances, Senator Dianne Feinstein (D-Calif.) and Senator Olympia Snowe (R-Maine) have proposed putting the Commodity Futures Trading Commission (CFTC) in charge of all carbon-trading markets.

According to *Environment & Energy Daily*, a highly regarded and nonpartisan news and information service, it appeared in September 2009 that forty-five senators would either certainly or probably vote for cap-and-trade legislation similar to ACESA, and thirty-four senators were either firmly opposed or very likely to vote against such legislation. That leaves a group of twenty-one senators on the fence, likely to determine the fate of U.S. climate policy legislation (and perhaps significantly affect the prospects for an international agreement in Copenhagen).[48] This group consists of fifteen Democrats and six Republicans, so if the vote broke along strict party lines, it would be possible to pass the legislation. The reality, however, is that many of the fifteen Democrats on the fence represent states that produce a large percentage of U.S. fossil fuel supplies (for example, Alaska, West Virginia, Pennsylvania, and Montana). The compromises needed to secure these votes will likely weaken, rather than strengthen, the provisions in ACESA. This would be very unfortunate.

Presidential leadership will be critical, both in terms of passing climate legislation in the Senate and in terms of achieving international consensus on a post-Kyoto agreement. Most pundits agree President Obama will have to take a much more active role in promoting a cap-and-trade bill in the Senate than he did in the House. Failure to pass climate legislation in the Senate would hand the Obama administration a major defeat, and it would be an enormous embarrassment if such a defeat took place before the Copenhagen meeting in December 2009. In many respects, this will be a make-or-break moment for the Obama administration, but the same can be said for all champions of climate justice. Unless or until the United States makes a binding commitment to substantially reduce its GHG emissions, China and other developing nations will refuse to entertain any form or scale of binding commitments. Unless or until nations like the United States accept their historical responsibility and current capacity to mitigate emissions and financially help poor nations adapt to climate change, developing nations will refuse to join a post-Kyoto agreement, because they will perceive it to be unjust.

When this book went to press health care reform was still dominating the congressional agenda and Democratic leaders in the Senate had pushed back the date for introducing climate legislation. While President Obama will not be able to control the pace and fate of climate policy decisions in the Senate, he does have the ability to enter into bilateral negotiations with other nations. Representatives of the Obama administration engaged in high-level discussions with energy and climate officials in China throughout 2009. Some analysts predict both nations will announce a joint set of goals and commitments on the eve of the Copenhagen conference, and that this may help to persuade developing nations that the U.S. is willing to accept responsibility with regard to various aspects of climate justice.

Even if the Senate does manage to pass climate legislation with a sixty-vote majority, it will require at least sixty-seven votes to reach the two-thirds majority necessary for the Senate to ratify an international treaty. It is possible the Democrats will add to their sixty seats in the 2010 elections, but it is also possible any 2009 vote on U.S. climate policy may cost some Democrats their Senate seats. It is precisely for this reason that the Obama administration is exploring other terms to describe any agreement that may emerge in Copenhagen or thereafter. It is too soon to know in what directions these options may lead. Suffice it to say, any form of agreement that adequately addresses the present climate crisis would be ethically justified.

Conclusion

Climate scientists frequently talk about dangerous tipping points that have the potential to trigger irreversible climate changes. In many respects, the United States and the international community have arrived at a political tipping point. After more than a decade of delay and obfuscation, we have now reached a point where a decision needs to be made. Failure to take aggressive action now to reduce emissions will perpetuate current rates of GHG emissions and condemn future generations to a rate and degree of warming unprecedented in human civilization. Never before have present generations been able to do so much for future generations.

"Where there is no vision, the people perish" (Proverbs 29:18 KJV). The only way change can come and justice will be done is if we envision a different future and then act on it. The concept of ecological justice and its related moral norms (sustainability, sufficiency, participation, and solidarity) sketch the broad contours of a way of life in which human beings can live more justly in relation to each other and more appropriately in relation to the ecological systems that support all forms of life on Earth. Application of the energy guidelines discussed in this volume reveal that a host of clean, renewable, and alternative energy options can replace the fossil fuels that are the main cause of the present climate crisis. In addition, the climate policy guidelines point us to ways individual nations and the entire international community can address climate change while also pre-serving the right to human development. We have the resources we need to bring about a different future. If only God would now open our eyes to see this vision. Perhaps the prophet Micah will be our best guide:

> He has told you, O mortal, what is good;
> and what does the LORD require of you
> but to do justice, and to love kindness,
> and to walk humbly with your God?
> (Micah 6:8)

6. Climate Justice Applied

Greenhouse Gas Reduction Strategies at Luther College

> *You don't wake up one morning and say Luther is going to be known for sustainability. A lot of things happen over a long period of time, until it comes to a tipping point.*
>
> RICHARD L. TORGERSON
> PRESIDENT OF LUTHER COLLEGE

Is it possible for the United States to reduce its greenhouse gas (GHG) emissions to 17 percent below 2005 levels by 2020? How feasible is it for the United States to reduce its emissions 42 percent by 2030, and ultimately 83 percent by 2050? This final chapter addresses these questions in a more personal and practical way by looking at the efforts my institution has taken to reduce its GHG emissions. The chapter will lead us to revisit many of the alternative and renewable energy options discussed in previous chapters, the policies designed to promote them, and the significant barriers that impede them. In many ways, this localized case study helps tie together the content of this book in a holistic way. While so many aspects of climate justice must be engaged at the national and international levels, there is also no substitute for local action. I don't think Luther's attempts to reduce its GHG emissions are unique or even particularly innovative, but they do reflect our attempts to grapple institutionally with some of the moral obligations associated with climate justice.

Located in the small town of Decorah in northeast Iowa, Luther College is an undergraduate liberal-arts institution with about 2,500 students and approximately 700 faculty and staff members. The college is affiliated with the Evangelical Lutheran Church in America and will celebrate its sesquicentennial in 2011. Because glaciers during the last ice age did not flatten this part of the state, Luther is situated in beautiful limestone bluff country. The main campus covers nearly two hundred acres and consists of eight major academic buildings, seven residence halls, one village of student townhouses, an athletic complex, a student union, and a large performing arts center. About 95 percent of our students live on campus. Connected by curving sidewalks, Luther's central campus also has the distinction of reflecting a historic landscape design mapped in the early 1900s by renowned architect Jens Jensen. Incorporating themes of light and shadow, woodlands and prairie, Jensen's plan helps Luther match the grandeur of its natural surroundings. The college also owns nearly eight hundred additional acres of the surrounding rural landscape, which includes two large woodlands, some productive farmland, and prairie areas. The Upper Iowa River runs through the northwest edge of campus.

Inspired by the landscape and the college's Christian heritage, environmental responsibility has been emphasized by many students and members of the faculty and staff at Luther over the life of the institution. In fact, the college's recently revised mission statement emphasizes, "We practice joyful stewardship of the resources that surround us."[1] Over the past decade, students have championed recycling, food composting, and food production on campus; faculty members have encouraged the college to invest in renewable energy and join the Chicago Climate Exchange; and the administration has made significant investments in geothermal energy systems, energy efficiency, prairie restoration, and the reforesting of college woodlands.

It is not surprising, then, that the president of Luther College, Richard Torgerson, became a charter signatory of the American College and University Presidents' Climate Commitment (ACUPCC) in January 2007. The ACUPCC is "a high-visibility effort to address global warming by garnering institutional commitments to neutralize greenhouse gas emissions, and to accelerate the research and educational efforts of higher education to equip society to re-stabilize the earth's climate."[2] Shortly after signing on, President Torgerson incorporated the ACUPCC commitment into Luther's new round of strategic planning. He charged one of three strategic planning task forces to develop a plan for how Luther could live up to its ACUPCC commitment and other environmental obligations. Comprising students, faculty, staff, regents, and friends of the college, the task force worked for twelve months beginning in April 2007 to address this task. The five-year strategic plan approved by the Luther College Board of Regents in May 2008 includes the following key recommendations related to reducing GHG emissions:

- Reduce Luther's carbon footprint by 50 percent and develop a plan to achieve carbon neutrality.
- Make sustainability a part of every student's learning experience.
- Model stewardship and sustainability in all college operations to reduce Luther's environmental impact and mitigate operational costs.
- Design and implement a campus land-use plan that affirms land stewardship, sustainability, and landscape designer Jens Jensen's original vision for the Luther campus in 1911.
- Continue sustainable and strategic enhancements of the plant and facilities with a focus on student learning, energy payback, campus needs, and economic return.
- Create a Center for Sustainable Communities to be a catalyst for change locally and regionally.

This chapter will focus only on strategies Luther has developed to reduce its carbon footprint 50 percent, but a great deal of work is taking place on the other key recommendations in the strategic plan, including many that are not listed here. It is safe to say that the eco-justice norms of sustainability and solidarity have helped motivate Luther's efforts to reduce its GHG emissions, but the truth is that the first steps we took were primarily driven by the energy guidelines that focus on cost and efficiency. We have learned that it is possible to achieve our economic and environmental goals simultaneously. In other words, it is possible to reduce our energy costs and also reduce our GHG emissions.

I am too close to the situation to assess objectively how well Luther's GHG reduction strategies satisfy the ecojustice norms and the energy and climate policy guidelines. This assessment is best left to the reader. That said, let's turn now to see what steps Luther has taken and may soon take to reduce its GHG emissions.

Luther's GHG Reduction Strategies

One of Luther's ACUPCC obligations is to inventory the college's GHG emissions. A student researcher worked closely with Luther's Director of Facilities in the summers of 2007 and 2008 to inventory all of Luther's emissions for the preceding six academic years. The Clean Air–Cool Planet Carbon Calculator (version 5) was used to conduct the study, and the inventory data and results are available online.[3] In most cases, every source of emissions was tied back to audited financial statements. As at most academic institutions, Luther's emissions fall into three categories: (1) direct emissions of GHGs associated with combustion of fossil fuels for heating and transportation; (2) indirect emissions associated with electricity purchases; and (3) other emissions associated with solid-waste disposal, including use of refrigerants, land use management, and college-funded air travel. Electricity purchases and heating-fuel consumption together currently constitute 84 percent of Luther's emissions.

Luther's GHG emissions peaked at 20,927 metric tons (MT) in the 2003–2004 academic year but were reduced to 17,672 MT in 2007–2008, primarily through a major investment in energy efficiency. In 2004, Luther College signed an energy services contract with our electric utility, Alliant Energy. After a preliminary audit of seventeen campus buildings, several potential projects with significant savings were identified, and the best selected. Luther then invested $1.5 million in various energy efficiency initiatives that had an average estimated payback period of seven years. The project with the most significant savings was the installation of an energy management and control system. The system controls the heating, ventilating, air-conditioning, and lighting systems for almost every room of every building on campus. Wireless capability is standard and allows monitoring of all building management functions from a single facility or remotely. This energy management system is a prime example of advanced metering technology that is one component of a smart electricity grid.

It took fifteen months to install the equipment for the various projects, but the time and money were well spent. Luther has reduced its peak 2004 electricity consumption by approximately 20 percent, a savings of approximately 4 million kilowatt-hours (kWh). These investments—together with a decision to fuel our heating plant with cleaner-burning natural gas rather than dirtier number 6 fuel oil—have resulted in a 15.5 percent reduction in Luther's GHG emissions. This significant level of reduction testifies to the huge potential that exists in the United States to consume energy more efficiently and to reduce emissions in a cost-efficient manner. If Luther's experience could be extrapolated across the United States, it might be possible for the nation to reduce its emissions to 17 percent below 2005 levels by 2020 almost with energy efficiency alone.

Luther's investment in energy efficiency and conservative budgeting produced even more financial savings than had been expected in our energy accounts. This enabled the college in the spring of 2008 to fund four professional feasibility studies that focused on ways Luther can make additional investments in energy efficiency and utilize wind, biomass, and solar energy. These studies have provided the foundation for a plan to cut our carbon footprint in half.

As I said, Luther's peak GHG emissions over the past seven academic years occurred in 2003–2004, when emissions totaled 20,927 MT. Therefore, to achieve our goal of a 50 percent reduction, Luther needs to reduce, avoid, or permanently sequester 10,463.5 MT of emissions. The college's investment in energy efficiency has already reduced emissions by 3,255 MT. Table 6.1 summarizes how we hope to achieve the remaining necessary reductions. The rest of this chapter explores these strategies in greater detail and identifies various barriers to their successful implementation.

Energy Efficiency and Conservation

The same firm that conducted our first energy audit did a second study in the spring of 2008 to identify additional opportunities to reduce energy costs and GHG emissions through investments in energy efficiency. The study identified twenty-one possible projects

Table 6.1. Luther College's Greenhouse Gas Reduction Strategies

Emission Reduction Strategy	Reduction (MT)	Reduction (% of Peak)
Energy efficiency	3,255 MT	15.5%
Wind energy	3,100 MT	14.8%
Biomass heat	2,970 MT	14.2%
Offsets	1,550 MT	7.4%
Total reductions	10,875 MT	51.9%

with paybacks ranging from 2 to 74 years. After reviewing these options, Luther may soon make a second investment of $171,318 in various measures that have a 4.1-year payback and are estimated to produce a 3.1 percent reduction in Luther's current electricity consumption of approximately 15 million kWh per year.

It is important to note that approximately 50 percent of the cost of Luther's energy efficiency studies has been paid for with funds that are levied by the state of Iowa via a system benefit charge imposed on all ratepayers that are customers of Iowa's investor-owned utilities. The Iowa Utilities Board imposes this fee in order to help the utilities they regulate achieve the state's goal of reducing energy consumption via investments in energy efficiency. This simple policy tool and very small additional expense has helped produce significant energy savings in the state.

We expect the related emission reductions from Luther's second investment in energy efficiency to offset the increased emissions associated with opening the college's new Sampson Hoffland Laboratories in the fall of 2008. This 64,000-sq.-ft. science facility was built to *Leadership in Energy and Environmental Design (LEED) Silver* standards but was recently certified as a LEED Gold building. LEED is a third-party certification program and the nationally accepted benchmark for the design, construction, and operation of high performance green buildings.[4] One of the college's ACUPCC commitments is that all new and renovated buildings will be built to LEED standards.

Luther has made some efforts to develop a culture of conservation on campus, but the amount of financial resources we have devoted to this task pales in comparison to that spent on implementing energy efficiency and studying the potential of renewable energy for our campus. As a result, we recently applied for and received a $45,000 seed grant from the Rocky Mountain Institute to develop a comprehensive and sophisticated approach to energy conservation and management that will benefit the college over several years. This will primarily involve a focus on training and education among students, faculty, and staff, but it will also include the acquisition of some hardware and software that will better enable us to monitor and evaluate energy consumption on campus. Funds from the seed grant will be used to retain the services of a professional consulting firm to help us design and implement an energy conservation campaign. Funds will also be used to purchase supplemental metering and communication technology equipment. We believe this investment in and focused attention upon energy conservation will help us expand the level of support for the American College and University Presidents' Climate Commitment on our campus while reducing our energy use and carbon footprint.

Wind Energy

According to the American Wind Energy Association (AWEA), the state of Iowa currently has 3,043 megawatts (MW) of installed wind turbine nameplate capacity in the United States, which is second only to the state of Texas, with 8,361 MW of capacity. Remarkably, AWEA estimates Iowa has the potential to produce 62,900 MW of electricity via wind energy.[5] Obviously, the wind blows often and hard across much of the wide-open state of Iowa, so it made sense for Luther to explore the potential of wind energy to help power our campus. The college first started to research this possibility in earnest after a group of students and faculty attended the ribbon cutting for Carleton College's 1.65 MW turbine in the fall of 2004. Inspired by Carleton's leadership, Luther commissioned a professional wind resource assessment for acreage the college owns near campus. The study concluded there was a sufficient wind resource at this site to power a commercial-scale wind turbine. This determination led Luther's administration to study the economics of this possibility carefully. At this point, some of the significant barriers emerged.

One of these barriers is the high cost of wind turbine technology and, until relatively recently, the difficulty of purchasing only one or two turbines, due to high global demand. The same turbine that cost Carleton approximately $1.5 million in 2004 costs around $2.4 million if you want to purchase only one today. Once delivery, construction, transmission, and interconnection costs are totaled, the installed cost for this turbine at Luther is around $3.7 million. That's a lot of money. Of course, wind turbines generate electricity that can be sold or consumed on-site in order to help finance the cost of the installation, but you need a lot of production or high electricity prices (and preferably both) to make the economics work. In Luther's case, the same turbine that generates about 4.5 million kWh per year up at Carleton would generate about 4.9 million kWh per year with Luther's wind resource.[6] That amount of production is significant because it represents about one-third of Luther's current annual electricity consumption.

In addition to the cost of a wind turbine, the second major barrier that has impeded Luther from investing in wind energy is our low cost of electricity. Luther enjoys some of the lowest rates in the nation. Nearly 80 percent of the electricity produced in our part of the U.S. electrical grid is generated by power plants fueled with coal and natural gas. These fossil fuels have historically been very inexpensive, and even though the cost of these fuels has increased recently, Luther still currently pays less than 6¢ per kilowatt-hour. This expense is divided into demand and electricity charges, which further lessens the economic incentive to switch to renewables. Approximately one-third of Luther's electricity bill is related to a demand charge, which reimburses the utility for maintaining infrastructure necessary to meet Luther's maximum electricity demand at any given time. Like lots of institutions in the Midwest, Luther's electricity bill peaks during the summer air-conditioning months. The other two-thirds of Luther's electricity bill constitute the actual cost of the electrical energy we consume, and this is the only portion of our bill that would be reduced through wind generation. Thus, if Luther wants to consume the approximately 5 million kWh that a 1.65 MW turbine would produce each year, we will offset only $200,000 in our electricity charges at approximately 4¢ per kilowatt-hour. With an annual revenue stream of $200,000, the simple payback on a $3.7 million project is just over eighteen years—and that doesn't include annual operating expenses.

One way to overcome the barrier posed by low electricity prices is to find ways to boost revenues or reduce expenses. Carleton College added to its revenue stream by tapping a 1.5¢ per kilowatt-hour cash subsidy that the state of Minnesota was offering at that time for wind projects. A couple of years later, St. Olaf College purchased a turbine identical to Carleton's with the assistance of a $1 million grant from the state of Minnesota. In both cases, the source of these funds came primarily from mitigation fees imposed on Xcel Energy to store spent nuclear fuel above ground in steel and concrete casks outside its nuclear power reactors. Xcel needed to do this because the federal government has not opened a permanent geological repository for high-level nuclear waste, and the utility was starting to run out of storage space in its reactor cooling ponds. The Minnesota legislature, recognizing the opportunity presented by this situation, required Xcel Energy not only to pay considerable annual fees to store this fuel but also to make additional investments in wind energy.

Sometimes I jokingly suggest Decorah ought to secede from the state of Iowa and join Minnesota 15 mi. to the north. Regrettably, Iowa does not have a cash production subsidy or substantial grant program to promote wind projects in the state. The federal government does offer the Renewable Energy Production Incentive (REPI) that currently pays a cash production subsidy of about 2¢ per kilowatt-hour, but this program is only for not-for-profit electrical cooperatives, public utilities, state governments, Indian tribal governments, and Native corporations.[7] Even if a private, liberal-arts college like Luther could qualify for REPI, it might not receive the full benefit of the subsidy because Congress has routinely failed to fully fund the REPI program with adequate appropriations. Private liberal-arts colleges face similar obstacles in accessing the relatively new federal Clean Renewable Energy Bonds program, which is also limited to not-for-profit electrical cooperatives and the other public entities just mentioned.[8]

The vast majority of federal and state incentives for renewable energy production are aimed at the for-profit sector. As we have seen, the federal Renewable Energy Production Tax Credit (PTC) has helped drive the rapid growth of the wind industry in the United States.[9] When the state of Iowa announced in 2005 that it was creating two production tax credit programs to stimulate renewable energy production in the state, Luther decided to form a separate for-profit entity, Luther College Wind Energy Project, LLC (LCWEP), in order to tap one of these incentives. In January 2007, the company became eligible for Iowa's 476C tax credit, which provides a tax credit for ten years equivalent to 1.5¢ for every kilowatt-hour of electricity that is generated and sold to a third party.

The formation of LCWEP has given Luther College additional ways to meet its goals for GHG reduction. If Luther chooses to be the sole investor in the company, then the production from a 1.65 MW turbine would be sold to our utility partner under a long-term power purchase agreement (PPA) at a price that is currently about 25 percent higher than our energy charge. Because the power will be sold and not consumed at Luther, LCWEP will also be able to tap Iowa's 476C tax credit, which will add another $75,000 to the annual revenue stream. Unlike the federal PTC, the state tax credit can be transferred once by sale to another party that carries a state tax obligation. Since LCWEP would not have a considerable state tax liability, sale of the state tax credit will increase the project's revenues. LCWEP will also transfer to Luther College at a nominal cost the renewable energy certificates (RECs), which represent all of the environmental attributes associated with the generation of electricity via renewable energy. Acquisition of these RECs will enable Luther to offset 3,100 MT of GHG emissions and further reduce its peak carbon footprint by 14.8 percent.

Luther could reduce its financial investment in the project if it folded additional investors into LCWEP. If these investors have sufficient federal tax obligations, then the company could benefit from various federal incentives for renewable energy production. These include the federal PTC mentioned earlier, the Business Energy Investment Tax Credit (ITC), or a grant from the U.S. Treasury equivalent to the ITC in lieu of the PTC, accelerated depreciation on qualified wind energy equipment, and other incentives.[10] While this option could cut Luther's capital investment in the project almost in half, it also poses risks that accompany any complicated business partnership that would last for at least five to ten years. For this reason, Luther is currently focused on other options.

Our preference would be for Luther College to purchase a 1.65 MW turbine and consume the power on campus from the outset. In fact, the college might now be able to tap Iowa's other production tax credit program, because a recent change allows not-for-profit institutions to tap the credit if the electricity generated is for self-use. To cope with the minimal annual revenue stream and avoid a drain on the college's annual budget that might require a hike in tuition, Luther is trying to raise $2 million in donations that would be used to reduce the $3.7 million estimated cost of the project. If we fall short in our fund-raising goal, Luther could soon tap about $240,000 a year in debt service that will be freed up once our $1.5 million investment in energy efficiency is paid off. If we did this, energy cost savings produced through investments in efficiency would be the financial key to a viable wind energy investment. That is a model other schools could replicate.

Alternatively, Luther is also actively considering becoming the sole investor in LCWEP in order to tap the increased revenue stream offered by the PPA sale, the 476C state tax credit, and the new Treasury grant option that Congress established in February 2009 as a part of the American Recovery and Reinvestment Act. This grant is in lieu of the PTC or ITC and is equivalent to 30 percent of the project's eligible wind energy property. Projects need to be completed in 2009–2010, or construction needs to have begun within this time frame. Not-for-profit institutions may not apply for the Treasury grants directly, but they may invest in eligible wind projects by forming a taxable C corporation.[11] On a $3.7 million project, this grant would be close to $1 million and would substantially reduce the amount of cash Luther would have to invest in the project to make it economically viable. This approach also can be replicated by other schools.

When this book went to press, there was some urgency around both these options, because Luther had been offered an opportunity to purchase a 1.65 MW turbine through a bundled turbine supply agreement. I hope that by the time this book is published, Luther will have been able to make this investment in wind energy, because it is a key part of our plan to cut our carbon footprint in half. Both options enable Luther to reduce its GHG emissions by 3,100 MT and to reduce the college's peak carbon footprint by 14.8 percent.[12]

Before leaving the topic of wind energy, I want to offer some remarks about two other matters that emerged as we worked on our wind project—matters that have both national or state policy implications. The first has to do with the subject of net metering. If you install a wind turbine (or any renewable electricity generation system) that produces more electricity than you can currently consume, this electricity needs to go somewhere. Net metering is a policy that allows you to sell your surplus electricity back to the utility at retail prices by effectively running your electricity meter backward when you are producing more than you consume. That's a good deal, but here's the rub: net metering normally has limits. In Iowa, net metering is limited to 500 kW of installed nameplate capacity. If you install a 500 kW wind turbine, then you can net meter 100 percent of any surplus production. If you install a 1,000 kW (1 MW) turbine, then you can net meter only 50 percent of any surplus production. Thus, if Luther installs a 1,650 kW (1.65 MW) turbine, we can net meter only 30.3 percent of surplus production; the remaining 69.7 percent would have to be sold to the utility as an "inadvertent delivery" at the current rock-bottom price of 2.1¢ per kilowatt-hour. That's not a very good deal. As a result, Luther will likely install only one 1.65 MW turbine because our consultant tells us we can consume the output from the turbine 98.5 percent of the time, which minimizes any inadvertent deliveries.

If Iowa had a net metering limit of 5 MW (ten times the current level), then Luther might consider installing enough turbines to produce all of the electricity we consume in a year, rather than simply installing one that will generate about a third of what we consume. For example, if we installed three 1.65 MW turbines for a total of 4.95 MW of nameplate capacity, those turbines would often produce much more electricity than Luther can consume. If Iowa had a 5 MW net metering limit, however, Luther would receive a retail credit for this surplus electricity that we could draw down when the wind is not blowing and our turbines are not producing.

Senators Robert Menendez (D-N.J.) and Bernie Sanders (Ind-Vt.) have recently proposed legislation that would create uniform national net metering regulations, and they have proposed that net metering be capped at 10 MW of nameplate capacity.[13] Such a measure would be a boon to investors in renewable electricity and distributed generation. With a 10 MW net metering limit, Luther might even consider installing enough turbines so that we could convert our central heating plant to electric boilers.

The other issue I want to discuss is limited transmission capacity, which is another significant barrier to renewably produced electricity in general and wind energy in particular. Luther ran into this barrier as we explored our options with the help of our consultant. While most of our study focused on sites near campus so that we could both see the turbine and consume the power, locations farther away also were considered. One of these sites is ten miles north of Decorah in a portion of the county that has a strong wind resource. The other main virtue of this site is that there are two high-voltage transmission lines in the area. When I realized this might be an ideal location for a 20 to 100 MW wind farm, I contacted a Luther graduate who at that time was working for John Deere Wind Energy. He came out and toured the area with me and agreed that the site has many desirable characteristics. The site was too far away from Luther to affordably ship power back to campus, so my goal was to acquire a small percentage of the RECs from the project in order to help Luther achieve its GHG reduction goals. We approached the utility that owns one of the transmission lines in the area, and it responded positively to the project idea. When we gathered at Luther for a meeting to discuss the possibility, however, it quickly became apparent that there was a problem. Although the utility's business development manager was eager to secure additional renewably produced electricity in order to satisfy various renewable portfolio standards in the states where the utility sells electricity, the utility's transmission manager said the project might take more than a decade to develop because there was insufficient transmission capacity in our region of the nation's electrical grid.[14] There was plenty of available room on their line, but not in the grid to which their line was connected. The wind literally went out of the sail at that point in the meeting. Here we had gotten our hopes up, only to have them dashed by insufficient transmission capacity.

This issue plagues projects all over the United States and recently was one of the main reasons that T. Boone Pickens decided to scale back his intention to build the biggest wind farm in the world in Texas. The United States must find the political will and financial resources to address transmission bottlenecks around the nation, because they pose an enormous barrier to increased generation of renewable electricity.

Biomass Energy

Not only does Iowa have many areas with a very good wind resource, it also has a huge potential for biomass energy. This is especially true with regard to biofuel production, and we have already explored some of the problems associated with corn-based ethanol in particular. Nevertheless, another use for sustainably produced biomass resources is to replace fuel oil and natural gas for space heating. In fact, portions of northeast Iowa where Luther is located are some of the most heavily wooded parts of the state. As a result, within 90 mi. of Luther are a fair number of sawmills that produce a significant volume of wood waste. Luther's professional feasibility study focused on tapping this fuel source to replace a portion of the college's natural gas consumption.

The study concluded that one 400 hp wood-fired boiler would supply approximately 59,502 MMBtu of steam heat and displace approximately 62 percent of the college's natural gas consumption in our central steam plant. This use of biomass would prevent the release of 2,970 MT of GHG emissions and thus enable Luther to reduce its peak campus carbon footprint by an additional 14.2 percent. This estimate of net emission reductions takes into account the emissions associated with delivering the wood chips to campus and hauling away the ash. Our consultant estimated the project would cost approximately $4.9 million, largely because it requires the construction of a new building next to our current heating facility. Nevertheless, the study projected the payback to be in the range of eleven to twelve years, assuming delivered natural gas prices at $10.50 per MMBtu and delivered wood chips at $50 per ton. These payback calculations need to be revised today, however, since delivered natural gas prices are currently about one third of what they were in 2008, and wood chip prices are also fluctuating.

In spite of the potential cost of this project, Luther continues to actively research this possibility as well as other biomass options. One of these options involves the installation of modular biomass gasification systems rather than one large biomass combustion boiler. Whereas combustion utilizes oxygen to burn biomass, gasification uses very little oxygen as it converts a solid or liquid fuel to a gas. A start-up company in a nearby town is ramping up production of its modular gasification system, and representatives of the company believe they can install enough of the modular gasifiers in our existing heating plant to meet up to 100 percent of our annual heating load. Because this would not require the construction of a new building, the estimated cost of the project is substantially reduced to approximately $2 million.

Of course, fueling either system requires a sufficient biomass supply, and there is the rub. Luther's steam plant supplies heat to approximately 1.1 million sq. ft. of buildings on campus. With winter temperatures that can dip to −20°F, the college can ill afford to have problems with its heating plant. Our consultant estimates a wood-fired combustion boiler would consume 4,850 tons of wood chips each year in order to generate enough heat to replace 62 percent of the college's natural gas consumption. That's a lot of wood chips. The college would have to store at least a three-day supply on campus and then either store an additional supply elsewhere on college property or have the wood chips delivered on a regular basis.

Concerned about the long-term availability, sustainable supply, and fluctuating cost of wood chips, some of us recently met with the manager of one of Iowa's largest sawmills. He discussed the vicissitudes of the U.S. biomass industry in the past few years but indicated he thought his mill might be able to supply about half of Luther's annual need for wood chips. One month later, we learned the company was in bankruptcy and the facility had been closed. Today the manager has pulled together new investors and reopened the plant, but this abrupt change in the status of the facility has caused us to rethink issues related to the long-term supply of wood chips.

We have similar concerns related to the long-term fuel supply for the gasification systems we are considering. The company that wants to sell us the gasifiers also wants to sell us the fuel. The gasifiers will be able to utilize a variety of feedstocks, including wood chips, but the primary fuel the company wants to use is surplus, treated seed corn. In our Midwest region, there are many seed corn production facilities. These producers sell a wide range of seed corn varieties, because growing conditions vary and can change rapidly. For example, the floods that drowned much of Iowa's cropland in the summer of 2008 required farmers to replant fields later with a different, faster-maturing variety of corn. Many of these types of seed corn are treated with herbicides, so the surplus at the end of each growing season cannot be disposed of in conventional ways; it must be sent to a landfill. The company that has designed the gasification system assures us that no toxic emissions result from its gasification process, and that it has permits from the relevant state and federal agencies to prove this, but the potential for these emissions remains a concern for us.

In many respects, an ideal solution would be for Luther to grow its own annual biomass heating fuel supply or to purchase it from farmers near the college. One option would be to combust or gasify diverse prairie grasses that are grown in a sustainable way. Dry prairie grasses have a heat value similar to that of wood chips, and they have the added advantage of sequestering carbon beneath the soil in their long root systems. Assuming a yield of 5 tons per acre, Luther would need to purchase the production from about 1,000 acres in order to secure enough fuel to displace 62 percent of our natural gas consumption. Unfortunately, there is currently no market for diverse prairie grasses, so it would be very difficult to acquire sufficient supply. Federal and state research projects are under way in the area, however, and Luther is exploring ways we might be able to join them or benefit from them. The new federal Biomass Crop Assistance Program (BCAP) has the potential to stimulate the production of sustainable biomass crops.[15] It will be very difficult for Luther to cut its carbon footprint in half without replacing a large amount of our heating fuel with a sustainable biomass alternative.

Offsets

I have already discussed one way that Luther could significantly reduce its GHG emissions by acquiring RECs from Luther College Wind Energy Project, LLC. While this is a theoretical possibility, Luther is already purchasing RECs from a nearby community wind project in St. Ansgar, Iowa. More specifically, Luther has contracted to purchase the entire production of RECs from this single turbine project that was commissioned in November 2008. The turbine is projected to produce approximately 2.5 million kWh of electricity per year. The related RECs will offset 1,550 MT of GHG emissions, enabling Luther to reduce its peak campus carbon footprint by an additional 7.4 percent.

The strategic planning task force that grappled with how best to live up to Luther's ACUPCC obligations recommended the college use offsets to reduce no more than 25 percent of Luther's emissions. Moreover, the task force recommended that Luther purchase these offsets only from projects in the area where we can know the developers and thus have greater confidence our offset purchases will result in real, additional, permanent, verifiable, and enforceable emission reductions while also helping the local economy.

President Torgerson, however, is not very comfortable with offsets. He likens them to indulgences that were sold during the Reformation. He would rather spend the college's scarce financial resources to reduce energy costs and GHG emissions via investments in energy efficiency and renewable energy on the Luther campus. It's hard to argue with that. As we have seen, there are good reasons to question the environmental integrity of many GHG offsets, and it would be very unwise and ethically inappropriate to use offsets as the primary way to reduce emissions. It would also be foolhardy to rely exclusively or even substantially on offsets to reduce an institution's carbon footprint because, while the offsets might be relatively inexpensive today, they will likely be far more expensive in the future. Nevertheless, it will not likely be possible for Luther to achieve the ACUPCC goal of "climate neutrality" without making use of some GHG offsets. The key will be to help develop a range of quality offset options in our area.

Other Energy-Related Initiatives at Luther College

Before I close this chapter, I want to summarize some other initiatives Luther has taken to save energy dollars and reduce GHG emissions.

Solar. Luther used savings from its energy efficiency initiative to commission a local expert to identify locations on campus where a 10 kW photovoltaic (PV) system could be installed. A system this size would generate approximately 15,000 kWh per year, which is the amount we estimate our fleet of electric vehicles currently uses. Three sites have been identified. The total installed cost is $70,000 to $77,000, depending on location and mounting options. As noted, the PV panels would produce only about 15,000 kWh per year, and thus would not make a significant impact on Luther's carbon footprint, but all of the locations would have high visibility and educational value.

The economics for the project would be greatly enhanced if our utility partner were to implement renewable energy incentives it has proposed to the Iowa Utilities Board in its new five-year energy efficiency plan. If adopted, these incentives would provide Luther with a 30 percent to 40 percent cash rebate on the costs associated with installing a solar electric or solar hot-water system.

Geothermal. Luther has made two substantial investments in geothermal technology. In 1999, Luther built Baker Village, a 33,000-sq.-ft. student-housing complex comprising several two-story townhouses. Luther's student environmental-concerns organization had encouraged the administration to utilize a geothermal system in order to capture the constant temperatures beneath the surface of the ground. It took some time to find architects and contractors familiar with geothermal, but eventually a system was installed that utilizes eighty-eight vertical closed loops at a 150-ft. depth.

In 2003, Luther built a two-level, 60,000-sq.-ft. building for the college's art and theater/dance departments. In collaboration with our electric utility, Alliant Energy, Luther chose a high-efficiency geo-thermal energy system to heat and cool the Center for the Arts. The system required drilling eighty-six wells to a depth of 300 ft. in order to tap the constant temperature of the earth below the ground. Local contractors drilled the wells and installed the 248-ton system, which includes fifty-two two-speed geothermal heat pumps ranging from 1 to 15 tons.

While these geothermal systems were initially more expensive than conventional heating and cooling systems to install, the added investment has already been paid back in energy savings in less than five years. The heating and cooling costs for Baker Village and the Center for the Arts are 40 percent below costs in other campus buildings.

Biodiesel. After years of student–faculty collaborative research and small-scale biodiesel production, Luther in 2007 invested $10,000 in an Ester Machine that converts waste vegetable oil into biodiesel. Our cafeteria fryer oil is no longer sent off as a waste product, but is now used to make biodiesel, which gets mixed with an equal volume of regular diesel for use in all the diesel engines that power Luther's lawn and garden equipment. We have produced about 3,000 gal. over the past two years and have nearly paid for the equipment in this short amount of time. Vehicles powered by campus biodiesel are easily identified by a sticker in the shape of a french fry holder that proclaims, "Fries to Fuel!"

Electric Vehicles. Over the past three years, Luther has purchased seven electric vehicles. The director of facilities determined that using electric utility vehicles instead of regular gasoline-powered vehicles for campus facilities services, dining services, security, and light hauling duties would substantially reduce the college fleet's GHG emissions and save money. The all-electric vehicles emit 76 percent fewer emissions and cost 84 percent less to operate than their gasoline-powered predecessors. The seven vehicles collectively reduce Luther's carbon emissions by an estimated 50,000 lb. annually.

Hybrid Passenger Fleet Vehicles. Over the past four years, Luther has purchased seven gasoline–electric hybrid vehicles to replace regular sedans in the college's vehicle fleet. President Torgerson drives one of these vehicles; the rest are part of the college's much-used rental fleet. With a fuel economy that is more than 50 percent better than the sedans they replace, these hybrid vehicles are also helping to reduce Luther's direct emissions from transportation.

The college also recently purchased a used pickup that is powered by compressed natural gas. The vehicle is used to pick materials on campus that can be recycled.

Bike Share Program. Luther responded to student suggestions and requests for alternative transportation on campus by creating the Luther Bike Share program in April 2008. This joint initiative was developed by Luther's sustainability coordinator and the director of Luther's Lifetime Wellness Program. The objectives were to promote physical fitness and environmental wellness, including the reduction of vehicle emissions. The program operates from Preus Library on campus, where students swipe their student identification card to check out a bicycle, free of charge, for the day. Currently, there are five one-speed cruiser-style bikes, fitting for short trips and flat terrain, and three eight-speed bikes, which are more suitable for longer rides and hills.

Conclusion

The investments in energy efficiency, wind, biomass, and GHG offsets described in this chapter are all realistic ways that Luther College can achieve the goal in our new five-year strategic plan to cut our carbon footprint in half. To be sure, some formidable barriers remain, but it is possible that this 50 percent reduction in our GHG emissions could even be achieved by the time the college celebrates its sesquicentennial in 2011. By comparison, the American Clean Energy and Security Act of 2009 only hopes to cut U.S. emissions 3 percent from 2005 levels by 2012. I hope I have demonstrated in this chapter that significant GHG emission reductions are possible in the U.S. economy, and that they can be achieved cost-effectively, so long as important barriers can be overcome.

As I wrote this book, I considered it very important to work simultaneously with my students and colleagues on Luther's GHG reduction strategies. Studying energy and climate policy issues while also pursuing Luther's goals has given me a new understanding about the complexities and barriers facing our nation and the world. It also gave me reasons to be optimistic and hopeful. From my experience at Luther and from my study of these issues, I know that God is at work in the world among all who labor tirelessly in so many venues to come to grips with the climate crisis we face today. I hope my efforts in these areas have in some small ways made a constructive contribution to climate justice.

Notes

Preface

1. Thomas R. Karl, Jerry M. Melillo, and Thomas C. Peterson, eds., *Global Climate Change Impacts in the United States* (New York: Cambridge University Press, 2009), 9, accessed at http://downloads.globalchange.gov/usimpacts/pdfs/climate-impacts-report.pdf.
2. Ibid.
3. Ibid., 12.
4. Ibid., 9. For an excellent summary of the report, see Michael D. Lemonick, "Report Gives Sobering View of Warming's Impact on U.S.," *Yale Environment 360* (June 30, 2009), accessed at http://www.e360.yale.edu/content/feature.msp?id=2166.
5. Karl et al., *Global Climate Change Impacts*, 29.
6. Tore Johnsen, "Listen to the Voice of Nature!" in *God, Creation and Climate Change: Spiritual and Ethical Perspectives*, ed. Karen L. Bloomquist (Geneva: Lutheran World Federation/Lutheran University Press, 2009).
7. Karl et al., *Global Climate Change Impacts*, 85.
8. *Minutes*, 2008, pt. I, pp. 934ff; *The Power to Change: U.S. Energy Policy and Global Warming: A Revised Social Policy Statement Adopted by the 218th General Assembly (2008)* (Louisville, Ky.: Presbyterian Church (U.S.A.), 2008). See http://www.pc-biz.org/Explorer.aspx?id=1537&promoID=10.

9. James B. Martin-Schramm, "The Automobile and Its Threats to Our Planetary Welfare," *WW* 28, no. 3 (Summer 2008): 260–72; "Human Rights and Climate Change," *J. Luth. Ethics* (February 2009), http://www.elca.org/What-We-Believe/Social-Issues/Journal-of-Lutheran-Ethics/Issues/February-2009/8-Human-Rights-and-Climate-Change.aspx; "Assessing Climate Policy Proposals: Ethical Guidelines," *J. Luth. Ethics* (April 2009), http://www.elca.org/What-We-Believe/Social-Issues/Journal-of-Lutheran-Ethics/Issues/April-2009.aspx; "Human Rights and Climate Change," in *God, Creation and Climate Change: Spiritual and Ethical Perspectives*, ed. Karen L. Bloomquist (Geneva: Lutheran World Federation/Lutheran University Press, 2009); James B. Martin-Schramm and Robert L. Stivers, *Christian Environmental Ethics: A Case Method Approach* (Maryknoll, N.Y.: Orbis, 2003), 37–45.

Introduction

1. All biblical citations are from the New Revised Standard Version unless stated otherwise.
2. Earth receives about 100,000 terawatts (TW) of energy each day from the sun. See p. 821 of Quirin Schiermier, Jeff Tollefson, et al., "Energy Alternatives: Electricity without Carbon," *Nature* 454 (August 13, 2008): 816–23, accessed at http://www.nature.com/news/2008/080813/full/454816a.html.
3. European Renewable Energy Council and Greenpeace International, *Energy Revolution: A Sustainable World Energy Outlook* (Brussels: EREC; Amsterdam: Greenpeace, January 2007), 60, accessed at http://www.greenpeace.org/raw/content/new-zealand/press/reports/global-energy-report.pdf.
4. William F. Ruddiman, *Plows, Plagues, and Petroleum: How Humans Took Control of Climate*, (Princeton, N.J.: Princeton University Press, 2005), 167.
5. Intergovernmental Panel on Climate Change (IPCC), "Summary for Policymakers," in *Climate Change 2007: The Physical Science Basis; Contribution of Working Group I to the Fourth Assessment Report of the Intergovernmental Panel on Climate Change*, ed. S. Solomon et al. (New York: Cambridge University Press, 2007), 12–14, accessed at http://www.ipcc.ch/pdf/assessment-report/ar4/wg1/ar4-wg1-spm.pdf. This mean projection is for the fossil-fuel-intensive A1F1 scenario, the worst of the six developed by the IPCC. See p. 13, Table SPM.3. Under this scenario, greenhouse gas concentrations are projected to increase from approximately 430 ppm of carbon dioxide equivalent (CO_2eq) in 2005 to 1,550 ppm CO_2eq by 2100. See p. 12, n. 14.
6. Ibid., 5.
7. IPCC, "Summary for Policymakers," in *Climate Change 2007: Impacts, Adaptation and Vulnerability: Contribution of Working Group II to the Fourth Assessment Report of the Intergovermental Panel on Climate Change*, ed. M. L. Parry et al. (Cambridge: Cambridge University Press, 2007), 8, accessed at http://www.ipcc.ch/pdf/assessment-report/ar4/wg2/ar4-wg2-spm.pdf.

8. U.S. Climate Change Science Program, *The Effects of Climate Change on Agriculture, Land Resources, Water Resources, and Biodiversity* (September 2007 public review draft), 7, accessed at http://www.climatescience.gov/Library/sap/sap4-3/public-review-draft/sap4-3prd-all.pdf.

9. James Hansen, "Why We Can't Wait," *The Nation*, April 19, 2007, accessed at http://www.thenation.com/doc/20070507/hansen.

10. James Hansen et al., "Climate Change and Trace Gases," *Philosophical Transactions of the Royal Society* 365 (2007): 1925.

11. See Hans Joachim Schnellnhuber, Wolfgang P Cramer, et al., *Avoiding Dangerous Climate Change*, (New York: Cambridge University Press, 2006); and Commission of the European Communities, *Limiting Global Climate Change to 2 Degrees Celsius: The Way Ahead for 2020 and Beyond*, (Brussels, January 10, 2007), accessed at http://eur-lex.europa.eu/LexUriServ/LexUriServ.do ?uri=COM:2007:0002:FIN:EN:PDF.

12. Kevin A. Baumert, Timothy Herzog, and Jonathan Pershing, *Navigating the Numbers: Greenhouse Gas Data and International Climate Policy* (New York: Worldwatch Institute, 2005), 31–33, accessed at http://archive.wri.org/pub lication.cfm?id=4093%20&z=?#pdf_files.

13. Netherlands Environmental Assessment Agency, "China Contributing Two Thirds to Increase in CO_2 Emissions," news release June 13, 2008, accessed at http://www.pbl.nl/en/news/pressreleases/2008/20080613Chinacontributing twothirdstoincreaseinCO2emissions.html.

14. Thomas L. Friedman, *Hot, Flat, and Crowded: Why We Need a Green Revolution—and How It Can Renew America* (New York: Farrar, Straus & Giroux, 2008), 154. Michael Northcott argues persuasively that colonial powers have created much of this energy poverty by relentlessly exploiting energy resources in other nations that used to be managed sustainably by their citizens. See Michael S. Northcott, *A Moral Climate: The Ethics of Global Warming* (Maryknoll, N.Y.: Orbis, 2007), 100–101. I return to the topic of energy poverty later in chapter 5 when I address "Greenhouse Development Rights."

15. Terry Tamminen, *Lives per Gallon: The True Cost of Our Oil Addiction* (Washington, D.C.: Island, 2006), 13.

16. David Sandalow, *Freedom from Oil: How the Next President Can End the United States' Oil Addiction* (New York: McGraw-Hill, 2008), 30.

17. Ibid., 18.

18. Tamminen, *Lives per Gallon*, 13–14.

19. Ibid., 22. Scientists are also exploring the impact of diesel exhaust on global warming. Diesel exhaust contains a type of particulate matter called "black soot," which is now estimated to be the second most potent greenhouse agent after carbon dioxide. Diesel emissions in the United States produce 50 percent of the black soot in the United States. Since black soot remains in the atmosphere only for one to several weeks (as opposed to 100 to 120 years for carbon dioxide), aggressive reduction of black soot emissions has the potential to rapidly reduce the impact of black soot on global warming. Thus, the reduction of diesel emissions would be beneficial not only to human health, but also to the health of Earth's climate. See John Lash, "Black

Carbon an Easy Target for Climate Change," *Policy Innovations* (Carnegie Council), February 9, 2009, accessed at http://www.policyinnovations.org/ideas/innovations/data/000084.

20. See Michael Ash, J. Boyce, G. Chang, M. Pastor, J. Scoggins, and J. Tran, Justice in the Air: Tracking Toxic Pollution from America's Industries and Companies to our States, Cities, and Neighborhoods (San Francisco: Creative Commons, 2009), 6–8, accessed at http://college.usc.edu/geography/ESPE/documents/justice_air_web.pdf.

21. Energy Information Administration, *International Energy Outlook 2007*, Report No. DOE/EIA-0484 (May 2007), accessed at http://www.eia.doe.gov/oiaf/ieo/world.html.

22. Jeff Goodell, *Big Coal: The Dirty Secret behind America's Energy Future* (New York: Houghton Mifflin, 2006), xii.

23. Ibid., xx.

24. Ibid., 122. See also Editorial, "Mercury and Power Plants," *New York Times*, July 25, 2009, accessed at http://www.nytimes.com/2009/07/25/opinion/25sat1.html.

25. Centers for Disease Control, *Second National Report on Human Exposure to Environmental Chemicals* (January 2003). Cited in Goodell, *Big Coal,* 135.

26. Katie Howell, "Home Heating Program Needed to Stop 'Slow-Motion Katrina,'" *Energy & Environment Daily,* September 26, 2008, accessed at http://www.eenews.net/EEDaily/2008/09/26/archive/7?terms=slow-motion+katrina. See also the Support LIHEAP website (http://www.supportliheap.org/).

27. Daniel J. Weiss and Alexandra Kougentakis, "Clean Energy, Clean Jobs," Issues page of Center for American Progress Web site, January 26, 2009, accessed at http://www.americanprogress.org/issues/2009/01/clean_recovery.html.

28. Energy Information Administration, *Short-Term Energy Outlook* (July 2007), accessed at http://www.eia.doe.gov/emeu/steo/pub/a4tab.html.

29. Sandalow, *Freedom from Oil,* 19.

30. Energy Information Administration, *Annual Energy Review 2008*, DOE/EIA-0384(2008) (Washington, D.C.: EIA, June 2009), fig. 3.7, p. 80, accessed at http://www.eia.doe.gov/aer/pdf/aer.pdf.

31. Evan Harrje, *The Real Price of Gasoline* (Washington, D.C.: International Center for Technology Assessment, 2000), cited in Tamminen, *Lives per Gallon,* 59.

32. Energy Information Administration, "World Proved Reserves of Oil and Natural Gas: Most Recent Estimates," January 9, 2007, accessed at http://www.eia.doe.gov/emeu/ international/reserves.html.

33. Estimate of civilian deaths since the start of the war (90,831 to 99,177) provided by IraqBodyCount.org, accessed at http://www.iraqbodycount.org/ (February 28, 2009); estimate of coalition military fatalities (4,251) provided by iCasualties.org, accessed at http://icasualties.org/Iraq/index.aspx (February 28, 2009).

34. Milton R. Copulus, President, National Defense Council Foundation, statement at *The Hidden Cost of Oil: Hearing before the Senate Committee on Foreign Relations,* March 30, 2006, 5.

35. National Petroleum Council, "Executive Summary," in *Facing the Hard Truths about Energy* (July 2007 prepublication draft), 25, accessed at http://www.npc.org/.

36. George W. Bush, "State of the Union Address by the President" (January 31, 2006), accessed at http://www.whitehouse.gov/stateoftheunion/2006/.

37. Barack H. Obama, "Address to Joint Session of Congress" (February 24, 2009), accessed at http://www.whitehouse.gov/the_press_office/Remarks-of-President-Barack-Obama-Address-to-Joint-Session-of-Congress/.

38. Energy Information Administration, "Crude Oil and Total Petroleum Imports Top 15 Countries," accessed at http://www.eia.doe.gov/pub/oil_gas/petroleum/data_publications/ company_level_imports/current/import.html (January 5, 2009).

39. Amnesty International, *Nigeria: Petroleum, Pollution, and Poverty in the Niger Delta* (London: Amnesty International Publications, 2009), accessed at http://allafrica.com/sustainable/resources/view/00011821.pdf.

40. National Petroleum Council, *Facing the Hard Truths about Energy*, 8.

41. Hillard Huntington, Executive Director, Energy Modeling Forum, Stanford University, statement at *The Hidden Cost of Oil: Hearing before the Senate Committee on Foreign Relations*, March 30, 2006, 13.

42. Alexander Vershinin, "Russia to Control Gas out of Central Asia," *Washington Post*, May 13, 2007, A16, accessed at http://www.washingtonpost.com/wp-dyn/content/article/2007/05/12/AR2007051201394.html.

43. Intergovernmental Panel on Climate Change (IPCC), "Climate Change 2007," Fact Sheet accessed at http://www.ipcc.ch/press/ar4-factsheet1.htm (June 16, 2009).

44. IPCC, *Climate Change 2007: The Physical Science Basis*, 2–3.

45. Ibid., 4–6.

46. Ibid., 10–13.

47. IPCC, *Climate Change 2007: Impacts, Adaptation and Vulnerability*, 7–9.

48. For updated scientific studies on the impacts of climate change on human health, see Anthony Costello, Mustafa Abbas, Adriana Allen, et al., "Managing the Health Effects of Climate Change," *Lancet* 373 (May 16, 2009), accessed at http://www.thelancet.com/climate-change.

49. IPCC, *Climate Change 2007: The Physical Science Basis*, 3–5. According to the IPCC, "very high confidence" refers to "greater than 90 percent probability."

50. Ibid., 5.

51. "Greenhouse Gases Rise despite Global Recession," *Environmental News Service*, April 21, 2009, accessed at http://www.ens-newswire.com/ens/apr2009/2009-04-21-03.asp. See also Worldwatch Institute, *State of the World 2009: Into a Warming World* (New York: Norton, 2009), 23.

52. Thomas R. Karl, Jerry M. Melillo, and Thomas C. Peterson, eds., *Global Climate Change Impacts in the United States* (New York: Cambridge University Press, 2009), 23–24, accessed at http://downloads.globalchange.gov/usimpacts/pdfs/climate-impacts-report.pdf.

53. See Hans Joachim Schnellnhuber, Wolfgang P Cramer, et al., *Avoiding Dangerous Climate Change* (New York: Cambridge University Press, 2006); and

Commission of the European Communities, *Limiting Global Climate Change to 2 Degrees Celsius.*

54. IPCC, *Climate Change 2007: The Physical Science Basis*, 12.
55. W. L. Hare, "A Safe Landing for the Climate," in *State of the World 2009*, box 2-2, p. 23.
56. Intergovernmental Panel on Climate Change, *Climate Change 2007: Synthesis Report; Summary for Policymakers* (Geneva: IPCC, November 2007), p. 66, n. 29, and p. 67, table 5.1, accessed at http://www.ipcc.ch/pdf/assessment-report/ar4/syr/ar4_syr.pdf. In a recent report, the European Renewable Energy Council and Greenpeace International claim, "Further research shows that to have an approximately 50 percent chance of keeping warming below 2 degrees Celsius, atmospheric greenhouse gas concentrations must stabilize below 450 parts per million (ppm) [CO_2eq]. For the chances of keeping warming below these levels to be considered 'likely,' total greenhouse gases must stabilize at 350–400 ppm [CO_2eq] or lower." See European Renewable Energy Council and Greenpeace International, *Energy Revolution: A Sustainable USA Energy Outlook* (Washington, D.C.: Greenpeace, February 2009), 5, accessed at http://www.greenpeace.org/raw/content/usa/press-center/reports4/energy-r-evolution-a-sustain.pdf.
57. J. Hansen, Mki. Sato, P. Kharecha, D. Beerling, R. Berner, V. Masson-Delmotte, M. Pagani, M. Raymo, D. L. Royer, and J. C. Zachos, "2008: Target Atmospheric CO_2: Where Should Humanity Aim?" *Open Atmos. Sci. J.* 2 (2008): 217–31, accessed at http://pubs.giss.nasa.gov/abstracts/2008/Hansen_etal.html.
58. Sir John Houghton, from the foreword in Richard Hawkins, Christian Hunt, Tim Holmes and Tim Helweg-Larsen, *Climate Safety: In Case of Emergency . . .* (London: Public Interest Research Centre, 2008), accessed at http://www.scribd.com/doc/8522620/Climate-Safety.
59. Richard Hawkins, Christian Hunt, Tim Holmes and Tim Helweg-Larsen, *Climate Safety*, 2.
60. Jean-Marie Macabrey, "Science: Researchers Warn that Sea Levels Will Rise Much Faster than Expected," *ClimateWire,* March 3, 2009, accessed at http://www.eenews.net/climatewire/2009/03/11/archive/1. See also Michael D. Lemonick, "As Effects of Warming Grow, IPCC Report Is Quickly Dated," *Yale Environment 360,* February 12, 2009, accessed at http://www.e360.yale.edu/content/feature.msp?id=2120.
61. Commonwealth Scientific and Industrial Research Organization, "Permafrost Melt Poses Major Climate Change Threat," news release, July 1, 2009, accessed at http://www.csiro.org/news/Permafrost-climate-change-threat.html.
62. Some climate scientists and other scientists disagree with the findings of the Intergovernmental Panel on Climate Change. See Craig Idso and S. Fred Singer, *Climate Change Reconsidered: The 2009 Report of the Nongovernmental International Panel on Climate Change (NIPCC)* (Chicago: Heartland Institute, 2009), accessed at http://www.nipccreport.org/index.html.
63. Susan Solomon et al., "Irreversible Climate Change Due to Carbon Dioxide

Emissions," *Proceedings of the National Academy of Sciences of the United States* 106, no. 6 (February 10, 2009): 1709. Accessed at http://www.pnas .org/content/early/2009/01/28/0812721106.full.pdf+html.

64. United Nations Development Programme, *Fighting Climate Change: Human Solidarity in a Divided World,* Human Development Report 2007/2008 (New York: United Nations, 2008), 2, accessed at http://hdr.undp.org/en/media/ HDR_20072008_EN_Overview.pdf.

1. Ethical Resources

1. Quoted by Andrew C. Revkin in "The Climate Bill in Climate Context," *New York Times,* June 26, 2009, accessed at http://dotearth.blogs.nytimes .com/2009/06/26/the-climate-bill-in-climate-context/.

2. Larry Rasmussen points out that, up to this point, sustainability was simply a term used to discuss the yield of forests and fisheries. See Larry Rasmussen, "Doing Our First Works Over," *J. Luth. Ethics* 9, no. 4 (April 2009), accessed at http://www.elca.org/What-We-Believe/Social-Issues/Journal-of-Lutheran-Ethics/Issues/April-2009/Doing-Our-First-Works-Over.aspx; For more background on the WCC's position in 1974, see World Council of Churches, *Study Encounter* 69, vol. 10, no. 4 (1974) 2. Cited in Rasmussen, "Doing Our First Works Over."

3. Paul Abrecht, ed., *Faith, Science, and the Future* (Geneva: World Council of Churches, 1978); and Roger L. Shinn, ed., *Faith and Science in an Unjust World* (Geneva: World Council of Churches, 1978).

4. World Council of Churches, *Accelerated Climate Change: Sign of Peril, Test of Faith* (Geneva: WCC Publications, 1994).

5 Ibid., 12–13. Cited in Rasmussen, "Doing Our First Works Over."

6. This statement was jointly adopted by the Presbyterian Church in the United States and the United Presbyterian Church in the United States of America. See *Minutes,* Presbyterian Church in the United States, 1981, pt. I, pp. 122, 413–25; and *Minutes,* United Presbyterian Church in the United States of America, 1981, pt. I, pp. 42, 86, 293–306.

7. Office of the General Assembly, *Restoring Creation for Ecology and Justice: A Report Adopted by the 202nd General Assembly (1990)* (Louisville, Ky.: Presbyterian Church (U.S.A.), 1990). See http://www.pcusa.org/environment/ restore.htm.

8. *Overture 02-57. On Revising the Denominational Policy on the Issue of Energy* (*Minutes,* 2002, pt. I, pp. 72, 596).

9. *Minutes,* 2008, pt. I, pp. 934ff; *The Power to Change: U.S. Energy Policy and Global Warming: A Revised Social Policy Statement Adopted by the 218th General Assembly (2008)* (Louisville, Ky.: Presbyterian Church (U.S.A.), 2008). See http://www.pc-biz.org/Explorer.aspx?id=1537&promoID=10. I served as the primary author of this statement.

10. Evangelical Lutheran Church in America (ELCA), *Caring for Creation: Vision, Hope, and Justice* (Chicago: Division for Church in Society, 1993), accessed

at http://www.elca.org/What-We-Believe/Social-Issues/Social-Statements/
Environment.aspx. Technically, ethical principles are a more specific form of
moral guidance than a broad moral norm. I prefer to describe sustainability,
sufficiency, participation, and solidarity as moral norms, because I refer later
to the "polluter pays" and "ability to pay" principles later in chapter five,
which focuses on climate policy.

11. See ELCA, *For Peace in God's World,* (Chicago: Division for Church in Society, 1995), accessed at http://www.elca.org/What-We-Believe/Social-Issues/
Social-Statements/Peace.aspx. See also ELCA, *Economic Life: Sufficient, Sustainable Livelihood for All,* (Chicago: Division for Church in Society, 1999),
accessed at http://www.elca.org/What-We-Believe/Social-Issues/Social-
Statements/Economic-Life.aspx.

12. ELCA, *Genetics and Faith: Power, Choice, and Responsibility* (Chicago: ELCA
Church in Society, Taskforce on Genetics, 2008), accessed at http://www
.elca.org/What-We-Believe/Social-Issues/Social-Statements-in-Process/
Genetics/Link-to-the-Study.aspx.

13. Ibid., 30.

14. National Council of Churches of Christ Eco-Justice Programs, "About Us,"
NCC Eco-Justice Web site, http://www.nccecojustice.org (accessed June 10,
2009).

15. This section on the ethic of ecological justice and its four moral norms is
excerpted from James B. Martin-Schramm and Robert L. Stivers, *Christian
Environmental Ethics: A Case Method Approach* (Maryknoll, N.Y.: Orbis,
2003), 37–45. It is used here gratefully with permission from Orbis Books.

16. Aristotle, *Nicomachean Ethics,* trans. Weldon, J.E.C., (Buffalo, N.Y.: Prometheus, 1987), Bk. V, Chap. VI.

17. See Sallie McFague. *Super, Natural Christians* (Minneapolis: Fortress Press,
1997), 172ff. See also Rosemary Radford Reuther, *Gaia and God: An Ecofem-
inist Theology of Earth Healing* (San Francisco: HarperSanFrancisco, 1992).

18. See James Nash, "Toward the Revival and Reform of the Subversive Virtue:
Frugality," *Ann. Soc. Christ. Ethics* (1995): 137–160.

19. Martin Hengel, *Property and Riches in the Early Church* (Philadelphia: Fortress Press, 1974).

20. Ibid.

21. How far to extend moral considerability to other species is a controversial issue. So too is the issue of moral significance. See James Nash, *Loving
Nature: Ecological Integrity and Christian Responsibility* (Nashville: Abingdon, 1991), 179ff.

22. James B. Martin-Schramm and Robert L. Stivers, *Christian Environmental
Ethics: A Case Method Approach* (Maryknoll, N.Y.: Orbis, 2003), 205–6. The
following list and descriptions of twelve guidelines are reprinted with the
gracious permission of Orbis Books.

23. Marianne Lavelle, "The Climate Change Lobby Explosion," Articles page,
Center for Public Integrity website, February 24, 2009, accessed at http://www
.publicintegrity.org/investigations/climate_change/articles/entry/1171/.

24. I published an initial draft of these guidelines in "Assessing Climate Policy

Proposals: Ethical Guidelines," *J. Luth. Ethics* 9, no. 4 (April 2009), accessed at http://www.elca.org/What-We-Believe/Social-Issues/Journal-of-Lutheran-Ethics/Issues/April-2009/Assessing-Climate-Policy-Proposals.aspx.

25. Martin Luther King Jr., "I Have a Dream," August 28, 1963, accessed at http://www.americanrhetoric.com/speeches/mlkihaveadream.htm.

2. Conventional Energy Options

1. Vijay V. Vaitheeswaran, *Power to the People: How the Coming Energy Revolution Will Transform an Industry, Change Our Lives, and Maybe Even Save the Planet* (New York: Farrar, Straus & Giroux, 2003), 19.

2. Ban Ki-moon, address to World Business Summit on Climate Change (Copenhagen, May 25, 2009). Cited in "World Business Leaders Hear Catastrophic Climate Warnings," *Environmental News Service*, May 25, 2009, accessed at http://www.ens-newswire.com/ens/may2009/2009-05-25-01.asp.

3. Intergovernmental Panel on Climate Change, *Climate Change 2007: Synthesis Report; Summary for Policymakers* (Geneva: IPCC, November 2007), fig. SPM.3, p. 5, accessed at http://www.ipcc.ch/pdf/assessment-report/ar4/syr/ar4_syr.pdf.

4. Environmental Protection Agency (EPA), *Inventory of U.S. Greenhouse Gas Emissions and Sinks: 1990–2007*, EPA 430-R-09-004 (Washington, D.C.: EPA, April 15, 2009), 3-1, accessed at http://epa.gov/climatechange/emissions/downloads09/InventoryUSGhG1990-2007.pdf.

5. Energy Information Administration, *Annual Energy Review 2008*, DOE/EIA-0384(2008) (Washington, D.C.: EIA, June 26, 2009), fig. 2.0, p. 37 accessed at http://www.eia.doe.gov/aer/pdf/aer.pdf. EIA reports the U.S. consumed 99.2 quadrillion Btus of primary energy in 2008. Renewable energy sources contributed 7.3 quadrillion Btus (7.4 percent). Petroleum, natural gas, coal, and nuclear power contributed 91.9 quadrillion Btus (92.6 percent).

6. Ibid.

7. Energy Information Administration, *An Updated Annual Energy Outlook 2009 Reference Case Reflecting Provisions of the American Recovery and Reinvestment Act and Recent Changes in the Economic Outlook* (Washington, D.C.: U.S. Department of Energy, April 2009), table A1, "Total Energy Supply and Disposition Summary," p. 16, accessed at http://www.eia.doe.gov/oiaf/servicerpt/stimulus/pdf/sroiaf(2009)03.pdf. See also Energy Information Administration, *Annual Energy Outlook 2009 with Projections to 2030*, DOE/EIA-0383(2009) (Washington, D.C.: EIA, March 2009), accessed at http://www.eia.doe.gov/oiaf/aeo/pdf/0383(2009).pdf.

8. Energy Information Administration, *Annual Energy Review 2008*, DOE/EIA-0384(2008) (Washington, D.C.: EIA, June 26, 2009), fig. 7.1, p. 206, and fig. 7.3, p. 210, accessed at http://www.eia.doe.gov/aer/pdf/aer.pdf.

9. Energy Information Administration, *Electric Power Monthly*, DOE/EIA-0226 (2009/06) (Washington, D.C.: EIA, June 2009), accessed at http://www.eia.doe.gov/cneaf/electricity/epm/epm_sum.html.

10. Pew Center on Global Climate Change, "Coal and Climate Change Facts," accessed at http://www.pewclimate.org/global-warming-basics/coalfacts. cfm (June 17, 2009). A recent study by the U.S Geological Survey, however, notes that economically extractable coal reserves could be substantially less abundant and may be as little as half the previously estimated reserves. See J. A. Luppens, D. C. Scott, J. E. Haacke, L. M. Osmonson, T. J. Rohrbacher, and M. S. Ellis, *Assessment of Coal Geology, Resources, and Reserves in the Gillette Coalfield, Powder River Basin,* Open-File Report 2008-1202 (Powder River Basin, Wyoming: U.S. Geological Survey, 2008), 32, accessed at http:// pubs.usgs.gov/of/2008/1202/pdf/ofr2008-1202.pdf.

11. Jonathan G. Dorn, "The End of an Era: Closing the Door on Building New Coal-Fired Power Plants in America," *Eco-Economy Updates* (Earth Policy Institute), March 31, 2009, accessed at http://www.earth-policy.org/ Updates/2009/Update81.htm.

12. EPA, "Executive Summary," in *Inventory of U.S. Greenhouse Gas Emissions and Sinks,* ES-4, accessed at http://epa.gov/climatechange/emissions/down-loads09/ExecutiveSummary.pdf.

13. James Hansen, "A Plea to President Obama: End Mountaintop Coal Mining," *Yale Environment 360,* June 25, 2009, accessed at http://e360.yale.edu/ content/feature.msp?id=2168. Hansen, America's most distinguished climate scientist, recently engaged in civil disobedience and was arrested for protesting mountaintop removal in Appalachia.

14. See Erik Shuster, "Tracking New Coal-Fired Power Plants" (National Energy Technology Laboratory, June 23, 2009), slides 6 and 13, accessed at http:// www.netl.doe.gov/coal/refshelf/ncp.pdf. These technologies are integrated gasification combined cycle (IGCC), supercritical and ultra-supercritical pulverized coal combustion, subcritical pulverized coal combustion, and fluidized bed combustion. More realistic estimates, according to experts both inside and outside government, are that perhaps a third of the remaining eighty-seven projects are being seriously pursued by utilities, and fewer than two dozen are likely to make it to the permitting or construction phases by 2010.

15. Debra Kahn, "Industry Ready for Federal Regs, AEP Executive Tells Congress," *Environment & Energy Daily,* September 7, 2007, accessed at http:// www.eenews.net/EEDaily/print/2007/09/07/4.

16. Massachusetts Institute of Technology (MIT), *The Future of Coal: Options for a Carbon-Constrained World* (Boston: MIT, 2007), ix, accessed at http://web. mit.edu/coal/The_Future_of_Coal.pdf.

17. Jon Luoma, "The Carbon Conundrum," *Popular Mechanics,* July 2008, 48–49.

18. Pew Center on Global Climate Change, "Coal and Climate Change Facts."

19. Energy Information Administration, "Frequently Asked Questions: Electricity," updated April 1, 2009, accessed at http://tonto.eia.doe.gov/ask/ electricity_faqs.asp#coal_plants. Of this total, 476 are "power plants" owned by electric utilities and independent power producers that generate and sell electricity as their primary business; 141 are industrial, commercial, and

institutional facilities, where most of the electricity generated is consumed on-site.

20. Pew Center on Global Climate Change, "Coal and Climate Change Facts." The Massachusetts Institute of Technology Energy Initiative recently published a report with a similar recommendation. The report also focuses on the potential of increasing the efficiency of existing power plants and other measures to reduce greenhouse gas emissions. See *Retrofitting of Coal-Fired Power Plants for CO_2 Emissions Reductions,* March 23, 2009, accessed at http://www.eenews.net/features/documents/2009/06/19/document_cw_01 .pdf.

21. Ben Gorman, "Coal: Enviros Fault Scaled-Back FutureGen Carbon Goal," *Greenwire,* June 16, 2009, accessed at http://www.eenews.net/Greenwire/ 2009/06/16/archive/3.

22. Center for Media and Democracy, "Clean Coal," *SourceWatch,* accessed at http://www.sourcewatch.org/index.php?title=Clean_coal (February 28, 2009).

23. Lisa Friedman, "China: A Sea Change in the Nation's Attitude toward Carbon Capture," *ClimateWire,* June 22, 2009, accessed at http://www.eenews. net/climatewire/2009/06/22/1/.

24. Energy Information Administration, "Energy in Brief: Major Sources and Users." Natural gas and coal both provide 23 percent, nuclear power 8 percent, and renewable energy 7 percent.

25. ABC News, "A Look under the Hood of a Nation on Wheels," January 31, 2005, ABC News/*Time* Magazine/*Washington Post* poll, accessed at http:// abcnews.go.com/images/Politics/973a2Traffic.pdf. Cited in David Sandalow, *Freedom from Oil: How the Next President Can End the United States' Oil Addiction* (New York: McGraw-Hill, 2008), 14.

26. Jay Inslee and Bracken Hicks, *Apollo's Fire: Reigniting America's Clean-Energy Economy,* (Washington, D.C.: Island, 2008), 14.

27. Daniel Yergin, *The Prize: The Epic Quest for Oil, Money, and Power* (New York: Simon & Schuster, 1991), 13–14.

28. Joyce Dargay, Dermot Gately, and Martin Sommer, "Vehicle Ownership and Income Growth, Worldwide: 1960–2030," *Energy J.* 28, no. 4 (2007), accessed at http://www.econ.nyu.edu/dept/courses/gately/Vehicle%20Own ership%20and%20Income%20Growth_abstract.htm.

29. Sandalow, *Freedom from Oil,* 19.

30. Ibid., 150.

31. Rachel Graham and Alexander Kwiatkowski, "World Oil Reserves Dropped Last Year in Russia, China," *Bloomberg.com,* June 10, 2009, accessed at http:// www.bloomberg.com/apps/news?pid=newsarchive&sid=aSwcNFu1JWJg.

32. Energy Information Administration, "Long-Term World Oil Supply: A Resource Base, Production Path Analysis," August 2004, accessed at http:// www.netl.doe.gov/energy-analyses/pubs/LongTermOilSupplyPresentation .pdf. See also, Howard Geller, *Energy Revolution: Policies for a Sustainable Future* (Washington, D.C.: Island, 2003), 13.

33. Terry Tamminen, *Lives per Gallon: The True Cost of Our Oil Addiction* (Washington, D.C.: Island, 2006), 83.

34. Ibid., 82.
35. Michael T. Klare, *Blood and Oil: The Dangers and Consequences of America's Growing Petroleum Dependency* (New York: Metropolitan, 2004), 10.
36. Ibid., 30.
37. Ibid., 32.
38. Ibid., 43.
39. Ibid., 4.
40. Ibid., 2.
41. Ibid., 5.
42. "Alternative Energy: U.S. Military Embraces Green Trend," *Greenwire,* December 5, 2007, accessed at http://www.eenews.net/Greenwire/2007/12/05/archive/9.
43. Michael T. Klare, "The Pentagon v. Peak Oil: How Wars of the Future May Be Fought Just to Run the Machines That Fight Them," *TomDispatch.com,* December 6, 2007, accessed at http://www.tomdispatch.com/post/174810/.
44. Jay Inslee and Bracken Hicks, *Apollo's Fire: Reigniting America's Clean-Energy Economy* (Washington, D.C.: Island, 2008), 14.
45. S. David Freeman, *Winning Our Energy Independence* (Salt Lake City, Utah: Gibbs Smith, 2007), 3.
46. Thomas L. Friedman, *Hot, Flat, and Crowded: Why We Need a Green Revolution—and How It Can Renew America* (New York: Farrar, Straus & Giroux, 2008), 96.
47. Sandalow, *Freedom from Oil,* 32. Only oil tankers with double hulls are now allowed to enter Prince William Sound. Terry Tamminen claims Exxon refurbished the *Exxon Valdez,* changed its name to the *SeaRiver Mediterranean,* and then petitioned the federal government for permission to allow this single-hull tanker to continue moving oil out of Valdez, Alaska. See Tamminen, *Lives per Gallon,* 33.
48. Tamminen, *Lives per Gallon,* 33.
49. Ibid., 39–40.
50. Energy Information Administration, *Emissions of Greenhouse Gases in the United States 2007,* DOE/EIA-0573(2007) (Washington, D.C.: EIA, December 2008), table 5, p. 13, accessed at ftp://ftp.eia.doe.gov/pub/oiaf/1605/cdrom/pdf/ggrpt/057307.pdf.
51. Freeman, *Winning Our Energy Independence,* 19. Approximately 9 percent of oil in the United States is used in the aviation industry, 5 percent in home heating, and the rest in industrial manufacturing.
52. Natural Gas Supply Association, "Overview of Natural Gas: Background," *Naturalgas.org,* accessed at www.naturalgas.org/overview/background.asp (July 1, 2009).
53. Clifford Krauss, "Drilling Boom Revives Hopes for Natural Gas," *New York Times,* August 25, 2008, accessed at http://www.nytimes.com/2008/08/25/business/25gas.html.
54. Katie Howell, "Natural Gas: Shales Could Provide Quarter of U.S. Supplies in Decade, Industry Says," *E&E News PM,* November 12, 2008, accessed at http://www.eenews.net/eenewspm/2008/11/21/archive/9.

55. Jad Mouawad, "Estimate Puts Natural Gas Reserves 35% Higher," *New York Times,* June 17, 2009, accessed at http://www.nytimes.com/2009/06/18/business/energy-environment/18gas.html?ref=business.

56. Katie Howell, "Natural Gas: Dems Plan to Reintroduce Bill to Regulate Drilling Technique," *Energy & Environment Daily,* June 5, 2009, accessed at http://www.eenews.net/EEDaily/2009/06/05/archive/7.

57. IHS Global Insight, *Measuring the Economic and Energy Impacts of Proposals to Regulate Hydraulic Fracturing,* prepared for American Petroleum Institute (Lexington, Mass.: IHS, June 2009), accessed at http://api.org/policy/exploration/hydraulicfracturing/upload/IHS-GI-Hydraulic-Fracturing-Natl-impacts.pdf.

58. Worldwatch Institute and Center for American Progress, *American Energy: The Renewable Path to Energy Security* (Washington, D.C.: Worldwatch Institute, September 2006), 24.

59. Energy Information Administration, "U.S. Nuclear Reactors," accessed at http://www.eia.doe.gov/cneaf/nuclear/page/nuc_reactors/reactsum.html (July 1, 2009).

60. Katherine Ling, "Yucca Mountain: Project's Estimated Lifecycle Cost Rises 38%—to $96B," *E&E News PM,* August 5, 2008, accessed at http://www.eenews.net/eenewspm/2008/08/05/archive/2.

61. Ibid.

62. Quirin Schiermier, Jeff Tollefson, et al., "Energy Alternatives: Electricity without Carbon," *Nature* 454 (2008): 817, accessed at http://www.nature.com/news/2008/080813/full/454816a.html.

63. U.S. Department of Energy, Office of Civilian Radioactive Waste Management (OCRWM), "Fact Sheet: What Are Spent Nuclear Fuel and High-Level Radioactive Waste?" accessed at http://www.ocrwm.doe.gov/fact/What_are_snf_and_hlrw.shtml (June 26, 2009).

64. OCRWM, "Fact Sheet: Yucca Mountain Project," accessed at http://www.ocrwm.doe.gov/fact/Overview_Yucca_Mountain_Project.shtml (June 26, 2009).

65. Katherine Ling, "Nuclear Waste: States Threatening to Halt Payments if U.S. Cancels Yucca Mountain," *Greenwire,* April 8, 2009, accessed at http://www.eenews.net/Greenwire/2009/04/08/archive/2.

66. Ling, "Yucca Mountain."

67. U.S. Department of Energy, *The Report to the President and the Congress by the Secretary of Energy on the Need for a Second Repository* (Washington, D.C.: Office of Civilian Radioactive Waste Management, December 2008), 10, accessed at http://www.ocrwm.doe.gov/uploads/1/Second_Repository_Rpt_120908.pdf.

68. Katherine Ling, "Nuclear Waste: Second Repository Necessary if Yucca Mountain Limit Isn't Lifted—DOE," *E&E News PM,* December 9, 2008, accessed at http://www.eenews.net/eenewspm/2008/12/09/archive/4.

69. Ling, "Nuclear Waste: States Threatening to Halt Payments."

70. Ling, "Nuclear Waste: Second Repository Necessary"; Matthew L. Wald, "Future Dim for Nuclear Waste Repository," *New York Times,* March 6,

2009, accessed at http://www.nytimes.com/2009/03/06/science/earth/06
yucca.html.

71. Ling, "Nuclear Waste: States Threatening to Halt Payments."

72. U.S. Department of Energy, Office of Civilian Radioactive Waste Management, *Report to Congress on the Demonstration of the Interim Storage of Spent Nuclear Fuel from Decommissioned Nuclear Power Reactors* (Washington, D.C.: Department of Energy, December 2008), accessed at http://www.eenews.net/features/documents/2008/12/09/document_pm_02.pdf.

73. Ling, "Nuclear Waste: Second Repository Necessary."

74. See James B. Martin-Schramm and Robert L. Stivers, "Skull Valley: Nuclear Waste, Environmental Racism, and Tribal Sovereignty," in *Christian Environmental Ethics: A Case Method Approach* (Maryknoll, N.Y.: Orbis, 2003), 218–52; James Martin-Schramm, "Skull Valley: Nuclear Waste, Tribal Sovereignty, and Environmental Racism," *Cresset,* Advent/Christmas 2006, 7–15, accessed at http://www.valpo.edu/cresset/2006/2006%20Advent%20Martin-Schramm.pdf.

75. Stephen Power, "Yucca Mountain: Obama Budget Takes Another Whack at Storage Site," *Wall Street Journal,* May 7, 2009, accessed at http://blogs.wsj.com/environmentalcapital/2009/05/07/yucca-mountain-obama-budget-takes-another-whack-at-storage-site/.

76. Ben German, "Nuclear Power: DOE Chief Says He Supports Building New Reactors," *Greenwire,* March 11, 2009, accessed at http://www.eenews.net/Greenwire/2009/03/11/archive/5.

77. Associated Press, "Funds to Shut Nuclear Plants Fall Short," *New York Times,* June 17, 2009, accessed at http://www.nytimes.com/aponline/2009/06/16/us/AP-US-Nuclear-Funds-Shortfall.html?.

78. "A Renaissance That May Not Come," *Economist,* May 19, 2001, 24–26.

79. Lester R. Brown, "The Flawed Economics of Nuclear Power," *Eco-Economy Updates* (Earth Policy Institute), October 28, 2008, accessed at http://www.earth-policy.org/Updates/2008/Update78.htm.

80. Amory B. Lovins and Imran Sheikh, "The Nuclear Illusion," draft, May 27, 2008, accessed at http://www.rmi.org/images/PDFs/Energy/E08-01_AmbioNucIllusion.pdf.

81. Rebecca Smith, "U.S. Chooses Four Utilities to Revive Nuclear Power Industry," *Wall Street Journal,* June 17, 2009, accessed at http://online.wsj.com/article/SB124519618224221033.html.

82. Christopher Mason, "Ontario Suspends Nuclear Reactor Plan," *Financial Times,* June 29, 2009, accessed at http://www.ft.com/cms/s/0/46f12ba8-64c8-11de-a13f-00144feabdc0.html?nclick_check=1.

83. Schiermier et al., "Energy Alternatives," 817.

84. See "Tritium Leak: Exelon Says It Found Source of Radioactive Leak at Dresden Nuclear Plant," *Chicago Tribune,* June 16, 2009, accessed at http://www.chicagotribune.com/news/local/chi-exelon-leak-16-jun16,0,545073.story; U.S. Nuclear Regulatory Commission, "Fact Sheet on Tritium, Radiation Protection Limits, and Drinking Water Standards" (July 2006), accessed at http://www.nrc.gov/reading-rm/doc-collections/fact-sheets/tritium-radiation-fs.html.

85. Energy Information Administration, "New Reactor Designs," accessed at http://www.eia.doe.gov/cneaf/nuclear/page/analysis/nucenviss2.html (July 1, 2009).

86. Public Citizen, "Nuclear Giveaways in the Energy Policy Act of 2005" (Washington, D.C.: Public Citizen, n.d.), accessed at http://www.citizen.org/documents/NuclearEnergyBillFinal.pdf (July 1, 2009).

87. Environmental News Service, "U.S. Would Turn Nine Tons of Plutonium into MOX Fuel," September 19, 2007, accessed at http://www.ens-newswire.com/ens/sep2007/2007-09-18-091.asp.

88. See Peter Fairley, "Nuclear Wasteland," *IEEE Spectrum,* February 2007, accessed at http://www.spectrum.ieee.org/energy/nuclear/nuclear-waste land. See also Katherine Ling, "Nuclear: Is the Solution to the U.S. Waste Problem in France?" *ClimateWire,* May 18, 2009, accessed at http://www.eenews.net/climatewire/2009/05/18/archive/1; and Frank N. von Hippel, "Nuclear Fuel Recycling: More Trouble than It's Worth," *Scientific American,* May 2008, accessed at http://www.scientificamerican.com/article.cfm?id=rethinking-nuclear-fuel-recycling.

89. Friedman, *Hot, Flat, and Crowded,* 32.

3. Alternative and Renewable Energy Options

1. Energy Information Administration (EIA), *Annual Energy Review 2008,* DOE/EIA-0384(2008) (Washington, D.C.: EIA, June 26, 2009), fig. 10.1, p. 282, accessed at http://www.eia.doe.gov/aer/pdf/aer.pdf.

2. EIA, *An Updated Annual Energy Outlook 2009 Reference Case Reflecting Provisions of the American Recovery and Reinvestment Act and Recent Changes in the Economic Outlook,* (Washington, D.C.: U.S. Department of Energy, April 2009), table A-1, p. 16. See also EIA, *Annual Energy Outlook 2009, with Projections to 2030,* DOE/EIA-0383(2009) (Washington, D.C.: EIA, March 2009), accessed at http://www.eia.doe.gov/oiaf/aeo/pdf/0383(2009).pdf.

3. Paul Komor, *Wind and Solar Electricity: Challenges and Opportunities,* Solutions White Paper Series (Arlington, Va.: Pew Center on Global Climate Change, June 2009), accessed at http://www.pewclimate.org/docUploads/wind-solar-electricity-report.pdf.

4. Charles F. Kutscher, ed., *Tackling Climate Change in the U.S.: Potential Carbon Emissions Reductions from Energy Efficiency and Renewable Energy by 2030* (Boulder, Colo.: American Solar Energy Society, January 2007), 5, accessed at http://ases.org/images/stories/file/ASES/climate_change.pdf.

5. European Renewable Energy Council and Greenpeace International, *Energy Revolution: A Sustainable USA Energy Outlook* (Washington, D.C.: Greenpeace, February 2009), 5, accessed at http://www.greenpeace.org/raw/content/usa/press-center/reports4/energy-r-evolution-a-sustain.pdf.

6. Worldwatch Institute and Center for American Progress, *American Energy: The Renewable Path to Energy Security* (Washington, D.C.: Worldwatch, September 2006), 21.

7. Ibid.
8. Editorial, "Energy Inefficient," *New York Times*, January 19, 2009, accessed at http://www.nytimes.com/2009/01/19/opinion/19mon1.html.
9. American Council for an Energy-Efficient Economy (ACEEE), "Energy Efficiency Progress and Potential," ACEEE Fact Sheet accessed at http://aceee.org/energy/effact.htm (July 2, 2009).
10. Bill Prindle, Maggie Eldridge, et al., *The Twin Pillars of Sustainable Energy: Synergies between Energy Efficiency and Renewable Energy Technology and Policy* (Washington, D.C.: ACEEE, May 2007), v, accessed at http://aceee.org/pubs/e074.htm.
11. Natalie Mims, Mathias Bell, and Stephen Doig, *Assessing the Electric Productivity Gap and the U.S. Efficiency Opportunity* (Boulder, Colo.: Rocky Mountain Institute, January 2009), 8, accessed online June 19, 2009 at http://ert.rmi.org/files/documents/RMI.CEGpaper.pdf.
12. Ibid., 17.
13. IBM advertisement, "Smarter Power for a Smarter Planet," *Wall Street Journal*, November 24, 2008, A7.
14. Jay Inslee and Bracken Hicks, *Apollo's Fire* (Washington, D.C.: Island, 2008), 58.
15. David Sandalow, *Freedom from Oil: How the Next President Can End the United States' Oil Addiction* (New York: McGraw-Hill, 2008), 111.
16. John Randolph and Gilbert M. Masters, *Energy for Sustainability, Technology, Planning, Policy* (Washington, D.C.: Island, 2008), fig. 13.13, p. 510.
17. Terry Tamminen, *Lives per Gallon: The True Cost of Our Oil Addiction* (Washington, D.C.: Island, 2006), 66.
18. John M. Broder, "Bush Signs Broad Energy Bill," *New York Times*, December 19, 2007, accessed at http://www.nytimes.com/2007/12/19/washington/19cnd-energy.html.
19. American Council for an Energy-Efficient Economy (ACEEE), "Fuel Economy Standards in the 2007 Energy Bill," update, ACEEE Web site, December 5, 2007, accessed at http://www.aceee.org/transportation/fueleconomyupdate.pdf.
20. Josh Voorhees, "Autos: White House Blends CAFÉ, Calif. Waiver to Create National Standard," *Energy & Environment Daily*, May 19, 2009, accessed at http://www.eenews.net/EEDaily/2009/05/19/archive/3. Passenger cars averaged 27.5 mpg in 2009 and now will need to average 39 mpg by 2016; light trucks averaged 23.1 mpg in 2009 and now will need to average 30 mpg by 2016.
21. "Energy Inefficient," *New York Times*. This example is so counterintuitive that it's worth breaking out the calculator: An SUV that gets 14 mpg would burn 1,071.4 gallons to travel 15,000 miles (15,000/14). An SUV that gets 16 mpg would burn 937.5 gallons to travel 15,000 miles (15,000/16). Thus the more fuel-efficient SUV saves 133.9 gallons. A sedan that gets 35 mpg would burn 428.6 gallons to travel 15,000 miles (15,000/35). A hybrid sedan that gets 51 mpg would burn 294.1 gallons to travel 15,000 miles (15,000/51). Thus trading up to the hybrid saves 134.5 gallons, which is almost identical to the 133.9 gallons of fuel savings in the SUV example.

22. American Institute of Architects, "Survey Shows Only 7 Percent of Voters Know Top Cause of Greenhouse Gas Emissions," news release, October 1, 2007, accessed at http://www.sustainablefacility.com/Articles/Industry _Watch/BNP_GUID_9-5-2006_A_10000000000000188671.

23. European Renewable Energy Council and Greenpeace, *Energy Revolution: A Sustainable World Energy Outlook,* (Utrecht, The Netherlands: PrimaveraQuint, January 2007), 72, accessed at http://www.greenpeace.org/new -zealand/press/reports/global-energy-report.

24. Worldwatch Institute and Center for American Progress, *American Energy*, 31.

25. European Renewable Energy Council and Greenpeace, *Energy Revolution: A Sustainable World Energy Outlook,* 74.

26. Britt Childs Staley, Jenna Goodward, Clayton Rigdon, and Andrew MacBride, Juice from Concentrate: Reducing Emissions with Concentrating Solar Thermal Power (Washington, D.C.: World Resources Institute, 2009), 16.

27. Worldwatch Institute and Center for American Progress, *American Energy*, 30.

28. Staley et al., Juice from Concentrate, 24.

29. Ibid., 23.

30. Yingling Liu, "Solar Power Experiences Strongest Year of Growth Yet," Worldwatch Web site, June 18, 2009, accessed at http://www.worldwatch .org/node/6156?emc=el&m=258906&l=4&v=97bdfc81f5.

31. Noelle Straub, "Renewable Energy: Interior Moves to Fast-Track Solar Development," *E&E News PM,* June 29, 2009, accessed at http://www.eenews.net/ eenewspm/2009/06/29/2/.

32. Liu, "Solar Power Experiences Strongest Year."

33. Worldwatch Institute and Center for American Progress, *American Energy*, 29.

34. See Database of State Incentives for Renewables and Efficiency (DSIRE) Web site, accessed at http://www.dsireusa.org/Index.cfm?EE=0&re=1 (June 19, 2009).

35. For an excellent resource, see Paul Gipe, "Electricity Feed Laws, Feed-In Tariffs, Advanced Renewable Tariffs, and Renewable Energy Payments," Articles page, *Wind-Works.org,* accessed at http://www.wind-works.org/articles/ feed_laws.html (June 19, 2009).

36. U.S. Department of Energy, "Vermont Passes a Feed-In Tariff, plus Other Green Measures," *EERE News,* June 3, 2009, accessed at http://apps1.eere .energy.gov/news/news_detail.cfm?news_id=12551.

37. An electric generator's capacity factor is the ratio of the electric energy produced by a generating unit for a given period of time to the electric energy that could have been produced at continuous full-power operation during the same period. Since sunlight is only available for certain hours each day, and clouds often obscure the sun, a PV panel can only produce electricity under certain conditions. Thus, the capacity factor of PV panels is much lower than the capacity factor of a nuclear power plant that might be operating 90 percent of time at all hours of the day.

38. Quirin Schiermier, Jeff Tollefson, et al., "Energy Alternatives: Electricity without Carbon," *Nature* 454 (2008): 821.

39. American Wind Energy Association, "Fighting Against Impact of Economic Crisis, U.S. Wind Energy Industry Installs 1,200 MW in Second Quarter," July 28, 2009, accessed at http://awea.org/newsroom/releases/AWEA _second_quarter_market_report_072809.html.

40. Worldwatch Institute and Center for American Progress, *American Energy*, 26.

41. Ibid., 6.

42. Ibid., 26.

43. Ibid.

44. Ibid., 27.

45. American Wind Energy Association (AWEA), "Production Tax Credit," Policy page, AWEA website, accessed at http://www.awea.org/policy/ptc.html (June 19, 2009).

46. American Wind Energy Association (AWEA), "American Recovery and Reinvestment Act of 2009," Legislative page, AWEA website, accessed at http://awea.org/legislative/american_recovery_reinvestment_act.html (June 19, 2009).

47. Government Accountability Office, *Federal Electricity Subsidies: Information on Research Funding, Tax Expenditures, and Other Activities That Support Electricity Production*, GAO-08-102 (Washington, D.C.: GAO, October 26, 2007), accessed at http://www.gao.gov/new.items/d08102.pdf.

48. Gilbert E. Metcalf, *Taxing Energy in the United States: Which Fuels Does the Tax Code Favor?* Energy Policy and the Environment Report (New York: Center for Energy Policy and the Environment, Manhattan Institute, January 2009), accessed at https://www.policyarchive.org/bitstream/ handle/10207/14601/eper_04.pdf?sequence=1.

49. See Ryan Wiser and Galen Barbose, *Renewable Portfolio Standards in the United States: A Status Report with Data through 2007* (Berkeley, Calif.: Lawrence Berkeley National Laboratory, April 2008), accessed at http://eetd.lbl .gov/ea/ems/reports/lbnl-154e.pdf.

50. American Wind Energy Association, "Renewable Electricity Standard," Policy page, AWEA Web site, accessed at http://www.awea.org/policy/renew ables_portfolio_standard.html (June 19, 2009).

51. Katherine Ling, "Transmission: East Coast Could Need up to $80 Billion in New Lines for Wind," *Greenwire,* February 9, 2009, accessed at http://www .eenews.net/Greenwire/2009/02/09/archive/5.

52. For more information about the dangers posed by electromagnetic fields, see European Environment Agency, "Radiation Risk from Everyday Devices Assessed," September 17, 2007, press room highlights, accessed at http:// www.eea.europa.eu/highlights/radiation-risk-from-everyday-devices-assessed. See also Edison Electric Institute, "Electric and Magnetic Fields," accessed at http://www.eei.org/industry_issues/environment/land/electric_ and_magnetic_fields (July 2, 2009).

53. Worldwatch Institute and Center for American Progress, *American Energy,* 27.

54. Allison Winter, "Energy Policy: Ethanol Gulping Two-Thirds of Federal Renewable-Energy Subsidies," *E&E News PM,* January 8, 2009, accessed at http://www.eenews.net/eenewspm/2009/01/08/archive/8.

55. Editorial, "The High Costs of Ethanol," *New York Times,* September 19, 2007, accessed at http://www.nytimes.com/2007/09/19/opinion/19wed1.html.

56. Worldwatch Institute and Center for American Progress, *American Energy,* 22.

57. U.S. Department of Agriculture, Economic Research Service (ERS), "Agricultural Baseline Projections: U.S. Crops, 2009–2018," ERS Web site, updated February 12, 2009, accessed at http://www.ers.usda.gov/briefing/Baseline/crops.htm.

58. "The High Costs of Ethanol," *New York Times.*

59. Joel K. Boure Jr., "Green Dreams," *National Geographic,* October 2007, accessed at http://ngm.nationalgeographic.com/2007/10/biofuels/biofuels-text.html.

60. Celia W. Dugger, "As Prices Soar, U.S. Food Aid Buys Less," *New York Times,* September 29, 2007, accessed at http://www.nytimes.com/2007/09/29/world/29food.html.

61. "The High Costs of Ethanol," *New York Times.*

62. Ford Runge and Benjamin Senauer, "How Biofuels Could Starve the Poor," *Foreign Affairs* (May/June 2007), accessed at http://www.foreignaffairs.com/articles/64915/c-ford-runge-and-benjamin-senauer/how-ethanol-fuels-the-food-crisis.

63. UN General Assembly, 62nd Sess., *Report of the Special Rapporteur on the Right to Food,* August 22, 2007, pg. 14, accessed at http://www.righttofood.org/new/PDF/A62289.pdf.

64. Boure, "Green Dreams."

65. Worldwatch Institute and Center for American Progress, *American Energy,* 23. There is clearly a great need for alternative fuels, but precaution is warranted, especially when genetic engineering is employed to develop new crops for biofuel production. Just as government incentives to spur corn-based ethanol production have had unforeseen and deleterious consequences, so too could genetic engineering of biofuels feedstocks if this research is not conducted carefully and regulated closely.

66. To further incentivize production, the Food, Conservation and Energy Act of 2008 included a new income tax credit of $1.01 per gallon for producers of cellulosic alcohol and other cellulosic biofuels. See Renewable Fuels Association, "Cellulosic Biofuel Production Tax Credit," accessed at http://www.ethanolrfa.org/resource/cellulosic/documents/CellulosicBiofuelProducer-CreditBrief.pdf (June 22, 2009).

67. U.S. Department of Energy, "EPA's Proposed Renewable Fuel Standard Tackles GHG Emissions," *EERE News,* May 6, 2009, accessed at http://apps1.eere.energy.gov/news/news_detail.cfm/news_id=12491. See also Renewable Fuels Association, "Cellulosic Ethanol," accessed at http://www.ethanolrfa.org/resource/cellulosic/ (June 21, 2009).

68. Environmental Protection Agency, "EPA Lifecycle Analysis of Greenhouse Gas Emissions from Renewable Fuels," EPA-420-F-09-024 (May 2009), accessed at http://www.epa.gov/oms/renewablefuels/420f09024.htm.

69. Joseph Fargione at al., "Land Clearing and the Biofuel Carbon Debt," *Science* 319, no. 5867 (February 29, 2008): 1235–38, accessed at http://www.sciencemag.org/cgi/content/abstract/1152747. See also R. W. Howarth, S. Bringezu, et al., "Rapid Assessment on Biofuels and Environment: Overview and Key Findings," in *Biofuels: Environmental Consequences and Interactions with Changing Land Use: Proceedings of the Scientific Committee on Problems of the Environment (SCOPE) International Biofuels Project Rapid Assessment, 22–25 September 2008,* ed. R. W. Howarth and S. Bringezu, 1–13 (Ithaca: Cornell University, 2009), accessed at http://cip.cornell.edu/biofuels /files/SCOPE00.pdf.

70. Ben German and Robin Bravender, "Climate: EPA Biofuels Rule among a Host of Changes to House Bill," *Energy and Environment Daily,* June 24, 2009, accessed at http://www.eenews.net/EEDaily/2009/06/24/4/.

71. Ben German, "Biofuels: EPA Rule Release Sparks New Round in Emissions Fight," *E&E News PM,* March 5, 2009, accessed at http://www.eenews.net/eenewspm/2009/05/05/archive/3.

72. John Ohlrogge, Doug Allen, et al., "Driving on Biomass," *Science* 324, no. 5930 (May 22, 2009): 1019, accessed at http://www.sciencemag.org/cgi/content/abstract/324/5930/1055.

73. Valcent Products, Inc., "Vertical Algae Technology," accessed at http://www.valcent.net/s/Ecotech.asp?ReportID=182039 (July 1, 2009).

74. Jad Mouawad, "Exxon to Invest Millions to Make Fuel from Algae," *New York Times,* July 14, 2009, accessed at http://www.nytimes.com/2009/07/14/business/energy-environment/14fuel.html.

75. Jonathan Watts, "China Recruits Algae to Combat Climate Change," *Guardian,* June 29, 2009, accessed at http://www.guardian.co.uk/environment/2009/jun/28/china-algae-carbon-capture-plan.

76. Greg Breining, "From the Sewage Plant, the Promise of Biofuel," *Yale Environment 360,* July 1, 2009, accessed at http://www.e360.yale.edu/content/feature.msp?id=2167.

77. Worldwatch Institute and Center for American Progress, *American Energy,* 32.

78. Ibid.

79 Ibid., 25.

80 "U.S. Geothermal: Leading but Lagging," *Wall Street Journal,* September 5, 2007, B13–B14.

81. Massachusetts Institute of Technology, *The Future of Geothermal Energy: Impact of Enhanced Geothermal Systems [EGS] on the United States in the 21st Century* (Boston: MIT, 2006), 1-1 and 1-3, accessed at http://geothermal.inel.gov/publications/future_of_geothermal_energy.pdf.

82. "Renewable Energy: Iceland Finds Geothermal Dirtier than Expected," *ClimateWire,* May 27, 2009, accessed at http://www.eenews.net/climatewire/2009/05/27/archive/7.

83. James Glanz, "Deep in Bedrock, Clean Energy and Quake Fears, *New York Times,* June 24, 2009, accessed at http://www.nytimes.com/2009/06/24/business/energy-environment/24geotherm.html.

84. Electric Power Research Institute, "Utility-Owned Geothermal Heat Pump

Ground Loop Piping Network Development," September 2007, 1, accessed at http://mydocs.epri.com/docs/public/000000000001015476.pdf.

85. Ibid., 2.

86. Worldwatch Institute and Center for American Progress, *American Energy,* 25.

87. Ibid., 33.

88. Jon R. Luoma, "Capturing the Ocean's Energy," *Yale Environment 360,* December 1, 2008, accessed at http://e360.yale.edu/content/feature.msp ?id=2093.

89. Worldwatch Institute and Center for American Progress, *American Energy,* 33.

90. Luoma, "Capturing the Ocean's Energy."

91. Debra Kahn, "Renewables: Regulatory Hurdles Loom High for Wave Power," *ClimateWire,* March 17, 2009, accessed at http://www.eenews.net/ climatewire/2009/03/17/archive/2.

92. Schiermier et al., "Energy Alternatives," 823.

93. The U.S. climate scientist James Hansen vehemently opposes a cap-and-trade approach to reducing carbon emissions and much prefers what he calls a tax-and-dividend approach. Hansen calls for a federal carbon tax of $115 per ton of CO_2, which would be passed on to all consumers of carbon-intensive fuels and which would add $1 to the price of a gallon of gasoline and raise $670 billion per year. Under Hansen's plan, each adult legal resident would get $3,000 per year from the federal government via automatic electronic deposits of $250 per month deposited in his or her bank account. Each family would also receive half shares for each child up to a maximum of two children per family. Thus, a family of four would receive a dividend of $9,000 per year to offset rising prices for energy and other goods. Hansen's proposal does not use the tax receipts for any other purpose. He relies on the high tax to stimulate investments in low- or no-carbon energy sources. He offers no subsidies for energy efficiency or renewable energy. While Hansen's proposal is dramatic and intriguing, in my opinion, it is impossible politically. See James E. Hansen, "Carbon Tax and 100% Dividend vs. Tax and Trade," testimony to the U.S. House of Representatives Ways and Means Committee," February 25, 2009, accessed at http://www.columbia.edu/~jeh1/2009/ WaysAndMeans_20090225.pdf.

94. See Gilbert E. Metcalf, *A Proposal for U.S. Carbon Tax Swap: An Equitable Tax Reform to Address Global Climate Change,* Discussion Paper 2007-12 (Washington, D.C.: Brookings Institution, October 2007), accessed at http://www.brookings.edu/~/media/Files/rc/papers/2007/10carbontax _metcalf/10_carbontax_metcalf.pdf.

95. I want to thank Bruce Rittenhouse, at the University of Chicago Divinity School, for his counsel on this topic. I also want to thank one of my students majoring in economics, Michael Kientzle, for his reminder about the power of subsidies to shape markets.

96. Pew Center on Global Climate Change, "Tax Policies to Reduce Greenhouse Gas Emissions," Congressional Policy Brief, Fall 2008, accessed at http:// www.pewclimate.org/docUploads/DDCF-Taxes.pdf.

97. Paul Voosen, "Climate: Sarkozy Outlines Plan for Carbon Tax in 2010," *Greenwire*, September 10, 2009, accessed at http://www.eenews.net/Green wire/2009/09/10/archive/4.

4. International Climate Policy

1. Quoted in "Gore, U.N. Chief Tell CEOs Ambitious Climate Change Deal Would Be Good for Business," *ClimateWire*, May 26, 2009, accessed at http://www.eenews.net/climatewire/2009/05/26/.
2. Quoted in "Seventeen Major Economies Pledge to Set Greenhouse Gas Limit by December," *Environmental News Service*, July 9, 2009, accessed at http://www.ens-newswire.com/ens/jul2009/2009-07-09-01.asp.
3. Thomas R. Karl, Jerry M. Melillo, and Thomas C. Peterson, eds., *Global Climate Change Impacts in the United States* (New York: Cambridge University Press, 2009), 14, accessed at http://downloads.globalchange.gov/usimpacts/pdfs/climate-impacts-report.pdf.
4. Intergovernmental Panel on Climate Change, *Climate Change 2007: Synthesis Report; Summary for Policymakers* (Geneva: IPCC, November 2007), 36, n. 5, accessed at http://www.ipcc.ch/pdf/assessment-report/ar4/syr/ar4_syr_spm.pdf.
5. Ibid., 36.
6. Ibid.
7. Ibid. One gigatonne is equivalent to 1 billion metric tons.
8. Ibid.
9. Intergovernmental Panel on Climate Change, "Summary for Policymakers," in *Climate Change 2007: Impacts, Adaptation and Vulnerability: Contribution of Working Group II to the Fourth Assessment Report of the Intergovernmental Panel on Climate Change*, ed. M. L. Parry et al. (Cambridge: Cambridge University Press, 2007), 3, accessed at http://www.ipcc.ch/pdf/assessment-report/ar4/wg2/ar4-wg2-spm.pdf.
10. Karl et al., *Global Climate Change Impacts,* 14.
11. Ibid., 13.
12. United Nations Framework Convention on Climate Change (UNFCCC), "Essential Background: Feeling the Heat," UNFCCC Web site, accessed at http://unfccc.int/essential_background/feeling_the_heat/items/2914.php (May 28, 2009).
13. United Nations, *United Nations Framework Convention on Climate Change* (New York, 1992), 2, accessed at http://unfccc.int/resource/docs/convkp/conveng.pdf.
14. The Kyoto Protocol focuses on six greenhouse gases: carbon dioxide, methane, nitrous oxide, hydrofluorocarbons, perfluorocarbons and sulfur hexafluoride.
15. United Nations Framework Convention on Climate Change (UNFCCC), "Kyoto Protocol," UNFCCC Web site, accessed at http://unfccc.int/kyoto_protocol/items/2830.php (May 28, 2009).

16. Senate Resolution 98 (Report No. 105-54), 105th Cong., 1st sess. (July 25, 1997), accessed at http://frwebgate.access.gpo.gov/cgi-bin/getdoc.cgi ?dbname=105_cong_bills&docid=f:sr98ats.txt.pdf.

17. United Nations Framework Convention on Climate Change (UNFCCC), "Kyoto Protocol: Mechanisms; Emissions Trading," UNFCCC Web site, accessed at http://unfccc.int/kyoto_protocol/mechanisms/emissions_ trading/items/2731.php. All of these allowances or credits are equal to 1 metric ton of CO_2eq. The United Nations tracks these allowances and offsets under the following categories:
    - A nation's annual emission allowances are called Assigned Amount Units (AAUs).
    - Emission reduction units (ERUs) are generated by a Joint Implementation project.
    - A certified emission reduction (CER) is generated from a Clean Development project.
    - A removal unit (RMU) is based on land use, land-use change, and reforestation practices.

18. David Adam, "Analysis: Has the Kyoto Protocol Worked?" *Guardian,* December 8, 2008, accessed at http://www.guardian.co.uk/environment/2008/ dec/08/kyoto-poznan-environment-emissions-carbon.

19. Robert Engelmann, "Sealing the Deal to Save the Climate," in *State of the World 2009: Into a Warming World* (New York: Norton, 2009), 177–79.

20. United Nations Framework Convention on Climate Change, "Decision 1/CP.13: Bali Action Plan," in *Report of the Conference of the Parties on its Thirteenth Session, Held in Bali from 3 to 15 December 2007* (March 14, 2008), 3, accessed at http://unfccc.int/resource/docs/2007/cop13/eng/06a01 .pdf#page=3.

21. United Nations Framework Convention on Climate Change, Ad Hoc Working Group on Long-Term Cooperative Action, 6th sess., "Negotiating Text," FCCC/AWGLCA/2009/8 (May 19, 2009), accessed at http://unfccc.int/ resource/docs/2009/awglca6/eng/08.pdf.

22. Ibid., 8.

23. Ibid., 9.

24. Murray Sheard, "Fair Weather: Who Should Pay for Climate Change Mitigation?" *Stimulus* 15, no. 4 (November 2007): 35, accessed at http://www .stimulus.org.nz/index_files/STIM%2015_4%20Sheard.pdf.

25. Ad Hoc Working Group, "Negotiating Text," 9.

26. Lisa Friedman, "Negotiations: Stern Takes a Cautious but Optimistic Approach to Climate Talks," *ClimateWire,* April 6, 2009, accessed at http:// www.eenews.net/climatewire/2009/04/06/archive/1?terms=stern+takes+a+ cautious.

27. Environmental Protection Agency, "Executive Summary," in *Inventory of U.S. Greenhouse Gas Emissions and Sinks: 1990–2007,* EPA 430-R-09-004 (Washington, D.C.: EPA, April 2009), 3, accessed at http://epa.gov/climate change/emissions/downloads09/ExecutiveSummary.pdf.

28. Elisabeth Rosenthal, "At U.N. Talks on Climate, Plans by U.S. Raise

Qualms," *New York Times,* April 9, 2009, accessed at http://www.nytimes
.com/2009/04/09/world/09climate.html.

29. Arthur Max, "U.N. Official Seeks G-8 Cash for Climate Change Fund," *San
    Francisco Chronicle,* July 6, 2009, accessed at http://www.sfgate.com/cgi-bin/
    article.cgi?f=/n/a/2009/07/05/international/ i170143D10.DTL.

30. Lisa Friedman, "Finance: Still No Money for Developing Nations, New G-20
    Documents Show, *Climatewire,* September 9, 2009, accessed at http://www
    .eenews.net/climatewire/2009/09/11/.

31. Reuters, "EU Considers Billions for Poor before Climate Talks," *New York
    Times,* July 25, 2009, accessed at http://www.nytimes.com/reuters/2009/07
    /25/world/international-us-eu-climate-aid.html.

32. Lisa Friedman, "Finance: Still No Money for Developing Nations, New G-20
    Documents Show, *Climatewire,* September 9, 2009, accessed at http://www
    .eenews.net/climatewire/2009/09/11/.

33. Ambika Chawla, "Government Proposals for Climate Change Mitigation,
    Adaptation, and Technology Transfer," in *State of the World 2009,* 182–83.

34. Lisa Friedman, "Nations: Climate Funding Is Entitlement, Not Aid India
    Says," *ClimateWire,* February 17, 2009, accessed at http://www.eenews.net/
    climatewire/2009/02/17/4/.

35. Ambika Chawla, "Government Proposals for Climate Change Mitigation,
    Adaptation, and Technology Transfer," in *State of the World 2009,* box 6-2,
    pp. 182–83.

36. Lisa Friedman, "Nations: World Leaders Say Poor Countries Need Urgent
    Aid," *ClimateWire,* June 8, 2009, accessed at http://www.eenews.net/
    climatewire/2009/06/08/4/.

37. George Zachariah, "Musings on Climate Justice: A Subaltern Perspective,"
    J. Luth. Ethics 9, no. 4 (April 2009), accessed at http://www.elca.org/What-
    We-Believe/Social-Issues/Journal-of-Lutheran-Ethics/Issues/April-2009/
    Musings-on-Climate-Justice.aspx.

38. Environmental Defense Fund (EDF), "The Cap and Trade Success Story,"
    Our Work page, EDF Web site (May 26, 2009), accessed at http://www
    .edf.org/page.cfm?tagID=1085. See also Environmental Protection Agency
    (EPA), "Cap and Trade," EPA Web site, accessed at http://www.epa.gov/
    captrade/ (July 11, 2009).

39. A. Denny Ellerman and Paul l. Joskow, *The European Union's Emissions
    Trading System in Perspective* (Arlington, Va.: Pew Center on Global Climate
    Change, May 2008), accessed at http://www.pewclimate.org/docUploads/
    EU-ETS-In-Perspective-Report.pdf.

40. Nathanial Gronewold, "Nations: In the Debate over International Carbon
    Trading, Going Slowly May Be Good," *ClimateWire,* June 15, 2009, accessed
    at http://www.eenews.net/climatewire/2009/06/15/3/.

41. Gary Gardner, "Equity and the Response to a Changing Climate," in *State of
    the World 2009,* box 6-1, pp. 170–71.

42. See the EcoEquity website, http://www.ecoequity.org.

43. Paul Baer, Tom Athanasiou, and Sivan Kartha, *The Greenhouse Development
    Rights Framework: The Right to Development in a Climate Constrained World,*

2nd ed. (Berlin: Heinrich Böll Foundation, November 2008), accessed at http://www.ecoequity.org/docs/TheGDRsFramework.pdf.

44. See the Christian Aid website, http://www.christian-aid.org.uk/.

45. See Heinrich Böll Foundation North America, "Overview," http://www.boell.org/overview.asp.

46. World Council of Churches, "Statement on the 10th Anniversary of the Kyoto Protocol" (September 28, 2007), accessed at http://www.oikoumene.org/en/resources/documents/executive-committee/etchmiadzin-september-2007/28-09-07-statement-on-the-10th-anniversary-of-the-kyoto-protocol.html.

Michael Northcott, the author of *A Moral Climate: The Ethics of Global Warming* (Maryknoll: Orbis, 2007), discourages appeals to rights language in Christian responses to climate change. In a recent unpublished paper prepared for a consultation on climate change sponsored by the Lutheran World Federation, Northcott argues on pragmatic grounds that "it is not the poor or the weak but the powerful who have most successfully mobilized rights claims in the law courts and economic markets." Moreover, Northcott claims, "The assertion of such rights lacks any theological or confessional base in the historic documents of the Christian tradition. More worryingly rights assertions are a foundational source of violence in the history of the modern world." Northcott argues that throughout Christian history, "the ways in which [Christian] communities exercise moral claims on one another have not traditionally been through the language of rights arising from rights or property claims but from obligations recognized in the law of love."

Are appeals to human rights grounded in the norm of justice incompatible with or less important than moral obligations rooted in the norm of love? This is a false dichotomy. Rights, in part, specify the content of our moral obligations to others and thus are an invaluable ethical category, particularly for grounding the moral and legal worth of all forms of life. Obligations imply that we owe something to others, and at least, what we owe them are their rights. The problem with a benevolence- and duties-based approach is that duties arise from within, and rights can only be requested, whereas in a justice- and rights-based approach, duties arise in response to those who are demanding their rights. The fact that rights-based appeals have been abused by the powerful does not change the fact that the concept of rights has been at the heart of successful attempts to achieve greater measures of freedom and equality around the world. While a rights-based approach to ethics can accentuate individualism and undermine community, this would be a distorted understanding of the mutual rights *and responsibilities* of members of a democratic society. Properly understood, a rights-based approach has the best potential for holding together the twin objectives of protecting individuals and the common good, because the purpose of rights is to foster relationality rather than undermine it.

I am indebted here to James A. Nash, who developed a rights-based approach to environmental ethics in his seminal volume, *Loving Nature: Ecological Integrity and Christian Responsibility* (Nashville: Abingdon, 1991).

47. Baer et al., *The Greenhouse Development Rights Framework,* 13.

48. Ibid., 28.

49. Ibid., 43.

50. Ibid., 45.

51. Ibid., 53.

52. Ibid., 10.

53. Baer et al., "Executive Summary," in *The Greenhouse Development Rights Framework,* table ES-1, p. 4. Gross domestic product is measured in U.S. dollars and in relation to purchasing power parity. The income categories (high, middle, and low income) are based on World Bank definitions.

54. See *United Nations Framework Convention on Climate Change* at http://unfccc.int/resource/docs/convkp/conveng.pdf.

55. Baer et al., "Executive Summary," in *The Greenhouse Development Rights Framework,* 4.

56. "United States federal budget," Wikipedia, accessed at http://en.wikipedia.org/wiki/United_States_federal_budget (May 29, 2009).

57. U.S. Department of State, Bureau of Public Affairs, "2008 U.S. Official Development Assistance," news release, March 30, 2009, accessed at http://www.state.gov/r/pa/prs/ps/2009/03/120982.htm.

58. Baer et al., "Executive Summary," in *The Greenhouse Development Rights Framework,* 4–5.

59. Ibid., 6.

5.   U.S. Climate Policy

1. Quoted in "Seventeen Major Economies Pledge to Set Greenhouse Gas Limit by December," *Environmental News Service,* July 9, 2009, accessed at http://www.ens-newswire.com/ens/jul2009/2009-07-09-01.asp.

2. Quoted in "Battle against Climate Change Is Like Fighting the Nazis: Al Gore Urges World Leaders to Unite," *Mail Online* (London), July 8, 2009, accessed at http://www.dailymail.co.uk/news/article-1198150/Battle-climate-change-like-fighting-Nazis-Al-Gore-urges-world-leaders-unite.html.

3. J. Andrew Hoerner and Nia Robinson, *A Climate of Change: African Americans, Global Warming, and a Just Climate Policy for the U.S.* (Oakland, Calif.: Environmental Justice and Climate Change Initiative, July 2008), accessed at http://www.ejcc.org/climateofchange.pdf.

4. See Redefining Progress, "About Redefining Progress," http://www.rprogress.org/about_us/about_us.htm.

5. Hoerner and Robinson, *A Climate of Change,* 1.

6. Ibid., 45–46.

7. Ibid. The authors point out that cap-and-trade systems require the long and complex task of determining baseline emission levels for thousands of polluters and the costly task of verifying emission reductions at thousands of locations. They also worry that powerful corporations will figure out how to game the system in terms of setting and revising the initial emissions cap.

Finally, the report emphasizes that cap-and-trade approaches can produce emission "hot spots" where emissions like mercury are concentrated disproportionately in communities of color.

8. Ibid., 48.

9. Ibid., 49.

10. Ibid., 51.

11. Ibid., 50.

12. James Hansen, testimony before U.S. Senate Committee on Energy and Natural Resources, Washington, D.C., June 23, 1988. Cited in Linda Starke, ed., *State of the World 2009: Into a Warming World* (New York: Norton, 2009), 6.

13. Robert F. Kennedy Jr., "Bush Backpedals on Environment," *Seattle Post-Intelligencer,* August 4, 2004, accessed at http://www.seattlepi.com/opinion/184710_kennedy04.html.

14. U.S. Conference of Mayors, "About the Mayors Climate Protection Center," accessed at http://usmayors.org/climateprotection/about.htm (May 31, 2009). I am proud that Decorah's mayor, Don Arendt, has signed the agreement.

15. See Ryan Wiser and Galen Barbose, *Renewables Portfolio Standards in the United States: A Status Report with Data through 2007* (Berkeley, Calif.: Lawrence Berkeley National Laboratory, April 2008), accessed at http://eetd.lbl.gov/ea/ems/reports/lbnl-154e-revised.pdf.

16. Obama for America, "Barack Obama's Plan to Make America a Global Energy Leader," accessed at http://obama.3cdn.net/4465b108758abf7a42_a3jmvyfa5.pdf (May 31, 2009).

17. Christa Marshall, "Finance: A Budget Plan That Stimulates a 'Cap-and-Tax' Climate Debate," *ClimateWire,* February 27, 2009, accessed at http://www.eenews.net/climatewire/2009/02/27/archive/3?terms=obama+auction+allowances.

18. John M. Broder, "E.PA. Clears Way for Greenhouse Gas Rules," *New York Times,* April 17, 2009, accessed at http://www.nytimes.com/2009/04/18/science/earth/18endanger.html?scp=1&sq=epa%20carbon%20dioxide%20april&st=cse.

19. Accessed at http://energycommerce.house.gov/Press_111/20090331/acesa_discussiondraft.pdf (May 31, 2009).

20. Pew Center on Global Climate Change, "At a Glance: American Clean Energy and Security Act of 2009," accessed at http://www.pewclimate.org/docUploads/Waxman-Markey-short-summary-revised-June26.pdf (July 11, 2009).

21. "Text of H.R. 2454: American Clean Energy and Security Act of 2009," 111th Cong., July 7, 2009, *GovTrack.us*, accessed at http://www.govtrack.us/congress/billtext.xpd?bill=h111-2454 (July 11, 2009).

22. *Darren Samuelsohn, Ben Geman, and Christa Marshall,* "U.S. Climate Debate: The House Climate/Energy Bill," Reports page, E&E Publishing, July 16, 2009, accessed at http://www.eenews.net/special_reports/us_climate_debate/hr2454/ (September 11, 2009).

23. Paul Komor, *Wind and Solar Electricity: Challenges and Opportunities,* Solutions White Paper Series (Arlington, Va.: Pew Center on Global Climate

Change, June 2009), 3, accessed at http://www.pewclimate.org/docUploads/wind-solar-electricity-report.pdf.

24. Congressional Budget Office, "H.R. 2454: American Clean Energy and Security Act of 2009," cost estimate, Washington, DC, June 5, 2009, accessed at http://www.cbo.gov/ftpdocs/102xx/doc10262/hr2454.pdf.

25. Pew Center, "At a Glance: American Clean Energy and Security Act."

26. Environmental Protection Agency, *Inventory of U.S. Greenhouse Gas Emissions and Sinks: 1990–2007,* EPA 430-R-09-004 (Washington, D.C.: EPA, April 2009), 2-27, accessed at http://epa.gov/climatechange/emissions/downloads09/InventoryUSGhG1990-2007.pdf. See figure 4.3 in the previous chapter.

27. Ibid., table ES-3, pp. ES4–ES6. Gross U.S. GHG emissions totaled 7.1 billion MT in 2005. A 17 percent reduction of 2005 levels (1.2 billion MT) means U.S. GHG emissions would be capped at 5.9 billion MT in 2020. U.S. GHG emissions totaled 6.1 billion MT in 1990. The 2020 cap of 5.9 billion MT is 3.3 percent less than the 6.1 million MT of U.S. GHG emissions in 1990. The original proposal to reduce emissions to 20 percent below 2005 levels would have produced a reduction to 6.85 percent below 1990 levels, which is almost equivalent to the 7 percent U.S. obligation under the Kyoto Protocol.

28. Yang Jun and Fei Liena, "More Needs to Be Done for U.S. to Fight Climate Change," *China View,* June 29, 2009, accessed at http://news.xinhuanet.com/english/2009-06/29/content_11616354.htm.

29. Yvo de Boer, address to Spanish Parliament Commission for Climate Change, Madrid, June 25, 2009, accessed at UNFCCC Web site, http://unfccc.int/files/press/news_room/statements/application/pdf/090625_speech_madrid.pdf.

30. Pew Center, "At a Glance: American Clean Energy and Security Act."

31. Samuelsohn et al., "U.S. Climate Debate."

32. "Text of H.R. 2454," *GovTrack.us,* 901.

33. Samuelsohn et al., "U.S. Climate Debate."

34. Pew Center on Global Climate Change, "Eight Myths about the Waxman-Markey Clean Energy Bill," Climate Policy Memo 2 (Arlington, Va., June 2009), 1, accessed at http://www.pewclimate.org/docUploads/Policy-Memo-2-8-Myths-July09.pdf.

35. Samuelsohn et al., "U.S. Climate Debate."

36. "Text of H.R. 2454," *GovTrack.us,* 780.

37. Ibid.

38. Ibid., 781.

39. Ibid., 1386–1427. See also Pew Center, "At a Glance: American Clean Energy and Security Act."

40. Environmental Protection Agency, *Inventory of U.S. Greenhouse Gas Emissions and Sinks,* ES-6. More exactly, the EPA lists U.S. GHG emissions in 2007 as 7,150.1 million MT of CO_2eq, which is equivalent to 7.15 billion MT or 7.15 gigatonnes (Gt) of CO_2eq.

41. Pew Center, "At a Glance: American Clean Energy and Security Act."

42. "Text of H.R. 2454," *GovTrack.us,* 741.

43. Anne C. Mulkern, "Lobbyists Battle over Escape Hatch on Carbon Penalties,"

Greenwire, June 12, 2009, accessed at http://www.eenews.net/Greenwire /2009/ 06/12/2/.

44. "Text of H.R. 2454," *GovTrack.us,* 785–92, 1386–90.

45. National Commission on Energy Policy, "Forging the Climate Consensus: The Case for Action," June 2009, accessed at http://energycommission.org/ ht/a/GetDocumentAction/i/10643.

46. Environmental Protection Agency, "EPA Analysis of the American Clean Energy and Security Act of 2009: H.R. 2454 in the 111th Congress," (EPA Office of Atmospheric Programs, June 23, 2009), slide 3, accessed at http:// www.epa.gov/climatechange/economics/pdfs/HR2454_Analysis.pdf.

47. Darren Samuelsohn, "Climate: House Allocation Formula 'Can't Hold' in Senate—Harkin," *E&E News PM,* July 21, 2009, accessed at http://www .eenews.net/eenewspm/2009/07/21/1/.

48. "Senate Climate Debate: The 60-Vote Climb," *Environment & Energy Daily,* updated September 11, 2009, accessed at http://www.eenews.net/eed/ documents/climate_debate_senate.pdf.

6.   Climate Justice Applied

1. Luther College, "Mission Statement," accessed September 10, 2009 at http:// www.luther.edu/about/mission/index.html.

2. ACUPCC, "About the American College and University Presidents' Climate Commitment," accessed September 10, 2009 at http://www.presidents climatecommitment.org/html/about.php.

3. See ACUPCC, "ACUPCC Reporting System," http://www.aashe.org/pcc/ reports.

4. U.S. Green Building Council, "LEED Rating Systems," accessed at http:// www.usgbc.org/DisplayPage.aspx?CMSPageID=222.

5. AWEA, "U.S. Wind Energy Projects," accessed at http://awea.org/projects/ (updated June 27, 2009).

6. Carleton College, "Turbine Monthly and Yearly Production," accessed at http://apps.carleton.edu/campus/sustainability/resources/utilities_data/ turbine_data/turbine_monthly/.

7. See North Carolina Solar Center (NCSC), "Renewable Energy Production Incentive (REPI)," Database of State Incentives for Renewables and Efficiency (DSIRE), accessed at http://www.dsireusa.org/incentives/incentive .cfm?Incentive_Code=US33F&re=1&ee=0.

8. See NCSC, "Clean Renewable Energy Bonds (CREBs)," DSIRE, accessed at http://www.dsireusa.org/incentives/incentive.cfm?Incentive_Code=US45F &re=1&ee=0.

9. See NCSC, "Renewable Electricity Production Tax Credit (PTC)," DSIRE, accessed   at   http://www.dsireusa.org/incentives/incentive.cfm?Incentive_ Code=US13F&re=1&ee=0.

10. For a comprehensive list of federal incentives, see NCSC, "Federal Incentives/Policies for Renewables and Efficiency," DSIRE, http://www.dsireusa

.org/incentives/index.cfm?state=us&re=1&EE=0http://www.dsireusa.org/incentives/incentive.cfm?Incentive_Code=US02F&re=1&ee=0. Unfortunately, the federal Department of the Treasury recently ruled that projects involving not-for-profit investors are not eligible for the new Section 1603 grants, which are to be issued by the Treasury Department in lieu of the federal PTC or ITC.

11. See U.S. Department of the Treasury, "American Recovery and Reinvestment Act: Payments for Specified Energy Property in Lieu of Tax Credits," accessed at http://www.ustreas.gov/recovery/1603.shtml (July 27, 2009).

12. Just before this book went to press we learned that LCWEP was awarded a $500,000 grant and a $1.3 million guaranteed loan by the U.S. Department of Agriculture's Rural Energy for American Program (REAP). LCWEP was eligible to apply for funding through this program because it is a rural, small business as defined by the Small Business Administration. REAP provides funds for feasibility studies, energy audits, energy efficiency, and renewable energy projects. More information is available at http://www.rurdev.usda.gov/rbs/farmbill/index.html. For more information on Luther's financing options, see http://www.aashe.org/blog/financing-large-wind-turbine-project-luther-college-experience.

13. Katherine Ling, "Electricity: New Senate Bill Backs Small-Scale Renewable Energy," *E&E News PM,* May 6, 2009, accessed at http://www.eenews.net/eenewspm/2009/05/06/archive/4.

14. Federal Energy Regulatory Commission, "Order Conditionally Accepting Tariff Revisions Addressing Queue Reform," 124 FERC ¶ 61,183 (August 25, 2008), p. 5, accessed at http://www.ferc.gov/EventCalendar/Files/20080825213947-ER08-1169-000.pdf.

15. See National Association of State Departments of Agriculture, "Biomass Crop Assistance Program (BCAP) Established," *NASDA News,* June 20, 2008, http://www.nasda.org/cms/7197/9060/16588/16614.aspx.

Glossary

Adaptation: Policy changes and different land use practices to deal with climate threats and risks. Examples include crop shifting to deal with changing weather conditions, sea wall construction and other flood prevention measures, and developing medicines and preventive behaviors to deal with spreading diseases.

Additionality: Achieved by projects that store more carbon or reduce greenhouse gas emissions by a greater amount than the baseline amount that would have been stored or emitted in the absence of the project. For example, projects under the Kyoto Protocol's Clean Development Mechanism and Joint Implementation must show that any emissions reductions are in addition to what would have occurred without the project.

Alternative Energy Options: Investments in energy efficiency and renewable energy technologies offer alternative ways to supply or produce energy in contrast to fossil fuels and nuclear power, the conventional energy sources in the United States.

American Clean Energy and Security Act (ACESA): The U.S. House of Representatives passed the American Clean Energy and Security Act of 2009, H.R. 2454, on June 26, 2009, by a vote of 219 to 212. This comprehensive national climate and energy legislation would establish an economy-wide, greenhouse gas (GHG) cap-and-trade system and critical complementary measures to help address climate change and build a clean energy economy.

American College and University Presidents' Climate Commitment (ACUPCC): A high-visibility effort to address global warming by garnering institutional commitments to neutralize greenhouse gas emissions, and to accelerate the research and educational efforts of higher education to equip society to re-stabilize the earth's climate. Presidents from 650 colleges and universities are currently signatories.

Annex Countries: Under the United Nations Framework Convention on Climate Change, Annex 1 countries include industrial or industrializing countries that agreed to reduce their greenhouse gas emissions to 1990 levels collectively. Annex 2 countries are industrial countries that also committed to provide technology, financial assistance, and other resources to developing countries.

Anthropogenic: Caused by human behaviors. The term is used in the context of global climate change to refer to greenhouse gas emissions that are the result of human activities, as well as other potentially climate-altering activities, such as deforestation.

Bali Action Plan: The United Nations Climate Change Conference that took place in Bali, Indonesia, in December 2007 adopted the Bali Action Plan (also known as the Bali Roadmap) as a two-year process to develop an international climate treaty to replace the Kyoto Protocol. The Bali Action Plan was designed to culminate in 2009 at the United Nations Climate Change Conference in Copenhagen, Denmark.

Biodiesel: A fuel typically made from soybean, canola, or other vegetable oils that can serve as a substitute for petroleum-derived diesel fuel or distillate fuel oil.

Biofuels: Liquid fuels and blending components produced from biomass (plant) feedstocks, used primarily for transportation. See *Biodiesel* and *Ethanol*.

Biomass Energy: A renewable energy source consisting of organic materials that can be burned or otherwise used as a source of fuel.

Biomass Waste Energy: Organic material of biological origin that is a byproduct or a discarded product. Biomass waste includes municipal solid waste from biogenic sources, landfill gas, sludge waste, agricultural crop byproducts, straw, and other biomass solids, liquids, and gases. It excludes wood and wood-derived fuels, biofuels feedstock, biodiesel, and fuel ethanol.

Cap and Trade: An approach to limiting and reducing greenhouse gas emissions that harnesses the power of markets to achieve this policy goal in a cost-effective manner. Once a maximum emissions level (a cap) is determined, annual emission allowances are distributed to emitters in an amount that is equal to the cap. Companies or governmental jurisdictions can sell or trade the emission allowances to parties whose permits are insufficient to cover their full emissions.

Carbon Capture and Storage (CCS): A process whereby carbon dioxide is separated and captured during energy production or other industrial processes and stored or sequestered rather than released into the atmosphere. Also known as carbon capture and sequestration.

Carbon Dioxide (CO_2): A naturally occurring gas that is a product of fossil-fuel combustion as well as other processes. It traps heat (infrared energy) radiated by the Earth into the atmosphere and thereby contributes to the potential for global warming. The global warming potential (GWP) of other greenhouse gases is measured in relation to carbon dioxide, which by international scientific convention is assigned a value of one.

Carbon Dioxide Equivalent (CO_2eq): The amount of carbon dioxide by weight emitted into the atmosphere that would produce the same estimated radiative forcing as a given weight of another radiatively active gas. Carbon dioxide equivalents are computed by multiplying the weight of the gas being measured (for example, methane) by its estimated global warming potential (which is 21 for methane).

Carbon Tax: A tax levied on carbon dioxide emissions to reduce the total amount of emissions by setting a price on pollution. A carbon tax can be used independently or in conjunction with a cap-and-trade approach. The tax revenues can be used to provide cost relief to consumers, to promote research and development, and to subsidize renewable energy and energy efficiency investments.

Clean Coal Technology: Any technology deployed at a new or existing coal-fueled facility that will achieve significant reductions in the emission of carbon dioxide, sulfur dioxide, or nitrogen oxides. Technologies include chemically washing minerals and impurities from coal, gasification, treating the flue gases with steam to remove sulfur dioxide, and carbon capture and storage technologies to sequester carbon dioxide.

Clean Development Mechanism (CDM): Allows a country with an emission-reduction or emission-limitation commitment under the Kyoto Protocol to implement an emission-reduction project in developing countries. Such projects can earn saleable certified emission reduction (CER) credits, each equivalent to one metric ton of carbon dioxide, which can be counted towards meeting Kyoto targets.

Climate Change: A term used to refer to all forms of climatic inconsistency but especially to significant change from one prevailing climatic condition to another.

In some cases, "climate change" has been used synonymously with the term "global warming"; scientists, however, tend to use the term in a wider sense to include natural changes in climate as well as climatic cooling.

Climate Justice: This new and growing area of research focuses on ethical dimensions of climate change as it impacts human communities and the rest of the natural world for present and future generations.

Climate Sensitivity: A measure of the climate system response to increased greenhouse gas concentrations. It is defined as the global average surface warming following a doubling of carbon dioxide concentrations.

Conventional Energy Options: Fossil fuels (coal, oil, and natural gas) together with nuclear power supply over 90 percent of all primary energy consumed in the United States.

Corporate Average Fuel Economy (CAFE): The sales weighted average fuel economy, expressed in miles per gallon (mpg), of a manufacturer's fleet of passenger cars or light trucks with a gross vehicle weight rating (GVWR) of 8,500 lbs. or less, manufactured for sale in the United States, for any given model year. The Energy Policy Conservation Act, enacted into law by Congress in 1975, established CAFE standards for passenger cars and light trucks.

Earth Summit: A term often used to refer to the United Nations Conference on Environment and Development that was held in Rio de Janeiro, Brazil, from June 3 to June 14, 1992. Also known as the Rio Summit.

Ecological Justice (Ecojustice): This new approach to ethics attempts to unite in one broad scope of moral concern the ethical obligations human beings have to present and future generations, as well as to all human and natural communities; it explores the intersections between social ethics and environmental ethics. Four moral norms are key to the ethic: sustainability, sufficiency, participation, and solidarity.

Ecosystem: A system that includes all living organisms (biotic factors) in an area as well as its physical environment (abiotic factors) functioning together as a unit.

Energy: Energy is the capacity of a physical system to perform work. Energy exists in several forms such as heat, kinetic or mechanical energy, light, potential energy, electrical, or other forms. Most of the world's energy comes from fossil fuels that are burned to produce heat that is then used to perform various tasks.

Energy Conservation: Taps the moral virtue of frugality and seeks to reduce energy consumption through behavioral changes in lifestyle practices.

Energy Efficiency: Utilizes available technology to use less energy to produce the same amount of goods and services.

Energy Information Administration (EIA): Established by the U.S. Congress in 1977 as an agency of the Department of Energy to provide policy-neutral data, forecasts, and analyses to promote sound policy making, efficient markets, and public understanding regarding energy and its interaction with the economy and the environment.

Environmental Protection Agency (EPA): Established by the U.S. Congress in 1970 in response to the growing public demand for cleaner water, air, and land. The mission of the EPA is to protect human health and the environment. The EPA leads the nation's environmental science, research, education, and assessment efforts.

Ethanol: A clear, colorless, flammable oxygenated hydrocarbon. Ethanol is typically produced chemically from ethylene, or biologically from fermentation of various sugars from carbohydrates found in agricultural crops and cellulosic residues from crops or wood. It is used in the United States as a gasoline octane enhancer and oxygenate (blended up to 10 percent concentration). Ethanol can be used also in high concentrations (E85) in vehicles designed for its use.

Ethics: Systematic reflection on moral questions that confront individuals and communities.

Evangelical Lutheran Church in America (ELCA): With denominational offices in Chicago, Illinois, the ELCA has approximately five million members in nearly 10,500 congregations across the United States, Puerto Rico, and the Virgin Islands.

Fossil Fuel: An energy source formed in the Earth's crust from decayed organic material. The primary fossil fuels are petroleum, coal, and natural gas.

Geothermal Energy: Hot water and steam extracted from deep beneath the Earth's crust for hot water heating or electricity generation. Geothermal heat pumps utilize the constant temperature of water or soil relatively close to the Earth's crust to provide heating and cooling services.

Global Warming: An increase in the near-surface temperature of the Earth. Global warming has occurred in the distant past as the result of natural influences, but the term is most often used today to refer to the warming that is occurring as a result of increased anthropogenic emissions of greenhouse gases.

Greenhouse Development Rights (GDR): The United Nations Framework Convention on Climate Change states that "parties should protect the climate system for the benefit of present and future generations of humankind, on the basis of equity and in accordance with their common but differentiated responsibilities and respective capabilities." It also states that "parties have a right to, and should, promote sustainable development." The concept of Greenhouse Development Rights safeguards the right to sustainable development while also equitably assigning responsibility for reducing greenhouse gas emissions. Thus, societies or countries below a certain income level are exempted from emission reductions and should work to raise their standard of living.

Greenhouse Gases (GHG): Those gases, such as water vapor, carbon dioxide, nitrous oxide, methane, hydrofluorocarbons (HFCs), perfluorocarbons (PFCs), and sulfur hexafluoride, that are transparent to solar (short-wave) radiation but opaque to long-wave radiation, thus preventing long-wave radiant energy from leaving the Earth's atmosphere. The net "greenhouse effect" is a trapping of absorbed radiation and a tendency to warm the planet's surface.

Hydroelectric Power: The production of electricity from the kinetic energy of falling water. Also called hydropower.

Intergovernmental Panel on Climate Change (IPCC): The leading body for the assessment of climate change, established by the United Nations Environment Programme (UNEP) and the World Meteorological Organization (WMO) to provide the world with a clear scientific view on the current state of climate change and its potential environmental and socio-economic consequences.

Joint Implementation (JI): One of three mechanisms for emissions trading set out in the Kyoto Protocol. Like the Clean Development Mechanism (CDM), it is a mechanism for financing individual projects aimed at reducing GHG emissions. JI credits are created by reducing actual emissions in a project compared to a hypothetical baseline in the future. Only Annex I countries with capped GHG emissions can utilize the Joint Implementation mechanism.

Justice: The proper ordering of things and persons within the world. For Aristotle, justice meant "treating equals equally and unequals unequally." This simple statement hides the complexities of determining exactly who is equal and who is not and the grounds for justifying inequality. In modern interpretations of justice, however, it leads to freedom and equality as measures of justice. It also leads to the concept of equity, which is justice in actual situations where a degree of departure from freedom and equality are permitted in the name of achieving other goods.

Kyoto Protocol: An international agreement linked to the United Nations Framework Convention on Climate Change. The major feature of the Kyoto Protocol is that it sets binding targets for 37 industrialized countries and the European community for reducing greenhouse gas (GHG) emissions. These amount to an average of 5 percent against 1990 levels over the five-year period of 2008–2012.

Marine Energy: An energy source associated with the waves, tides, and currents of the oceans that cover 70 percent of the planet.

Mitigation: Policies and behaviors designed to reduce greenhouse gas emissions and increase carbon sinks.

Offsets: An offset is a financial instrument that represents the reduction, removal, or avoidance of greenhouse gas emissions from a specific project that is used to compensate for greenhouse gas emissions occurring elsewhere. One carbon offset represents the reduction of one metric ton of carbon dioxide or its equivalent in other greenhouse gases.

Parts Per Million (ppm): A way of expressing very dilute concentrations of substances. Just as *percent* means out of a hundred, so *parts per million* means out of a million. Carbon dioxide is usually measured in parts per million. According to the U.S. Mauna Loa Observatory, the atmospheric concentration of carbon dioxide as of August 2009 was 385.92 ppm, an increase of more than 100 ppm since 1750. Some other greenhouse gases are often measured in parts per billion (ppb).

Participation: This ecojustice norm focuses on the respect for and inclusion of all forms of life in human decisions that affect their well-being. Participation is concerned with empowerment and seeks to remove the obstacles to participating in decisions that affect lives.

Photovoltaic Energy: Direct-current electricity generated from sunlight through solid-state semiconductor devices that have no moving parts.

Presbyterian Church (U.S.A.) (PCUSA): With denominational offices in Louisville, Kentucky, the PCUSA has approximately 2.3 million members, more than 10,000 congregations, and 14,000 ordained and active ministers.

Solidarity: This ecojustice norm highlights the communal nature of life in contrast to individualism and encourages individuals and groups to join in common cause with those who are victims of discrimination, abuse, and oppression. Solidarity calls for the powerful to share the plight of the powerless, for the rich to listen to the poor, and for humanity to recognize its fundamental interdependence with the rest of nature.

Sufficiency: This ecojustice norm emphasizes that all forms of life are entitled to share in the goods of creation. Sufficiency emphasizes the meeting of basic needs, sharing, and equity; it repudiates wasteful and harmful consumption.

Surface Temperature (global): An estimate of the average surface air temperature across the globe most commonly expressed as a combination of land and sea temperature. When estimating climate change over time, only abnormal changes to the mean surface temperature—not daily, seasonal, or other common variations—are measured.

Sustainability: This ecojustice norm is defined as the long-range supply of sufficient resources to meet basic human needs and the preservation of intact natural communities. Sustainability expresses a concern for future generations and the planet as a whole, and emphasizes that an acceptable quality of life for present generations must not jeopardize the prospects for future generations.

Technology Transfer: The flow of knowledge, equipment, and resources to help developing nations and other entities adapt to or mitigate climate change.

United Nations Framework Convention on Climate Change (UNFCCC): An international treaty approved at the United Nations Conference on Environment and Development (UNCED), informally known as the Earth Summit, held in Rio de Janeiro, Brazil, June 3–14, 1992. The treaty seeks to stabilize atmospheric greenhouse gas concentrations at a level that will prevent dangerous anthropogenic interference with the climate system.

World Climate Conferences: The World Meteorological Organization (WMO) has sponsored three world climate conferences in Geneva, Switzerland. The First World Climate Conference was held February 12–23, 1979. The second conference was held from October 29 to November 7, 1990. The third conference took place from August 31 to September 4, 2009, and focused on climate predictions and information for decision-making at the seasonal to multi-decadal timescales.

World Council of Churches (WCC): The WCC brings together 349 churches, denominations, and church fellowships in more than 110 countries and territories throughout the world, representing over 560 million Christians and including most of the world's Orthodox churches, scores of Anglican, Baptist, Lutheran, Methodist, and Reformed churches, as well as many United and Independent churches.

Index

Iran, 11, 55–56
Iraq, 10–11, 25, 56–57, 184n33
Isaiah, 27, 33
Israel, 11, 27, 33

Japan, 55–56, 79, 81, 84, 107, 115–16, 132
Jeremiah, 27
Jesus, xiv, 2, 27, 30–34, 36, 110
jet fuel, 98
John Deere Wind Energy, 173
Joint Implementation Mechanism, 116, 123, 126, 216
jubilee legislation, 2, 31
justice, social, 22–24, 130. *See also* climate justice; environmental justice

Kansas, 88
Ki-moon, Ban, 45, 111, 189n2
King, Martin Luther, Jr., 42, 189n25
Kuwait, 11, 56
Kyoto Protocol, 52, 115–18, 123, 126, 129, 138, 141, 146–48, 153, 202n14–15, 203n17–18, 205n46, 208n27, 211, 212, 213, 216
land use
    changes, 13, 18, 96, 203n17
    management, 164
    practices, 21, 110, 152, 211
landfills, 62, 93, 151
landfill gas, 107, 212
Latin America, xi
Lautenberg, Frank, 156
Leadership in Energy and Environmental Design (LEED), 166
Lieberman, Joseph I., 142–43, 156
liquefied natural gas, 61
livestock facilities, 93
lobbyists, 37, 41, 148, 155–56, 208n43
Lorde, Audre, 125
Louisiana, x
love, 23, 25–29, 32–33, 37, 54, 110, 159, 205n46
Low Income Home Energy Assistance Program (LIHEAP), xxii, 8, 140, 184n26

low-income households, U.S., 8, 138, 140
Luther College, xii–xviii, 161–80
Luther College Wind Energy Project, LLC (LCWEP), xxii, 169–71, 176, 210n12
Luther, Martin, xv
Lutheran World Federation, x, xvii, 181n6, 182n9, 205n46
Lutheranism, xiv

Maldives, 124
marine energy, 103–5, 217
Markey, Edward, 143, 148–49, 207n20, 208n34
mass transit, 109
Massachusetts Institute of Technology, 51, 102, 190n16, 191n20, 200n81
McFague, Sallie, 188n17
Menendez, Robert, 172
merchant power plants, 149
mercury pollution, 7, 50, 102, 184n24, 206n7
Metcalf, Gilbert E., 106, 198n48, 201n94
methane, 13, 14, 21, 59, 62, 93, 111–12, 151, 202, 213, 216
methane hydrates, 62
Mexico, 11, 61, 95, 123, 132
Micah, 27, 159
Middle East, xvi, 56, 61
Midwest, U.S., x, 91, 168, 175
migratory bird flyways, 91
militarism, 33
Minnesota, 54, 98, 168–69
Mississippi, 78
Mississippi River, 95
mitigation, national obligations. *See* greenhouse gas emissions
Montana, 157
Montreal Protocol, 120
MOX fuel, mixed uranium and plutonium oxide, xxii, 68–69, 195n87
Multilateral Adaptation Fund, 123

Nash, James, 188n18, 188n21, 205n46

National Academy of Sciences, 21, 97,
    186n65
National Commission on Energy Pol-
    icy, 153, 209n45
National Council of Churches of Christ,
    xxii, 25, 188n14
    Eco-Justice Program, 25, 188n14
National Petroleum Council, 10,
    185n35, 185n40
national renewable electricity standard
    (RES), xxiii, 90, 143
natural gas, xii, 3, 38, 46–48, 52, 59–62,
    69, 165, 168, 214–15
    consumption, U.S., 60
    distributors and utilities, U.S.,
        144, 146, 149–50
    Luther College consumption,
        168, 173–75, 179
    power plants, 64, 87–89
    prices, U.S., 106
    production, U.S., 53, 61
    ratepayers, U.S., 156
    shale gas, U.S., 60
    subsidies, U.S., 89
    supplies, 11, 184n32, 189n5,
        191n24, 192n53–54,
        193n55–56
Natural Gas Supply Association, 60,
    192n52
Natural Resources Defense Council, 60
net metering, 171–72
Netherlands Environmental Assess-
    ment Agency, 5, 183n13
New York, 78
New Zealand, 116
Nickels, Greg, 141
Niger Delta, 11, 185n39
Nigeria, 11, 57, 185n39
nitrogen fertilizer, 95
nitrogen oxides, 7, 12, 213
nitrogen trifluoride, xxii, 146
nitrous oxide, xxii, 13, 14, 111–12,
    202n14, 216
Nixon, Richard M., 56, 79
North Dakota, 88
Northcott, Michael, 183n14, 205n46
Northeast, U.S., 91, 99, 156

Norway, xi, 123
nuclear fission, 64
nuclear generating units, U.S., 63
nuclear power, xii, xv, 46–48, 62–69, 89,
    105, 107, 109, 154, 189n5, 191n24,
    211, 214
    spent nuclear fuel, 64–66, 108,
        193n63
    spent nuclear fuel, dry-cask
        storage, 66, 169
    subsidies, 62
nuclear power plant reactors, 59, 62,
    64–65, 68–69, 89, 100, 102–3, 108,
    193n59
nuclear proliferation, 68, 109
Nuclear Regulatory Commission
    (NRC), xii, 62, 64, 68, 194n84
nuclear waste. See also Yucca Mountain;
    radioactive waste
    high level, 64–65, 67, 69, 169
    interim storage facility, 194n72
    reprocessing, 64, 68
nuclear war, 24
Nuclear Waste Policy Act, 65
nuclear weapons, 109

Obama, Barack H., 8, 11, 51–52, 66, 81,
    89, 107, 121, 125, 137, 142, 157–
    58, 185n37, 190n13, 207n16
obligation, moral, 5, 162, 205n46
oceans, 57, 103, 217
    salinity, 13
    temperatures, 13
official development assistance (ODA),
    xxii, 123, 133, 135
offsets, greenhouse gas emissions, 97,
    151, 217
    Clean Development Mechanism,
        138, 152
    domestic greenhouse gas, U.S.,
        151–56
    European Union Emission
        Trading System, 115–17
    international greenhouse gas,
        118, 124–27, 152–54, 203n17
    Luther College, 166, 168, 170,
        176–79

offshore wind resource, 76, 89
oil, xii, 3, 11, 38, 46–48, 52–59, 61–62,
    69, 98, 107, 109, 214. *See also*
    petroleum
    consumption, U.S., 51, 53, 58,
        192n51
    demand, global, 8
    exporting nations, 11, 139
    foreign dependency, U.S., 50, 54,
        56–57
    imports, U.S., 8, 10–11, 52, 79,
        81, 185n38
    industry, 10, 51
    Luther College, fuel oil, 165,
        173
    peak global, 54–55, 58, 192n43
    prices, 11, 77, 79
    production, U.S., 8, 53, 54
    production, global, 54–55, 58
    refiners, 146, 149, 154
    reserves, 10–11, 54, 184n32,
        191n31–32, 192n33
    spills, 12
    subsidies, 10, 89
ozone, 7, 111
ozone layer, 120
Pachauri, Rajendra, 111, 117
Pacific Northwest, U.S., 99, 156
paleoclimate evidence, 20
palm oil, 95, 98
participation, norm of, xii–xiii, 24–26,
    28, 30, 33–35, 37–39, 41, 44,
    46, 57, 59, 75–76, 82, 86–87, 92,
    98–99, 103, 119, 135, 145, 158,
    187n10, 214, 217
particulate matter, 6–7, 12, 183n19
Paul, 2, 27–28, 30–32, 34, 36
peace, 3, 21, 24–25, 37, 39, 45–46,
    54–55, 58, 61, 75–76, 83, 87, 98,
    105
Pennsylvania, 157
perfluorocarbons, 112, 202n14, 216
permafrost, 21, 109, 186n61
Persian Gulf, 56–57
petroleum, 7, 52–56, 59, 189n5, 215.
    See also oil
    demand, U.S., 96

fuels, 8, 12, 58, 97
    imports, 185n38
    production and consumption,
        U.S., 53
    products, 58–59
Pew Center on Global Climate Change,
    51, 72, 150, 190n10, 190n18,
    191n20, 195n3, 201n96, 204n39,
    207n20, 208n34
Philippines, 121
photovoltaic (PV) solar, xxii, 83–87,
    104, 217
    Luther College, 177
Pickens, T. Boone, 173
platinum, 105
plutonium, 64, 68–69, 195n87
Polluter Pays Principle, 128–30, 187n10
population
    growth, 24
    India, 131
    policy, xix
    United States, 61
    world, 6, 16
poverty, 6, 8, 22, 24, 28, 31, 34, 37, 41,
    133, 135
power grid, U.S., 87, 108
power purchase agreement (PPA), xxii,
    170
prairie restoration, 162
precipitation, x, 13, 16–17
Presbyterian Church, (U.S.A.), xii, xvi–
    xvii, xxii, 25, 217
    Advisory Committee on Social
        Witness Policy, xvi–xvii, xxi
    Theological Educators for Presby-
        terian Social Witness, xvii
present generations, 21, 29, 37, 42, 50,
    158, 218
Private Fuel Storage, LLC, 66
prophets, biblical, 27, 33
public transportation, U.S., 106, 109
Puget Sound, 104
Putin, Vladmir, 57

radioactive waste, 64–65, 193n63, 193n67,
    194n72. *See also* nuclear waste
rapeseed, 95

Rasmussen, Larry, v, xvii, xix, 187n2
Reagan, Ronald, 56
realism, xvi, 5, 124, 133
recession, global, 60, 89, 185n51
REDD, reducing emissions by preventing deforestation and forest degradation, xxii, 117
Redefining Progress, 137, 206n4
Reed, Brandon, xviii
Reformation, 176
refrigerants, 164
renewability guideline, 38–39, 46, 75, 86, 91, 99
renewable electricity standard (RES), xxiii, 90, 143–44, 198n50
renewable energy, 48, 52, 62, 70–71, 73, 75, 83–110, 126, 142, 189n5, 211–13
  incentives and mandates, 72, 87, 89–90, 99, 106–7, 143, 169–70, 177, 197n34, 199n65, 209n7–10
  Luther College, 167–78
  market barriers, 108
  research and development, U.S., 89, 106, 150, 213
  share of total U.S. primary energy consumption, 72
  sources, 3, 71, 74, 76, 144
  subsidies, U.S., 90, 94, 199n54
  total production and major sources, U.S., 100
Renewable Energy Certificates (REC), xxii, 170
Renewable Energy Production Incentive (REPI), xxii, 169, 209n7
Renewable Energy Production Tax Credit (PTC), xxii, 89, 169
Renewable Fuels Standard (RFS), xxiii, 96–97, 108
renewables portfolio standard (RPS), xxiii, 90, 207n15
residential sector, U.S., 47, 78, 83, 86, 108, 156
responsibility
  historical, 42, 44, 119–21, 124, 135, 145, 148, 154, 157
  moral, 5, 42, 135

Responsibility-Capacity Index (RCI), 129–35
Reuther, Rosemary Radford, 188n17
right to development, 41, 129, 130, 135
righteousness, 23, 27, 30–31
risk guideline, 39, 46, 65, 67–68, 75, 83, 86, 92, 103
Robinson, Nia, 138–39, 206n3
Rocky Mountain Institute (RMI), xxiii, 78, 167
Rossing, Barbara, xvii
Russia, 5, 11, 57, 61, 64, 115, 132, 185n42, 191n31

sacraments, 29
Safe Drinking Water Act, 61
Sanders, Bernie, 156, 172
Saudi Arabia, 11, 56–57
sea ice, x, 17, 20
sea levels, rising, x, xi, 3, 16–18, 19, 20, 186n60
  global mean, 13, 15
sewage treatment plants, 93, 98, 200n76
Skull Valley Goshute Indian Reservation, 66, 194n74
smog, 7, 58
Snowe, Olympia, 156
Society of Christian Ethics, xvii
soil erosion, 76, 95
solar energy, 3, 37, 72, 83–87, 91, 165
solidarity norm, xii–xiii, 5, 24–26, 28, 35–39, 41–42, 44, 46, 50, 52, 58–59, 61, 65, 67, 69, 75, 82, 86, 98–100, 119, 133, 135, 145, 158, 163, 187n10, 214, 217
South Africa, xiv, 121, 123, 132, 154
South Carolina, 78
Southeast Asia, 96
Southwest, U.S., x, 83–84, 102, 109
Sovereignty Principle, 128
Soviet Union, 117, 126
Spain, 84, 86, 108, 116
species, xi, 26, 30, 32–33, 35, 59, 98, 188n21
  threatened and endangered, 3, 18, 84, 99, 101, 138
St. Olaf College, 168

Stern, Todd, 121, 123, 203n26
stewardship, xvi, 23, 29–31, 36, 77,
    162–63
Stivers, Robert, v, xix, 38
Stockholm Environmental Institute,
    129
subsidiarity, 44, 119, 124, 145, 155
subsidies, government, 10, 62, 87,
    89–90, 92, 94, 99, 106–7, 198n47,
    199n54, 201n93, 201n95
Suez Canal, 11
sufficiency norm, xii–xiii, 2, 24–26, 28,
    30–32, 37–39, 41, 44, 46, 59, 61, 75,
    82, 86–87, 98–99, 101, 103, 119, 135,
    145, 158, 187n10, 214, 217
sugarcane, 98
sulfur dioxide, 7, 12, 126, 213
sulfur hexafluoride, 112, 202n14, 216
sustainability norm, xii–xiii, 23–26,
    28–30, 32, 37–39, 41, 44, 46, 50,
    52, 58–59, 61, 64, 67, 69, 75, 83,
    86, 91, 98–100, 103, 119, 145,
    158, 161, 163, 187n2, 187n10,
    214, 218
sustainable development, xvi, 98, 138,
    216
switchgrass, 93, 96
Switzerland, 102, 123, 218
    Basel, 102
system benefit charge, 166

technology transfer, 118, 121–24, 127,
    204n33, 204n35, 218
teleological moral theory, 129
temperature, global average surface, 3,
    15, 18, 21, 120
Texas, x, 88, 90, 167, 173
theology of the cross, 36
tidal power, 103–4
Torgerson, Richard L., xviii, 161–63,
    176, 178
transportation sector, 6, 43, 47, 52, 55,
    58, 78
tropical cyclones, 16
Tufts University, 106
turbine supply agreement, 171

underground geological repository. *See*
    carbon capture and sequestration;
    Yucca Mountain
United Kingdom, 23, 116
United Nations, 118. *See also* Inter-
    governmental Panel on Climate
    Change; Kyoto Protocol
    Climate Change Conference in
        Copenhagen, xiii, 118–19,
        121, 157–58, 212
    Development Programme
        (UNDP), 21, 187n64
    Food and Agriculture
        Organization (FAO), 95
    Framework Convention on
        Climate Change (UNFCCC),
        112, 114, 141, 146, 148,
        202n12–13, 202n15, 203n17,
        203n20–21, 206n54, 212,
        215–16, 218
    Special Rapporteur on the Right
        to Food, 95
Union Theological Seminary, xix
Union of Concerned Scientists, 82
United States
    Climate Change Science
        Program, 3, 183n8
    Department of Agriculture
        (USDA), xxiii, 97, 152, 155,
        199n57, 210n12
    Department of Energy (DOE),
        xxi, 51, 65–68, 78, 83, 97, 99,
        103, 215
    Department of State, 133, 206n57
    Department of the Interior, 84
    Department of the Treasury,
        209n10, 210n11
    Energy Information Adminis-
        tration (EIA), xxi, 9, 10,
        47–49, 53, 55, 60, 63, 71–73,
        77, 88, 94, 100, 215
    Environmental Protection
        Agency (EPA), xxii, 7, 46,
        49, 58, 81, 96–97, 103, 122,
        126, 141–43, 151–53, 155, 215
    Geological Survey (USGS), xxiii,
        49, 190n10

United States (*continued*)
    Global Change Research
        Program, ix, x, xi, 17–18, 112
    House of Representatives, 12,
        97, 139, 143–44, 148, 154,
        156, 201n93, 211
    Mayors Climate Protection
        Agreement, 141, 207n14
    Minerals Management Service, 58
    Senate, xii, 66, 115, 142–45, 148,
        156–58
    Supreme Court, 49, 81, 142
University of Minnesota, 98
Upper Iowa River, ix, 162
uranium, 11, 68–69
urban planning, 109
urgency guideline, 42, 44, 119, 120, 135,
    145, 148, 154–55, 171
utilities, electric and gas, U.S., 49,
    59, 65–67, 84, 86, 90, 144, 149–50,
    156, 166, 169, 190n14, 190n19

Vaitheeswaran, Vijay V., 45, 189n1
Venezuela, 11, 57
Vermont, 86, 197n36
viability, political, 42, 44, 119, 124, 135,
    145, 148
volatile organic compounds, 7, 12

war, 10, 24–25, 32, 55–57, 98, 184n33
Warner, John, 142–43, 156
Washington, state, 86, 141
wastes, municipal and agricultural, 71
water, 1, 60, 84, 98–99, 102–5, 125. *See
    also* Safe Drinking Water Act
    pollution, oil-related, 57
    quality, 58, 61
    resources, 103, 109
    supplies, 16, 18, 58, 95
    vapor, x, 111
wave energy, 103–4, 201n91

Waxman, Henry, 143, 146, 148–49, 208n34
wealth, 11, 31, 34, 57, 59, 70, 128
West Virginia, 157
Western Europe, 104
wheat, 95
wildlife conservation, 95
wind, 1
    energy, 71–72, 76, 87–93, 98–99,
        107–8, 144, 165–67, 169,
        171–72, 179
    farm, 67, 172–73
    industry, 93, 169
    patterns, 13
    resource, 168, 173
    turbines, xviii, 72, 76, 93, 168,
        171
windfall profits, 126, 149–50
Wisconsin, 54, 86
wood, 71, 93, 99, 212, 215
    chips, 174–75
    stoves, 6
    waste, 173
World Bank, 121, 132, 206n53
World Climate Change Fund, 123, 132
World Climate Conference, 114, 218
World Council of Churches, xii, xxiii,
    23, 129, 218
World Resources Institute, 5, 147,
    197n26
World War II, 32, 56
Worldwatch Institute, 20, 127

Xcel Energy, 169
Xinhua, 147

Yergin, Daniel, 54, 191n27
Yucca Mountain, 65–69, 193n60,
    193n6–65, 193n68, 194n75

Zachariah, George, 125, 204n37
Zimbabwe, xi

DEATH IN VENICE

Making and Unmaking a Master

TWAYNE'S MASTERWORK SERIES

Robert Lecker, General Editor

DEATH IN VENICE

Making and Unmaking a Master

T. J. Reed

TWAYNE PUBLISHERS • NEW YORK
Maxwell Macmillan Canada • *Toronto*
Maxwell Macmillan International • *New York Oxford Singapore Sydney*

Twayne's Masterwork Studies No. 140

Death in Venice: Making and Unmaking a Master
T. J. Reed

Twayne Publishers
Macmillan Publishing Company
866 Third Avenue
New York, New York 10022

Maxwell Macmillan Canada, Inc.
1200 Eglinton Avenue East
Suite 200
Don Mills, Ontario M3C 3N1

Library of Congress Cataloging-in-Publication Data

Reed, T. J. (Terence James), 1937–
    Death in Venice : making and unmaking a master / T. J. Reed.
        p.   cm.—(Twayne's masterwork studies ; no. 140)
    Includes bibliographical references and index.
    ISBN 0-8057-8069-6 —ISBN 0-8057-8114-5 (pbk.)
    1. Mann, Thomas, 1975–1955. Tod in Venedig. I. Title. II. Series.
PT2625.A44T6455   1994
833'.912—dc20
                                                                    94-4252
                                                                    CIP

10 9 8 7 6 5 4 3 2 1 (hc)
10 9 8 7 6 5 4 3 2 1 (pb)

Printed in the United States of America

Contents

Note on Translations and References

I quote Mann's novella in the Bantam Books translation by David Luke, referring both to it and to the other stories in that volume by simple page numbers in parentheses in my text. Of the three existing versions of *Death in Venice*, Luke's is the only one by a professional German scholar, and he corrects many literal errors in what was previously the sole copyrighted translation into English, by Helen Lowe-Porter. I have, however, sometimes made slight changes to the English, tacitly or expressly, so as to get closer to the effect of the original. The movement is always towards a more literal rendering of the German.

Other references have been kept to a minimum. Passages from works of Thomas Mann other than the stories in the Luke selection are located by volume (roman numeral) and page of the standard German collected edition. References are again given in parentheses in the text. For letters, I provide date and recipient only. All translations from works and letters are my own. The form *DüD* in the footnotes refers to the relevant volume of *Dichter über ihre Dichtungen*, a collection of the author's statements about his own work. For full details of all these sources, see the Bibliography.

Thomas Mann and his family in front of their country house at Tölz.

Photograph courtesy of the Thomas Mann Archive, Zurich.

Chronology: Thomas Mann's Life and Work

1875 Paul Thomas Mann born on 6 June as the second son of Johann Heinrich Mann, a leading businessman and senator of the north German Hansa city of Lübeck.

1892 On the death of Senator Mann, the family grain firm goes into liquidation. Thomas Mann and his brother Heinrich are left with sufficient means to live independently and try to establish themselves as writers.

1893 Leaves school and moves south to Munich, where his mother has settled.

1894 His first story, *Fallen*, is published in a Naturalist literary journal, *Society (Die Gesellschaft)*.

1896–1898 Prolonged stay in Italy—Rome and Palestrina—with his brother Heinrich. Further short fiction appears in the leading literary journal of the day, the *New Review (Neue Rundschau)*, published by the house of Samuel Fischer.

1897 At Fischer's invitation, begins work on a novel.

1898 Publishes his first volume of collected short fiction, *Little Herr Friedemann*.

1900 Completes the novel *Buddenbrooks* in May. Samuel Fischer, skeptical about the chances of such a massive work by a barely known author, suggests that Mann abridge it. The young author persuades him to publish it as it stands.

1901 *Buddenbrooks* appears, in two volumes, and is well received.

1902 Fischer brings out a single-volume cheap edition of *Buddenbrooks*. It becomes a best-seller, establishing Thomas Mann's fortunes and a broad popular reputation.

1903 The volume *Tristan* appears (six stories, including *Tonio Kröger*).

1905	Marries Katia Pringsheim, daughter of a wealthy Jewish academic family. Completes his only drama, *Fiorenza*, set in Renaissance Florence. Melodramatic and stylistically overelaborate, it never succeeds on the stage.
1905–1910	Works on a number of projects that are destined never to be completed: a novel on Munich society, "Maya"; a historical novel on Frederick the Great of Prussia; a major aesthetic essay, "Intellect and Art." Frustrated at his inability to make progress with them.
1909	Publishes the novel *Royal Highness*, on the surface a romance about a Ruritanian prince, but meant as an allegory of the artist's life. As the second novel from the author of the highly regarded *Buddenbrooks*, it is judged to be lightweight.
1910	Starts writing a further artist allegory, the story of the confidence trickster Felix Krull. Progress is difficult. Feels increasingly frustrated with his uncompleted projects and worried about how to repeat the success of *Buddenbrooks* with an unquestionable masterpiece.
1911	Vacation journey to the Adriatic island of Brioni in May. On 18 May, receives news of the death of the eminent composer Gustav Mahler, whom Mann had met the previous year. From 26 May to 2 June, stays on the Lido, Venice. Begins to write *Death in Venice*.
1912	*Death in Venice* completed in June. Published in the October and November numbers of the *New Review*.
1913	Begins work on *The Magic Mountain*, planned as a similar-length novella and comic pendant piece ("satyr-play") to *Death in Venice*.
1914	Outbreak of war. First essay in defense of Germany.
1915	Polemics continue, in particular against his brother Heinrich. In no mood for fiction, devotes himself to a long, brooding work of cultural-cum-political-cum-autobiographical reflections.
1918	*Considerations of an Unpolitical Man* appears just before World War I ends.
1918–1922	First reaction to Germany's military defeat is bitter withdrawal and a search for any remaining congenial forms of conservatism. Disturbed by increasing right-wing violence, resolves to make the best of the new sociopolitical situation. Public statement in defense of the new state in speech "Of German Republic." From then on, moves steadily towards social democracy.

Chronology

1924	Publishes *The Magic Mountain*. The intended novella has grown into a massive novel, taking issue allegorically with the social and political problems of the day.
1926–1933	Active as a member of the literary section of the Prussian Academy of Arts, where the cultural and ideological issues of the Weimar Republic are fought out by leading writers of left and right.
1929	Publishes *Mario and the Magician*, an allegorical tale of Italian fascism. Receives the Nobel Prize for Literature, but expressly for his first novel, *Buddenbrooks*. (The prize committee's most influential member disapproves of the liberalism implicit in *The Magic Mountain*.)
1933	Mann travels abroad in February, giving a lecture on Richard Wagner in various cities. Reports of the lecture are made the pretext for a hate campaign against him by Nazis and fellow-travelers. (Since the early thirties, he has been prominent as a defender of the Weimar Republic and an opponent of rising Nazism.) Mann's family warn him to stay abroad. It is the beginning of exile. After short stays in various places in France and Switzerland, settles in the autumn in Küsnacht near Zürich. *The Tales of Jakob*, the first volume of the four-part *Joseph and His Brethren*, is published in Germany, despite its Jewish subject.
1934	Makes first visit to the United States in May and June. Publishes the second volume of the tetralogy, *The Young Joseph*.
1936	Volume 3, *Joseph in Egypt*, appears. The Nazis deprive Mann of his German nationality. He takes Czech citizenship.
1938	Emigrates to the United States and holds a visiting professorship at Princeton.
1939	Publishes *Lotte in Weimar*, a novel about the older Goethe.
1940	Moves to Pacific Palisades, California.
1941	Becomes Germanic consultant to the Library of Congress.
1942–1945	Makes anti-Nazi broadcasts to Germany for the BBC.
1943	*Joseph the Provider* completes the Joseph tetralogy. Begins writing *Doctor Faustus*.
1944	Takes U.S. citizenship.
1947	*Doctor Faustus* published.
1949	Publishes *The Genesis of Doctor Faustus: Novel of a Novel*, which describes the roots of the work in the events of the time.

1950   Death of brother Heinrich.

1951   Publishes *The Holy Sinner*, a parodistic retelling of the medieval legend of Pope Gregory.

1952   Disturbed by McCarthyism and drawn to Europe for cultural reasons, but unwilling to return to Germany. Settles in Switzerland for his remaining years.

1954   Publishes *Confessions of the Confidence Trickster Felix Krull*, a completed first part of the novel begun in 1911 and abandoned in the twenties.

1955   Thomas Mann dies on 12 August in Zürich.

LITERARY AND HISTORICAL CONTEXT

1

A Culture and Its Pressures

The Germany Thomas Mann was born into in 1875 was just four years old. Until 1871 it had never existed as a unified state, and it had no coherent society of the kind England and France had long had. From the early Middle Ages down to the beginning of the nineteenth century, social and political realities for Germans were the local ones of the 300 territories, ranging from large principalities to independent cities, which made up the loose federal structure of the Holy Roman Empire of the German Nation. And when Germany did unite under Prussian leadership, it remained in some ways strongly regional and centrifugal. Political power might now be centralized in Bismarck's Berlin, but in places geographically or temperamentally remote from Berlin the old local ethos persisted: Mann's native Lübeck, for example, and Munich, the city to which he moved at the age of 18.

Culture too went on being divided as it always had been among the larger regional cities. Thomas Mann's move was taking him to an important artistic center, away from the cultural and economic backwater of Lübeck on the far north coast. His first novel, *Buddenbrooks*, seems at first sight dominated by the provincial reality he had left behind, a monument to a characteristic way of life. But the novel's immense success lay not in the local materials but in its precocious craftsmanship—the maturely unruffled style, the deft variations of technique and tempo that maintain narrative interest, the sovereign control of a long and complex history, the perfect balance struck between a relentless theme (*Decline of a Family* is the novel's subtitle), and the richness of figures and episodes that embody it. Mann was already, in his twenties, an accomplished European modern, nourished by the writing of Tolstoy and Turgenev, Flaubert, the Goncourt brothers, Maupassant and Bourget—and, above all, schooled in skeptical analysis by his reading of Nietzsche.

He was also a modern in his mode of work, rejecting emotion and inspiration in favor of discipline, detachment, and application. Like Flaubert, he scorned those who wrote easily (including, as his notebooks show, his novelist elder brother Heinrich) and labored over every sentence with ascetic devotion. This is the type of writer he makes Gustav von Aschenbach in *Death in Venice*, a dedicated and disciplined "moralist of achievement" (203). And as one of many strokes borrowed from his own experience, he locates Aschenbach in Munich. That background and the issues it focused for Thomas Mann are necessary factors in understanding the story.

If Mann would have been out of place staying in the provincial backwater of Lübeck, he was also out of place in Munich. Partly it was a matter of the southern city's all too easygoing character, which was at odds with Mann's sober north German ethos and moral sensibility, but partly also it was because of the domination of the visual arts in Munich, a city of painting and painters and models and artists' studios. Some of these artists, fashionable portrait painters especially, were established and celebrated, even ennobled with a "von" to their name.[1] But though they too must have been sufficiently "moralists of achievement" to work at their success, for Thomas Mann the very nature of visual art denied it the moral status of literature. Art could only represent the surface of things, whereas literature penetrated to the depths of experience. No literary mode had done this with more grim determination than late-nineteenth-century Naturalism, which was in its heyday when Mann began to write. His emphasis was to be different from Zola's and Ibsen's and Gerhart Hauptmann's, less on the social, more on the psychological and pathological depths. He also felt less confident than the Naturalists did that reality had now been—or ever could be—exhaustively explored by science or sociology.[2] Nevertheless, they were analysts all, probing life in order to portray it. In comparison, the visual arts seemed to him positively misleading. By celebrating the beautiful surface of life and its beautiful successful people, they hid from view the abyss of human suffering which literature's "sacred torch" could illuminate. Mann treated that issue, and used the torch image, in the brilliant satirical short story *Gladius Dei*, set in a turn-of-the-century Munich "resplendent" with sunshine and art, on which the grotesque hero calls down divine punishment (73ff.). What for Mann was worse, Munich's love of art seemed to lead to a contempt for literature; though in gloomy moments he even felt, as a note for "Intellect and Art" says, that "enmity to literature" was "innate in Germans" at large.[3]

Society is not often in harmony with new departures in literature. Since the late eighteenth century, when the age of patronage in European culture ended, writers had increasingly felt alienated from bourgeois society by its "philistine" lack of imagination. Their criticisms and artistic provocations only alienated it in turn from them. In the Germany of Wilhelm II, the criticism of social ills was felt by a settled and complacent bourgeoisie to be itself a social ill. The kaiser himself, never slow to utter on any subject, said as much: the task of culture was the fostering of ideals. The critical portrayal of life was an unnecessary and ill-willed disturbance. Behind this façade of high principles lay ultimately a requirement of political conformity.

The gap between society and literature was widened by theories that art had its origins in biological decadence or even pathology. *Buddenbrooks* might seem to have bridged the gap by its success with a broad bourgeois readership. But while bourgeois readers enjoyed it for its richness as a family saga, its theme was precisely that the roots of art lay in decadence. It showed the "decline" of a merchant family which reaches its genealogical end point in the hypersensitive, musically gifted boy Hanno. He dies. But the real artist who shared his background, Thomas Mann, survives as a self-conscious outsider, cut off from the normality and competence of his Lübeck family background.

The story *Tonio Kröger*, however, soon made plain just how painfully Mann felt himself to be "not a human being but something strange, something alien, something different" (157), how powerful his fascination was with the contrasting "bliss of the commonplace" (161), how strong his impulse to achieve rapport with and recognition by the "fair-haired and blue-eyed, the bright children of life" (192), as Tonio Kröger idealizingly calls them.

Such recognition had been achieved by painters. Hence for Mann they belonged more to the realm of "Life" than to the realm of "the Spirit," where literature was located. But this meant that the visual art he rejected did also offer ways of adapting. To fulfill his social yearnings perhaps he only needed to turn away from the dark depths towards the beauties of the outside world, away from analysis to a more strongly plastic representation (an element which *Buddenbrooks*, after all, did not lack)? Since the turn of the century, critics who claimed to be more in touch with the needs of the majority than the avant-garde could ever be had been calling for an end to distasteful probings and for a new "healthy" emphasis. Young writers were able to make their mark by following this lead, as Mann thought he saw when he surveyed the literary scene. And if they succeeded by meeting the demand for healthy "regeneration," could an older writer with different tendencies still compete and keep his public? Mann saw himself in the situation of the old architect in Ibsen's play *The Master Builder*, whose work and status are threatened by a younger man. Looking at other leading writers of his own generation—Gerhart Hauptmann, Hugo von Hofmannsthal—Mann found they were perceptibly edging towards health and regeneration, "trying to get on the bandwagon," as he called it ("Intellect and Art," n. 103).

Mann's own response, which would shape Aschenbach's career too, was to conceive such change as a natural phase in a career. What was a writer's stock-in-trade in younger years (pathology, analysis) might give way naturally to something less radical and more easy on the public palate. But actually to plan such change seems dubious. In an essay, Mann talks about the Romantic poet Adelbert von Chamisso writing a "wild" youthful book and then "hastening to grow out of the chrysalis stage" and become a "master" (IX, 57). "Hastening to grow" seems a contradiction, a confusion of an act of will and a natural process. To "become a master" also in its way contradicts Mann's whole conception of the artist: the destined outsider becomes an insider. Yet it was something Mann consciously aspired to. It crops up more than once in letters to his brother Heinrich. It seems to have meant for him writing a new work that would match *Buddenbrooks* for scale and quality. He had done good things since that first novel—*Tonio Kröger* and *Tristan* of 1903, for example—but they were short, while his second full-length novel, *Royal Highness* of 1909, was found lightweight by comparison with its predecessor. Meantime, Mann's attempt to break into theater, the costume drama *Fiorenza*, had turned out, in his own words, a "fiasco" (letter to Heinrich Mann, 18 February 1905. He had plans enough, all for impressive subjects—a Munich social novel ("Maya"), a historical novel on Frederick the Great of Prussia, the essay on "Intellect and Art" that would summarize the cultural issues of his day. But time went by and nothing came of them: "One consumes oneself in plans and despairs of beginning" (letter to Heinrich Mann, 11 June 1906). Works that might have made him a pillar of the national culture remained jottings in a notebook. It was a decade in the doldrums.

Mann was also too honest not to have doubts about these ambitions. Did not the status of a master involve a settled complacency essentially untrue to art? He only needed to look at his brother. Heinrich had stayed independent of society. He was more inclined to criticize than to court it, and an alternative guidebook to the Munich scene declared him "proof against titles and all public distinctions." He was also plainly skeptical about the effects Thomas's "good" marriage would have on his writing. Thomas was aware of all this.[4] There are jottings in his notebooks where he insists to himself that he does not want to be a "national figure"[5]; for a time he plans a novella on how the old Goethe's dignity was undone (at 74 he fell in love with a girl of 17).[6] So at the conscious, self-critical level, the precarious nature of dignity is clear to him. And yet. . . .

This unstable pattern—of cultural change and challenge, of personal ambition and frustration, of inner uncertainty, uneasy conscience, and compositional problems—is the material from which Mann creates Gustav von Aschenbach. But he projects him safely beyond his own doubts and difficulties, as an older and fully established writer who has completed works Mann had not, "Maya," the Frederick novel, "Intellect and Art," and who, in order to get that far, has taken decisions Mann had not—yet. From being the kind of writer Mann had so far been, Aschenbach has turned himself into the kind of writer Mann was thinking of becoming. *Death in Venice* asks what consequences such a change would have. So, as Mann more than once implied (XII, 201, 517), the story is an experiment, one conducted by an author with the possibilities of his own career. And perhaps it also questions ultimately the very notion of "career," because, for all the hard work that is entailed by a "morality of achievement" like Aschenbach's, it is something different from the simple devotion to writing as such that marks certain pure spirits in the record of literature like Kafka and Emily Dickinson.

These issues were suddenly crystallized in story form by the events and figures of Mann's own journey to Venice in 1911: the strange foreigner at the North Cemetery in Munich, the sordid ship, the repellent dandy, the unlicensed gondolier, Tadzio and his family (the very boy has even, in his own old age, been traced), the failed attempt to leave the city, the cholera epidemic, the honest English travel clerk, the malicious street singer—"it was all given, it really only needed fitting in, and showed in the most astonishing way its capacity to be interpreted for compositional purposes" (XI, 124). In other words, inner and outer worlds came together for the writer.

The mixture proved nevertheless to have a will of its own. So far from allowing themselves to be freely disposed into a pattern, the materials (in Mann's later phrase) "precipitated" as a crystalline formation does and found their own form (XI, 123f.). It is, after all, the nature of true experiments that they do not allow their results to be prearranged, they are conducted with real, independent forces. Perhaps for that very reason Thomas Mann could feel, disturbingly yet exhilaratingly, that he was being borne along by the compositional process and its complexities rather than consciously guiding it. In more ways than one, the work surprised him. But then, as he reflected, that is what literature does for the writer. "Every work is a fragmentary actualisation of our essence and the only way we have of finding out what that essence is" (ibid.). *Death in Venice* was in this sense not so much given a tragic ending by the author; to be more exact, it found it. There are signs it could have been something quite other. The experiment worked itself out. In the process of being written, the story uncovered just who and what its author was.

2

The Perils and Paradoxes of Art

Death in Venice is the culmination of Mann's early series of "artist" stories. At first sight it seems to have the limited reference of what modern writers like Henry James, Rilke, Kafka, Broch, Joyce, and Hesse have virtually made into a subgenre; but the psychological course and tragic outcome of Mann's novella have a wider relevance. It treats love and death, passion and control, and the relation of creativity to morality. It lays bare the workings of the conscious and unconscious life and shows the complicity of character and will in the making of an individual's fate. It also embodies some striking paradoxes. It is an intensely private work couched in the tone of elevated public utterance, and it uses a style of polished formality to recount the breakdown of formative power. Its own power is the greater for pointing beyond the seemingly random anecdote of an erotic encounter in an exotic setting. It is also unintendedly part of a larger whole. The way an ordered existence and a carefully established mastery are overthrown by the "alien god" of deep impulse fits a pattern present in Mann's work from the early tale of a cripple's disastrous infatuation (*Little Herr Friedemann* of 1897), via the passion of Potiphar's wife for Joseph (*Joseph in Egypt* of 1936), to a final high point in the "hellish intoxication" of *Doctor Faustus* in the 1940s. In telling how a writer's self-discipline gives way to self-abandonment, *Death in Venice* already points all unknowingly to the roots of a larger catastrophe. For the forces of the "alien god" Dionysus are latent in the collective as well as the individual psyche. That is how Mann saw fascism from American exile in the thirties and forties, and that is why *Doctor Faustus*, written between 1943 and 1947 in an effort to understand the causes of the "German catastrophe," still has echoes of the Venetian novella. Taken together, this sequence of works is a profound contribution to human psychology and its archetypal portrayal.

To convey psychological insights that contribute to the dark larger picture, *Death in Venice* brilliantly combines two distinct kinds of narrative that would seem to clash: the realistic mode inherited from nineteenth-century fiction and the mythic mode which began to fascinate writers at the end of that age, when realism reached its limits. Mann's handling of myth in this his first systematic exploring of its potential can stand comparison with any other modern work. His layering of the mythic and the realistic modes is so deft that the movement between them is unobtrusive; the hints of something more-than-everyday are so rooted in everyday reality, and that reality is heightened with such delicate suggestiveness, that the narrative holds together as a unity. The writer who falls in love with a beautiful boy and dies of cholera is also the fated victim of a god, his vacation a necessary passage to death at an appointed place. In the real figures along his route, leading him on and mocking him as he goes, we fleetingly recognize mythic gods by their traditional attributes of physical form and costume. The Polish boy has his own mythic identity as Hermes, the guide of souls to the underworld. Venice itself is not just a random setting but an apt meeting place halfway between the traditional Indian origins of the god Dionysus and a Western culture that refuses to recognize him. Literature itself, as Aschenbach practices it, is part of that refusal: in mythic terms, he is devoted too exclusively to another, more placid god, Apollo. Overall, myth gives a resonance of universality to the novella's specific circumstances, and hence to the protagonist's tragic fall. There but for the grace of God goes anyone.

In another context, of course, the "specific circumstance" of Aschenbach's encounter and infatuation with Tadzio also makes *Death in Venice* a, if not the, classic narrative of homosexuality to set alongside those of Gide and Proust. Though sexual orientation is not itself the moral issue of what Mann later called his "moral fable" (VIII, 1069), no other motif could have brought together Mann's real experience and a handful of latent themes in such a compelling way. Certainly homosexual love was not, as has sometimes been claimed, the coolly taken decision of a writer at home in all forms of decadence who simply added this one more to his repertoire. It was intimately important for Mann himself and had been there for the observant eye before *Death in Venice* (for example, in *Tonio Kröger*). Mann's Venice experiences took him to the brink of new possibilities of public statement, before traits of personal and literary character and the social climate of the day combined to close off those possibilities and dictate the story's final shape.

Death in Venice also stands out among works of modern fiction by the radical doubt it casts on style and ultimately on the pretensions of art. It hardly seems so at first. From the very beginning it signals a style of its own in an unmissable manner. Every word is clearly being weighed, every phrase polished and placed for dignified effect. Readers sometimes find this excessive, some students are put off by it. They are in noteworthy company. D. H. Lawrence in his review of 1913 complained that the style lacked "the rhythm of a living thing" and that no sense of "unexpectedness" was allowed by its "carefully plotted and arranged developments."[1] Yet the style does not take the form it does merely to impress for its own sake. In the word Mann used when early critics said he had been presumptuous—that is, had used a grand manner to claim master status for himself—the style was "mimicry," that is, a means to evoke the world as a fastidious Aschenbach would see it.[2] This would make Lawrence's criticism a tribute to Mann's success, for the ring of the text had convinced him that the Thomas Mann of 1912 was declining into lifelessness at 53. But 53 is the fictional Aschenbach's age; the Mann who wrote the novella was 35.

On this view, the slightly too grandiose manner would be a conscious strategy. More, it would be the embodiment of a critical theme. (Moral for students: trust your impressions, at least long enough to ask what produced them.) For, once Aschenbach's dignified status has been destroyed by passion, it follows that the dignified style which was the artist's way of presenting himself to the public must itself have been a hollow façade. Aschenbach himself reflects not long before he dies that "the magisterial pose of our style is a lie and a farce," and that all the other pretensions of an accepted public figure are just as precarious: "Our fame and social position are an absurdity, the public's faith in us altogether ridiculous, the use of art to educate the nation and its youth is a reprehensible undertaking that should be forbidden by law" (261).

Yet this skepticism cannot be the last word—and not just because we should hardly be discussing Mann's work at all but for the continuing "use of art to educate." Even if the novella's style has elements of "mimicry," it is still the vehicle that carries the narrative at every point, even when the angle of vision is clearly not Aschenbach's. Moreover, the highly wrought character does fit Mann's own aspirations at the time he was writing the story. The descriptions of Tadzio especially could be seen as, at least in the first instance, Mann's own attempts at "plastic" form in response to the demands of his day, as well as being his response to a male beauty of which he was intensely appreciative. Nor can the sensuous writing that evokes Venice in its beauty and sordidness be only a rendering of Aschenbach's perception, since it conveys more than just his perspective; it is surely also Thomas Mann being graphic and sensuous in his own right, attempting something like the classicism to which Aschenbach had turned in his maturity. "A new classicism must come" (X, 843), Mann himself had written in 1911—written it there in Venice, on notepaper headed "Grand Hotel des Bains, Lido, Venise," in an essay which corresponds to that last "page and a half of exquisite prose" Aschenbach composes on the beach, with Tadzio in full view as his inspiration (236). "Mastery" and "classicism" were not just an achievement of Aschenbach's, constructed and coolly viewed by a detached narrator. And did not Mann himself, for all his doubts about art, go on to attain, as much as any writer in our century has done, the kind of fame and unquestioned public standing that he queries so radically in Aschenbach?[3]

So if skepticism undermines this novella, the reverse is also true. That is perhaps the most intriguing of its paradoxes.

3

Reception

OPINIONS

The most obviously striking features of *Death in Venice* are its homosexual subject and its highly wrought style. The story's reception has been shaped by the way critics have responded to these features and seen (or failed to see) their relation to each other. It has only become clear in recent years just how closely the two are linked.[1]

Mann was naturally uneasy about the effect his subject would have. As he waited for the first public reactions, he wondered whether he had not after all produced, in a phrase from the text, something "absurd and forbidden" (215). Attack came not just from the expected quarter. The poet Stefan George, who practiced his own neo-Grecian cult of a beautiful 16-year-old youth—the dead Maximilian Kronberger, celebrated as "Maximin"—declared that *Death in Venice* had "drawn the highest things down into the sphere of decay."[2] The leading homosexual propagandist of the day, Kurt Hiller, called the story "an example of moral narrowness" which was unexpected from the author of *Buddenbrooks*, and he accused Mann of putting love for a boy on a par with cholera.

Surprisingly, there was not the mass expression of moral outrage that might have been expected from the guardians of public decency. There were rejections of homosexuality, but no suggestion that Mann or his story was defending it. It was easy to assume that a specialist in decadence had found another decadent subject. The literary treatment seemed to confirm this. The novella's final form as what Mann was later to call a "moral fable," the devices that distance the narrator from his character, the elevated style and noble tone, which are themselves a form of detachment, and, of course, the tragic ending (one Catholic critic even suggested Aschenbach's death was a necessary punishment for his "sinful thoughts")—all these elements visibly put Mann on the "right" side.

The story's elevated style was seized on by friend and foe. Mann's archenemy Alfred Kerr touched a sore point with his sneer that Mann was always writing about "real writers" (*Dichter*) without being one himself. Linked with this was the other by now clichéd criticism that the text lacked "life" because its author could make no direct "naive" contact with life (Carl Busse)—an insight Mann had handed to critics on a plate by the confessions of *Tonio Kröger*. Writers like Mann and Flaubert, it was alleged, had to make a virtue of necessity and create what they could from a deficiency of "life," whereas "real" creativity like that of the Greeks or of Goethe sprang from a superfluity of life which flowed spontaneously into art. These criticisms hark back to the irrationalism of Nietzsche, for whom Flaubert was *the* example of modern creativity. They are echoed again in D. H. Lawrence's demand for a live organic style.[3]

Friendly voices too were declaring that the new work put its author in a class with Flaubert, the linkage now meant as praise for a stylistic tour de force. *Death in Venice*, it was argued, had turned psychology into high literary art and created an objective portrait from the analysis of a subjective condition. Both camps were taking the style at face value as its author's, the one in order to decry its lifelessness or pretensions, the other so as to praise its achievement. Neither thought to link the story's own style with its theme of the moral dubiousness of style itself.

In due course Mann himself proved able to forget the story's warning of what "classical" style and "mastery" might conceal. By 1918 an interviewer was telling him that the younger generation now preferred his traditional mode of writing to the wild innovations of the Expressionists, and that the key work in establishing a new German tradition was *Death in Venice* with its "remarkable atmosphere of classicity."[4] Mann accepted this with a good grace. The "new classicity," which in Venice he had declared "must come," apparently *had* come, and in the form after all of the Venice novella itself. His growing repute now made it possible to reclaim as his own the style he had distanced from himself as "mimicry."

It was less easy to reclaim the homosexual subject as equally his own. In the following decades, as Mann became an established international classic (which, of course, means more than having written works with outwardly "classical" qualities), the stylistic mastery of *Death in Venice* went on being emphasized. Arguably this was at least in part a displacement activity of critics that allowed them to pass over in silence the story's taboo subject, or at any rate not to probe the author's own relation to it. Mann gave scarcely a public hint of how close that relation was. Only when his letters began to be published did it become clear that there had at first been an affirmative and only after that a critical treatment of the theme.[5]

It remained for a more recent phase of criticism to read both this change of direction and its public aftermath, Mann's management of the reception process through his own authorial comments, as a failure of nerve. *Death in Venice* became "a provocation that was never understood" and that was made to seem "harmless" by the later statements of both author and commentators. And yet, when the critic asks, "What is left of an artist's boldness if he is not prepared to stand by it with his social persona?" the answer is not as simple as the rhetorical question implies.[6] It is easy now to ridicule *Death in Venice* for its "cultivated" treatment of a taboo theme, and to belittle Thomas Mann for timidity about his sexual orientation. But forthright confession and confrontation may not be the best literary tactic for changing the attitudes of society, as the case of Oscar Wilde shows. In contrast, the high formality and moral components of *Death in Venice* made it a difficult target to attack, and over the years this has had important consequences for the way its subject is viewed. Alfred Kerr's sarcastic comment that the novella had made "pederasty acceptable to the cultivated middle classes" has some truth in a more straightforward sense.

Old attitudes, of course, remained in force, and as late as the year before Mann died a letter from a German correspondent attacked *Death in Venice* as a "perverted" and "irresponsible" work. Mann replied by invoking the country he had just left against the continent he had returned to: "In America it is regarded as 'classical,' a sign surely that even and especially in that puritanical sphere it is not felt to be immoral." The story is indeed not immoral, he insists, because it is a "confession, the product of a thinking conscience and a pessimistic love of truth" (letter to Jürgen Ernestus, 17 June 1954). With notable patience—one wonders whether Aschenbach in his great days would have "performed the social . . . duties entailed by his reputation" (200) quite as conscientiously as this—the old writer tries once more to explain the familiar issues, down to that final querying of the public's trust in art and artists. But he now goes a step further: "In all this sceptical and suffering pessimism there is much truth, perhaps exaggeration of the truth and therefore only half-truth." In other words, revelations are not the final word, because the honest act of making them is part of the moral picture. So if *Death in Venice* "betrays the dignity of art and the artist," then his correspondent "might consider whether it is not through this conscientious betrayal that the artist's dignity is regained." And what Mann did not openly confess always lay just beneath the story's surface. It has become clear in later perspective.

ADAPTATIONS

Part of a work's reception is the way it is adapted in other media. In 1921 Thomas Mann was delighted by the portfolio of illustrations for

Death in Venice drawn by Wolfgang Born. Mann liked the shift away from the Naturalistic mode and from the story's more obvious "sensationalistic" motifs. Born had picked up the fleeting reference to Saint Sebastian (202) as an emblem for Aschenbach's work, and in the drawing entitled "Death" he had drawn Aschenbach with a startling likeness to Gustav Mahler, even though he could not know Mann had secretly used Mahler's features as a model for his description of Aschenbach (206). So language could after all communicate things seen, as visual art does.

More complex and challenging are the two major adaptations of more recent date and the critical questions they raise: Luchino Visconti's film, with Dirk Bogarde in the role of Aschenbach; and Benjamin Britten's opera, in which the Aschenbach role was created by Peter Pears. Whatever qualities each of these works has within its own art, they offer a stark contrast as adaptations, the one making radical changes, the other following as far as the medium allows the lines of the original.

Visconti's changes undo thematic links that hold Mann's novella together, and he adds motifs which further confuse the issue. His Aschenbach has been turned into a composer, perhaps on the mistaken assumption that Mann borrowed more from Mahler than his given name, facial features, and the public impact of his death. Making Aschenbach a musician breaks the story's causal connection between the protagonist's literary aesthetic and his passion for Tadzio. There is no equivalent in music for the change of emphasis in Aschenbach's career from critical insight to the appreciation of external beauty, or at any rate no attempt is made to provide one. And there is no possibility of showing that Aschenbach's art has been repressing Dionysus, since music is by its nature *the* Dionysian art. Another vital part of Mann's conception is removed when the composer's new work is hissed at a public performance, and when the invented figure of a friend, in an abstract discussion that bears no relation to anything in the novella, positively rants at him. This is plainly not a respected Aschenbach, much less a pillar of the national culture. But if there is no master status to undo, any revelation that makes art and the artist questionable loses most of its point. The story is reduced to the homosexual encounter, with a boy rather less innocent than Mann's Tadzio. Visconti adds a reference to a later Mann work (the boat that brings Aschenbach to Venice has the same name as the prostitute-love of the composer in *Doctor Faustus*); but this seems gratuitous and does not make up for the loss of motifs that do matter in the story he is adapting. We are left with the adagio from Mahler's Fifth Symphony haunting the background and the atmospheric beauty of Venice, which a camera can hardly miss. What the film does miss is the chance to do something the medium is ideally suited to, namely, portray the silent solitary figure, whose inner monologue could have been made up from the fragments of thought the text attributes to him.

Benjamin Britten's librettist tries to do something like this, but the operatic medium is less accommodating than film would have been.[7] It is hard for opera to thrive on silence, and from the first the libretto has to make Aschenbach in his isolation (there are no invented characters for him to talk to here) explicitly describe himself and analyze his problems. This would be awkward enough in any operatic situation, but it is especially so when part of the story's point is that the character fails to recognize what is going on inside him. Mann's subtle transitions from narrator voice to character, from suppressed or semiawareness to full realization, have to be made more abrupt in the opera. But against that, Britten and his librettist strive to be faithful to both the detail and the spirit of the original, as the composer always had been in his settings of literary works (Melville's *Billy Budd*, Crabbe's *Peter Grimes*, Shakespeare's *A Midsummer Night's Dream*, James's *The Turn of the Screw*, and Wilfred Owen's poetry in the *War Requiem*). Their one drastic innovation, turning Tadzio into the glorious victor in a balletic beach festival of athletics, mistakes his delicate beauty for superior robustness. Structurally, however, the parts composed for the competing voices of Apollo and Dionysus make the tragic point of the work and are true to the novella's deepest conception.

When they met years earlier, Thomas Mann apparently expressed a hope that the young Britten would make an opera of *Doctor Faustus*. It would have been a daunting task to compose even samples of the composer hero's extensive—and in part diabolically inspired—oeuvre. But short of that grandiose idea, Mann would have been well pleased that of all his works *Death in Venice* should be set by a composer close to it in spirit, whose own last work it was before he died.

READING THE TEXT

4

Unease and Omens

The opening chapter of *Death in Venice* does two contradictory things at once. It builds up the dignified world of an established writer and at the same time shows it beginning to crumble. We are drawn into taking Gustav von Aschenbach's status seriously—perhaps even a touch solemnly—yet we are also invited to have doubts.

All this is done in two ways: through direct statement and through the subtler suggestions of narrative style. That Aschenbach since his fiftieth birthday has enjoyed noble rank, and that he can "feel calmly confident" in the "mastery" which has "brought him national honour" (199)—this information is clear. But his prestige is also encoded in the kind of elevated phrases that describe his writing and his daily routine. His current work has reached "a difficult and dangerous point which demanded the utmost care and circumspection, the most insistent and precise effort of will" (195), a choice of words that makes the highest claims both for the importance of the task and for the standing of the craftsman. This is not any old writer, but one who has long been fulfilling the larger commissions of the European mind (198). Even so banal a thing as Aschenbach's afternoon rest seems almost ceremonial in the original German, where his "refreshing daily siesta" (195) is called, literally, an "unburdening slumber" (VIII, 444). Much the same is true of the terms in which, unobtrusively, Aschenbach's every perception and response to experience is evoked. There is a detached superiority in the way he "briefly surveyed" the scene of popular enjoyment at an open-air restaurant in the Englischer Garten (195) before continuing his dignified progress. Later, faced with two possible explanations for the sudden appearance of the outlandish stranger who sets the tragic course of events in motion, there is a fastidious detachment and dignified formality in the way Aschenbach, "without unduly pondering the question, inclined to the former hypothesis" (196). These are only the more prominent details in a prose of consistently high stylistic register. What it introduces us to is a personal world of intellectual achievement and control, of legitimate authority, of public standing long and easily taken for granted. This is the mode of life of a master.

Like his positive pretensions, Aschenbach's problems too are conveyed in part by explicit statement and in part by less direct means. This distinction becomes more important than in the positive buildup, because the less direct means now come nearer to suggesting how grave the situation is and they suggest to us what is not clear to Aschenbach. Indeed, they mark the point where a crisis begins to work itself out. The explicit narrative statements only tell us what Aschenbach himself is aware of, what he is prepared to admit—that he is meeting with difficulties in his work on the current book; that he feels a "growing weariness which no one must be allowed to suspect nor his finished work betray by any telltale sign of debility or lassitude" (198); and that he even has a suspicion something may now be wrong with the whole spiritual economy which has made it possible for him to be so grandly productive in the past: "Was enslaved emotion now avenging itself by deserting him, by refusing from now on to bear up his art on its wings, by taking with it all his joy in words, all his appetite for the beauty of form?" (199).

To this extent Aschenbach is a worried man, but perhaps not yet more than that. Creative professional work like his *is* stressful in modern times. One reason the public of the day has acclaimed him, we later learn, is that the characters in his novels embody precisely this contemporary truth. Through these figures he has spoken up for "all those who work on the brink of exhaustion" (203). His own art has always been hard work, a heroic struggle inspired by a "morality of achievement." So the difficulties he has met with when the story opens may be just one more phase in that struggle, a consequence of his years that may be mitigated, if not wholly overcome, by "not bending the bow too far," i.e., by simply taking a break. His decision to do that seems reassuringly rational; it is what results when a sudden violent impulse has been brought under the control, typically, of "common sense and self-discipline" (198).

The reader is not meant to assent to all this rational taming and tidying of Aschenbach's experience. For we have been made to feel how disturbing the experience was that brought on the travel impulse. The discrepancy between the violent power of the disturbance and Aschenbach's almost trivializing reaction is meant to tell its own story. Dramatic irony is already being established because we see deeper than the character does. Though much is done to draw us into his viewpoint—for example, the repeated "now" in the opening paragraph discreetly enlists our sympathy for this hard-driven writer whose work has "now reached a difficult and dangerous point," and whose afternoon repose is "now so necessary to him"—there are also clear hints of an alternative viewpoint, an alternative way both to understand what happens and, eventually, to judge it. This interplay between two viewpoints is a central feature of the story, and it is made possible by the subtle and pervasive modern technique known as "free indirect style" (in German, *erlebte Rede*). What at first sight seems to be narrator statement is often only the character's view, skillfully eavesdropped. Once we sense this, doubt undermines his—and our—certainties.[1]

But what does happen in this first chapter that is so overwhelming for Aschenbach? And why is his reaction inadequate? Waiting at a tram stop by the North Cemetery in Munich, he sees a stranger standing outside the mortuary chapel. Their eyes meet and Aschenbach is faced down, but he at once puts this from his mind. Only on the tram does he think of looking round for the man, but he is no longer anywhere to be seen, on board the tram or in the street. On the face of it, the incident is no more than slightly odd. The man's appearance, at least until he grimaces, is only "slightly unusual," a matter of some features of his dress and his non-Bavarian ethnic type, and the confrontation is only a minor embarrassment. At first sight, normality has not been much disturbed. Yet Aschenbach, immediately after their eyes meet, has a startlingly intense vision:

> Whether his imagination had been stirred by the stranger's itinerant appearance, or whether some other physical or psychological influence was at work, he now became conscious, to his complete surprise, of an extraordinary expansion of his inner self, a kind of roving restlessness, a youthful craving for far-off places, a feeling so new or at least so unaccustomed and forgotten that he stood as if rooted, with his hands clasped behind his back and his eyes to the ground, trying to ascertain the nature and purport of his emotion. (197)

The conclusion Aschenbach comes to is dismissive and reductive: what the vision sprang from was "simply a desire to travel" (197). The original German makes it plainer that this is Aschenbach's inner voice speaking, reassuring himself: "It was wanderlust, nothing more." The "was" may sound as if this has the narrator's authority; as often with free indirect style, there is no single feature of syntax or vocabulary that would link the utterance unambiguously with the character. Yet those "nows" in the opening paragraph already have begun to draw us into his viewpoint. Our hunch—and everything in the later course of the story will confirm it—is that the narrator's voice is infiltrating and presenting the character's view. "It is wanderlust, nothing more" is what Aschenbach says to himself, or thinks, or vaguely feels as one of those impressions that make up our consciousness for much of the time without necessarily being put into words. The narrator gives it clear formulation, but he also, by turning the character's "is" into the "was" of narrative, makes it into a fact of the fiction like any other. The diagnosis may not be true, but it is what the character feels in response to experience. Thought and feeling are no longer what they seemed in earlier fiction, coolly detached agencies, a sovereign self-consciousness standing to some extent above events and the more able to cope with them. They have become integrated into events, they *are* the crucial events. This change relates to free indirect style and its view of the world in general, but it is also quite specifically relevant to Aschenbach, whose thinking does not cope with events, indeed, in some respects has consciously given up the effort to do so. All this, free indirect style communicates with the lightest of touches.

What makes Aschenbach's explanation fall so pathetically short is the power of the vision, which even he immediately afterwards has to admit to himself. (It *is*, I think, still Aschenbach's thought we are hearing, for at least a further half-sentence, as he reflects on "the nature and purport of his emotion" and half goes back on his first, all-too-glib explanation.) For the words "It was wanderlust, nothing more" come at the start, not the end, of a paragraph; they are not a conclusion, they start an exploration. The text goes on after a semi-colon, "but in the form of a veritable attack, intensified"—and what now follows renders Aschenbach's inner experience, again without implying that he verbalized it himself in this form—"intensified to the point of passion, of hallucination even. His desire became visionary, his imagination, which had not yet come to rest after the hours of work, conjured up an exemplary picture of all the wonders and terrors of the manifold earth, which it strove to embrace all at once; he saw, saw a landscape" (197). And what then unfolds is the picture of a tropical swamp, a water-wilderness of almost lewdly luxuriant plants and grotesque or threatening creatures ("the glinting eyes of a crouching tiger" [197]). The vision in all its detail is held together in a single long sentence, whose rhythmic force is sustained by the absence (in the original) of major punctuation rests, its visionary power renewed by the simple repetition of the dominant verb "saw." By omitting the pronoun "he" before these repetitions, the original conveys the intensity of Aschenbach's vision. Each (so to speak) unprefaced recurrence of the same verb is like a catching of his breath as a new wave of vision hits the involuntary watcher even before the last one has ebbed. The syntactic-stylistic effect is brought out by a comparison not just with the English translations, but with a weaker version of this paragraph in a 1912 bibliophile edition of the story.[2] No wonder that, from this visionary seeing, Aschenbach's "heart throbbed with terror and mysterious longing" (197). What he feels stirring is plainly a good deal more, after all, than just wanderlust.

But in what sense more? What can such an intense and exotic vision credibly be caused by, and what can it plausibly imply when it suddenly overcomes a staid twentieth-century character who has merely had a somewhat odd encounter? "His heart throbbed with terror and mysterious longing"—at a banal tram stop in a realistically described modern Munich. The story's opening pages are topographically precise and matter-of-fact, with their names of districts and streets and the Englischer Garten and the open-air restaurant. These are all places where Aschenbach is at home, and the kind of places where the modern reader, whether he happens to know Munich or not, in principle feels at home. Such everyday locations are certainly not as a rule the setting for intense visions and threatening epiphanies.

Yet despite the familiarity of setting, what we are told does nevertheless have a faintly alien feel. This is the edge of a populous city, but "as it happened . . . there was not a soul to be seen" in the vicinity of the tram stop, and "not one vehicle" passing along two main thoroughfares. That is not impossible, of course, any more than it is impossible to explain how the stranger was suddenly there, even if it is "not entirely clear" (196). Plausible explanations can similarly be found for his violent grimace (perhaps the sun was in his eyes, or perhaps he had a permanent facial deformity). And no doubt yet more explanations could be found for his equally sudden disappearance, though the chapter ends before Aschenbach can pursue them. But these circumstances, none of which strain credulity when taken singly, have a cumulative effect. Specifically, they make the stranger's appearance seem like a dramatic entrance staged just for Aschenbach. The theater, moreover, is one of death—a perfectly real chapel, of course, in the actual North Cemetery of Munich,[3] yet suddenly appropriated by this stranger with his bared teeth and his "air of imperious survey" for the purpose of a mysterious communication to his audience of one. It all creates "an extraordinary expansion" of Aschenbach's "inner self," and it opens a visionary window in his imagination, stirs unwonted emotions, and (as it turns out) fatefully alters the course of his life.

So although we are on the real streets of Munich in the year 19 . . and will shortly be on the equally real beaches and squares and canals of Venice, we are not quite at ease in either city. Indeed, we are less at ease from the outset than Aschenbach himself, who naturally enough soon regains his balance and sense of normality. We are seemingly located in modern reality and modern realism, but we are near the edge of such certainties as they offer. True, there has been nothing decisive to carry us into a different reality and a different literary mode, as there is in (say) the first sentence of Kafka's *Metamorphosis*, which pushes us decisively over the edge into the surreal by announcing that the protagonist awoke one day to find himself transformed into a beetle. Nor will there be anything that does so in the rest of the story; Thomas Mann will not—either here or, except very rarely, in his other works—abandon his footing in reality and realism. But already a touch of the uncanny has crept into Aschenbach's experience. That element, and with it our uncertainty and unease, will persist and grow. Together they will gradually suggest that there are more things in Munich and Venice than are dreamt of in Aschenbach's or in realism's philosophy.

All this, as already suggested, is a message to the reader rather than to Aschenbach. That remains largely true for the rest of the story: Aschenbach will only feel the disturbing effect of his experiences at the immediate level; he will notice the disturbing episodes and figures accumulate but will not see them as signs, much less glimpse the pattern they constitute. By the end of this first chapter, when they have only just begun, he seems fully settled again in his mind. Visionary terror and longing have begun to turn into a travel timetable; he has a plan to go south, though, as he reflects to himself, "not quite to where the tigers were" (199). That is the relaxed, almost complacent humor of a man who now feels sure of himself again. The remark will later rebound on him when, in a sense, the tigers come to meet him halfway. But for the present the force of his vision is already fading. By the time he begins his journey he seems to have forgotten it.

In this he is like other "sensible" Mann characters who experience vivid revelations or epiphanies that briefly lift them out of their real, and realistically presented, lives. In a late chapter (X, 5) of *Budden-brooks*, the weary and disillusioned Thomas Buddenbrook glimpses the ideal son who might have mastered life as he himself no longer can, and as his all-too-delicate real son never will. In a sudden compensating vision brought on by reading (and somewhat misunderstanding) the philosophy of Schopenhauer, he feels a mystical unity with all those human beings who have gone before him, especially those who had the strength and spontaneity he lacks. Something similar happens in *The Magic Mountain*. In its central chapter, "Snow," Hans Castorp skis out from his sanitarium, gets lost in a storm, drinks port, and in his befuddled state has a half-waking dream that embodies and resolves the social and existential issues that are daily argued out in the abstract, usually way above his head, by his two philosophic mentors, Settembrini and Naphta. Both these episodes contain an essential truth about the themes of their respective novels and about the situation each character is living out. The curtain briefly parts, and we share with the fictional figure a symbolic or allegorical message. After the revelation it closes again, and for realism's sake (it would not be plausible for his life to be transformed by it), the character forgets. The reader, of course, is meant not to. Similarly here, our remembrance of that swamp-labyrinth of "terror and mysterious longing," towards which the aggressive stranger has somehow pointed Aschenbach, remains a precondition for our understanding of everything that follows.

Indeed, placed this early in the action it is a kind of omen. There are further omens in these opening pages—the death's-head grimace of the stranger's distorted features; the cemetery chapel as the chosen setting for his entrance; the chapel's "Byzantine" structure and its apocalyptic beasts, tacit pointers to the Byzantine architecture of Venice and the city's emblem, the Lion of St. Mark. But these omens, which hint at what will finally happen and the place where it will happen, only confirm expectations that have already been raised in the reader by the story's title—of death, and of Venice. Aschenbach's vision, on the other hand, goes deeper than such externals as event and location. It hints at the reasons that lie behind his fate, or rather, more dynamically, at the forces stirring in him which his Venetian adventure will release.

5

Portrait of the Artist as an Older Man

Before Aschenbach can leave Munich, there is a fortnight's unavoidable delay during which he puts his personal and literary affairs in order. This routine matter is disposed of by the opening sentence of the third chapter, which flows on naturally from the close of the first. While we wait for that to happen and for the narrative proper to resume, we have the interpolated chapter 2 to read. It too tells a story, but not of external events. It recounts Aschenbach's career to date, reviewing the forms his literary work has taken and the issues and values his development embodies. It begins with the "works of his maturity," on which his reputation mainly rests, then treats his genetic origins, his fame and how he "manages" (200f.) it, his always delicate constitution, and the austere discipline he had to practice if he was to be productive. It discusses the special type of characters he created and their appeal to the contemporary public; the specific nature of his earlier work; his recent deliberate turn away from that literary mode; and the nature of his chosen new style (202ff.). It hints at possible dangers; seeks to justify a writer's becoming an established, even an establishment figure; and finally gives the few simple facts of Aschenbach's personal life and a sketch of his physical appearance (205f.).

All this is couched in a formal style that matches the high register of chapter 1. There we began to move in the world of a dignified major figure; now we are given the full justification of that status, that is, we learn what achievements have earned it. The narrative problem of how to make an artist-figure convincing *as* an artist is solved by a piece of mock literary biography. It may seem an easy way to give substance to a fictional figure, arbitrarily making up a distinguished career and inventing a set of impressive-sounding works. That would be so if the only thing needed were to equip the character with any old imagined past from which he could move forward into some equally arbitrary fictive future. But a fiction that is to express its writer[1] and persuade its readers must create its own necessities. Art is not, in a trivial, random sense, "free." Aschenbach's fictional "reality" is extrapolated backwards as well as forwards from the point at which we first meet him. Who he is must be consistent with how he acts. His past and the attitudes that have formed in him by the time the story starts are an important key to understanding its action and its ethical issues. Indeed, since he has enjoyed virtually no private "lived" life outside his creative career, apart from a brief happy marriage, what the text calls the "intensified life" of art becomes crucial. Aschenbach's temperament is traced back to a set of general causes, the mixture of austere Prussian and more "fiery" Bohemian blood. That is typical of Thomas Mann's conception of what makes artists. But beyond those preconditions, a very specific development has shaped the man who goes to Venice. We understand him not just as "*an* artist" but as "this particular artist" (not, as the Luke translation puts it, "this particular *kind* of artist").

Aschenbach's career is remarkable for two things. On the one hand there is the scope and nature of his work, on the other there is the way he has in recent years consciously shaped it. Roughly speaking, the first accounts for his standing, the second ultimately for his fall. The "works of his maturity" were calculated to meet all the demands an age might make on a major writer. He has treated a significant phase in German history in the massive novel about Frederick the Great. He has created a picture of contemporary society in the equally large-scale novel *Maya*. He has given a firm moral response to the aporias of modern relativism in the "powerful tale" entitled

A Miserable Wretch. And he has shown a command of the complex issues underlying the art of his day in the essay *Intellect and Art*. History, society, ethics, aesthetics; the greatest German monarch as a triumphantly handled subject; the greatest German aesthetic theorist (Schiller) as the obvious term of comparison—all this surely makes Aschenbach the complete literary master.[2]

And no less so because his achievement has cost great effort and discipline, more than anyone would guess from the outward appearance of "solid strength and stamina" (202) which his works present. That illusion is part of his triumph. His massive oeuvre has been built up with infinite pains from innumerable small inspirations. Aschenbach is a "moralist of achievement" (*Leistungsethiker*), an artistic exponent of the Protestant work ethic. For him, genius is not a matter of effortless superiority; everything great, he has somewhere written, is achieved against the grain, under pressure, "as a defiant 'Despite.'" He lives by that principle. It is typified by the early morning cold shower and the sacrificial religious devotion with which he "offers up" his morning hours to art. It is epitomized by the command "See it through!" (*Durchhalten*) which he has taken over from Frederick the Great as his own motto, and by the image a "subtle observer" has applied to the never-relaxed Aschenbach, that of a clenched fist which never relaxes. (The relaxing of Aschenbach's hands will mark the stages of his emotional adventure.)

Not surprisingly, the characters who people his books all have something of this same "heroism of weakness." The writer has projected his own mode of being into his fictions.[3] This fragile heroism constitutes, we learn, the "affinity" and "congruence" between him and his public that are in turn the deepest reasons for the acclaim his writing has won. So as well as a grand review of the named works that made Aschenbach's mature reputation, we get a second survey, this time of figures to which the public was drawn because of that affinity. They are figures not named, from works not named.[4] But the enigmatic hints of their fate and function suggest they are characters from earlier works; they do not obviously fit the plot of the "works of his maturity." Nevertheless, they belong alongside them in making the foundation of Aschenbach's eminence in the national culture.

Not so another aspect of Aschenbach's early work. Whereas he was able from the first to captivate bourgeois readers by his "palpably live literary representation, which had no intellectual axe to grind,"[5] at the same time he appealed to a less staid youthful readership by his "skepticism and irony," by being "problematic" and "radical," and by formulating "breath-taking cynicisms about the questionable nature of art and the artist." The key concepts of this practice were "knowledge" (*Wissen*) and, especially, "insight" or "analytical clarity" (*Erkenntnis*).[6] This is an aspect of his youth Aschenbach has since emphatically rejected, and the metaphors that evoke it imply that he was right to do so: "He had been in thrall to intellect, had exhausted the soil by excessive analysis and ground up the seed-corn of growth" (204). Intellect and analysis are here presented as contrary to nature: they tyrannize the free mind like an addiction, they consume resources that should be carefully husbanded for a productive future. So for Aschenbach to have put away these youthful things was a necessary part of that "ascent to dignity" which the text declares is the goal of every great talent (203).[7]

Even so, the way Aschenbach's resolve is narrated makes it sound like a paradox, even a provocation. It was, we are told, the "profound decision of the mature master to deny knowledge, to repudiate it, to pass over it with head held high, insofar as it was in the least degree calculated to paralyse, discourage or devalue the will, feeling, even passion" (204). The paradox and provocation lie in applying the metaphor of depth ("profound decision") to the rejection of all deeper understanding, and in labeling as "shallow by comparison" the original youthful impulse to take analysis as deep as it would go. It is, allegedly, "shallow" not to see that when analysis is thus pressed to the extreme it becomes a bottomless "abyss." Similarly, while we might think it was lax to reject the rigorous pursuit of knowledge, the text alleges on Aschenbach's behalf that in moral terms (paradox again) it is analysis itself that leads to laxity: "the laxity of the principle of compassion that to understand all is to forgive all"—Madame de Staël's famous aphorism "tout comprendre, c'est tout pardonner."[8]

The logic implied here can be put in a rhetorical question: when we know every last factor that lay behind, say, the behavior of a criminal, and if we accept that the criminal was indeed totally determined by these factors, how can there still be such a thing as moral blame? Psychology becomes an excuse to excuse everything. The notion of responsibility has been dissolved, and there is no ground left under our feet for moral judgment. In that sense, an abyss does indeed open beneath us. And as Tonio Kröger finds (153), for the writer who practices these things the abyss of knowledge and irony and skepticism into which he is constantly peering, if not himself actually falling, inevitably separates him from the society of ordinary people. Such unremitting analysis is also labeled (it may be implied that Aschenbach himself labeled it) the "indecent psychologism of the age." This is the dilemma Aschenbach has shown the way out of with his story *A Miserable Wretch*, where he has used forthright moral language to condemn vile actions (204). One imagines an almost Victorian voice thundering forth.

At the same time as Aschenbach came to believe that true "profundity" required a paradoxical return to a more "superficial," simpler view of morality, by coincidence (or is it, the text inquires, something more than coincidence?), his literary style suddenly took on a new "purity, simplicity, symmetry." These are all likewise "superficial" qualities, in the literal sense that they are aspects of the visible surface of things, undisturbed by analytical probing and benefiting from its absence. They are, moreover, qualities traditionally associated with the "classical" in art and literature, and the classical in turn is the category in which we expect to find many of the artists and writers who are by common agreement revered as "masters." It is therefore no surprise to find the two terms side by side in the sentence that summarizes Aschenbach's present position and aspirations as an artist: his mature works, we are told, had "an evident, indeed an intentional stamp of the Masterly and the Classical" (204). So the relation between art and knowledge, between analytical depth and unproblematic surface, is the issue on which at some point in his mature years Aschenbach's career has pivoted. We may guess that it was a central issue in his essay *Intellect and Art*, and we can perhaps assume that his argument resolved it—as is usual with artists who theorize—in a way that prepared and justified the shift in his own artistic commitment from "intellect" to "art."

So far, the narrator's rhetoric has suggested approval of Aschenbach's work and sympathy with his literary evolution—in simple terms, it has gone along with what must be the public's view of this great writer. But now, towards the end of the chapter, the rhetorical flow changes its course. In place of approval and sympathy, the narrator sounds notes of doubt. The authority of Aschenbach's new aesthetic, its adequacy as a response to experience, is questioned. Doubt begins with the word *intentional*. Can an intentional—literally, "a willed"—stamp of the classical and the masterly be wholly genuine? The word *stamp* already suggests something imposed from without. Should we be convinced by an appearance of classical mastery? Can the problems of art be truly resolved and the course of an individual artist's development be rightly settled by "decision" and imposition, rather than by a natural growth from within? Is it possible, is it legitimate, to *will* literary maturity?

The text poses rhetorical questions in this vein. It asks whether "moral resoluteness beyond knowledge and beyond subversive, inhibiting insight" (204f.) does not necessarily involve "a moral oversimplification of the world and of human psychology." This takes back the earlier paradoxical play with what is truly "profound" and what is "shallow" and comes closer to the commonsense view that neglecting or rejecting the knowledge and insight we have, or might acquire, can only be risky. This means that the moral achievement claimed for Aschenbach, the alleged "miracle of reborn naiveté" (204), may after all be merely a matter of sweeping uncomfortable questions under the carpet. It may involve turning a blind eye to too much. It is symptomatic that Aschenbach has excluded, as Louis XIV is said to have done, "every unrefined word" from his linguistic usage (205). How much of the world must that not involve excluding too?

And just as Aschenbach's moral (self-)simplification was also matched by a new attention to beauty of form in his work, so the doubts about his new morality are accompanied by doubts of the narrator's about formal beauty. Form may have a moral value because it is the product of the artist's disciplined work, and yet it may still be amoral, even immoral, as a finished product because the criteria to which it appeals do not necessarily have any substantive link with morality. Worse, beauty may even try to override moral values. The narrator, it seems, is still capable of the skeptical probing that has been renounced by his fictional colleague. Once again, as in chapter 1, he has first built up and then questioned something established, in this instance Aschenbach's thinking in aesthetics, together with the ethics that went with it.

But a brisk "Be that as it may!" has already anounced that we are breaking off the abstract argument and starting back towards the story track. The narrator stops only to defend Aschenbach's acceptance of public status, the outward forms of which were the conferring of the name-prefix *von* (Aschenbach "sensed the inner appropriateness of this honor" [205]) and the use of selected pages from his works as models of prose in school reading books. Finally we learn what little there is to know about Aschenbach's brief and now distant family life and are given a sketch of his outward appearance, for which the narrative borrows the features of Gustav Mahler, as it has already borrowed the composer's given name.

This detailed account of Aschenbach's career, interpolated into the narrative, shows Thomas Mann's need (and perhaps his sense of the reader's need too, in a dense and complex story) to have an explicit statement of the issues it embodies. In this it is like the lengthy discussion of an artist's problems in the central section of *Tonio Kröger* (153ff.), where that earlier writer-figure unburdens himself of his inner conflicts to his sympathetic painter friend Lizaveta Ivanovna. Or it is like the letter which Spinell writes to Klöterjahn in *Tristan* (122ff.), pouring out his hatred for the "unconscious type" of the bourgeois and declaring his mission to "analyze" it. All such abstract presentation, like the essayistic digressions found in much modern fiction, runs the risk of making the work of art seem overly schematic, and perhaps also of tapping off energies which the author might have used to shape the issues concretely. It needs, in other words, some aesthetic justifying. This particular example seems at first sight even more abstract than the discussion in *Tonio Kröger*, which is at least staged as a conversation-piece, with dialogue plausibly distributed between Tonio and Lizaveta in a real situation which has its own subtly suggested atmosphere. We are in the painter's studio, where Russian cigarettes and tea and sympathy are offered, a sunlit Munich is outside the north-facing windows, and there is "painter's fixative and the scent of spring" in the air (154), a disharmonious mixture which becomes for Tonio Kröger an emblem for the opposition between art and life they are discussing.

Yet the second chapter of *Death in Venice* does have its own situation and atmosphere too. It is not just an interruption in the narrative flow to provide information. As suggested above, it is "mock literary biography," a pastiche of what might be found in a standard reference work—a dictionary of national biography or an authoritative literary history. It has the ring of a measured public appraisal, and that inevitably gives a feeling of near-finality; for reviewing a life of achievement makes the great man's career seem nearly complete, especially when the fault lines in his work which will bring about that completion are highlighted. Altogether, it is like the obituary which journals of record keep ready, in need only of a last updating, for the day when the great public figure will die. To that extent the whole chapter is one more omen for the story that now resumes.

6

Destination, Destiny

What Aschenbach travels to find, as an escape from his literary impasse, is "something strange and random" (206). Yet apparently not quite random. There can still be right and wrong choices. His first stay, on an Adriatic island, is unsatisfactory. Aside from the particular annoyances of climate and clientele, he has an obscure sense of not yet having arrived at his proper destination. The German wording ("den Ort seiner Bestimmung") suggests a place he was "meant" to reach, without making clear whose is the intention. Suddenly he realizes where that must be, and acts. The account of this realization and his redeparture builds up to the final and culminating word of the paragraph: "Venice" (207).

This brings the narrative into line with its title, and in that sense Aschenbach is now on the right path. But "right" means that it will lead him to the other element decreed in the title, death. "Destination" is also destiny. It is his own instinct that has moved him in this fateful direction; throughout the story his actions do not just assent to a pattern of fate, they have a hand in creating it. But its reality *as* fate is also suggested, if not openly asserted—for to assert that ancient idea would sit oddly in a modern text. In this instance it is as if Aschenbach has subconsciously followed the symbolic pointers of chapter 1: the "Byzantine" mortuary chapel and the "two apocalyptic beasts" that hinted at Venetian style and the Lion of St. Mark. These were part of the weird encounter with that imperious stranger who dramatically embodies the external force of fate. To put it crudely (though this the text never does), "something" came for Aschenbach. There are further hints of an alien force that is concerned to keep him on his "chosen" path. The ship's purser sells him a ticket with a glib sales pitch, "almost as if he were anxious that the traveler might have second thoughts about his decision to go to Venice" (207f.). After serving Aschenbach, he calls for the next customer. There is none. As with the deserted Munich streets and the empty setting of the mortuary chapel, the stage is empty but for Aschenbach; it is as if things were set up solely for his benefit.

But decidedly not to his taste. The boat to Venice is not at all this dignified writer's usual scene. It is "ancient . . . dingy and black with soot," and everything on it is sordid—the "grubby hunch-backed sea-man," the purser's "cavelike cabin" where Aschenbach's change is "dropped . . . on the stained tablecloth," the steward in a "grease-stained frock-coat," the "wretched meal," the captain who drinks all morning belowdecks with a group of loud apprentices (207ff.). Most sordid of all, in among these young men, and loud in his grotesque pretensions to be one of them, there is the hideous old fop, scrawny and wrinkled, with false teeth, but with rouged cheeks and garish clothes, mutton dressed as lamb (208). If voyaging to Venice is the "right" path, it is a dubious and disturbing one. "How was this possible?" Aschenbach asks himself. Tired and disorientated, he has "a feeling that something not quite usual was beginning to happen, that the world was undergoing a dreamlike alienation, becoming increasingly deranged and bizarre" (208f.). Not for the last time, he tries to get a grip on the situation: "Perhaps this process might be arrested if he were to cover his face for a little and then take a fresh look at things" (209). But at that moment "he had the sensation of being afloat": the ship has begun to move away from the quay. Just when he wanted to steady things, he is on an unsteady element—again, not for the last time. Venice is itself half water, "the yielding element" (212), and, in a phrase of Georg Simmel's, "the ambiguous city."[1]

Even arrival there turns out to be a mixed experience. There is irksome delay while waiting for the health and customs authorities (who, significantly for what happens later, only perform their duties "perfunctorily"); though there is also the "dazzling composition of fantastic architecture" seen when this "most improbable of cities" is approached from seaward (211). But any appreciation of beauty is disturbed by the old fop, now helplessly drunk, who importunes Aschenbach with "bleated" farewells and compliments to his "sweetheart." Repellently, he half loses his false teeth as he does so. Beauty mixed with sordidness is in the very grain of this novella. And a more specific pattern can be picked up here: when the "false youth" burbles out the foolish formality, "We commend ourselves to your kind remembrance," it is not just a meaningless request of his to Aschenbach, but a hint from narrator to reader. False youth and cosmetic rejuvenation are motifs that will recur, and the narrator needs our powers of "remembrance" to accomplish his ends.

Patterns and recurrence from now on are crucial. The narrative strategy consists in making us see them without making them too obvious. They are designed to structure the story's reality, but as with the notion of "fate," which they help to realize, they cannot be declared "real" by the criteria of realistic narrative. By the same token, they are not seen by Aschenbach, who inhabits the, to him, real world, even if it does sometimes seem disquietingly out of joint through the bizarre encounters of travel. Thus the unlicensed gondolier in his coffin-black gondola, who rows an unwilling Aschenbach all the way to the Lido instead of to the vaporetto station, is sinister enough in himself, with his refusal to obey his passenger and his grim words when asked about the fare, "You will pay"—without even, in the original German text, the polite address "signore" to soften them. But everything about him also echoes the earlier Munich encounter: the alien ethnic type (not a Bavarian in the Munich context, not an Italian here in Venice), the reddish hair, the straw hat, the prominent teeth. The two surely cannot (can they?) "be" the identical man. But the narrative does not say they are; there is no overt cross-reference to the earlier passage. Their similar features are not even described with the exactly identical wording that is found in the simpler forms of leitmotiv, and those similarities of feature are differently explained in the two passages: the Munich stranger's teeth were bared by a grimace as he looked into the sun (or was it a permanent deformation?), whereas the gondolier's are, naturally enough, bared by the effort of rowing. The explanations are entirely plausible. But they do not explain the uncanny likeness itself, once we have noticed it. If we have not (and the student at first reading may very well not—one student certainly remembers not noticing), then the explanations, with their own obtrusive uncertainties, are an extra way to *make* us notice it. In fact, a certain slowness to notice is arguably something the narrative strategy counts on: we are meant to feel the force of our attachment to reality and to realism, even as we feel the pull away from them. And the full literary effect then depends on our suggestibility to pattern, on our gradually more willing suspension (or at least half-suspension) of disbelief. We entertain the pattern these figures and their similarities make as a significant fiction, one that suggests an alternative reality that is not yet clearly comprehensible but is starting to be as strong as the "normal" one.

Significance, after all, commonly depends on patterns of repetition; conversely, any pattern of repetition begins to create meaning. A repeated scientific observation points to an underlying law, a repeated human action hints at a constant character, the repetition of a word or phrase underlines the coherence of an argument. From early in his career, Thomas Mann had used recurring motifs to create meanings beyond the randomness of mere fact, which was all that late Naturalism, the extreme form of nineteenth-century realism, set out to record. An appreciative early critic described Thomas Mann's literary method as "naturalism on the way to symbolism."[2] An obvious example is the way the outsider figures in his early work are linked from one story to another by a set of shared physical attributes, and their more robust opposites are linked by a different and equally consistent set. The reader takes in (or is taken in by) this schematic account of the way body and mind relate, and of the social consequences, while enjoying the narrative. The thesis behind the fiction is not quite met head-on, to be accepted or disagreed with. It takes an effort for the reader to stand back and ask what, beneath surface appearances, is the reality and necessity of things behind this allusive art. Is biological decline and spiritual refinement the reality behind the decline of the Buddenbrooks, as the novel gently and cumulatively persuades us? With *Death in Venice*, there will be an analogous question: just what is finally asserted as the reality behind Aschenbach's death?

For the present, there is a pause. Aschenbach is installed in his Lido hotel, and after the vicissitudes of travel resumes his status amid a discreet luxury that very much *is* his scene. The narrative can take stock of "the phenomena of his journey to this place," in a double sense, for his judgment can be read as a comment on the story's own balancing act and its likely effect on the reader: "Without presenting reason with difficulties, without even really offering food for thought, they were nevertheless fundamentally strange in nature, as it seemed to him, and disturbing no doubt through precisely this contradiction" (215). Once again, by denying that the events of Aschenbach's journey are even food for thought, the narrative makes them just that for any reader who has been insensitive enough so far *not* to find them unsettling. In fact, by now we should be alert to the probability that any word of reassurance means its opposite; we read it as part of a code of contrary suggestion. But a phase has been concluded. Aschenbach seems safe again in cocooning civilization, and this is emphasized by the note on which the paragraph ends. It evokes in appropriately formal language the sheltering refinements offered by a first-class international hotel. Aschenbach "gave the room-maid certain instructions for the enhancement of his comfort" and then "had himself conveyed . . . to the ground floor" (215). Disturbances have apparently been left behind him. The next encounter will be disturbing in a quite different way.

It is with the Polish boy Tadzio, who, insidiously, is one of the most refined products of this high-society civilization. That makes the encounter deceptively unthreatening. After the first shock of seeing "that the boy's beauty was perfect" (216), Aschenbach hastens to classify it safely with art, with "Greek sculpture of the noblest period," for example, the *Boy Extracting a Thorn*, and on the other hand links it with social privilege and family pampering (216f.). But there is a clue to the deep impression the boy's beauty has made. While he and his siblings wait for their mother, Aschenbach delays going in to dinner, "comfortably ensconced in his deep armchair, and incidentally [*übrigens*] with beauty there before his eyes" (217). Is his extra motive for lingering really so incidental? And if the boy, on his way in to dinner, turns and looks Aschenbach in the eyes, is it really just "for some reason or other" (218)? Or is the narrative's code of contraries again suggesting some deeper significance? True, beauty occupies Aschenbach's conscious mind over dinner, but it is in the (for an artist) perfectly natural form of abstract reflections on how it comes about. Reflection, appreciation, the pleasure of a connoisseur suddenly faced with an embodiment of the thing he most values, namely beauty—such detachment is the keynote of Aschenbach's responses. He seems secure and relaxed, his benevolence expressing itself through cultivated allusion and a touch of humor. He quotes a classical hexameter so as to cast Tadzio in the role of a latter-day Phaeacian (the Phaeacians are a relaxed, carefree people described in book 8 of Homer's *Odyssey*). In no time the narrative text itself drops into a matching hexameter rhythm: on Tadzio's collar "rested the bloom of the head in unsurpassable beauty" (220). Aschenbach's silent comment on the boy, "Good, good!" is a piece of "cool professional approval," as if of an artistic masterpiece.

His enjoyment, nature appreciated as art, is surely itself high civilization; the writer is in his element. It continues on the beach, where civilization as a whole is taking its ease "on the brink of the element," i.e., the sea. For the artist always struggling to achieve perfection, the sea is a competing if paradoxical perfection, total limitlessness in contrast to the firm limits of form. It offers a temptation to escape and rest which is already a kind of self-abandonment (221). It is also the background against which the boy's "truly godlike beauty" comes and goes, still kept psychologically at arm's length by a fund of cultivated comment. Thus when Tadzio is kissed by Jascha, Aschenbach again finds an apt quotation, this time from Xenophon's *Recollections of Socrates*. But both the action and, for all its easy humor, the Greek allusion start to touch on the theme of homosexual love, while the sounds of the boy's name, "ruling the beach" through the cries of his family, add a radically new excitement, they are "something at once sweet and wild." And when the boy emerges from the sea, perfect form from perfect formlessness, "the sight inspired mythic imaginings . . . of the origins of form and the birth of the gods." Aschenbach, for all his professional detachment, hears within himself the "beginnings of song" (223f.). Cool appreciation of statuesque form is mixed with the spirit of music.

But also with some confused and latently violent reactions: Aschenbach, the creator of literary beauty, feels "paternal favor" for the live being who "possesses beauty," but also a strange satisfaction that this delicate boy will "probably not grow old." There is an impulse to cherish, but also to destroy: something must be disturbing him deeply to evoke this response. And a third impulse makes itself felt between those two: the writer scans his mirror for the signs of age, "his gray hair, his weary sharp-featured face," then recalls all the achievements and distinctions he can think of. The anxious appraisal of what he has become in the flesh is followed almost desperately by a compensating appeal to what he has created in the spirit (224f.).

But all this passes without any sign that Aschenbach is clear about what is driving him. Once again, the stuff of the narrative is a not fully explained unease. Is that a factor in Aschenbach's physical malaise, which in turn makes him try to leave Venice? Or is it all just the oppressive sirocco weather? (*The Magic Mountain*, which was first designed as a sequel and "satyr-play" to *Death in Venice*, and perceptibly shadows its plot line in detail, will make a firm link between emotional, climatic, and bodily conditions; though it stays teasingly ambiguous about whether, in the high-Alpine atmosphere of Davos, love brings on illness or illness brings on love.) Is Aschenbach's malaise perhaps even a subconscious impulse to escape—it will prove to have been his last chance—from what he is not yet aware is his fate? It is true that climate is a factor he expressly recognizes; it is an old enemy that apparently routed him once before and made him cut short a visit to Venice. The sultriness, the sirocco, produce "simultaneous excitement and exhaustion" (225). His decision is immediate and rational; his will, which has been flaccid during the adventures and misadventures of travel and arrival, is firm enough now to arrange departure.

Yet something undermines his firmness. A new morning with hints of a change in the weather already makes him regret his decision. But it is not the only thing that leads him to delay and delay leaving, despite the urgings of the hotel staff. "It was indeed getting very late by the time he rose. It so happened that at that same moment Tadzio entered through the glass door" (227). But this is not a story in which *any*thing just "so happens." Using the casual to suggest the causal is another feature of the code of contraries, which by now the reader should be reading with ease. Aschenbach's sotto voce farewell to the boy is the key to this part of the text. Can any reader of the next few pages, which describe the botched departure, seriously believe that "what he found so hard to bear, what was indeed at times quite unendurable, was *evidently* the thought that he would never see Venice again, that this was a parting for ever" (228; italics mine)? It would have been more "evidently" so without that word, which we take at our peril for a firm statement by an omniscient narrator. After our accumulated practice, we can now only read the explanation as once more couched in free indirect style, and therefore as a façade behind which Aschenbach conceals the truth from himself, though not from a narrator who is only feigning nescience. His regrets at the prospect of never again seeing Venice thinly overlay his real regrets at leaving Tadzio. That deeper reality duly shows in the language: Venice is a "beloved city," and Aschenbach is a failed lover, no longer prepared (as he was the night before) to admit his own physical inadequacy and draw the consequences.

The botched departure is a classic piece of narrative even in this virtuoso text. There are sad images and rhythms for the "voyage of sorrow" to the station; then a quick sequence of confusion and delight in the scene on the platform (made more immediate in the original by a shift to the present tense, which the English translations do not try to render); and then the sprightly rhythms of the return to the Lido, with "the rapid little boat, spray before its bows, tacking to and fro between gondolas and vaporetti," the very embodiment of joyful release. Aschenbach is as happy as a "truant schoolboy." The literal German sense—an "escaped" schoolboy—sets off an even more ironic sequence. For what Aschenbach has escaped from is his attempted escape from Venice. The irony is that for the first time he himself now sees things as the work of a higher agency, but a wholly benevolent one. So he can relish "returning to places from which one had just taken leave, turned round by fate," and correcting a "grievous mistake." He can be secretly delighted by the incompetence that ought by rights to have infuriated him. He can welcome what is outwardly a "stroke of misfortune," a "visitation" (229). He can inwardly laugh at the commiserations of the hotel staff: "Pas de chance, monsieur" ("Bad luck, sir"), says the lift attendant. But there is, of course, a double irony that reverses Aschenbach's own reversals. He is indeed a "fugitive" (230), now recaptured and returning to a new room. The lift attendant's innocent words can even be read as true, as a darker frame outside Aschenbach's glee, giving their true ominous sense to the accidents that have brought him back.

So Aschenbach's first recognition of a destiny underlying his adventures is both right and wrong, both clarity and illusion: he is right about the coherence, but wrong about its ultimate direction. The mistake draws him willingly on towards his fate.

On one thing, however, he attains a clarity without illusion. Reinstalled, relaxed after the excitement, and musing with disapproval on his own "irresolution, his ignorance of his own wishes," he sees from his high window Tadzio coming back from the beach. Aschenbach shapes a jaunty phrase of mental greeting but feels it "die on his lips," feels "the enthusiasm of his blood," and knows the true reason departure felt so desolating, "that it was because of Tadzio" (230). This, then, is the "late adventure of the emotions" that he half anticipated as the boat lay off Venice (210)—its origins lie that far back, though Aschenbach does not make the connection. But his visible response points much farther back still, to the needs of a toiler in the spirit who had "'only ever lived like *this*'—and the speaker clenched the fingers of his left hand tightly into a fist—'and never like *this*'—and he let his open hand hang comfortably down from the arm of the chair" (201). Aschenbach has sacrificed physical and emotional life over years of intense creativity. That disciplined will has asserted itself only with difficulty, and then flagged altogether, when challenged by the bizarre figures and events of the journey. Now he willingly gives up the struggle with an emblematic "opening and outspreading of the arms," a "gesture of ready welcome and calm acceptance" (230). It is the first time since the world started to be out of joint that Aschenbach, the devotee of beautiful surfaces who long ago gave up the indecencies of psychological analysis, has looked deeply into himself. But it is too late now to make a difference.

7

Idyll

What follows is a fatal happiness, but happiness nonetheless. After his failed departure, Aschenbach puts off all thought of leaving Venice and settles in for a season. The weather seems to confirm the rightness of what has happened: the opening of the new chapter is all heat and light—the burning sun, the radiance on the sea, the glowing sand. Aschenbach idles as it was never in his nature to do before. Away from his strict routines as a "moralist of achievement" at his summer house in the mountains, there is all the time in the world to do so. "This place bewitched him, relaxed his will, gave him happiness" (231). He savors this ideal existence by recalling some lines of Homer's—Greek allusions will come thick and fast from now on—about the "Elysian land . . . where lightest of living is granted to mortals" (232; *Odyssey*, book 4, ll. 563ff.). He is consciously living an idyll.

At its center is of course the chance to observe Tadzio "almost constantly" (232). The narrator lingers over those observations as lovingly as his protagonist does, and to more literary effect. Like Aschenbach, he soon knows "every line and pose of that noble, so freely displayed body" (233), but unlike his character, he captures them in language. For Aschenbach, the boy is "more beautiful than words can express"; he concludes that language "can only praise sensuous beauty, but not reproduce it" (240). But the disclaimer makes us aware—and is probably meant to—how much Thomas Mann has managed to do just that. It is one of the ironies of free indirect style that the narrator can find words for the passionate perceptions of his character and take credit for formulating what his character despairs of saying—even while the narrative suggests it was fully present to Aschenbach's mind and on the very tip of his tongue.

These set-piece descriptions are aesthetic in a complex sense. First, Thomas Mann sets out to create verbal equivalents of plastic art—that was a conscious ambition at the time he wrote the story, and specifically to celebrate the boy was its first inspiration (see below, p. 83f.). Secondly, a last remnant of aesthetic disguise still conceals Aschenbach's true feelings. Though he has now realized that the pain of departure was caused by leaving Tadzio, and though he gives himself up unreservedly to the pleasures of the beach, still he sees the boy in artistic terms: in motion or at rest, running, standing, or lying, poised or posed, with his "finely chiseled arm" (233) and his "marble-pale skin" which the sun seems never to burn, Tadzio is like an animated statue. Watching him can be called "contemplation and study" (232)—the delight it gives is of a cultivated, aesthetic kind. Admittedly, its sensuousness has moved it away from Kant's austere aesthetic principle of "disinterested pleasure" and towards the one Nietzsche borrowed from Stendhal, that "beauty is a promise of happiness." Even so, it is enough to hold off for a while Aschenbach's final frank avowal of his passion. And this last, in every sense formal resistance appears strengthened when Aschenbach draws a parallel between Tadzio and his own literary aesthetic, between the beauty of the boy's living form and the "slender form" that he the writer, "filled with sober passion," labors to "set free from the marble mass of language" (234). But the parallel reminds us that the concern with beauty, a new devotion to surfaces rather than depths, was the chosen aesthetic path of the mature, deliberately classical Aschenbach, and is what has made him extra responsive—ultimately, that is, susceptible—to Tadzio. Beauty of form is an obvious link between them, but the analogy is deceptive: the beauty the writer creates is an end product of his "sober passion"; live human beauty may be the start of an anything but sober one.

Just as clear is what links Aschenbach's present state of mind and feeling with the aesthetic path *not* chosen, that is, with the "immature" values of his early work which he consciously discarded. This is made quite explicit by the narrative. In another minidrama of confusion akin to the failed departure from Venice, he tries to establish a "normal" relationship with Tadzio by speaking a few casual words. Failure again results. When he catches up with the boy, "a strangled and trembling voice" is all he could have managed, "he felt his heart, perhaps partly because he had been walking so fast, hammering wildly inside him" (237). The words "perhaps partly" are a façade-explanation of the kind the story has made us used to. At all events, it is now "too late" to achieve his aim. That is Aschenbach's view ("he thought at that moment"), and it is still perhaps Aschenbach thinking—though with free indirect style it is hard to be sure—in what follows: "But was it too late? This step he had failed to take would very possibly have led to . . . a wholesome sobering." In the next sentence, however, the "dual voice" has certainly split, and it is the narrator we hear critically recognizing that it really is too late and that "wholesome sobering" has been consciously refused: "The aging lover no longer wished to return to sobriety . . . the intoxication was too precious to him." The explanation of why this is so echoes what chapter 2 told us about Aschenbach's mature development: "Aschenbach was no longer disposed to self-criticism; taste, the intellectual mold of his years, self-respect, maturity and late simplicity all disinclined him to analyze his motives and decide whether what had prevented him from carrying out his intention had been a prompting of conscience or a disreputable weakness" (237). Aschenbach's "profound decision" to give up probing into motives ("indecent psychologism") has become a "late simplicity" that now determines his actions and omissions. The "too late" of this particular incident is part of a more general and necessary "too late."

Earlier warnings are being fulfilled. But some of Aschenbach's own reflections take us on to quite new ground. The form he strives to "set free from the marble mass of language" is described as "a model and mirror of intellectual beauty" (234). These words excite him because they suddenly suggest a yet more elevated way of seeing Tadzio's beauty: this too is a "model and mirror" of something higher, beyond the individual's bodily being. Looking at Tadzio, Aschenbach can feel he is "gazing on Beauty itself, on Form as a divine thought, on the one and pure perfection which dwells in the spirit and of which a human likeness had here been lightly and graciously set up for him to worship" (234).

This is not a notion from early-twentieth-century Venice, or Germany, but from ancient Greece. It is more, however, than the kind of decorative allusion that comes readily to the cultivated traveler, like the "Elysian idyll" evoked at the start of the chapter or the various decorative myths that will occur later (239). This one goes deeper, putting Aschenbach's devotion to Tadzio in a new and potentially ennobling context. It begins when he imagines Socrates in conversation with a young Athenian, Phaedrus, outide the walls of the city, and remembers the doctrines Plato put forward in the dialogue called by the young man's name. Plato's philosophical dialogues, the *Phaedrus* and the *Symposium*, give beauty a special place as the only meeting point between the realm of absolute values (the "Ideas" or ultimate forms) and human sensuous experience. All other absolutes of that transcendent realm—which, according to Plato's metaphysics, human beings knew before they were born but necessarily forgot when they entered on earthly existence—are abstract and beyond direct experiencing. Only beauty can appear, visible and tangible, before our eyes. When it does, we undergo a shock of recognition as we remember (for Plato, all education and initiation is a process of remembering) the higher realm we once knew. Since that is where all reality resides, beauty itself cannot be seized or possessed. But it can be known more directly than any other of the ultimate forms, provided that, even while the individual beautiful object or person is being loved, the lover looks beyond them and pays homage to the reality from which their shape is borrowed. The true lover loves intensely, but always symbolically.

Strange though this subtle doctrine may seem to a materialistic age,[1] it can be understood at least at a simple level by asking whether the lover of a beautiful person or the owner of a beautiful work of art could ever be said to *possess* the actual beauty of person or work. For the quality of beauty exists in a different dimension from the living being or material object that manifests it, whether or not we choose to think of this other dimension in Plato's manner as an actual realm of transcendent reality. Beauty is an appearance, a form, a relationship between physical elements, an intangible essence of tangible bodies which may consequently generate in us a distinct way of seeing and responding—distinct, that is, from the normal impulses of desire, acquisition, or use. Eighteenth-century German philosophy coined the term "aesthetic" to capture this experience. To that extent Plato is the father of modern aesthetics—even though his insistence that the reality of beauty (as of all other phenomena) lies in a transcendent realm is at odds with the concreteness and earthliness of art. This will be a crucial point at the novella's end.

But meantime, what *should* the human response to beauty be, if not straightforward physical enjoyment and complacent possession? Plato's answer is: a spiritual activity that will measure up to the high, indeed quasi-religious source of inspiration. For him, physical love and procreation flatly did not. Christian Europe was later to idealize relations between the sexes, but for the Greeks they had no romantic aura. Love between men did. It seemed (a logically somewhat shaky argument) to have more spiritual potential precisely because it lacked a biological function. The *Phaedrus* talks of "spiritual begetting" as something analogous to, but higher than, the production of physical offspring. Homosexual love might lead men to write poetry, to pursue philosophy, or to act bravely in a common cause. They might be inspired to emulation, to creation, to reflection, they might die together (some celebrated pairs of young men did) in opposing tyranny or defending their homeland. That these things were possible did not of course make them always actual. It was equally possible for a lover to fall short of the ideal, not reach beyond gratification, fail to see what higher reality was signaled in the beloved. This meant that the lover's response to beauty would be a judgment on the lover. Aschenbach, who is consciously savoring and quoting to himself what he remembers of the *Phaedrus* dialogue (235), duly recalls Plato's warning against "the lusts of the profane and base who cannot turn their eyes to Beauty when they behold its image and are not capable of reverence" (235).

How does his own case stand? Positively, it would seem. His mind is certainly clear about the issues, and "at this point of [his] crisis and visitation"—the terms make it clear that this is an important turning point—he goes back to his art (236). Not by directly describing Tadzio, but by working with the boy in sight, so that he can "let his style follow the lineaments of this body which he saw as divine" (236). The boy's beauty is the writer's inspiration, and he is mindful of its transcendent source. This meets the demands of Plato's ideal, and the text duly echoes words from the *Phaedrus* on spiritual begetting: "How strange those hours were! How strangely exhausting that labor! How mysterious this act of intercourse and begetting between a mind and a body!" (236).

If more is needed to make this appear a wholly positive turn, there is the way it relates to the problems that set the story going. Aschenbach's act of writing achieves—ecstatically—what the Venetian journey was meant to achieve in a more humdrum way, as a simple break from his frustrating labors: namely, the return of his creative powers and an end to the problem of writer's block that first sent him out for that afternoon walk back in Munich. His pleasure in writing again, and writing well, is correspondingly acute. Thought and feeling interpenetrate, and "never had he felt the joy of the word more sweetly, never had he known so clearly that Eros dwells in language" (235f.). To the happiness of carefree days in the sun is added the happiness of a restored creativity. It seems the writer's situation is doubly idyllic.

So it comes as a surprise, if not a shock, to find that the "mysterious . . . act of intercourse and begetting between a mind and a body" is finally presented in a negative light. For as Aschenbach finishes his "page and a half of exquisite prose . . . with its limpid nobility and vibrant controlled passion," we get a jaundiced comment from the narrator: "It is as well that the world knows only a fine piece of work and not also its origins, the conditions under which it came into being," for such knowledge "would often confuse readers and shock them." More negative still, as Aschenbach puts his work away, "he felt worn out, even broken, and it felt as if his conscience were accusing him as if after some act of debauchery" (236).

It is hard to see how Aschenbach has fallen short, at least in intention. Yet there has been an earlier clue that Platonic spirituality will be hard for him to achieve. No sooner had he entertained the thought of Tadzio as "model and mirror . . . of Beauty itself" than the narrator commented (more emphatically in the original than in the translation): "That was intoxication; and unhesitatingly, avidly even, the aging writer bade it welcome" (234). And if this warning note was sounded as a lead-in to the "Platonic" phase, what follows immediately after that phase is the incident where Aschenbach fails to establish a normal contact with Tadzio—which is presented not simply as a failure, but as a positive preference for intoxication, a refusal to be sobered. It begins to look as if the writer's consuming emotion for the boy can no more transform itself into pure Platonism than it could earlier pretend to be pure aesthetic contemplation. There is thus no way of escape for Aschenbach in the spirit, any more than there was in the body when he tried to leave Venice. He is in the grip of some larger, still unidentified force.

Towards the end of the chapter, Aschenbach, unsobered and in a heightened "poetic" state, draws on yet more classical allusion, or the narrator does so on his behalf: the beauty of dawn over the sea is rendered in figures of Greek myth as he muses on Tadzio (238). And in what is now unambiguously Aschenbach's own vision, the boy is transformed into the youth Hyacinthus, who died a tragic death because two gods both jealously loved him. Here the mythic "fine writing" becomes cloyingly sentimental and overdone. But it is fairly clearly the character's excess, not the narrator's, for the latter's cool, detached voice returns on the same page to make a psychological generalization from Aschenbach's relation to Tadzio: "For one human being loves and honors another as long as he is not in a position to judge him, and longing is the product of deficient knowledge" (239). A familiar word has returned, *Erkenntnis*, the analytic knowledge which the young Aschenbach pursued to excess but which his later self forswore altogether as something too subversive for literary decency (203f.). The suggestion is plain: it would have helped him here.

With no ordinary relations initiated between them, Aschenbach and Tadzio live in a tense mutual awareness. For the boy could hardly not notice such persistent attention, and he begins to respond to it, passing closer than necessary to his admirer's place on the sands, as if drawn by the magnet of powerful feeling. The unspeaking relation between them is in its way controlled and formal. But the formality is precarious, and a sudden encounter is all it takes to let that powerful feeling break through and declare itself fully. They meet unexpectedly, and Tadzio smiles at his admirer from close range: "It was the smile of Narcissus as he bows his head over the mirroring water, that profound, fascinated, protracted smile with which he reaches out his arms towards the reflection of his own beauty" (241). Again the image of the mirror, but now in a very different sense. It is no longer Tadzio who is the mirror, certainly not the "model and mirror" of absolute beauty into which Aschenbach's Platonic reminiscing has idealized him. Nor is he even the boy of the mythic simile who innocently fell in love with his own image. Rather his is the knowing smile of one who senses the power of his beauty over others, consciously enjoys both the power and the beauty, and uses his admirer—Aschenbach is now the mirror—to reflect his beauty back to him. Tadzio's knowingness is as far from the Platonic ideal as Aschenbach himself seems fated to remain.

For the last paragraph of the chapter shows the writer in desperate disarray. His composure is shattered by the "fateful gift" of that smile, he struggles to find adequate expression of his moral outrage at it. Yet moral outrage is hardly relevant, since beauty of form, as we were long ago warned, need not have any connection with morality, and may totally override it (205). So it proves. The openness of this first ever avowed communication between them drives Aschenbach into the open. In a posture not of relaxed acceptance, as at the close of chapter 3, but of overwhelmed physical helplessness, he utters in the climactic last lines of this chapter the inner truth he has repressed for so long.

8

Alien God

In the fifth act of a tragedy, events take an ever clearer direction and move with growing speed down an incline of inevitability. When the catastrophe comes, it may bring with it an understanding of its own causes, and even an insight into some profound principle—for the character, that is. If he achieves this most sophisticated form of what Aristotle called *anagnorisis* (recognition), then the gap of dramatic irony that has all along separated the protagonist from the onlookers or readers is at least partly closed. The tragic victim is thereby restored in some measure to the larger community, even if it is only for a brief moment before being finally destroyed. So there is a paradoxical double movement in these closing stages: deeper into tragedy, but as a way—the only way left, and also the price—of rising above tragedy. All these possibilities are fulfilled in *Death in Venice*.

The act of avowing his love has removed most of Aschenbach's scruples. Where once he relied on chance encounters, he now positively pursues Tadzio—on foot through the streets, with the disturbing possibility that their intricate twists and turns may at any moment bring him embarrassingly face to face with the family; and more melodramatically on the canals, half thrilled and half ashamed at the "roguish compliance" (244) with which he is served by a gondolier to whom this kind of intrigue is routine. And that is only part of the changed relation to Tadzio. The boy is now far from being an aesthetic phenomenon, the object of "devotion and study" as envisaged in the Platonic ideal. He has become the "idol" of a lover driven by "mad compulsion"—the original German echoes the Greek word *mania*, meaning a condition in which alien forces have overwhelmed and taken possession of the conscious mind. The emphasis has shifted markedly away from beauty.

That also applies to the treatment of Venice. After the idyll on the Lido, the city now comes into view more and more as the scene of the pursuit and is itself morally dubious to match the foreground action. From the start Venice has been a disorienting mixture: it is land surrounded, infiltrated, even threatened by water. Water is the "element" on whose brink "civilisation" is so precariously perched (220). It is "the yielding element" on which Aschenbach's weakening will was first shown up in the episode of the unlicensed gondolier (212); even further back, at the start of his sea journey to Venice, the "sensation of being afloat" made him feel "an irrational alarm" and disoriented him further as he strove to get a grip on increasingly bizarre experiences (209). Now his new and conniving gondoliers take him "gliding and swaying"—a forward motion at once unsteady and unhindered—through the "labyrinth" of canals where they are at home but he is, in every sense, lost. Likewise in the maze of bridges, alleyways, and "filthy culs-de-sac," under the oppressive heat and in the "stagnant malodorous air" (244). There is still beauty, but it now comes paired always with decrepitude or sordidness. There is the Oriental magnificence of St. Mark's Basilica with its glowing interior, but mingled with its heavy incense there is "the smell of the sick city" (243), the chemicals being used against cholera. Lovely blossoms trail down crumbling walls and "Moorish windows [are] mirrored in the murky water"; the marble steps of a church dip below the surface of the dirty flood (244). Beggars and dealers feign and swindle. "This was Venice, the flattering and suspect beauty, half fairytale, half tourist trap" (245).

It is now about to be a tourist trap in a literal and potentially fatal sense. If the honest travel clerk is right, visitors will soon be imprisoned in the plague-ridden city by the cordon sanitaire, which is the internationally agreed way to contain major epidemics.[1] But for the time being, the authorities, from commercial motives which are those of the swindling traders and beggars writ large, are hushing up the sickness that will be the direct cause of Aschenbach's death. To him, though, his cholera seems not a threat but a confirmation, an accomplice even, of his passion; the city has its own dark secret, and one kind of disorder winks at another. The sequence in which he uncovers the facts, from the first "uncanny" signs of "the sickness" (241) until he forces the travel clerk's full admission, is part of the tragic action's firm final line. It is also the final stage in Aschenbach's corruption, because even while he teases out the truth from those who desperately or reluctantly conceal it, he has not the least intention of using it for anyone else's good—nor, admittedly, for his own in any normal sense. He revels in the embarrassment of the people he quizzes and the alarm of those who anxiously watch it happen. For all his shocked tone when he first discovers what is going on—"'They want it kept quiet!'. . . 'They're hushing this up!'" (242f.)—he is no moral crusader. Knowledge, the guiding light of his intellectually radical younger years, now gives him a purely formal ironic superiority, the means to irresponsible play in a situation of deadly earnest. Thus when the hotel manager explains away the smells of chemical that are pervading Venice as a routine police precaution, the irony of Aschenbach's reply—"'Very praiseworthy of the police'" (247)—rebounds on him: he is as silent and therefore as guilty as the Venetians. The idea of warning Tadzio's family is something he toys with only briefly, for he has already "realised with a kind of horror that he would not be able to go on living" if Tadzio were to leave (243), as in a slightly different sense it proves. So when he imagines the "decent action which would cleanse his conscience" (255)—not to mention perhaps saving the boy's life in the process—it is like a vignette implausibly transplanted from the conventional kind of fiction where unselfish acts are performed in undisturbed awareness of lofty moral values. But Aschenbach is living at the level of instinct; he enjoys a quite different awareness, of sharing and keeping the city's guilty secret, and this only intoxicates him further. His state has already been called "drunken ecstasy" (245), and ecstasy literally means being outside oneself. An action that would sober him and "give him back to himself again" is the last thing he wants. Hence "he said nothing, and stayed on" (255), a sentence which in the German original is even shorter and denser, four terse monosyllables ("er schwieg und blieb") that stand out against the elaborate syntax all around them like an erratic block in a landscape. Their simple directness makes a subtle connection, recalling the equally simple phrase that registered Aschenbach's first response to Tadzio, his perception "that the boy's beauty was perfect" (216). It is ironic that the noble simplicity of the one has led inexorably to the brutal simplicity of the other.

Aschenbach's fate has three clearly distinguishable factors determining it: the material factor of disease, the moral factor of complicity, and the psychological factor of willing self-abandon. The narrative has traced them all and thus made a comprehensive, realistic case. But the roots of the matter go deeper, to a coherence that is not just that of modern realism. Those alien forces that have taken over Aschenbach's conscious mind, as suggested by the word *mania*, begin to be identified, indeed, they take on a personal identity: "His head and his heart were drunk, and his steps followed the dictates of that dark god [*Dämon*] whose pleasure it is to trample man's reason and dignity underfoot" (244). Though unnamed—and he will stay unnamed—the mythic identity at the center of the story is beginning to emerge.

But he has also lurked there from the first, has been present through literary allusion. Myth has all along been interwoven with realism in the sequence of figures who have marked out the route to Venice, setting Aschenbach off on it, guiding him and furthering his progress along it, prefiguring his fate. To this sequence the last chapter adds (248ff.) the grotesque and sinister street singer who performs for the hotel guests. Like the Munich figure and the gondolier, he is once more an alien type ("not of Venetian origin"), with enough of their leitmotiv features to ring a bell—hat, snub nose, prominent Adam's apple, red hair, "threatening" furrows on the brow. Missing this time are the fiercely bared teeth that in those other figures suggested a traditional death's-head. But instead there is the concentrated carbolic stench that is virtually part of the man ("he seemed to be carrying his own suspect atmosphere about with him" [249]) and is every bit as eloquent of death, for we now guess what the chemical signifies.

Unlike the distant, imperious Munich figure (but like the unlicensed gondolier), the street singer can actually be talked to at the level of realistic narrative: he answers and balks Aschenbach's questions. To that extent he crosses the gap between mythic and real, just as in the course of the scene he crosses the physical distance between performer and audience. These two movements become, indeed, almost one. As he approaches Aschenbach, the "sauciness" of the performance turns into an obsequious bowing and scraping. But once artistic distance is restored, he reasserts his own kind of authority. The uproarious dialect laughing-song that ends his act is opaque in meaning, but transparent in intention: the tables are turned on the audience, they themselves become the show, and the "humble" performer treats the spectacle of his spectators with an ever wilder and more infectious mockery until—as his ultimate triumph—he finally gets them to join in the laughter. The figure's will to power, and his sense of the true power relation between him and the audience as he manipulates their responses, are evident. At the very end of his comic exit, before slipping away into the darkness, he "suddenly discarded the mask of comic underdog" and "uncoiled like a spring to his full height." We remember the "air of imperious survey" (196) with which his Munich doppelgänger looked out from his own quasi-theatrical vantage point and faced down his quarry.

Aschenbach has not laughed. It is as if the song were secretly aimed at him and he must try "to fend off an attack or flee from it" (251); as if the mocking laughter were the voice of the "dark god" who now controls his actions, and who will shortly appear to devastating effect on another stage, that of Aschenbach's sleeping mind.

Before this high point of the mythic causal line in his dream, there is also a high point of the literal causal line, which is the detailed account of cholera. From the English clerk in the travel bureau Aschenbach learns not just the nature of the disease, its symptoms and course in the individual patient, but the history of its recent spread through Asia and Russia to the moment when it arrived in Venice. After this dense medical and epidemiological information, it will only remain for Aschenbach to contract the disease by an obvious means, the "overripe soft strawberries" (260). We will need no second telling what, at this level, he dies of. But the travel clerk's account is not just bald fact. The disease becomes in turn a symptom, of a moral failure not unlike Aschenbach's. Fear of lost tourist business has been stronger in Venice "than respect for truth" (254). The complicity of city and lover is not just an external coincidence; commercial and erotic self-interest share a common resistance to knowledge. Another link is also made. The cholera has its origins in the Ganges Delta, "that wilderness of rank useless luxuriance, that primitive island jungle shunned by man, where tigers crouch in the bamboo thickets" (252f.). This surely is the world of Aschenbach's Munich vision, the "primeval wilderness of islands" where he saw "between the knotted stems of the bamboo thicket the glinting eyes of a crouching tiger" (197). He has come "not all that far, not quite to where the tigers were" (199), but still to a wilderness of islands, merely one where the primeval has long been overlaid by a city civilization. Here something has reached out for him from that truly primeval setting he so unaccountably envisioned on his Munich stroll. The sober details and background of disease connect with something more mysterious; fact connects with fate.

Aschenbach makes no such connection himself. The sense that a pattern is coming together remains ours, not his. True, he does once look back to that moment in Munich and remembers from it "a white building adorned with inscriptions" and the "strange itinerant figure" who first awakened his longing to travel. But he does not remember the vision of jungle wilderness, and his thoughts of the building and the figure merely fill him with repugnance because they remind him of home, "of level-headedness and sobriety, of toil and mastery." Decisively, it is in this paragraph that he contemplates but rejects the "decent action" of warning the Polish family and takes a final resolve to say nothing and stay on (255). And this paragraph stands in the text between the story's two extremes: it is a border and a bridge between realism and symbolism, between the factual account of disease and the mythic dream of an ancient orgy. Aschenbach's outward acceptance of the cholera risk leads over into his deeply inward final surrender to the god of intoxication.

For the orgiastic practices he experiences in the dream are those of the ancient Greek cult of Dionysus, the god of natural growth and regeneration and rebirth, of wine and drunkenness, of collective feeling and instinct, of ecstatic inspiration. Dionysus was an "alien god" in two senses. His worship came from Asia Minor, or even, it was sometimes said, from India, and spread like a wave over Greece. But his cult was also essentially alien to Greek religious tradition, so that there was strong resistance to his invasion.[2] This is seen graphically in Euripides' drama *The Bacchae*, where Pentheus, king of Thebes, refuses to recognize Dionysus in person and even tries to imprison him. The god, naturally enough, escapes. More significantly, so do Pentheus's own deeper desires to witness the orgies of the Dionysian cult and finally to take part in them in female disguise, whereupon he is unmasked and torn apart by the celebrants (including his own mother) along with their sacrificial animals. So Euripides' play already poses the question: is the god so wholly "alien" after all, or does he not rather touch irrational impulses which are already present deep in human beings? If the god is "alien" only in the sense that human beings refuse to *recognize* those impulses in themselves—or, put mythically, refuse to recognize him and try instead to imprison him, as Pentheus does—then the story becomes a parable of what in modern times is known as repression.[3]

Aschenbach too has long practiced repression, attempted to sublimate impulse in the cause of artistic creation. It was the crisis of that practice at the start of the story that led to the question, "Could it be that the enslaved emotion was now avenging itself by deserting him, by refusing from now on to bear up his art on its wings?" (199). His whole journey has been the pursuit of liberation for that emotion, initially unconscious, then fleetingly "wondering whether . . . some late adventure of the emotions might yet be in store for him" (210), and now fully aware, overriding "art and virtue" so as to enjoy "the advantages of chaos" (255).

Even at this late stage, like the Greeks and like Pentheus, Aschenbach resists with "a profound and spiritual resistance" the forces of the alien god that have "irrupted" into his soul. But, again as with Pentheus, it seems truer that those forces were latent in him rather than external. For when the dream starts, he has no perception of himself as separate from the orgiasts' actions, "rather the scene of the events was his own soul" (255); by the end he and the celebrants are one, "the dreamer now was with them and in them. . . . They were himself as they flung themselves, tearing and slaying, on the animals" (256).

Aschenbach's Socratic reminiscences and his mythologizing on the beach were classical knowledge; they helped him to maintain some distance from his experience, to understand it in a secure context. The dream is no such comforting story chosen from his cultural resources. The graphically envisioned Dionysian orgy thrusts up from the unconscious and allows not the least detachment. The details come direct from raw experience, the "long-drawn-out final *u*" is not, or not just, a version of the well-known howl of Dionysian worshipers, "Io! io!"; nor is it truly "like no cry ever heard" (256). On the contrary, it clearly echoes the cry that fascinated Aschenbach, the long *u* of the Polish vocative that dominated the beach in the cry "Tadziu!" and now dominates Aschenbach's dreaming mind. "Loathing," "fear," the "honorable will to defend to the last what was his and protect it against the Stranger," are no match for this ever louder howling which "swelled up to an enrapturing madness" (256f.).

After his dream, Aschenbach has no resistance left. Nor does he have scruples any longer about his pursuit of Tadzio being noticed; he is concerned only about his own aging appearance. That he now has himself "rejuvenated" by cosmetics puts him on a level with the tipsy old fop who so repelled him on the boat to Venice. Less obviously, his false rejuvenation is the end of a line which began with his high aesthetic preference for the surface of things rather than the truth below it: cosmetics as the ultimate art of the false surface. Correspondingly, the three monosyllables he mutters to the voluble hairdresser who fusses around restoring his appearance harshly suggest a low point of thought and the death of verbal mastery.

Harshness might seem the story's final keynote. The pursuit of the Polish family leaves Aschenbach sweating and exhausted in an ever more deserted and stinking Venice. The narrator's tone is sardonic, even sarcastic, as he sets the writer's past prestige as a cultural pillar of the community against what he has now become. "He sat there, the master, the artist who had achieved dignity" (260): the paragraph that follows is a complete rehearsal of all those literary achievements and claims to public respect which were recorded in chapter 2. But their effect now is nullified, even reversed, by what has become of the great writer. The narrator seems intent on a total moral repudiation of his character.

Yet thought and verbal mastery are not quite dead in Aschenbach. He still has something to contribute to the meaning of his own story. It is true that the paragraph which opened with sarcasm ends by denying any such possibility. It dismisses the thought processes of which Aschenbach's "drooping, cosmetically brightened lips shaped the occasional word" as a "strange dream-logic" (260). But when the dream-logic is displayed in full, its argument proves to be both coherent and incisive. It goes back, once more, to Plato. Aschenbach has earlier remembered the doctrines of Plato's *Phaedrus* dialogue. Now he speaks as if from within that dialogue, to Phaedrus, whom perhaps he associates in his mind with Tadzio. But it is effectively a monologue: there is no answering voice. And Aschenbach speaks not as one of the characters Plato used in the dialogue, but as himself, as the artist he is and as a representative of the whole artist guild. In this capacity he makes the crucial claim that, by the very nature of artists, their difficulties in living up to Plato's ideal are especially, even uniquely, acute.

This short, dense section of text interweaves the Platonic doctrine of beauty with the particular shape of Aschenbach's career right down to its last stage of deterioration; it draws the conclusion that there simply was no right path for him. Whatever he did—and, more generally, whatever any artist does—must be tragically wrong in one direction or another. The analytical knowledge of which he was once a devotee, "sympathizes with the abyss," it even "*is* the abyss." Yet to turn away from that abyss (which was the point of Aschenbach's "profound decision") and become instead a devotee of beauty only leads to another abyss. For it means seeking the spirit through the senses—and can that ever be free of risk? His musings put this as an open question to the imagined Phaedrus, a trick that Socrates, as the intellectual hero of Plato's dialogues, typically uses when the conclusion he is working towards has become unmissable but he wants his interlocutor to be humbled by admitting it: "Or do you think (I leave it to you to decide) that this is a path of dangerous charm, an errant and sinful path which must of necessity lead us astray?" (267). The answer is not in doubt. So it seems the flight from one extreme, one abyss, can only lead to another. But this is not just a confession, it is the modern artist's answer, dressed in Platonic pastiche, to Plato and his doctrine of a transcendent reality: a defensive plea that if beauty really is so overwhelmingly present to the senses, then the artist, of all people, simply cannot rise above it or go beyond it. To do so would be to deny its—and his—fundamental nature. The risks of beauty are rooted deep in his calling. Artists, such is Aschenbach's sweeping generalization, "are not capable of self-exaltation, only of self-debauchery" (261). It is a gloomy conclusion. (But then Plato, who wanted no art or artists at all in his ideal republic, would scarcely have been surprised.)

The scene, plainly, goes beyond literary realism. Suddenly the Aschenbach who just now was at the end of his physical and moral tether is lucidly drawing the lesson from his almost completed tragic fate and passing a categorical judgment on the possibilities—or rather, the impossibilities, the impasse—of the life and commitment of writers. It is a coherent overview, an exact and bitter recognition. And precisely this coherence and persuasive quality reflect back on the dismissive way the narrator introduced Aschenbach's thoughts, as "strange dream-logic." If the logic seems neither strange nor in any pejorative sense dreamlike, then not only was that label inappropriate, but perhaps everything about that paragraph—the judgment it contains, the sarcastic tone, the moralistic emphasis—was far from being the last word either. Perhaps they were some kind of narrative feint? For by now we are used to the idea that a style can be false, even a façade, and one of Aschenbach's conclusions in these Platonic musings is that "the magisterial poise of our style is a lie and a farce" (261). And one of the things the false style of his "deliberate classicism" went in for was emphatic moral judgments that "weighed vileness in the balance and found it wanting" (204). So when the narrative voice at this late stage in the story practices just such a moral emphasis, it is strangely, almost obtusely, untouched by what the story has taught us about the hollowness of self-confident moralizing. By now, surely, this and any uncomprehending contempt has only a very shaky claim to legitimacy.

Because for anyone who has eyes to see, the story has traced back Aschenbach's moral attitudes and actions to their aesthetic causes, the causes in turn to the course of his career, and the career to cultural pressures. These, for all his conscious "profound decision," shaped the consciousness that did the deciding. We *understand* Aschenbach too well by now to be able simply to repudiate him, and that means accepting that his fate is tragic. He himself in his maturity rejected the whole notion of understanding, and the forgiveness that proverbially goes with it, because of "the laxity of that compassionate principle" (204). Wanting to have and give simple moral assurance in a complex world, he restored such traditional concepts as that of a "vileness" which could be straightforwardly weighed and found wanting. That left no room for tragedy, which since the time of Aristotle has been largely defined by the compassionate understanding it arouses: showing the fearful necessity of a human being's fate, it invokes our pity. The irony is that Aschenbach's moral fall puts him in need of the compassion he once scorned. The narrative has made the case for it, and at the end he himself comes to see the necessity with which his fate unfolded: "We necessarily go astray, necessarily remain dissolute emotional adventurers" (261). The refusal of understanding rules itself out of court, and with it all overconfident moralizing, whether Aschenbach's, which events have discredited, or that of the sarcastic narrator. Strikingly, Aschenbach is not above pleading his own cause. His whole Platonic speech is a discreet way of appealing to our sympathy. For when he addresses an imagined and silent Phaedrus, the effect is as if he were directly addressing us; though outwardly his speech has the detached wisdom and gestures of superiority which we associate with a Socratic teacher ("Mark well . . . I must tell you"), its substance is a frank description of his own case. Didactic authority here rests on confessional authenticity—it is the one source of authority Aschenbach does have left, just as the only lesson he can teach is the impossibility of pedagogy, and even that only to an imagined pupil.

But the story's tragic understanding goes still deeper, is more complete, than Aschenbach's own. When he uses Platonic categories to understand the case of artists generally, he is strangely silent about the "alien god" who was the driving force and climax of his own. He speaks of "intoxication"—that much is now clear to him—but not of its lord. Though he has experienced Dionysus directly in his dream, has awoken from it a definitively changed man, "unnerved, shattered, and powerlessly enslaved to the demon-god" (257), yet he seems not consciously to know him. (The only god he does name, true to the conceptions of the Platonic dialogues, is Eros.) Perhaps he has suppressed or lost his knowledge of Dionysus in the transition to waking life or subsequently. That would repeat the pattern of his Munich vision, and with it those other instances in Mann's fiction when a character is granted a dramatic vision but soon, realistically enough, forgets it (see above, p. 31f.). So if Aschenbach's late reflections have brought him back to the analytic knowledge he once turned his back on, it is only a partial knowledge. He tells himself a story that is not quite the full story. For deeper even than the Platonic problem he ponders there lies the Dionysian element, the ultimate source of passionate feeling and potential destroyer of order. Aschenbach's conscious mind has not plumbed that abyss.

Even the insight he does achieve comes too late, in the same way that each successive advance of knowledge in the course of the story came too late: the recognition at the close of chapter 3 that parting from Tadzio was what made leaving Venice so painful, or the recognition at the end of chapter 4 that he is in love with the boy. Both these partial recognitions are wisdom after the event, only possible once the event cannot be reversed. They are thus more like appendages to the action than integral parts of it. In the same way, the last and fullest recognition contained in Aschenbach's monologue is in both senses a conclusion. It is the product of a development which is now essentially complete and cannot be affected by it.

The story's ending, after the drama and degradation of the Dionysian dream, after the sarcastic moral judgment, after the Platonic meditations, is very matter-of-fact. The brief narration of Aschenbach's actual death feels like a coda. The foreign visitors have heard rumors and gone, it is prematurely end-of-season, the beach is autumnal and bleak; a photographer's tripod stands there deserted. There is also a different feel about Aschenbach's final sight, or rather vision, of Tadzio—no more the desperate pursuit that led up to his moment of truth in the little Venetian square, no more the sensuously perceived idol, nor even the aesthetic form celebrated earlier. Yet the close too has a touch of the unreal, and we can choose (as so often with Thomas Mann) either to accept it as a suprarealistic effect or to put the sense of unreality down entirely to the fevered mind of the character, as the phrasing allows—"to him it was as if . . . as if . . ." (263). The real boy who has just suffered humiliation at the hands of his long-subordinate companion moves off to sulk; he becomes unreachable not just for Jascha but in a new way for Aschenbach too. He is "a quite isolated and unrelated apparition . . . in front of the nebulous vastness." And where once his beauty had blocked off any view of a spiritual Beyond, he now positively points—or it seems to Aschenbach that he points— beyond himself and out to sea, "outward, into an immensity rich with unutterable expectation." So when the sick man tries to get up from his deckchair and follow "as so often," he is no longer pursuing an object of desire but following the directions of a "soul-summoner," a mythic guide on a journey beyond Venice (263).

The final paragraph with its three laconic sentences registers Aschenbach's death and in so doing propels us abruptly out of the claustrophobic Venice setting. His death is the end of a private history, but it is also a public event in a world that has no knowledge of that history. For this world, his reputation remains intact. So it can be "respectfully shocked" at the passing of a still unquestioned master.

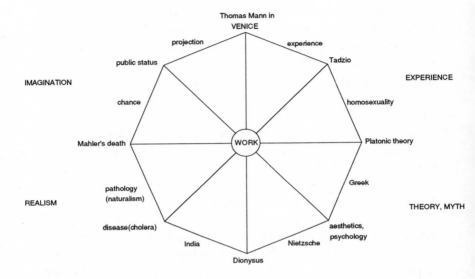

The diagram is a simple attempt, suggested by Thomas Mann's image of *Death in Venice* as a "crystal," to show both the story's thematic richness and the unplanned connections which its events, figures, motifs, and ideas turned out to have. These separate elements are named at the points of the octagon, while the nature of the connection between each and its neighbor is suggested by the label against the line that joins them. For example, reading anticlockwise from the apex, *Mann in Venice in 1911* is linked to (Aschenbach's) *public status* by imaginative *projection*; while a sense of what it is like when an artist of such status dies comes from the *chance* that *Mahler's death* occurred during Mann's journey. In the other direction, the link with *Tadzio* is through Mann's Venice *experience*, and the connection with the next point onwards, *Platonic theory*, is via *homosexuality*. And so on. The connecting process comes full circle, and the elements with their connections feed into the work at the center. Each quarter of the octagon also groups the elements by a general affinity, which is indicated in CAPITALS. These four concepts represent the large and disparate areas which the story succeeds in bringing together.

9

Connections, Genesis

In his *Sketch of My Life*, published in 1930, Thomas Mann picks out two things about the writing of *Death in Venice*. One is that the novella had a will of its own which carried it well beyond the meaning he intended to give it. The other is that the resulting text, which had formed spontaneously like a crystal, was more than usually multifaceted and rich in connections; and the notion of "connections," he says, is for him central to the very idea of significance.

These two things, the story's "will" and its richness of reference, are in the end only one. For it was precisely the way objects and events turned out to have interconnected meanings—meanings not planned but discovered as he wrote, an "innate symbolism"—that gave him at times a feeling he says he had not known before of being "carried serenely along" by the work's own impetus in a kind of "absolute movement" (XI, 123f.). As the connections emerged, the novella composed itself.

That is not to say that it *wrote* itself; the act of writing was as laborious as always for Thomas Mann, with doubts and shifts and despairs. But the process of composing—literally, "putting together"— a pattern of meanings could seem at least in retrospect as if it had been achieved by the materials of the story themselves and the many associations they brought with them. These came, moreover, from disparate sources, yet they proved to be compatible, sometimes by the most remarkable coincidences. The result was literary meaning that was complex but not contradictory: actual experience turned out to have potentially rich associations within the complex codes of culture. For a writer who from his beginnings had striven beyond the narrow limits of Naturalism, this was a deeply satisfying demonstration of how much more could be latent in mere reality than was accommodated in Naturalism's view of the world.

Yet the process by which those associations "came together" and "proved compatible" took place over time, not in a single revelatory instant. To that extent Thomas Mann's image of a sudden crystallization is misleading. The significances of the novella were a matter of accretion and interaction, of clarifying the relations between elements, while all the time the author's changing attitudes were reshaping his materials and his theme. The story has a story; its genesis shaped its significance.

Should we probe behind the product for the process? The text warns (though, of course, it ignores its own warning): "It is as well that the world knows only a fine piece of work and not also its origins"—i.e., Tadzio as inspiration for the last page and a half of Aschenbach's career—"for knowledge of the sources of an artist's inspiration would often confuse readers and shock them, and the excellence of the writing would be of no avail" (236). Yet arguably the opposite is true of Aschenbach's own story. *Death in Venice* works its way through intricate aesthetic and moral issues and is shaped by the phases in which its author worked his way through them. Knowing "the conditions under which it came into being" may actually sharpen our understanding of the issues and make the writing of more, not less "avail." To live always only with resolutions is to forget what problems are.

VENICE

Not the least significant thing was the location itself. In 1911 Thomas Mann traveled to Venice with his wife Katia and his brother Heinrich.

Like Aschenbach, he was escaping from a difficult stage in his current work which had temporarily exhausted his nervous energies (letter to Heinrich Mann, 24 March 1911). He had been to Venice before, and its fascination for him must always have been intensified by its background of associations with figures he admired to the point of passion. Richard Wagner had composed part of his *Tristan and Isolde* there in 1858—his autobiography, just published in 1911, made much of that phase—and had died there in 1883. Friedrich Nietzsche had stayed there and written evocative poetry about the city, also published only recently in his autobiography *Ecce Homo* (1908). And the homosexual poet August von Platen—a favorite writer for Mann, who knew many of his poems by heart—had been there in the 1820s and published the set of eloquent *Sonnets from Venice*. Platen too died in Italy, in flight from Venice and a threatening cholera epidemic. The city could hardly have been closer to Thomas Mann's most private culture through its associations with homoeroticism (Platen), with things decadent (Wagner), and with the ambition to overcome them (Nietzsche). Through these and many other links, as well as through its sheer bizarre extravagance, Venice had for some time been the favorite city of Europe's "decadent" writers generally: "No other swamp creates such violent fevers," wrote Gabriele d'Annunzio, not at all in a critical spirit.[1]

But when things with a seemingly "innate symbolism" happened to Thomas Mann in Venice, the city ceased to be just cultural background. It became a source of specific motifs that would interweave with the "adventure of the emotions" that Aschenbach looks forward to when his steamer arrives off Venice. This passage is itself an example. As anticipation stirs in the traveler, it is Platen he remembers and recites to himself; the text half quotes a sonnet of Platen's which celebrates the first sight of Venice's buildings rising from the waves (210).[2] Indeed, linking Aschenbach's expectations with the well-known homosexual poet makes almost too strong a motif, or at least a premature one—if, that is, we are to believe that Aschenbach's first admiration for Tadzio is innocently aesthetic. Later, when he is pursuing the boy through the labyrinth of canals and the narrative reminds us how the arts "once rankly and voluptuously blossomed" in this "insalubrious air" and "composers were inspired to lulling tones of somniferous eroticism" (245), the reference to Wagner's richly sensuous music is also no longer cultural background but part of the case that is being built up against art's elevated claims. And Nietzsche. . . . But Nietzsche is everywhere in the work, dictating its terms and pervading its substance.

NIETZSCHE: PSYCHOLOGY AND MYTH

Nietzsche claimed to be the greatest living authority on decadence, on the grounds that he was both a decadent himself and its very opposite,[3] i.e., a critic of his age and a vehement preacher of psychological and cultural health. It was avowedly from him that Thomas Mann learned the "psychology of decadence" which shaped the inward "decline of a family" in *Buddenbrooks* (XI, 556). This, though, was only part of the early debt. In the 1890s the young Mann immersed himself in Nietzsche, whose writings were a cult that swept all before it. Mann's thinking was marked from an early stage by Nietzsche's first book, *The Birth of Tragedy from the Spirit of Music* of 1872. Its scholarly aim—Nietzsche wrote it when briefly a professor of classics at the University of Basel—was to show the dynamic that underlay Greek tragedy. Against the clichéd view of the ancient Greeks as statuesquely serene figures in an ideal Mediterranean landscape, he evoked the forces they had to hold in balance before their art could come about. That meant giving full value to the violent primal impulse in human makeup as well as to formal control. Beyond the matter of Greek tragedy, this was a dramatic pre-Freudian picture of the necessary tensions that underlie all culture. And like Freud, Nietzsche brought abstraction alive by embodying it in the figures of myth, in his case, the Greek pairing of Dionysus and Apollo. Dionysus was the god of fundamental productive and destructive energies, of nature, spring, regeneration, wine and intoxication, who drew human beings by their inchoate drives into the collective and allowed them to glimpse the tragic realities of existence; Apollo was the god of light and artistic form who shaped those drives and insights into the clarity and order of dream, individuality, a detached art. The affinities of Dionysus were with music, the art of direct emotional overflow, not representation of some external object; Apollo's affinity was with the firm, clear outlines of sculpture. When these contrary but also complementary impulses were held in productive tension, they gave Greek tragedy its power and plasticity. Dionysian experience gave it its depth; Apollo's shaping hand gave it its form. The beauty of the finished work made life bearable despite its tragic nature; art created an illusion that was psychologically necessary if life was to continue. Paradoxically, the Greeks as creators of beautiful forms—including their gods—were "superficial because they were deep."[4]

Yet surely, Nietzsche thought, the Dionysian and Apolline impulses, and the forms they were capable of generating, were not peculiar to the Greeks? If they could only be brought into balance once again, they might regenerate late-nineteenth-century German culture, which in his view badly needed it. It was excessively cerebral, and its creativity was weighed down by the accumulated knowledge and reflective consciousness of an "advanced" civilization—a diagnosis which meant incidentally that Germany needed Dionysus more urgently than it needed Apollo. In the music dramas of Wagner, whom at this stage Nietzsche idolized, he saw his hopes of an artistic rebirth and a new tragic culture for Germany already on the way to being fulfilled.

Nietzsche's is a powerful and graphic account of art and of the forces that go into its making. It also points up fundamental problems. Imbalance between the two elements will clearly lead to artistic failure. Too much Dionysian energy unchecked by Apolline form, and the work of art will be chaotic; too much Apolline control without a Dionysian impulse to tax and extend it, and a bloodless formalism will result. Nietzsche's theory also implies dangers for the maker of art. (It can scarcely be expected that something as valuable as great art will be risk-free.) For the artist, keeping the two impulses in balance, harnessing them through a discipline of work and integrating them in a manageable way of life, will itself be a creative act. If the balance is lost and the discipline breaks down, there may be a serious crisis. When Aschenbach and his narrator join in that early question—"Could it be that enslaved emotion was now avenging itself by deserting him, by refusing from now on to bear up art on its wings, by taking with it all his joy in words, all his appetite for the beauty of form?" (199)—they are glimpsing (though Aschenbach does not pursue the insight further) the loss of that essential balance and integration. In the vision he has just had of a rank, luxuriant jungle and the beast of prey lurking there, what has stirred in his unconscious is the attraction of the wilder primal impulses which his years of discipline have kept too strictly subjugated. Even before this, the very first sight of the stranger has made him "conscious . . . of an extraordinary expansion of his inner self." That is exactly how the effect of Dionysian possession was described in the scholarly work on which Thomas Mann drew for his knowledge of the cult.[5]

So even this early in the narrative there is already a discreet mingling of psychology and myth. The two things may seem to us fundamentally different ways of understanding human behavior. Psychology sees it as resulting from inner processes, myth represents it as obeying the external compulsion of a god or following the set pattern of an archetypal story. Yet the one mode can embody the other, as it had already done in Nietzsche's originating essay, and long before him in the mythic creations of the culture he was analyzing: "We appropriate these names from the Greeks, who made the profound mysteries of their view of art accessible to anyone with insight, not in concepts, but in the strikingly clear figures of their gods" (*The Birth of Tragedy*, sect. 1). *Death in Venice* proceeds similarly. It links the psychological and the mythic modes from the start and represents an inner breakdown as the thrilling yet vengeful visitation of a god. For it to do this, the reader only has to sense the special quality of that first ominous figure in Munich. Exact identification is not needed. It is enough, to start with, if the bizarre confrontation lifts events and our response to them out of the ordinary, if the bared teeth suggest a death's-head. That sensitive the novella's title should already have made us. The bared teeth of later figures will confirm the intuition of something extra-ordinary. Aschenbach's first gondolier may be recognized as a ferryman across death's river, and perhaps even, with a very modest knowledge of ancient mythology, as Charon. His curt "'You will pay'" (214) is a strong hint, a touch too ambiguously threatening to be merely part of the realistic narrative. Other recurrent details—the broad-brimmed hat and the staff, the physical appearance and attitudes—may be noticed by the reader later and may be seen as attributes of Hermes, guide of souls to the realm of the dead, or of Dionysus himself. The more precise the identification, the more our experience of the work is enriched and unified along the lines of Thomas Mann's syncretistic conception. But even short of precise identification, importantly, the reader may still sense the function of the recurring figures, which is to give narrative coherence to the process of psychological breakup that has already begun in Munich and whose consequences the journey spells out.

But if psychology and myth are two ways of talking about that one process, why does cholera enter into it as the literal cause of death? On the face of it, only because there was a cholera epidemic in Italy in the summer of 1911. But what Thomas Mann called "innate symbolism" then makes its connections. Cholera originated in India, spreading across Asia and penetrating Europe from early in the nineteenth century. And it was from India that the religion of Dionysus was traditionally said to have come, spreading (as Thomas Mann's sources put it) like an epidemic[6] across Asia Minor and Greece. So Aschenbach's vision of a jungle swamp contains the causes of his destruction at more than one level: psychological—it is a metaphor of his repressed impulses ("The moralist hates the primeval forest," wrote Nietzsche, taking it as a symbol for "the whole previous history of the mind and those of its possibilities that have not yet been drunk to the lees"); mythic—it is a place associated with the god of those impulses; and naturalistic—it is the source of the fateful disease. Similarly with the lurking tiger. He is at home in the literal jungle where cholera originates. But he is also a Dionysian animal: tigers drew the god's chariot in the myth. What is more, the tiger, along with lions and leopards, is a metaphor of the primal and primitive which crops up frequently in German writing around the turn of the century, a further debt to Nietzsche and the vocabulary of his vitalism.[7]

Homosexuality: Greece versus Wilhelmine Germany

The release of a writer's repressed impulses did not have to mean homosexual passion. Mann's first idea for the theme of lost dignity in a great writer, around 1906, was a heterosexual subject: the episode of the old poet Goethe falling in love at 74 with a girl of 17. This belongs, strictly speaking, more to the prehistory of *Death in Venice* than to its genesis. It is a quite different conception and has only one thematic strand in common with the one that replaced rather than grew out of it, namely, late loss of dignity through sexuality. Its main interest lies in the contrast it offers: it allows us to see just how much richer and more unified a conception grew out of what happened in Venice. As in the case of the cholera motif, outward events brought inner complexity with them unbidden, especially through the homosexual element. The writer's admiration for young male beauty allowed the further theme of blindness or self-deception. (There was no self-deception, or possibility of it, in Goethe's attraction to the young Ulrike von Levetzow.) Aschenbach's failure or refusal to recognize his own feelings could then be connected with his mature rejection of self-knowledge, and at the same time with the new aesthetic priority he has for some time been giving to visual beauty, an Apolline ideal under cover of which Dionysian feeling can get a hold. (Paradoxically, the more total the commitment to Apollo, the more complete the later surrender to Dionysus.) And since these new aesthetic directions of Aschenbach's were career temptations of Mann's own, the subject Venice offered him had the potential to capture his whole literary situation. And not just in any detached way. This was an actual "adventure of the emotions" for him to come to terms with, more real and more pressingly immediate than a mere anecdote from some famous past life, especially one from a writer's old age which for obvious reasons it would have been difficult for Thomas Mann to identify expressively with. The tale of Goethe's late infatuation was in any case grotesque rather than serious, material for something perilously close to a routine debunking of greatness.[8] In contrast, the erotic excitement Mann apparently experienced in Venice brought home to him the precariousness of private morality and public reputation in a real and threatening way.

Not that the impact of young male beauty was the surprise for Thomas Mann that it is, when at last he recognizes it, for Aschenbach. Mann was well aware of his own sexual ambivalence. His attachment to the painter Paul Ehrenberg had been the great emotional experience of his life in the years that led up to his marriage in 1905. *Tonio Kröger* of 1903 was in a sense addressed to Paul Ehrenberg, designed to show him that inside the cool ironist he thought he knew there was a sensitive and suffering human soul. But if that is the background to Tonio's yearning for acceptance by Hans Hansen, the literary treatment remains very discreet: homoerotic feeling is there only as a boyhood phase, followed in the normal sequence by Tonio's crush on Ingeborg Holm. There is a similar sequence or mixture in later works like *The Magic Mountain* and *Felix Krull*. Mann's feelings for Paul Ehrenberg were not transposed directly into fiction until many years later, in the Leverkühn-Schwerdtfeger relationship of *Doctor Faustus*, and discreetly enough even then. Thomas Mann's ambivalence about his own ambivalence prevented him from being the kind of pioneer his French contemporary André Gide became, with the confessional frankness of the novel *L'Immoraliste* (*The Immoralist*, 1901) and his autobiography *Si le grain ne meurt* (*If it die*, 1921), and the equally explicit arguments of his dialogue *Corydon* of almost exactly the same date as *Death in Venice* (printed—but in only 12 copies—in 1911, published fully in 1924 [see "Über die Ehe," X, 196]). Thomas Mann, by contrast, remained as timid and reticent in fiction and autobiographical statement as he did, on the evidence of his diaries, in real life.

Except, that is, this once. The emotions inspired by his Venice experience—or (to say no more than we can know for certain) its power to inspire persuasive images of what a consuming passion would be like—produced one of the rare classics of homosexual feeling.

But how affirmative a treatment could it be? Here "literature" meets "society" head-on. For if, on the one hand, the writer had an intimate and challenging experience to convey, on the other he had the expectation, or rather the near-certainty, that the result would meet with little sympathy. This was Europe not long after the trials and imprisonment of Oscar Wilde (1895–97). Gide in France, we saw, felt he had to hold back his *Corydon*. In Germany, accusations of homosexuality had recently (1902, 1906) caused scandals and a suicide at the highest levels of Wilhelmine society, reaching up to the kaiser's own circle.[9] If we add this larger background to that of Thomas Mann's stay in Venice, it seems likely that he turned to Plato for sympathetic confirmation from a society of very different outlook, as well as for deeper insight into his experience and its implications. Ancient Greece, certainly Athens at the time and social level of Plato, so the *Symposium* and *Phaedrus* suggest, had not been hostile to homosexuality in the way modern Europe was. Even four centuries after Plato, the Platonic tradition was alive in Plutarch's dialogue *Erotikos*, where the relative value of homosexual and heterosexual love is still being argued out as an open question. Mann was to draw on that work too—a new translation appeared opportunely in 1911.

But the Greek texts did not offer mere cozy reassurance; they set austere standards and creative aims for the lover. If Nietzsche's theory of Dionysian and Apolline impulse provided the story's dynamics, the Greek dialogues provided its ethics. Mann's work notes include substantial passages transcribed from all three dialogues, and there is no hint that they have been gathered and are being deployed merely as materials from which to construct Aschenbach's alien responses and reflections. With no framework of critical comment, they look as if they are there simply for the light they throw on the nature and possibilities of homosexual feeling.

Its possibilities for literary creation, barring some distinct moral failure in the lover, were plainly great (see above, p. 55f.). What is more—and this makes a connection between the two kinds of Greek source—the same was potentially true of the Dionysian force. For despite the destructive violence of his cult, Dionysus is also a god of regeneration and new growth. In psychological terms, freeing the writer's long pent-up and overexploited emotions might have meant literary rejuvenation. So far, so good. What is more, journeys in literature commonly transform the traveler. That, unobtrusively, is the pattern in *Tonio Kröger*: the writer achieves renewal by a journey back to the roots of natural feeling, albeit only to its social roots and through very much gentler adventures. Add to this the fact that Mann himself had got safely back from Venice without being destroyed by passion or disease, and was once more writing freely; not, it is true, on the *Felix Krull* project, which he had been unable to push further at the psychological low point before his vacation, but on the Venetian subject itself, the story of a (for better or worse) transforming passion. It is not clear why it had to be for worse, why it had to be death in Venice rather than new poetic life. Yet when Aschenbach writes with Tadzio there before him on the beach, we are firmly told, not that he feels elevated and spiritually fulfilled, but that he feels debauched and that his conscience accuses him after it.

This is the pivotal point in the story and in the conduct of its moral argument. How much so is clear if we remember an earlier moment, and the potential it suggested. It is the scene where the sight of Tadzio running out of the sea inspires "mythical images" in Aschenbach's mind (224), and he feels "song" stir inside him. No mere trivial ditty either, but *Gesang*, the word used in German for high poetry. At that point there is no necessary obstacle to literary renewal. There is perhaps even a hint, in the combination of Tadzio's statuesque form and Aschenbach's inward song, that the Apolline and the Dionysian are being brought together.

That the outcome did not absolutely have to be tragic, and that the novella might have followed a very different line and still been faithful to Mann's Venice experience (including its regenerative effect on him) and to his classical sources is not just a matter of gratuitous speculation. For his later accounts of how the story was written suggest that a more affirmative work did nearly come about. These retrospects of Thomas Mann's testify to the nature and power of his original inspiration, but they also confess its—or to be more precise, his—limitations.

The first of these retrospects is in verse. It is the opening of his only nonprose work, the *Song of the Child* of 1919, and the unfamiliar situation of composing in verse leads him to reflect yet again on what kind of writer he is. One episode and its bitter lesson sticks in his mind:

> Remember? Intoxication, a heightened exceptional feeling
> Came over you yourself on one occasion and threw you
> Down, your head in your hands. To hymnic impulse your
> spirit
> Rose, amid tears your struggling mind pressed urgently
> upward
> Into song. (VIII, 1069)

He is speaking of the very beginnings, the Venetian beginnings it would seem, of *Death in Venice*; the dominant note of this recollection several years after the event is regret at a literary failure. He speaks of an "ancient shame" and a "secret defeat," even though the novella that resulted won great public acclaim. For despite his "intoxication," he could not sustain the "hymnic impulse" which, for once in his sober prose-writer's life, had begun to generate "song" (once more the word in the original is the elevated *Gesang*). "Unhappily," he goes on:

> things stayed just as they had been:
> There began a process of sobering, cooling, and mastering—
> Lo! what came of your drunken song was an ethical fable.[10]

In other words, having been (almost) carried away, he went back to being the kind of writer he had always been, the morally aware, intellectual, analytical *Schriftsteller*. It was another failure to win what he had always coveted and so often been refused by critics: the status that German usage denotes but never quite defines when it confers the title "Dichter." The word literally means "poet," though it connotes not verse but literary quality and public acceptance. For example, at the end of *Tonio Kröger* the title figure, and with him no doubt his author, had looked forward to achieving that status through a new emotional commitment to ordinary life.[11] In his notes for the essay "Intellect and Art," Mann had tried various arguments: now to claim the title, now to challenge the German ways of thinking that gave it its special aura. And in the first upsurge of what was to become *Death in Venice*, he perhaps felt the title within his grasp, only to see it elude him once more. If anything could have secured it, it was surely a work of impassioned inspiration—perhaps for good measure in verse too, which is what particularly recalls it to his mind as he begins to write *Song of the Child*. Now he can only try to cut the Gordian knot of that old issue and claim that the title of "Dichter" ought by rights to be his on the strength of his work as it always has been and still is:

> for where from the outset his love of a language
> Joins with all other loves and mingles with all that he
> goes through,
> Let us be bold and give the writer this name—he deserves
> it.

Yet clearly the old failure to follow that original Venice impulse still rankles. As he presents it, the failure sprang from a deep-rooted literary character. But intertwined with issues of literary form, social scruple was also at work, whether fully conscious or internalized as a taboo. This second element does not have to be guessed at, since it is part of the explanation Thomas Mann gives in a second retrospect which is probably the fullest and frankest self-interpretation he ever penned.

Mann's letter of 4 July 1920 to the young poet Carl Maria Weber is meant to remove any impression the novella might have given that "a mode of feeling [that is, homosexuality] which I respect because it is almost necessarily infused with *mind* (far more necessarily so than the 'normal' mode) should be something that I would have wanted to deny or, insofar as it is accessible to me (and I may say it is so with scarcely any reservation), would have wished to disavow." He tries to locate the possible causes of misunderstanding. The first is, in the story's own Nietzschean terms, "the difference between the dionysian spirit of lyricism whose outpouring is irresponsible and individualistic, and the apolline spirit of objectively committed, morally and socially responsible epic narration." In other words, a passionately felt private experience is all very well for lyrical poetry but will and must be toned down before being put in front of the public in prose narrative. That is, it would be irresponsible not to tone it down, and such toning down is an intrinsic part of epic form.[12] Hence his striving after "a balance of sensuality and morality," a morality that would offset the sensuality of the work. Yet this, he says, cannot hide the fact that "at its core" it is "hymnic in character, indeed of hymnic origin," and he quotes the lines from *Song of the Child*, already discussed above, which evoke the Venice experience and his first response to it. If those lines mean that he began by writing in verse, then the occasional full hexameter and the numerous fragments of hexameters that critics espied long ago[13] embedded in the prose of *Death in Venice* may be remnants of such a first form. That makes it the more sadly apt that Mann should have recorded the defeat of his efforts at hymnic song in a different "song" composed in hexameters. Apt and ironic, since *"Gesang vom Kindchen"* is as far removed as possible from the celebration of homosexual love. It celebrates the christening of his sixth child.

Mann calls the process of cooling into prose "the *artistic* reason" (his emphasis) for what then looked like an unsympathetic attitude to homosexuality. But the social element is strong, and explicit. He told Weber there were also what he calls "purely intellectual" reasons, though in fact these are in some measure artistic: "the *naturalistic* attitude of my generation, so alien to you young people, which compelled me to see the 'case' *also* in pathological terms (the climacteric) alongside and mingling with the symbolism of Tadzio as Hermes psychopompos." But then, he confesses, there was the most deeply personal element: "the absolutely un-'Greek,' the fundamentally protestant, puritanical ('bourgeois') character which I share with the story's protagonist; in other words, our deeply mistrustful, deeply pessimistic attitude to passion itself and in general."

The letter continues and becomes almost an essay, moving out from the themes of *Death in Venice* to the larger context of Mann's intellectual world at the time he wrote it, and the place of homosexual feeling and its artistic products within that world. His overriding aim is to defend the novella against the charge of being negative. But alongside this defense and the virtual full confession of his own homosexual feeling there is an equally clear confession of the limits—artistic, social, personal—beyond which he could not or would not go. The full force of Dionysus was not something for society, or for prose fiction, or for this particular prose writer. Those constraints were plainly crucial in making the story what it became.

Perhaps no more was needed to transform the "hymnic" conception, despite its Platonic possibilities—which are strikingly not even mentioned in the letter to Weber. But well on in the writing of the novella, reservations about Plato were added to those about Dionysus. An essay by Georg von Lukács published in 1911,[14] probably autumn, analyzed Plato-Socrates' cultivation of yearning as a principle of spiritual growth, but frankly declared such yearning to be hopeless: it could have no spiritual fulfillment on earth, so it was forced to take on the lower forms for which some sort of fulfillment is possible. Lukács writes of men and of poets that "their exaltation is always tragedy. . . . In life . . . yearning must remain love: that is its happiness and its tragedy." That pessimism is the keynote of Aschenbach's speech to Phaedrus near the close, and formulations from Lukács's essay can be recognized in Thomas Mann's text, the wording in each case pushed to a more drastic extreme. "Our yearning must remain love,—that is our pleasure and our shame." And, "We are not capable of self-exaltation, we are capable only of self-debauchery" (261). Hence Thomas Mann's conclusion in the work note (no. 4) that contains his excerpts from Lukács: "Dignity can be saved only by death ('tragedy,' the 'sea,'—recourse, rescue and refuge of all higher love)." This image of a sea into which the lover would move out may have been long in his mind as a possible ending for the novella, but perhaps in the positive sense of Plato's "sea of beautiful forms" to whose shore the true initiate comes, to be pointed onwards by the single being that first inspired his love. That passage from the *Symposium* (210d) is transcribed in Mann's work notes (no. 16). But in the finished story, there is no suggestion, or certainly not a firm one, that Aschenbach has achieved any such initiation. "Sea" has become instead the real Adriatic beside which he dies, at most a symbol for the uncertain promise of death into which Tadzio beckons his lover on.

If death it was to be, then the feel of those moments when a great figure departs this life was also by chance one of the experiences of Thomas Mann's Italian journey. In the summer of 1911 Gustav

Mahler had just returned gravely ill from an American tour, "and his princely decline into death in Paris and Vienna" could be followed "step by step in the newspaper bulletins" (XIII, 149). The hushed respect of that occasion whispers in the novella's last line.

Since *Death in Venice* is a complex story about complex issues, it ought not to surprise anyone to find that its genesis was also complex. Like the plot of the story itself, the genesis is a history of conflicting impulses within a writer, some universally human, some specific and individual, some internalized from the surrounding culture. The whole mixture was inherently unstable. That as well as the delicacy of the subject is why Thomas Mann more than once while writing it spoke of an "impossible conception"; was still stuck for an ending at a stage when arrangements to publish were well advanced; was desperately concerned to complete the story somehow; and then, when at last it was finished, did not know what to think of it.[15]

All this hardly fits Mann's image as the most sovereignly intellectual among modern writers. That is no great loss. Intellectualism is neither a sufficient nor a necessary quality in a writer. Ideas and reflection may put much into the melting pot out of which the work comes, and clearly did so in this story, but the work itself cannot be wholly planned. Encounters with experiences and ideas remain unpredictable and challenging. A writer so intellectual as to have everything immutably cut-and-dried would simply be out of live touch with the things that matter enough to make literature, and that make literature matter to us. Being, on the contrary, *in* touch meant being carried by the complexities of the work, not just in the beneficial sense of Thomas Mann's comments with which this chapter began, but in the sense of being moved in different directions by the pressures of subject and sources and society and his response to all of them. It is then an achievement if the writer can in some degree master and unify the mixture. "Mastery," in other words, cannot result merely from the ambitious planning of "great works," such as occupied Thomas Mann in the years before 1910, any more than it had been able to result from the laborious working up of slight motifs into disproportionate structures—the dialogues of *Fiorenza* that ponderously overstate an idea already more briskly done in *Gladius Dei*, or the allegory of *Royal Highness* which spends 350 pages elaborating Tonio Kröger's parallel between the artist and "a prince walking incognito among the people" (157). Those really *are* products of "intellectualism." To create works that are less perfunctory, less predictable, there must be something that demands to be shaped, that extends the author's capacities of mind and verbal skill beyond plan and intention and leaves the text as its necessary trace. That this was so in *Death in Venice* sets it apart from the works, written and unwritten, of Thomas Mann's doldrum years.

There is more than one reason for wanting to trace the processes that shaped a work of art. Such inquiry helps us appreciate the work as an achievement, and it also sharpens our understanding, both of the text and of its reception: for example, the shifts of authorial position that led Thomas Mann at different times to claim the text's qualities for himself as "classical" and to disclaim them as conscious "mimicry,"[16] or those inner contrasts of tone which have made one critic suggest the novella has "two authors."[17] There has sometimes been resistance to any following up of Thomas Mann's genetic hints.[18] Yet to do so is not a gratuitous practice, and certainly not a matter merely of conjecturing stages prior to the final text, but rather of feeling the full force of the text itself. Thomas Mann, after all, did not tell Weber only that the work was of "hymnic origin," he said the finished text itself still *was* "at core hymnic in character." Unlike his later image of a crystal, which is apt for the work's many facets, the image of a core still visibly present despite outward changes exactly fits those passages where a "Platonic" lyrical enthusiasm has had a moral framework built immediately around it.[19] And on a larger scale, chapter 2, interpolated (when?) into the narrative line and already implying the outcome of the experiment, provides an analogous moral framework for the whole novella. We know what psychological and social pressures made these frameworks necessary, just as well as we know what emotions created the dangerous core they were designed to surround. This ambivalence is the key to understanding the style and structure of *Death in Venice*. In a sense the story did indeed have "two authors," but neither of them was the kind of bloodless artificial narrator-construct modern criticism routinely assumes when analyzing narrative. They were alternating personas of the real author himself, whose motto could well have been the words of Goethe's Faust: "Two souls, alas! dwell in this single breast."[20]

By 1930, as we saw, Thomas Mann could look back on a confusion from which he had climbed free, could recall that his novella had surprised him about himself, and could say that it meant more than he had meant it to mean. That makes the situation sound settled. It was firmly—was it not?—a moral fable, and safely part of the past. But the story's story was even then not ended. The growth of its meaning still had some way to go.

10

History: or, What Dionysus Did Next

History is almost the first note *Death in Venice* strikes: the world in which Aschenbach takes his afternoon walk is overshadowed by a threat to the peace of Europe. But from that point on, the narrative treats an intensely inward subject that has no obvious link with public events. Aschenbach is admittedly a public figure, and the story's outcome suggests how precarious and doubtful such a status is. But this is presented first of all as a psychological and moral problem in the individual artist's life; in its widest application, it concerns the mutual relation between writers and the community that reads and respects them, a social but hardly a historical matter. The story thus seems at first sight to be continuing Thomas Mann's obsession with the artist's (that is, ultimately, his own) problems, an obsession that excluded almost everything else, and certainly excluded public affairs and events, from his artistic vision of life before the First World War. Typical of this is the passage of *Tonio Kröger* where the artist—and the narrative is taking him seriously, not showing him up as unduly self-absorbed—tells Lizaveta Ivanovna that "no problem, none in the world, is more tormenting than the business of being an artist [*das Künstlertum*] and its effects on human beings" (158).

Most readers nowadays will respond to that statement with incredulity and quickly call to mind a whole clutch of problems—social, political, moral—that are both more "tormenting" and more obviously "in the world" than the self-concern of a fictive, and behind him an actual, artist. After that opening reference to the threat of a European war in some unspecified year early in the twentieth century, the historical note is not struck again. It thus seems to have been a purely decorative motif, or at most a way to set Aschenbach's private destiny in a framework of larger menace, part of the deliberate solemnity of a narrative which, we saw, uses omens to create suspense and suggest tragic necessity.

Yet the novella does bear on German history in an indirect way. Besides being filled with ominous figures and happenings, *Death in Venice* is also a kind of omen itself. Rather than reflecting the history of its own time or an earlier time, as works of literature are commonly thought to do, its connection is with events that still lay far in the future when it was written. They obviously therefore could not affect the author's literary intention. But this may only make the story's historical reference the more real and the more impressive.

What the novella turned out long afterwards to have uncovered (or so it seemed to Thomas Mann) was an important root of Nazism. In Aschenbach's attitudes and decisions, with their tragic private consequences, hindsight showed Mann a pattern which on a larger scale had helped to shape politics, with devastating public effects. It was not simply, or even particularly, the Prussian-ness of Aschenbach's discipline of life and work and its fragility, on which the Marxist critic Georg Lukács put such historical emphasis.[1] After all, if "Prussianism" specifically was significant in German history, it was through its continuity, not its breakdown. Thomas Mann's psychological insight went deeper. His story traces the fate of an all-too-conscious master-artist who has grown impatient with psychology and analysis, desires a simplified view of the world and the human mind, attempts a new "resoluteness" beyond moral complexity—and as a consequence has no defense against destructive self-abandon. These elements of a powerful anti-intellectual syndrome were, so Mann wrote in 1938, very much tendencies of the time, they were in the air long before the word "fascism" existed, and are scarcely recognisable in the political phenomenon that bears that name. Yet in spirit they are in some measure connected with it, morally they served to prepare the way for it. I had these tendencies in me as much as anyone, I included representations of them here and there in my work, for example in the formula of a "reborn naïveté" in the drama *Fiorenza* [VIII, 1064; cf. 204]. What I wanted to point out in our conversation was simply how understandable it is that I must hate and despise the depraved shape reality has given to spiritual things I carried in me twenty, thirty years ago.

This in a letter of 30 May 1938 to his American friend and patron Mrs. Agnes E. Meyer. It had come as a shock to her when Mann in conversation first made the link between fascism and his own work. How could anything in the intellectual history of this great humane writer be even remotely connected with the vileness of Nazism? In the America of the thirties, what is more, he was the foremost German exile spokesman against the Nazis. As events moved towards war he was trying to raise American consciousness of what Nazism meant and to break down isolationist attitudes. Surely (it must have seemed to Mrs. Meyer) it took an excessively sensitive moral conscience to link himself with that regime, even with its remotest intellectual history?

Yet Thomas Mann was refusing, precisely, to do what Aschenbach had done with such tragic results, namely, to be uncomplicatedly "resolute" and to adopt his fictional figure's "morally simplistic view of the world and of human psychology" (205)—refusing to do so even now, in a historical situation which seemed to make simplification permissible if ever it could be. Though his writings and broadcasts of the thirties and forties are entirely resolute in using the "massive power of the word" against Hitler's Germany, and though he was later to call the Nazi period a "morally good time" because it made moral priorities plain (XI, 253f.), still it was only in a historical emergency and for the most urgent political purposes that it was proper to divide the world into black and white, good and bad. It was not an option for the more complex view that is characteristic of art or of historical understanding.

So when in 1939, the year after his exchange with Mrs. Meyer, Thomas Mann wrote the essay "Brother Hitler" (XII, 843), he brought out precisely the features that were common to himself and the man he most cordially hated. Perhaps he was already groping towards a grand historical fiction of his time and obscurely felt that it would only be possible to grasp its spiritual history if he went beyond simple moral outrage at what had happened, however justifiable in this case moral outrage might be. In retrospect, Mann saw himself as part of that history, sharing responsibility for it as a German, specifically as an artist and intellectual, and more specifically still as the kind of artist he had been. What had occurred in Germany was not a takeover of the good by the bad, but the distortion of a single culture from within. The thread needed careful untangling.

That is the message of Mann's lecture "Germany and the Germans," given at the Library of Congress in 1945 (XI, 1126). The message is then immensely and movingly elaborated in what he called "the novel of my epoch," *Doctor Faustus*. He began it in 1943, with the Second World War still raging, and published it in 1947. It traces the dilemmas and temptations to which the twentieth-century German mind, individual and collective, was exposed, dilemmas and temptations that are shown to have affected both the subtleties of art and the currents of public thought and feeling that prepare political change. Thomas Mann sees the symptoms everywhere: impatience with the seeming dead-end of European civilization; a consequent rejection of basic concepts like justice and truth; a deliberate retrogression into instinct and unreason; a preference for primitive rather than refined methods in the most diverse areas. This willing self-abandonment is presented in Thomas Mann's chosen myth as a surrender to ultimately demonic forces—*Doctor Faustus* is, of course, a remake of the German moral fable of Faust. But it is also a remake, enlarged and intensified, of his own "moral fable," *Death in Venice*, even though his new protagonist is a musician, not a writer. Thomas Mann says in one of the work notes for *Doctor Faustus* that he has long carried the idea for a

"Faust" about with him (it was first sketched in a notebook of 1905) and that "deeper moral associations have accreted." Some of them came from *Death in Venice* and from later reflection on the themes he had treated in the novella. This is implied in the same note, which diagnoses the deepest impulse of his modern Faust figure, Adrian Leverkühn, and of the nation he allegorically represents, as "the desire to escape from everything bourgeois, moderate, classical [added: "Apolline"], sober, industrious and dependable into a world of drunken release, of bold, dionysian genius, beyond society, indeed superhuman." And this "intellectual-spiritual fascism" is further diagnosed as a "dionysian denial of truth and justice."[2]

These preparatory notes for *Doctor Faustus* show how different a degree of prior clarity Thomas Mann brought to the later work. And in line with this, the new protagonist shares his author's awareness of contemporary processes—intellectual, psychological, artistic—even while he is living through them. Where Aschenbach had been drawn on all unknowingly from a change in his approach to art, via a crisis in his productive routine, to an encounter which is first revivifying and then destructive, Adrian Leverkühn in contrast sees with total lucidity his own place in the history of music, understands the impasse of modernity, knows that only drastic means will get him out of it, embraces (in realistic terms) syphilitic infection, or (in mythical terms) a pact with the devil, and makes inspired music from the pathologically heightened condition ("intoxication") that finally leads to his mental collapse. A parallel is pointed with the equally pathological condition (in literal terms) or the devilish pact (in mythic terms) through which Germany gained its brief intoxicating triumphs of the thirties and forties before the collapse and defeat of 1945. Figures, major and minor, and other motifs link the late novel with the earlier novella. But the fundamental relation is between on the one hand a work that captured a tendency of its age all unknowingly as a seismographic trace, and on the other hand the mature analysis that knows how to read it. In other words, where *Death in Venice* is a historical document, *Doctor Faustus* is a work of history. But so accurate does the document seem to its author that it decisively marks the ideas and structure of his most ambitious novel. In this respect too *Death in Venice* is what Thomas Mann called it, an experiment, one on whose results he later felt able to rely.

To help understand Thomas Mann's feelings of complicity in German guilt, we have to go back and see stage by stage just how, and how far, he participated in the historical processes of his time and place. If irrationalism is the villain, then long before *Death in Venice* there were the self-doubts of the artist and intellectual Tonio Kröger, seemingly harmless in his wistful self-subordination to "Life" and the simple value of "normal" people. This lyrical masochism or "self-betrayal of the intellect" (XII, 26) has its roots in the late-nineteenth-century notion that artistic and intellectual activity arises from decadence, cultural value from the decline of vital forces. How could any artist embrace his calling and its associated values wholeheartedly when it was a widely held belief in his society (and, as a child of his time, he believed it himself) that they arose from vital deficiency? This is the motive for Mann's flirtation around 1910 with allegedly postdecadent efforts at "regeneration" (but what could have been more decadent than such hectic overcompensation?), as documented in his notes for the essay "Intellect and Art." Much of the complex of problems and temptations manifest in those notes, but left unresolved as a set of issues he could not yet master, went into the imagined career of Aschenbach. Aschenbach, besides completing other unfinished projects of Mann's listed in the first paragraph of chapter 2, has finished his equivalent of that essay and solved the equivalent of those problems, it is evident in what way. His tragic history duly shows the perils of the anti-intellectualist position that he thereby arrived at: what happens when you think you have achieved a "reborn naïveté," when you become morally resolute, deny analysis, reject "the abyss," and devote yourself to an unproblematic beauty of the surface.

If the novella was indeed an experiment, and if tragedy was its outcome, then that hard-won conclusion ought to have warded off all such temptations for good. Yet in the years immediately following, something like Aschenbach's impulses reassert themselves, admittedly in a very different outward guise. Within two years of the appearance of *Death in Venice*, the "grave threat" to the peace of Europe which haunts its first paragraph was fulfilled. From the start of the First World War in August 1914, national emotions and basic instincts seized even the most sophisticated citizens of the European combatant nations. Writers and intellectuals were no more immune to war fever than anyone else. With few exceptions, they supported not just war but the national policies that had led ever more inexorably to war. Thomas Mann was prominent and vocal among them. This is not the place to analyze general causes or attribute political guilt. The striking thing for present purposes is the way Thomas Mann's internal development had long since assigned him his place in an embattled Germany with a logic that was clear to him, though it came as a shock to those few literary colleagues (not least his brother Heinrich) who stood out against the nationalistic fervor. They declared themselves astonished that he, renowned as the cool intellectual, the detached ironist, did not join them. Yet in fact this greatest of all societal stresses, war, was precisely the signal and pretext to come into the fold that Tonio Kröger, with his longing for "life in its seductive banality" (163), had needed. In an essay of autumn 1914 called "Thoughts in War," Thomas Mann rejects intellect, critical consciousness, and civilization as shallow and "western" in contrast with a German culture which is altogether profounder and nonrational and therefore compatible with such primitive practices as "pederasty" and "orgiastic cult forms" (XIII, 528). In these wild utterances we can hear obvious echoes of *Death in Venice*, as well as of arguments left unresolved in the notes for the never finished essay "Intellect and Art." We can also recognize in them Tonio Kröger's suspicion of intellect and longing for the "bliss of ordinariness," but driven now to feverish extremes by the atmosphere of the first months of conflict. Near the end of the war, and of the massive work of self-justification and polemic that he spent the war years writing, *Considerations of an Unpolitical Man*, Thomas Mann himself makes the link between the yearnings of that novella and his (to some) unexpected political behavior. He quotes a long passage from *Tonio Kröger* to explain why he, the intellectual and outsider, necessarily leapt to Germany's defense in 1914. He was championing a community which for him represented "Life," and the clue had been there for all to see in his celebrated story of ten years earlier:

> I wrote: "It is absurd to love Life and nevertheless to be trying with all the skill at one's command to entice it from its proper course, to interest it in our melancholy subtleties, in this whole sick aristocracy of literature. The kingdom of art is enlarging its frontiers in this world, and the realm of health and innocence is dwindling. What is left of this realm should be most carefully preserved: we have no right to try to seduce people into reading poetry when they would much rather be looking at books full of snapshots of horses." It can be seen that I was applying those words and concepts to moral and intellectual things, but unconsciously there is no doubt a political will was alive in me, and it is again clear that one doesn't have to be a political activist and demonstrator, that one can be an "aesthete," and still, at a profound level, be in touch with things political. (XII, 586, quoting VIII, 303 [Luke translation, 162; cf. 140ff.])

It is a perceptive self-analysis. The bonds of communal feeling had been waiting to be pulled tight by some great crisis like war. But it is easy to see how for Heinrich Mann, as a critic of German actions and of the Wilhelmine society that had generated them, the national passions of his brother and other intellectuals called to mind a different story. In his essay "Zola" of 1915, overtly about the French novelist's conflict with the state over the Dreyfus case but alluding constantly to Germany and its intellectuals in 1914, Heinrich wrote that "it is the fate of reason periodically to grow weary, to abandon itself, and to surrender the field to the orgies of a complicated naiveté, the outbreaks of a deep and ancient anti-reason." The phrasing here recalls, no doubt deliberately, the Dionysian orgies in *Death in Venice*, which are ultimately the result of Aschenbach's "complicated naiveté."[3] It was certainly not implausible to see the collective emotions of intellectuals in time of war as a deeply Dionysian phenomenon.

The wartime controversy between the two brothers estranged them from each other for almost a decade; they were not reconciled until 1922. But Heinrich's reading of the politics of 1914 as a manifestation of atavistic impulse was then virtually taken over by Thomas as a key to understanding the rise of fascism in the twenties and thirties. Most observers concentrated on the externals, the "normal" political factors that had brought this extreme movement into being. There was the unpopularity of the Weimar Republic among Germans, which sprang from its origins in the traumatic defeat of 1918 and the way a new form of state was felt to have been imposed on Germany by the victors. There was the resentment many felt (and were incited to feel by right-wing politicians) against the Versailles Treaty, which had imposed punitive reparations payments and contained a clause recognizing Germany's exclusive guilt for the First World War. The instability of the Republic was also thought to stem from its frequent changes of governmental coalition and its repeated economic crises (the reparations burden, the hyperinflation, the consequences of the Wall Street crash). Altogether, certainly, few modern states have had to contend with such pressures and with such fierce internal opposition, from left as well as right, not just to the specific government in power but to the republican form of state itself.

Thomas Mann did not discount any of these things, but he believed they were only the occasions, not the essence, of fascism. They were the surface conditions that served to let loose deeper and darker forces in German society—and also (which undercut the standard explanation of German fascism from purely German circumstances) in other European countries. Mann was speaking of Europe generally when he wrote in 1925: "The anti-liberal backlash is more than clear, it is crass. It shows itself politically in the disgust with which people turn away from democracy and parliamentarism, turning faces of dark resolve towards dictatorship and terror" (IX, 166). This political development seemed to him at root an irrational acceptance of primitive forms, and not just an unconscious one. The fascist ideology drew on a tradition of explicit irrationalism—Nietzsche, Klages, Sorel, and others—to scorn and attack rationality, reflection, the critical mind, and any group that was committed to these things: the hated West, the hated intellectuals, the hated Jews. (For propaganda purposes, the three groups were easily and deliberately confused with each other.) Against the liberal values such people represented, fascism embraced and preached a tribal irrationality. The political consequence was an uncritical, near-ecstatic submerging of individuality in the collective which nobody who has seen original newsreel of an Italian or German fascist rally will think it far-fetched to call intoxication.

But was it right to call it a Dionysian intoxication? Or was that unnecessarily to dishonor an ancient deity and a vital element in the human makeup? In a letter to Thomas Mann of 13 August 1934, the mythologist Karl Kerényi, just back from observing at firsthand the behavior of young Germans, called it "a bad, non-dionysian (I might say dysdionysian) madness." The originator of the term "Dionysian," Nietzsche himself, had at first distinguished between the Dionysian element in Greek tragic culture and a cruder barbaric version found elsewhere in the ancient, and indeed the modern, world. In this other version, "the wildest beasts of nature were unleashed, to the point of a loathsome mixture of voluptuousness and cruelty" (*The Birth of Tragedy*, sect. 2). Later, fatefully, Nietzsche lost sight of this distinction and his revulsion against barbarism receded, to be replaced by an undiscriminating enthusiasm for cruelty as a sign of cultural health, most notoriously in his celebration of the "blond beast" of primitive warrior-nobilities. And in notes towards unfinished works just before his writing career ended in insanity, he asks with positive longing, "Where are the barbarians of the twentieth century?"[4]

By the late 1920s the barbarians had arrived. Nearly every essay Thomas Mann wrote and nearly every speech he made in the years up to 1933, whatever else its topic and whatever its thesis, is also a dismayed response and a call for opposition to the new irrationalism in German political behavior and what passed for German thinking. His Berlin speech of 1930, "German Address: An Appeal to Reason," is the high point and summary of his commitment. To borrow the phrase with which he had described Aschenbach's weighty responsibilities, Mann himself was more than ever "preoccupied with the tasks imposed on him by . . . the collective European psyche" (198)—now in the most literal sense, because the European psyche had become "collective" to a terrifying degree. To see and say what was going on in its depths required a psychopathologist, and it is a bitterly apt comment of Mann's that in the Nazi annexation of Austria in 1938 Hitler's real target was a certain aged analyst working in Vienna.

This reminds us that Mann's mode of explanation for fascism was not unique to him. In his *Civilization and Its Discontents* of 1930, Freud similarly saw the patterns of social behavior determined not by influences operating on the social surface, but by forces deep in the psyche. In the postscript to his *Autobiographical Study*, he declares that "the events of human history . . . are no more than a reflection of the dynamic conflicts between the ego, the id and the super-ego, which psychoanalysis studies in the individual—they are the very same processes repeated upon a wider stage."[5] Carl Gustav Jung argued much the same, especially in his thirties essay "Wotan." And as early as 1924, D. H. Lawrence wrote a "Letter from Germany" that conveys a sense of terrible regression, of "time . . . whirling with mysterious swiftness to a sort of death. Whirling to the ghost of the old Middle Ages of Germany, then to the Roman days, then to the days of the silent forest and the dangerous, lurking barbarians."[6] The letter was not printed until ten years later, when events had confirmed Lawrence's extraordinary insights. Mann's diary entry for 19 October 1934 registers an unsurprising approval: "Admirable what a sure eye for essentials in Lawrence's letter about Germany and its return to barbarism at a time when Hitler was not yet even talked of."

But fascism was not just an alarming factor in the outside world, to be treated only in essays and speeches. In 1929 Mann published *Mario and the Magician*, the tragic-grotesque study of an audience under the hypnotic sway of a brutal yet subtle performer. Set in Italy, it is both an atmospheric literal record of the new national assertiveness fascism had promoted in national communities, and an allegory of fascism itself with its brutal yet subtle propaganda methods. But the central figure, Cipolla, is also a kind of artist, and there are hints that he works with Dionysian means, achieving "a drunken dissolution of critical resistance" in his audience and driving them to an "orgy of dance" (VIII, 700f.).

By the time of his exchange with Mrs. Meyer, then, Thomas Mann could look back over this whole history in which *Death in Venice* was the most telling document. Despite his honorable resistance to the irrational in its gross Nazi form, he could feel disquiet at being part of the culture of an age that had veered so sharply towards irrationality, at seeing how closely his own work had been involved in that trend and thus "in touch with things political" in a much grimmer sense than his words of 1918 intended.

This deep disquiet is the driving force behind the confession that *Doctor Faustus* contains. Unless we are cynical enough to suspect that Mann's confession is just a last fling of Mann's self-centeredness, a desperate effort to get into the historical act at any price, then in the light of his overall political record it must seem the act of an unduly sensitive conscience. Yet it deserves to be taken seriously for at least two reasons. One is its consistency. It is the logical conclusion of a life's work which itself took seriously the part ideas and psychological forces play in human affairs; Mann's need to confess his own real involvement was the acid test of that belief. The other reason is its ethical value. When a historical evil that pervaded a nation comes to its end, most of those who have been involved rush to exculpate themselves and to accuse others. People rewrite history to prove that they were the innocent victims and point the finger at the guilty agents. Self-justification is the rule. Self-scrutiny and confession are the exception, the more sorely missed because they might have offered a more promising route back to social normality. In that respect, *Doctor Faustus* is not just a great and complex novel, it is an exemplary human act.

Whatever view is taken of that, it may at least now be clear how *Death in Venice* relates to the politics and history of Mann's lifetime, and how far the life story in which it stands gives a larger sense to Tonio Kröger's claim that "no problem, none in the world, is more tormenting than the business of being an artist."

Appendix: A Selection from Thomas Mann's Work Notes for Death in Venice

[*This appendix is meant to give the reader some sense of what "sources" and "influences" mean in the concrete detail of Mann's compositional practice, and of how they look to the scholar in their raw state. I therefore provide no cross-references either within Mann's text or to his sources. The highly motivated reader may try tracing them independently, e.g., in the dialogues of Plato and Plutarch discussed in chapter 7 and listed in the Bibliography. The less motivated but still interested reader can find them ready-traced in the critical editions also listed there. For the full German text, see Primary Works in the Bibliography.*]

1. Tadzio's smile is the smile of Narcissus seeing his own reflection—he sees it in the face of the other person, he sees his beauty in its effects. This smile also has something of the coquetry and tenderness with which Narcissus kisses the lips of his shadow.

4. *Connections from Ch. II to V*
   Forebears, sterling service
   Love of fame and *capacity* for fame.
   "See it through." Discipline. War service. Under the tension of great works. The "Despite" principle.
   Ascent of a problem-individual to dignity. And now! The conflict is: from a position of "dignity," from a hostility to knowledge and

second naiveté, from an anti-analytic condition, he gets involved in *this* passion. Form is sin. The surface is the abyss. How acutely for this artist who has achieved "dignity" art once more becomes a problem! For the artist, Eros is the guide to things intellectual, to spiritual beauty, for him the path to the highest things passes through the senses. But that is a path of perilous delight, an aberration, a path of sin, although there is no other. "Poets will always be denied this kind of noble exaltation. Their exaltation is always tragedy. . . . In *life* (and the artist is the man of life!) yearning must remain *love*: that is its happiness and its tragedy."—Realisation that the artist *cannot* attain dignity, that he necessarily goes astray, remains a bohemian, a gipsy, a libertine, an adventurer of the emotions. The composure of his style appears to him as lies and foolishness, decorations, honours, ennoblement highly ridiculous. This dignity can be saved only by death ("tragedy," the "sea,"—recourse, rescue and refuge of all higher love).

The artist's fame a farce, the trust of the masses sheer stupidity, education through art a risky undertaking that should be prohibited. Ironic that boys read him. Ironic that he has become "official," been ennobled.

6. "Only beauty is at one and the same time visible (perceivable, bearable by the senses) *and* delightful," i.e. a part of the divine, of eternal harmony. . . . We would be destroyed by the others, as Semele was. Thus beauty is the way of the sensuous person, the artist, to what is "delightful," divine, eternal, harmonious, intellectual, pure, ideal, *moral*: the only path and—a perilous path, which almost inevitably leads astray, leads to confusion. Love of beauty leads to what is moral, i.e. to the rejection of sympathy with the abyss, of psychology, of analysis; leads to simplicity, greatness and a fine austerity, to a reborn naiveté, to form, but precisely thereby back to the abyss. What is moral? *Analysis?* (The destroying of passion?) It has no austerity, it is knowing, understanding, forgiving, without composure and form. It has sympathy for the abyss, it *is* the abyss. Or *form*? Love of beauty? But it leads to intoxication, to desire and so equally to the abyss.

8. *Madness as the correlative of form and measure.* Known among the Greeks: at the time of their fullest development *madness* (μανια), a temporary disturbance of psychological equilibrium, a condition in which the conscious mind is overwhelmed, a state of *possession* by alien forces, gained far-reaching importance as a religious phenomenon. This overflowing of emotion has as its opposite pole in Greek religious life: the calm and measured feeling with which heart and gaze are raised to the gods.

Home of the cult of Dionysus is *Thrace.* Celebrated on mountain-tops *by night, by the light of burning torches.* Noisy music, *the crashing of brazen cymbals, the thundering of great hand-drums, and the deep tones of flutes whose "harmony lures to madness."* The inspired celebrants dance with wild exultation in furious, swirling, stumbling circles over the high fields. Mainly women, in long flowing garments sewn from fox-fur or with deerskins over them, with horns on their heads too, with streaming hair, snakes in their hands, and *brandishing daggers or thyrsus staves, whose points are hidden under ivy.* Their *wildness goes to the extreme*, they finally fling themselves on the animals chosen for sacrifice, hack and tear and bite off the bloody flesh, and swallow it raw. And so on.—The aim is mania, over-excitation, rapture, excess of emotional stimulation to the point of visionary states. Only through over-excitation and expansion of their being can humans achieve contact and connection with the god and his hosts. *The god is visibly present or at least near, and the din of the festival is meant to draw him fully to them.*

Ekstasis. Hieromania, in which the soul, escaped from the body, is united with the divine. It is now with and in the god, in the state of *enthusiasmos.*

9. *Daemon* as a name for the higher powers as a whole, especially when it was thought something unfavourable could be attributed to the deity, particularly a *bewitchment of the human being to do evil*, even in a satanic way. The daemon who *drives the man of noble striving into error and transgression* is the deity in person.

Dionysos: His significance is far from exhausted with the delights of wine and intoxication; he can offer quite different excitements and thus corresponds to a large area of ancient life, indeed of human nature generally, about which the ancients never spoke explicitly.

The mask of the hellenic fertility god conceals a half-alien being. One of the personifications of the "suffering" (dying and resurrected) god, whose cult was celebrated with excited lamentation and jubilation, had taken on in Asia Minor too and among the Phrygians and Thracians a particularly wild, noisy activity, and in repeated intrusions had substituted himself for the Greek Dionysus. The god is described as an *alien, intruding violently from outside.* . . .

10. In response to this experience he yields up all at once the last remnant of his strength and his capacity for intoxication. Exit raving.

Mercury had the task of guiding souls down to the underworld and hence was called psychagogos and psychopompos.

12. In the market-place of Chalcis the monument to the Pharsalian Cleomachus, who won victory for the Chalcidians and died with his beloved (darling) looking on. The Chalcidians, who had previously loathed pederasty, after this heroic deed began to esteem it particularly and hold it in high honour. . . .

The bravest peoples, the Boeotians, Lacedaemonians, Cretans, were most given to love, and just as many of the ancient heroes, e.g. Meleager, Achilles, Aristomenes, Cimon, *Epaminondas. Along with the last-named his darling Caphisodorus fell at the battle of Mantinea* and lies buried beside him.

14. "For the friend is more divine than the beloved. The friend bears the god in himself."

15. *From Agathon's speech: "But the god is young and his figure is delicately formed.* . . . Where he meets with a rough response, Eros flees, and he will dwell only in the gentle soul. . . . And finally, do we not know *that in the mastery of the arts too only that person shines and is admired whom Eros has taught,* and that all those the god has not touched remain in the shade and without fame? . . . Eros is the creator of all tenderness, voluptuousness, grace and yearning among

mankind.—In all labours, in every fear and every desire, *in the word*— there he is a sure guide, there Eros is a help and rescue."

16. ". . . and so in the sight of this multifarious beauty let him no longer yearn like a slave for the beauty of this one boy and desire the beauty of this one human being, and be common and petty . . . but rather, *arrived at the shores of the great sea of beauty*, here create many noble words and thoughts with the *inexhaustible urge to wisdom*, until then he is strong and mature and has a vision of that unique knowledge, which is the knowledge of the Beautiful. . . . Yes, Socrates, the person who, because he was able to love the beloved in the right way, begins to make the ascent from below and to see that eternal beauty, *that person has come to the end and is perfected and initiated*. . . .

17. *Phaedrus.* "Whenever anyone catches sight of something beautiful here on earth, he remembers the true beauty, and his wings grow, and he would gladly fly back to it. . . . *And is considered as one possessed.* But I say to you, this divine bliss is genuine like no other."
    [. . . . .]
    "The uninitiated and corrupt man is not easily brought to the sight of beauty when he sees an earthly copy. He is blind and not capable of *reverence* . . . indeed, he does not shrink from sexual enjoyment and is without shame in his unnatural desires. But when the initiate, one of those *who looked much upon beauty in that higher realm*, sees *a face of divine semblance, which mirrors that great beauty*, or the beautiful form of a body, then he trembles and a sacred fear comes upon him as it did before. . . ."

18. Infinity compressed into one, perfect beauty standing on the earth, captured in *one* human figure.—Intoxication and adoration.
    He sees the eternal forms, Beauty itself, the unified ground from which every beautiful form springs.

20. Eros and *word*. (In the word—there he is a sure guide. Relationship of the eloquent Athenians to him. Writing on the beach.)

Only that person shines in art whom Eros instructs. His art too was a sober service in the temple of Thespiae. Eros has always been in him. Tadzio was always his king. His love of fame too was Eros.

22/24. *Cholera asiatica*

The mortality rate varies according to the severity of the epidemic and to how old the patients are. It reaches 60–70 percent. About half the population is immune.

Since a long way back the disease has been native to certain parts of Eastern India. Since 1817 it has shown a striking tendency to spread to other countries. In 1816, scattered smaller concentrations developed in the Ganges estuary. In the following year the disease *spread* over the whole sub-continent, by the end of 1818 it had already *taken in* the whole of Eastern India, *devastated* the islands of the Indo-Chinese archipelago, in 1820–21 it *spread* over the whole of China and by 1823 it had *penetrated* via Persia as far as Astrakhan. . . .

[*This is the start of a lengthy note sequence—it makes some six printed pages—on the history of cholera, the symptoms and course of its various forms, the details of the Hamburg epidemic, and the means of combating the disease.*]

Hygiene:

In Italy in accordance with a law of 1865 there is a Health Council under the Minister of the Interior, a Health Council in every province, one in each district, and Health Committees in the municipalities.

International regulation on quarantine measures: set going for cholera by congresses, among others one in 1892 in Venice. States undertook to inform each other immediately cholera was discovered, and further settled the nature and extent of surveillance of persons when cholera threatened, and especially of affected or suspected ships.

Quarantine:

People who have fallen ill with cholera-like symptoms may be detained, others only medically examined (at the customs point). Travellers arriving from an affected place are subjected at their destination to five-day surveillance by the medical authorities.

The *Ganges* flows into the Bay of Bengal, forming together with the Brahmaputra the largest delta in the world. The south of the delta, a luxuriantly overgrown *very unhealthy* swamp and island labyrinth, is called the *Sunderban*.

$$\begin{array}{r} 1911 \\ \underline{-53} \\ \text{born } 1858 \end{array}$$

$$\begin{array}{r} 1858 \\ \underline{30} \\ 1888 \end{array}$$

23. [*Newspaper cutting with a profile photograph of Gustav Mahler.*]

26. Development of his style: towards the classical and settled, traditional, academic, conservative.

Alongside the cloistered tranquillity of his outward life, extreme blasé fastidiousness of his nerves through art. (And through the adventures of his material: bloody episodes in the Frederick novel.)

As far removed from the banal as from the eccentric.

"*Despite.*" His works achieved not only against the pressure of his delicate constitution, but also against his *mind*, against scepticism, mistrust, cynicism directed at art and artists themselves. The heroic Hamlet.

27. District Court, Provincial Court, Provincial Court of Appeal.

Liegnitz 66,620 inhabitants. Garrison. Provincial and District Court. Grammar School.

His type of hero

Gustav Mahler

Courtesy of the Thomas Mann Archive, Zurich.

Poetry only to begin with, then prose writer

Problematic youth: scepticism about artists and their world. Knowledge, irony. Then increasing dignity.

30. [*Newspaper cutting on a current cholera epidemic in Italy, from the* Münchener Neueste Nachrichten *of 5 September 1911.*]

31. Begins to follow him. (By day he pursues him without a break, at night he watches—.) (Love gives the lover freedoms—to become a slave.)

Pandering Venice.

On what paths!—Tries to get a moral grip. Remembers his forbears, his courageous life. Eros and bravery. New impressions of the "sickness." The manager. The musician. The Englishman. The epidemic.

Complicity.—Wild dream of the alien god.

Broken nerve and complete demoralisation. Hair coloring and waving. Pursuit through a sick Venice. The strawberries. Realisation by the cistern. Last view and dissolution.

Notes and References

Where works are referred to in abbreviated form, full details are given in the Bibliography.

Chapter 1

1. Mann had in mind mainly such painters as Franz von Lenbach or Franz von Stuck. His argument about the "superficiality" of all visual art is itself superficial if applied to greater artists, like Rembrandt or Van Gogh. There is no sign Mann had noticed the avant-garde painters in Munich—Wassily Kandinsky, Franz Marc, Paul Klee, August Macke—who formed first the New Artists' Association and then, in the year *Death in Venice* was begun (1911), the Blaue Reiter group. See Kolbe, *Zauber*, 212ff. It is a tantalizing question whether Mann knew Douanier Rousseau's painting *Le Rêve* of 1911, where jungle and tiger are the dream vision of the female figure, as they are of Aschenbach in chap. 1 of Mann's novella. (Reproduced in Schmidgall.)

2. An entry in his earliest preserved notebook quotes a French aphorism, "To think that everything has been discovered is to take the horizon for the limit of the world," and comments, "Naturalists please note!" *Notizbücher 1–6*, 21.

3. Note 10. The full German text of Mann's notes for this never completed essay ("Geist und Kunst") is printed in Scherrer and Wysling, 152–223.

4. See the letters to Heinrich Mann of 27 February and 23 December 1904, which have a strong element of self-justification.

5. See Thomas Mann, *Notizbücher 7–14*, 120.

6. Ibid., 186.

Chapter 2

1. "German Books: Thomas Mann," *Blue Review* (July 1913), reprinted in D. H. Lawrence, *A Selection from Phoenix* ed. A. A. H. Inglis (Harmondsworth: Peregrine, 1971), 283.

2. Cf. letter to Paul Amann, 10 September 1915: "The most embarrassing thing was that people interpreted the 'hieratic [i.e., high-priestly] atmosphere' as personal pretension, whereas it was nothing but mimicry" (*DüD* 1, 406). Elsewhere (e.g., letter to Josef Ponten, 6 June 1919, *DüD* 1, 412) Mann uses instead the more common literary term "parody."

3. Mann became aware of this paradox himself. In his 1940 Princeton lecture "On Myself" (XIII, 150) he speaks of "a strange *dual-track quality* [*Doppelgleisigkeit*—italics his] in poetic thinking" such that he had been able in an essay to claim that literature is a valuable guide for young people, whereas in a story he had drawn savagely pessimistic conclusions about any pedagogical role for artists and writers. What Mann does not draw attention to is the important point: which of these things came first? That is, the story does not retract the opinion (which would be a normal enough sequence); rather the opinion is reasserted after and despite the tragic findings of the story.

Chapter 3

1. There are three good surveys (all in German) of the response to *Death in Venice*. They overlap only partially in content and approach. Vaget, *Kommentar*, provides a condensed description; Bahr, *Dokumente* the most substantial extracts; and Böhm, *Selbstzucht*, the sharpest argument. Full references for articles which I mention only by author's name are given in the above volumes.

2. See the section "Maximin" in the volume of George's poems *Der siebente Ring* (1907), especially the poem "Kunfttag I"; and also his foreword to *Maximin: Ein Gedenkbuch* (1906). George's comment on *Death in Venice* must have been privately reported to Thomas Mann, probably by his friend Ernst Bertram, who was a member of the George circle. Mann quotes it in the important letter to Carl Maria Weber discussed in chap. 9.

3. See chap. 2, n. 1.

4. O. Zarek, "Neben dem Werk," reprinted in *DüD* 1, 411f.

5. First argued in the earlier of the two critical editions of *Death in Venice* listed in the Bibliography, *Der Tod in Venedig*, ed. T. J. Reed (1971), and in Reed, *Uses of Tradition*. The novella's genesis and its bearing on our understanding and interpretation of the text are discussed in chap. 9.

6. Böhm, *Selbstzucht*, 321. Böhm acutely suggests (323ff.) that Mann's repeated references to the "original" (but really quite different) subject of the old Goethe's (heterosexual) love was "Informationspolitik"; that is to say, a piece of public relations, in fact, virtually "disinformation." A similar view was already implied in the otherwise largely favorable essay on *Death in Venice* by the novelist Wolfgang Koeppen in 1976: "Thomas Mann had a deep-rooted morality of guilt and punishment. He would never willingly put himself among disorderly persons. Tonio Kröger wanted to be like everyone else. A contra-

diction in the artist's existence; Thomas Mann suffered it. . . . 'See things through' [Frederick the Great/Aschenbach's motto "Durchhalten"]—how? By subordinating himself to convention, or by resisting it? For a long time the writer might content himself with his success. The beautiful boy was absorbed into his biography. The disgusting horror-figures of old worn-out, misused, poor homosexuals receded, were replaced by approved [i.e., mythological] figures from the encyclopedia. Passion, the urge of love, is a happiness granted only to the gods. For August von Platen there was death . . . , for Mann-Aschenbach the game with fate, which the more prudent of them won." *Frankfurter Allgemeine Zeitung*, 7 February 1980, excerpted in Bahr, *Erläuterungen*, 163.

7. Myfanwy Piper, *Death in Venice*, an opera in two acts, set to music by Benjamin Britten, opus 88 (London: Faber Music, 1973).

Chapter 4

1. Technically, free indirect style removes the signs which earlier fiction used for distinguishing the character's temporal standpoint from the time frame of the narrative: a verb of thinking or saying in the past tense, followed by direct speech ("She realized: 'This is really happening'"); or by indirect speech ("She realized that this was really happening"), where the character's present tense has become a past tense like that of the main clause by the normal principle of English sequence of tenses. Free indirect style does not thus distinguish narrator's from character's standpoint. It gives us the character's experience in a main clause, but in the narrative past tense ("This was really happening"). With narrator and character drawn thus close together, ambiguity can arise. This is lessened when (as often happens) a fragment of the character's "present-time" experience—typically, an adverb or pronoun—is carried over unchanged into past-tense narration and confirms that we have character, not narrator-viewpoint: "*This* was really happening"; "The water got deeper *here*"; "*Good God*, it could not be done"; "*Now* things were going better." The technique is present systematically as early as Jane Austen in English and Goethe in German. Its most intensive development and subtlest use come with Flaubert in French and with Henry James in English.

For a concise account of the phenomenon and its history, with illuminating examples, see Roy Pascal, *The Dual Voice: Free Indirect Speech and Its Functioning in the Nineteenth-Century European Novel* (Totowa, N.J.: Rowman and Littlefield, 1977).

2. No. 13 in the series *Hundertdrucke* published in Hans von Weber's Hyperion Verlag, Munich. The alternative version of the paragraph in question is reprinted as a variant in my 1983 edition of the German text of *Death in Venice*, 83. (It has also strayed, unaccountably and unexplained, into a recent [1992] reprint of the German text by S. Fischer Verlag.)

3. This does not mean that every detail corresponds to the facts observable on the ground. Divergences like the absence of the "scriptural passages" on the façade, or of obtrusive features in the Venice of 1911, are noted by Krotkoff, "Symbolik," and by Leppmann, "Time and Place."

Chapter 5

1. This function of the story—to serve as an "experiment" in shaping a career and to explore the consequences—means that the "necessities" must have roots in the author's creative world and his problem-filled present. This does not reduce everything to autobiographical statement, since the story goes to dramatic extremes which are pure invention, and achieves general, not merely personal insights. Still, the distinction is a fine one. Readers who are afraid of falling into biographism may prefer to disregard the cross-references between Aschenbach's and Thomas Mann's work in the further notes to this chapter.

2. On "Frederick," "Maya," and "Intellect and Art" as projects of Thomas Mann's, cf. chap. 1, p. 7. On *A Miserable Wretch*, see Hans Wysling, "'Ein Elender': zu einem Novellenplan Thomas Manns," in Scherrer and Wysling (106–22). The transfer of these works to Aschenbach's imaginary oeuvre would have made it difficult for Mann to continue and complete them, so he must have already abandoned the idea by 1912. But he did in 1915 write a long historical essay, "Frederick and the Grand Coalition," and materials from "Intellect and Art" went into (among other works) "Thoughts in War," *Considerations of an Unpolitical Man*, and the 1920s essay "Goethe and Tolstoy." Similarly, many of the themes and figures sketched for "Maya" were used much later in the chapters of *Doctor Faustus* that portray Munich society.

3. A corresponding passage to Aschenbach's "defiant 'Despite'" is Mann's own short essay "Uber den Alkohol" of 1906 (XI, 718). The idea's source is probably Nietzsche's identical statement in *Ecce Homo* ("Zarathustra," sect. 1)—ironically, only one page away from the famous description of the "old-fashioned" inspiration that Nietzsche enjoyed when writing his *Zarathustra*. This was permanently tantalizing for such a laboriously creating modern like Thomas Mann. Cf. *Doctor Faustus*, chap. 25, VI, 316f.

The image of the tense or relaxed hand originated not in any of the literary and philosophical sources from Cicero to Goethe which scholars have conjectured, but in a comment on Hugo von Hofmannsthal made in conversation by the Austrian writer Richard Beer-Hofmann (cf. letter to John Conley, 20 November 1946, *DüD* 1, 443). Hofmannsthal was also the original exemplar of those who "work on the brink of exhaustion" (203). See letter to Heinrich Mann, 7 December 1908.

4. They could not, of course, be named, since—unlike the unfinished projects—they were already publicly Thomas Mann's. Cf. Thomas Mann to

his French translator, Félix Bertaux, 29 March 1924 *DüD* 1, 420f., where he says the figures evoked in his text "resemble," respectively, Thomas Buddenbrook, Lorenzo de' Medici and Savonarola in *Fiorenza*, Prince Klaus Heinrich in *Royal Highness*, and Felix Krull. The phrase used by a "shrewd commentator" to summarize the ethos behind these figures of Aschenbach's (202f.) is the one actually used about Thomas Mann by the critic Samuel Lublinski in his survey of contemporary writing, *Die Bilanz der Moderne* (Berlin: Cronbach, 1904), 226.

5. In Mann's oeuvre, the equivalent work, which captivated a broad popular readership with its "palpably live literary representation," is of course his immensely successful first novel, *Buddenbrooks*.

6. On the literary practice of "insight" and "knowledge," see Tonio Kröger's conversation with Lizaveta Ivanovna (159f.). Significantly, it is already causing that earlier writer-figure extreme discomfort and prickings of conscience.

7. The "ascent to dignity" as an ambition of all artists is alleged by Thomas Mann in "Intellect and Art," n. 59.

8. Cf. again the central dialogue in *Tonio Kröger*. It is expressly the principle "tout comprendre, c'est tout pardonner" that leads Tonio to describe the condition he calls the "nausea of knowledge" (160).

Chapter 6

1. See Thomas Mann to Erika and Klaus Mann, 25 May 1932: "Ambiguous is really the most modest adjective one can give the city (Simmel suggested it)" *DüD* 1, 435.

2. Ernst Bertram, "Das Problem des Verfalls" [1907], reprinted in Bertram, *Dichtung als Zeugnis* (Bonn: Bouvier, 1967.

Chapter 7

1. Mann is not alone in reviving it at this time. Apart from Stefan George's austere circle, there is a striking literary parallel in Rilke's *Duino Elegies*, where love is invoked as the source of a deeper understanding and a spiritual energy that can (and should) carry human beings beyond the beloved. See especially the lines in the First Elegy:

> . . . is it not time that our loving
> made us free from whatever we love, so we tremblingly stand it:
> as the arrow the bowstring, whence gathered for leap-off
> it may be *more* than itself. For of what use is staying?

Plato may have been the source for both writers. Rilke was a friend of Rudolf Kassner, whose versions of *Phaedrus* and the *Symposium* Thomas Mann used, and a letter of Rilke's to Ilse Sadé written at the precisely relevant time and place—5 March 1912 from Castle Duino—shows him reflecting on love in terms avowedly borrowed from Plato's *Symposium*.

Chapter 8

1. By a nice coincidence, the man whose diplomatic travels and persistence established this principle ("the question of international hygiene passes and surpasses political frontiers") was Dr. Adrien Proust, father of the novelist. See George D. Painter, *Marcel Proust: A Biography*, vol. 1 (London: Chatto & Windus, 1961), 2.

2. Mann's knowledge of the Dionysus cult and its rituals came from the scholarly work of Nietzsche's friend Erwin Rohde, *Psyche: Seelencult und Unsterblichkeitsglaube der Griechen*, 4th ed. (Tübingen: J. C. B. Mohr, 1907).

3. The question naturally arises whether Thomas Mann was consciously working in Freudian terms. He tells us that at this stage he had not yet read Freud, but that psychoanalytic theory was "in the air," and that he may conceivably have read things that originated in the Freudian school (letter to Joyce Morgan, 28 February 1951, *DüD* 1, 445f.). Manfred Dierks has suggested ("Schreibhemmung und Freud-Lektüre: Neuer Blick auf die Novelle *Der Tod in Venedig*," *Neue Zürcher Zeitung*, 23–24 June 1990) that the psychological situation and story line of *Death in Venice* follow, and must therefore have been influenced by, Wilhelm Jensen's novel *Gradiva* (1903), as analyzed in an essay of Freud's. But given Mann's disclaimer of a direct Freudian influence, and the fact that the plot follows his situation and experiences of 1911, the hypothesis seems unnecessary. Moreover, the story's psychological theme, the breakup of a controlled life into chaos, was a constant with deep roots in Mann's work (see above, p. 10f.). Dierks had earlier argued in his *Studien* that the story line of *Death in Venice* followed that of Euripides' *Bacchae*. It is not clear how many such determinants a plot line can accommodate.

Chapter 9

1. Gabriele d'Annunzio, *Il fuoco* (1900; reprint, Milan, 1951), 94.

2. The sonnet is the one beginning "Mein Auge liess das hohe Meer zurücke."

3. "Authority on decadence": letter to Malwida von Meysenbug, 18 October 1888; "decadent . . . and its very opposite": in the chapter of *Ecce Homo* entitled "Why I Am So Wise," sect. 2.

4. In this epigrammatic form, the idea comes in a much later work, *Nietzsche contra Wagner*, epilogue, sect. 2.

5. Rohde, *Psyche*, 2:11f.

6. Ibid., 2:42, 47.

7. Friedrich Nietzsche, *Beyond Good and Evil*, sects. 197 and 45. On Nietzsche's beasts of prey as symbols of vitalism in early twentieth-century writing (Mann, Rilke, Benn, Kafka), see my essay "Nietzsche's Animals: Idea, Image and Influence," in *Nietzsche: Imagery and Thought*, ed. Malcolm Pasley (London: Methuen, 1978).

8. To that extent it might have followed out one strand of the short story "A Weary Hour" of the year before. There Mann had decidedly identified with Schiller, among other things with his love-hate for the, to outward appearance, effortlessly creative Goethe. This view is taken to a psychological extreme by Peter von Matt, who suggests that Thomas Mann needed to "kill off" Goethe, the supreme German literary figure, in order to supplant him as *the* "national writer." See "Zur Psychologie des Nationalschriftstellers," in *Perspektiven psychoanalytischer Literaturkritik*, ed. S. Goeppert (Freiburg: Rombach, 1978).

9. The industrialist Alfred Krupp committed suicide in 1902 as a result of journalistic revelations, which were then officially played down. In 1906 Prince Philipp zu Eulenburg, a close friend of Kaiser Wilhelm II, was at the center of similar allegations which led to court proceedings.

10. The word for "song" in this case is *Lied*. But as "*drunken* song," its associations are again high rhapsodic utterance, and specifically the Dionysian elements in Nietzsche: "The Drunken Song" is the title of the last section but one of Nietzsche's *Thus Spake Zarathustra*.

11. The Luke translation of this passage (191) sets "true writer" against "*littérateur*," essence against profession. There is not much more one can do in English to render a distinction which, in bad German criticism, has always appealed to mysticism and snobbery rather than to argument and demonstration.

12. The purely *stylistic* point is put less solemnly in a letter of three weeks later: "I know how difficult it is, when the song [*Lied*] moves in the higher register, not to go over the top into kitsch. In 'D.i.V.' there were tricky passages." Letter to Hans von Hülsen, 22 July 1920, *DüD* 1, 416.

The *social responsibility* point echoes Mann's contribution to Munich debates on art, sex, and society just before and after *Death in Venice*. See Kolbe (158ff.) on Mann and the censoring of Frank Wedekind's plays, and especially the formal opinion Mann gave on the question of literature and public morality in the case of a Munich bookseller who had been attacked for listing erotica in his catalog. (See "Ein Gutachten," in Thomas Mann, *Aufsätze, Reden, Essays*, ed. Harry Matter, vol. 1, *1893–1913* [Berlin: Aufbau, 1983],

220ff.) This statement recognizes that society's demand for sexuality to be "as far as possible hushed up and hidden" is justified, but that art has always disregarded it. Art is "not family entertainment" but a "deep and dangerous thing" that has a "demonic" element rooted in sexuality. This cannot be denied without denying art itself.

At first sight, that is more liberal than the Weber letter because it speaks out for all art, rather than sacrificing a "socially irresponsible" mode (lyric) to save a "socially responsible" mode (narrative). Yet it thereby leaves *all* art in conflict with conservative bourgeois society. The lyric/narrative distinction on the other hand offers a tactical means to infiltrate society by making a taboo subject acceptable. Or is the tactical means merely a surrender? Either way, Thomas Mann was never an "anything goes" liberal. See, just after the Weber letter, his positive but deeply shaken response to the erotic poetry, both homo- and heterosexual, of Verlaine (letter to Paul Steegmann, 18 August 1920). The poems in question are still not included in "complete" works of Verlaine. See Verlaine, *Hombres/Femmes*, dual-text edition, with (virtuoso) translations by Alistair Elliot (London: Anvil Press, 1979).

13. See Hofmiller, "Thomas Mann's *Tod in Venedig*."

14. Georg von Lukács, "Sehnsucht und Form," in the volume of essays *Die Seele und die Formen* (Berlin: Fleischel, 1911).

15. From the letters of 1911–13: *delicacy*: "a very strange subject . . . serious and pure in tone, treating a case of pederasty in an ageing artist. I hear you saying 'hm hm!' But it is all very proper" (to Philipp Witkop, 18 July 1911); *impossible conception*: "tormented by a work which has turned out in the course of execution to be more and more an impossible conception" (to Ernst Bertram, 16 October 1911), "a novella with a daring, perhaps impossible subject" (to Alexander von Bernus, 24 October 1911) [both *DüD* 1, 395], and, "a serious, daring subject. . . . Very important to me to hear from you whether I have made it possible" (to Joseph-Emile Dresch, 21 April 1913, *DüD* 1, 401); *arrangements . . . well advanced* (to Hans von Hülsen, 4 April 1912, *DüD* 1, 396); "still stuck for an ending" (to Heinrich Mann, 27 April 1912); *desperately concerned* (to Albert Ehrenstein, 3 May 1912); *did not know what to think* (to Ernst Bertram, 21 October 1912).

16. On "classical" qualities, see above, p. 13f.; on "mimicry," cf. above, p. 12f., 17.

17. See Cohn, "Second Author." Professor Cohn is tolerant enough of my genetic aproach to say (139) that it only "appears to differ radically" from her intratextual method and is close to it in spirit. So close, one might say, that the "two authors" hypothesis, as she deploys it, is ultimately a metaphor for the real emotional and moral conflict I traced in the writing of the work. Her method may indeed be "a necessary interpretive move for a reader bent on affirming the aesthetic integrity of Mann's novella"—though it is not clear why

we should be *"bent on* affirming" anything that the work of art does not present so persuasively that ingenious hypothesis is not needed to explain discontinuities. At all events, by showing up the real stresses that caused the discontinuities, the genetic approach offers an answer to a textual question—admittedly at the price of emphasizing that the literary work has its roots in (to use a word unfashionable in literary theory) life.

18. Two critics—Vaget, *Kommentar* (199), and Luke, introduction, xli—reject critical accounts that "postulate a 'hymnic origin'" or "postulate a change of course." This is neither frank nor fair. "Postulate" insinuates the critic is offering a speculative hypothesis of his own. But the "hymnic character and origin" ("the *so-called* hymnic origin," says Vaget for good measure [200]) and the "change of course" are Thomas Mann's own unambiguous—confessional, rueful—statements. They are clearer and more fundamental genetic evidence than is commonly found in literary studies, and a conscientious scholar cannot properly neglect them. Luke grudgingly concedes (xlii) that "there *may* have been some shift of emphasis (as *seems to be suggested* by the last two lines of the passage from *Song of the Child*)." When one recalls what those lines actually say:

> There began a process of sobering, cooling, and mastering—
> Lo! what came of your drunken song was an ethical fable

it becomes clear how extraordinary is Luke's refusal to allow words their meaning. Nobody claims that we can (in Luke's phrase) "reconstruct *with certainty* the process of the story's composition," nor that we *"need"* any other version of the story. But that must not be an embargo on attempts to understand, for reasons given in my text, what was obviously an intricate and intense process. And it certainly cannot be a license for reasserting, as Luke does, flatly against the clear sense of Mann's own testimony, that "it is *more likely* that a complexity of conflicting elements was fully present from the beginning" (xlii, all italics mine).

19. Cf. Mann's text p. 234; and of the preparatory note with that passage (work note no. 18), where the Platonic formulations are given as in Plato's text, without any interpolated moral reservations. Is that only because the note contains preparatory, not yet fully processed material? Or do text and note stand on different sides of a genetic divide? Mann later claimed (letter to Paul Amann, 10 September 1915, *DüD* 1, 416)) that the "Greek cultural material" (*Bildungs-Griechentum*) was only a "spiritual refuge of the experiencing subject." Even this statement is ambiguous: does it refer to the "experiencing subject" within the story? Or to the one that had the experiences from which the story originated?

20. Goethe, *Faust*, pt. 1, l. 1112.

Chapter 10

1. In various essays of the mid-1940s. The relevant passages are usefully excerpted in Bahr, *Dokumente*, 165ff. Lukács gets closest when he speaks of *Death in Venice* and Heinrich Mann's *Professor Unrat* as "great harbingers of that tendency which signalled a barbaric underworld within modern German civilisation as its necessary complementary product" (167). Thomas Mann singles out this passage for quotation in his book *The Genesis of Doctor Faustus* (XI, 239).

2. Thomas Mann Archive, Zürich, ms. 33, fol. 8 and 9.

3. Heinrich Mann, "Zola," in the essay volume *Geist und Tat* (reprint, Munich: dtv, 1963), 210. Thomas Mann himself came strangely close to such a recognition. As early as October, he says that reading war propaganda makes you "as savage as if you were in the trenches," speaks of war as "the great blood-drunkenness" (*der grosse Blutrausch*), and suggests that "after the moral orderliness [*Sittsamkeit*] of half a century people are thirsting for horrors,— the whole thing can hardly be explained any other way." He even calls his forthcoming "Thoughts in War" "unspeakably journalistic, a product of corruption" (letter to Annette Kolb, 28 October 1914). The "overcoming" of these insights so that it was still possible to publish the article is itself surely a form of "complicated naiveté."

4. See *Genealogy of Morals*, pt. 1, sect. 11; on barbarians, see the "Nachlass" note in Nietzsche, *Werke*, vol. 3, ed. Karl Schlechta (Munich: Hanser, 1962), 90.

5. *Freud: Standard Edition*, trans. James Strachey, vol. 20 (London: Hogarth Press, 1959), 72.

6. Lawrence, *Selection*, (see n. 1 to ch. 2) 120.

Bibliography

Primary Works

Fiction

Gesammelte Werke. 13 vols. Frankfurt am Main: S. Fischer, 1974. The standard collected, though not complete, edition.

English translations of *Buddenbrooks*, *The Magic Mountain*, *Joseph and His Brethren*, *Doctor Faustus*, and other works by Thomas Mann mentioned in the text are published by Alfred A. Knopf (New York) and by Secker and Warburg (London) in translations by Helen Lowe-Porter. Many of these texts are available as Penguin paperbacks. Alfred A. Knopf has recently launched a retranslation program, beginning with a version of *Buddenbrooks* by John E. Woods (1993).

Death in Venice and Other Stories. Translated with an introduction by David Luke. New York: Bantam Books, 1988.

Der Tod in Venedig. Edited with an introduction and notes by T. J. Reed. Oxford: Clarendon Press, 1971 (and reprints).

Der Tod in Venedig: Text, Materialien, Kommentar. Edited by T. J. Reed. Munich: Hanser, 1983. Contains a complete annotated transcript of Mann's work notes for the story (reprinted in Bahr, *Erläuterungen*). Interested readers are referred to the notes in these critical editions of the German text of *Death in Venice*, which trace Mann's quotations and sources in more detail than it is the job of the present volume to do.

Letters, Diaries, Notebooks

For full details of the original German editions of Mann's diaries and the numerous volumes of correspondence, see *Thomas-Mann-Handbuch*, edited by Helmut Koopmann (Stuttgart: Kröner, 1990), xvif.

The Letters of Thomas Mann. 2 vols. Selected and translated by Richard and Clara Winston. London: Secker and Warburg, 1970.

Diaries 1918–1939. Translated by Richard and Clara Winston. London: André Deutsch, 1983.

Notizbücher 1–6. Edited by Hans Wysling and Yvonne Schmidlin. Frankfurt am Main: S. Fischer, 1991.

Notizbücher 7–14. Edited by Hans Wysling and Yvonne Schmidlin. Frankfurt am Main: S. Fischer, 1992.

Dichter über ihre Dichtungen. Edited by Hans Wysling. Munich: Heimeran, 1975–82. A three-volume collection of Mann's statements about his work, drawn largely from letters, some of them not previously published. Those on *Death in Venice* are contained in vol. 1, 393–448.

"Geist und Kunst" [the notes for the project "Intellect and Art"]. In Scherrer and Wysling, *Quellenkritische Studien*. No English translation exists at present.

Thomas Mann's Main Sources for Death in Venice

Burckhardt, Jacob. *Griechische Kulturgeschichte.* 4 vols. Stuttgart: Kröner, 1898.

*Lukács, Georg von. *Die Seele und die Formen.* Berlin: Fleischel, 1911.

*Plato. *Das Gastmahl* [*Symposium*]. Translated into German by Rudolf Kassner. Leipzig: Diederichs, 1903.

Plato. *Phaidros.* Translated into German by Rudolf Kassner. Leipzig: Diederichs, 1904.

Plutarch. *Erotikos* [*On Love*]. In Plutarch, *Vermischte Schriften*. Leipzig: Müller, 1911.

*Rohde, Erwin. *Psyche: Seelencult und Unsterblichkeitsglaube der Griechen*, 4th ed. 2 vols. Tübingen: Mohr, 1907.

*Thomas Mann's own copy, with his annotations, is preserved in the Zürich Thomas Mann Archive.

Translations of Plato's *Symposium* and *Phaedrus* dialogues can be found in Penguin Classics, in the four-volume Jowett edition (Oxford University Press), and in the one-volume *Collected Dialogues*, edited by Edith Hamilton and

Huntington Cairns, Bollingen Series 71 (Princeton University Press, 1961, and frequent reprints).

Plutarch's dialogue *Erotikos*, translated by W. C. Helmbold, is in vol. 9 of the *Moralia* in the Loeb bilingual edition (Cambridge, Mass.: Harvard University Press, 1969).

Nietzsche's *Birth of Tragedy*, the most important of his works for *Death in Venice*, is available in Penguin Classics, translated by R. J. Hollingdale, and in a version by Walter Kaufman (New York: Random House, 1967).

Biography

Bürgin, Hans, and Hans-Otto Mayer. *Thomas Mann: A Chronicle of His Life.* University of Alabama Press, 1969. The bald facts of Mann's life usefully given in calendar sequence.

Hamilton, Nigel. *The Brothers Mann: The Lives of Heinrich and Thomas Mann.* London: Secker and Warburg, 1978. A readable and well-informed biography of the two men and their uneasy relationship.

Kolbe, Jürgen. *Heller Zauber: Thomas Mann in München 1894–1933.* Berlin: Siedler, 1987. The liveliest biographical work on Mann to date. A well-written and well-documented account—with many atmospheric period photographs—of the Munich background to Mann's (and Aschenbach's) life.

Mendelssohn, Peter de. *Der Zauberer: Das Leben des deutschen Schriftstellers Thomas Mann. Erster Teil 1875–1918.* Frankfurt am Main: S. Fischer, 1975. The first part of what was to be the "official" biography, left unfinished at the death of its author. Already immensely long (1185 pages) because so leisurely in style and so devoted to the detailed narration of unimportant things, it yet manages to leave out much that is essential—for our purposes, the whole issue of Mann's homosexuality and its bearing on *Death in Venice*. The Paul Ehrenberg relationship, too central to be missed, is treated with coy evasiveness. A slighter second volume, edited by Albert von Tschirnding (Frankfurt am Main: S. Fischer, 1993), is subtitled *Jahre der Schwebe 1919 und 1933* and contains two further chapters.

Winston, Richard. *Thomas Mann: The Making of an Artist 1875–1911.* London: Constable, 1982. Likewise unfinished through the death of its author. Broaches the issues de Mendelssohn avoided but finally trivializes them: Mann "perhaps exaggerated" his own homosexual feelings, "as he exaggerated all the little ailments . . . he recorded in his diary" (273).

BIBLIOGRAPHY

Secondary Works

A useful list of German and English items, more substantial than there is space for here, is provided in Ehrhard Bahr, *Erl äuterungen und Dokumente zu Thomas Mann "Der Tod in Venedig"* (Stuttgart: Reclam, 1991), 181–95.

Alberts, Wilhelm. *Thomas Mann und sein Beruf.* Leipzig: Xenien-Verlag, 1913. The first monograph on Mann's work to that date, with a stop-press chapter on the newest work, *Death in Venice*, that illustrates contemporary attitudes.

Böhm, Karl Werner. *Zwischen Selbstsucht und Verlangen: Thomas Mann und das Stigma Homosexualität.* Würzburg: Königshausen und Neumann, 1991. Part of a new criticism which appraises Mann's homosexuality and its effects frankly and sympathetically (see also Härle). Polemical towards earlier writers' evasiveness in the face of the evidence. A necessary corrective, though it risks reducing Mann's inspiration and problems to a single source.

Cohn, Dorrit. *Transparent Minds: Narrative Modes for Presenting Consciousness in Fiction.* Princeton, N.J.: Princeton University Press, 1978.

———. "The Second Author of *Der Tod in Venedig.*" In *Critical Essays on Thomas Mann*, edited by Inta M. Ezergailis (Boston: G. K. Hall, 1988), 124–43.

Acute work on the techniques of psychological analysis used in modern fiction.

Dierks, Manfred. *Studien zu Mythos und Psychologie bei Thomas Mann.* Berne and Munich: Francke, 1972. Strongly psychoanalytic approach combined with keen pursuit of sources.

Good, Graham. "The Death of Language in *Death in Venice.*" *Mosaic* 5, no. 3 (1972): 43–52. Concentrates on the role and implications of silence in the story.

Härle, Gerhard. *Männerweiblichkeit: Zur Homosexualität bei Klaus und Thomas Mann.* Frankfurt am Main: Athenäum, 1988. Similar to Böhm, but with a more psychoanalytic approach. Interpretation is sometimes pressed beyond plausibility to make a case.

Heller, Erich. *The Ironic German.* London: Secker and Warburg, 1957. The first attempt at a synoptic view to be produced after Mann's death in 1955. Still a lively read.

Hofmiller, Joseph. "Thomas Manns *Tod in Venedig.*" *Merkur* 9 (1955): 505–20. Reprint of a 1913 article which already spotted essentials about the story's form.

Krotkoff, Herta. "Zur Symbolik in Thomas Manns *Tod in Venedig.*" *Modern Language Notes* 82 (1967): 445–53. Compares Munich realities with Mann's realism (see also Leppmann).

126

Leibrich, Louis. *Thomas Mann: Une recherche spirituelle*. Paris: Aubier, 1975. A comprehensive but concise study by the most prominent French Thomas Mann scholar.

Leppmann, Wolfgang. "Time and Place in *Death in Venice*." *German Quarterly* 48 (1975): 66–75. Does for Venice 1911 what Krotkoff does for Munich.

Lukács, Georg. *Essays on Thomas Mann*. Translated by Stanley Mitchell. London: Merlin Press, 1964. Fruits of his lifelong sympathetic interest in Mann's work which, where necessary, was stronger than his Marxist axioms.

Reed, T. J. *Thomas Mann: The Uses of Tradition*. Oxford: Clarendon Press, 1974. Interprets Mann's works singly and collectively as a response to and use of German literary, intellectual, and political traditions.

———. "'Geist und Kunst': Thomas Mann's Abandoned Essay on Literature." *Oxford German Studies* 1 (1966): 53–101. Reconstructs the lines of argument of Mann's "Intellect and Art" project and analyzes the conflict of elements that prevented him from completing it.

Scherrer, Paul, and Hans Wysling. *Quellenkritische Studien zum Werke Thomas Manns*. Berne and Munich: Francke, 1967. Masterly genetic and source studies—from the first two curators of the Zürich Thomas Mann Archive—of completed and uncompleted works by Mann, casting much light on his preoccupations and compositional methods. The collection includes the full annotated German text of the notes for "Geist und Kunst" ("Intellect and Art").

Schmidt, Ernst A. "'Platonismus' und 'Heidentum' in Thomas Manns *Tod in Venedig*." *Antike und Abendland* 20 (1974): 151–78.

———. "'Künstler und Knabenliebe': Eine vergleichende Skizze zu Thomas Manns *Tod in Venedig* und zu Vergils zweiter Ekloge." *Euphorion* 68 (1974): 437–46. Two studies by a classicist of the novella's classical sources and affinities.

Seidlin, Oskar. "Stiluntersuchungen an einem Thomas-Mann-Satz." In Seidlin, *Von Goethe zu Thomas Mann* (Göttingen: Vandenhoeck & Ruprecht, 1963), 148–61. The style analyst's approach to a sentence which can also be treated illuminatingly by the positivist scholar (see Wysling, "Aschenbachs Werke").

Vaget, Hans Rudolf. *Thomas Mann-Kommentar zu sämtlichen Erzählungen*. Munich: Winkler, 1984. A concise treatment of all Mann's shorter fiction, with accounts of its reception and an extensive discussion of secondary works.

Wysling, Hans. "Aschenbachs Werke: Archivalische Untersuchungen an einem Thomas-Mann-Satz." *Euphorion* 59 (1965): 272–314. The alternative approach to Seidlin's.

Other Works

Dodds, E. R. *The Greeks and the Irrational*. Berkeley: University of California Press, 1971. Authoritative study of the earliest documented forms of irrational beliefs.

Dover, K. J. *Greek Homosexuality*. London: Duckworth, 1978. Detailed and dispassionate study of homosexual practices and attitudes to them among the Greeks.

Mitchell, Donald, ed. *Benjamin Britten: Death in Venice*. Cambridge Opera Handbooks. Cambridge: Cambridge University Press, 1987. A collection of essays on various aspects of the opera—its genesis, music, production, and relation to the novella and to the film.

Schmidgall, Gary. *Literature as Opera*. New York: Oxford University Press, 1977. Has an excellent and wide-ranging chapter on Britten's opera which shows equally good judgment on the essentials of the novella.

Index

abyss, 36, 67, 70, 96
adaptations, 18–21
aesthetics, 35, 52, 55, 66
alien, 28, 42–43, 62
"alien god," 10, 28, 59–71
allegory, 32, 95
anagnorisis. *See* recognition
analysis, 6, 36–39, 50, 57, 84, 96
animal imagery, 79
anti-intellectualism, 92–93, 96
Apollo, apolline, 11, 20, 76, 77, 80,
    85, 95
archetypes, 11, 78
Aristotle, 59, 69
art, visual, 4, 19, 68
artist story, 10, 91, 102
avantgarde, 6
Aschenbach: "achievement, moralist
    of," 4, 33, 35, 47, 51, 67, 74;
    aesthetic, 39, 46, 52, 75;
    career, 33–40; compositional
    process, 35, 52–53, 56, 95;
    "decision" to change direction,
    33, 36, 53, 69; death, 71; evo-
lution, 34; family life, 39; final
    recognition (anagnorisis), 70;
    happiness, 48–49, 51–52; ini-
    tial vision, 27–32; love, con-
    fession of, 58–59; maturity,
    33–34, 53; "master"-status,
    25–26, 33–34, 67, 71; parent-
    age, 34; "reborn naiveté," 38;
    typical characters, 26–27; *von*
    title, 39; will, 48–49; works,
    33–35, 36
Austen, Jane, 115

barbarism, 100–101
beauty, 5, 38–39, 43, 46, 47, 53–55,
    58, 60, 62, 67, 80; of surface,
    37, 50, 66
Beer-Hoffmann, Richard, 116
Benn, Gottfried, 119
Bertram, Ernst, 114
Bismarck, Otto, Prince von, 3
Blaue Reiter, der, 113
block, writer's, 26–27, 56, 83
Bogarde, Dirk, 19

129

Index

homosexuality, 12, 15–16, 17–18, 19, 21, 55, 57–59, 75, 80–82, 85
"hymnic origin," "hymnic core," of *Death in Venice*, 84–86, 89, 121

Ibsen, Henrik, 4, 6
Ideas, platonic. *See* Forms, platonic
idyll, 51–58, 60
intoxication, 57, 62, 70, 72, 76, 84, 95, 100
irony, 36, 52, 61; dramatic, 59
irrationalism, 16, 94, 96, 99, 100
isolationism, 93

James, Henry, 10, 20, 115
Jensen, Wilhelm, 118
journey motif, 82–83
Joyce, James, 10
Jung, Carl Gustav, 101
jungle symbol, 28, 64, 78–79

Kafka, Franz, 8, 10, 31, 119
Kandinsky, Wassily, 113
Kant, Immanuel, 52
Kassner, Rudolf, 118
Kerényi, Karl, 100
Kerr, Alfred, 16, 18
Klages, Ludwig, 99
Klee, Paul, 113
knowledge: (*Erkenntnis*), 36–38, 57, 64, 70, 80
Koeppen, Wolfgang, 114
Kronberger, Maximilian, 15

Lawrence, D. H., 12, 16, 100
laxity, moral, 36, 69. *See also* understanding
leitmotiv, 44, 62–63. *See also* recurrence
Lenbach, Franz von, 113
Levetzow, Ulrike von, 80
lie, art as a, 68

"life," as value, 6, 16, 84, 97
literature: moral status of 4; analytic quality of 4; German hostility to, 5; as social criticism, 5; as "spirit," 6; and society, 81
Louis XIV, 38
Lublinski, Samuel, 117
Lukács, Georg (von), 87, 92

Mahler, Gustav, 19–20, 88, 110
mania, 60, 62
Mann, Heinrich (brother), 4, 7, 74, 75, 97, 98, 116
Mann, Katia (wife), 74
Mann, Thomas: ambitions to be a "master," 7; American exile, 11, 92–93; artist-stories, 10; compositional process, 8–9, 73, 83–89, 116; homosexual orientation, 15, 17, 85; intellectuality 88–89; irrationalism confessed, 102; marriage, 7; political opposition to Nazism, 93; puritanism, 86; self-discovery through writing, 9–10; sense of complicity in German history, 96; temptation to change literary mode, 6–7; uncompleted projects, 7, 96, 116; underlying pattern in works, 10–11; vacation in Venice, 8, 74–75

WORKS
Brother Hitler, 94
Buddenbrooks, 3, 5–7, 16, 32, 76, 117
Considerations of an Unpolitical Man, 97, 98, 116
Doctor Faustus, 11, 20, 81, 94, 95, 102, 116
Fiorenza, 7, 89, 93, 117
Frederick and the Great Coalition, 116

131

Index

Schiller, Friedrich, 35, 119
Schopenhauer, Arthur, 32
Schriftsteller, 84
science, 5
sea, as ideal, 46; as refuge, 87
self-simplification, 38, 94
Shakespeare, 20
Simmel, Georg, 43
skepticism, 13–14, 36, 39
sobriety, 53, 62, 64, 84
Socrates, 46, 54, 66, 68, 87
song, 83–84, 119
society, 5, 81, 85, 88–89, 95, 99
sordidness, 42–43, 60
Sorel, Georges, 99
spirit, 6, 47, 55, 57, 67
Staël, Madame de, 36
Stendhal, 52
Stuck, Franz von, 113
style, 10, 12–13, 15–17, 25–26, 68;
    free indirect (narrative
    mode), 27–29, 48, 52,
    115
symbolism, 32, 44–45, 54, 75, 84

taboo, 17, 85
thesis, 44
theater, 30, 42
Tolstoy, Lev Nikolaevich, 4
tragedy, 36, 59, 69, 76, 87, 92, 96,
    101
Turgenev, Ivan Sergeyevich, 4

understanding, 36–37, 69–70

Van Gogh, Vincent, 113
Venice: as a city of decadence, 75;
    composition begun in, 13, 84;
    cultural associations of 74–75;
    description of, 13, 60; effect
    of climate, 47; as real setting,
    31–32; as tourist trap, 60;
    Mann's vacation in, 8, 74–75
Verlaine, Paul, 120
Versailles treaty, 99
verse, 83, 85–86
Vienna, 101
vitalism, 79

Wagner, Richard, 75–77
Wall Street crash, 99
Weber, Carl Maria, 85–87
Weber, Hans von, 115
Wedekind, Frank, 11
Weimar Republic, 99
Wilde, Oscar, 18, 82
Wilhelm II, kaiser, 5, 119
World War I, 91–92, 97–99
World War II, 93–94

Xenophon, 46

youth, as cultural value, 36, 43

Zola, Emile, 5, 98

The Author

T. J. Reed is Taylor Professor of German Language and Literature at the University of Oxford, and a Fellow of the Queen's College. He was born in Blackheath, London, in 1937, went to a London grammar school, and took his degree in modern languages at Brasenose College, Oxford, in 1960. He has taught at Oxford for over 30 years, 25 of them as Fellow and Tutor in German at St. John's College. His publications include *Thomas Mann: The Uses of Tradition* (1974); *The Classical Centre: Goethe and Weimar 1775–1832* (1980); *Goethe* (1984); *Schiller* (1991); critical editions of Thomas Mann's *Der Tod in Venedig*, for both English (1971) and German readers (1983); a verse translation of Heine's satirical poem *Germany, A Winter's Tale* (1986); and numerous articles on German literature and ideas from the mid-eighteenth century to the 1990s. He co-edits the yearbook *Oxford German Studies* and is editor of the *Oxford Magazine*, the university's house journal. He was elected a Fellow of the British Academy in 1987. He is married, with two children. Outside the family, he is happiest when teaching or mountain walking.